FAST TRACK TO A 5

Preparing for the **AP***
**United States History
Examination**

To Accompany
The American Pageant
by David M. Kennedy, Lizabeth Cohen, and Thomas A. Bailey

Mark Epstein
Greenwich High School, Greenwich, Connecticut

McDougal Littell A Houghton Mifflin Company
Evanston, Illinois   Boston   New York

Printed in the U.S.A.

ISBN: 0-618-25051-4

123456789-QUD-09 08 07 06 05

CONTENTS

ABOUT THE AUTHOR

MARK EPSTEIN has taught for twenty years at Greenwich High School in Greenwich, Connecticut. He began teaching AP U.S. History eight years ago, and since then his students have compiled a 4.6 group average on the AP examination. In 2002 he was named a Greenwich Public Schools Distinguished Teacher.

PREFACE

"The past is not dead," declared the great American novelist William Faulkner. "It is not even past." With this observation, Faulkner neatly expressed the fact that forces at play in our world today have historical roots. Anyone interested in understanding the world in which we live must have a clear and deep understanding of the historical forces that shaped it.

I had extremely valuable help when I was writing this book. Charles Robinson and Chris Kazanas reviewed the rough drafts, and their comments provided important insights for organization, content, and presentation; Margot Mabie helped to make this work more readable and accessible.

This book is dedicated to the teachers, staff, and students of Greenwich High School, past, present, and future; to my wife, Janet, and my children, Ethan, Stephanie, Benjamin, and Carly; and to my father, Sheldon Epstein, whose determination in the face of adversity is testimony to the resilience of the human spirit.

Mark Epstein
Greenwich High School
Greenwich, Connecticut
November 2004

Part I

Strategies for the AP Test

PREPARING FOR THE AP* EXAM

Advanced Placement is a challenging yet stimulating experience. Whether you are taking an AP course at your school or you are working on AP independently, the stage is set for a great intellectual experience. As the school year progresses and you burrow deeper and deeper into the course work, you can see the broad concepts, movements, conflicts, resolutions, and personalities that have shaped the history of the United States. Fleshing out those forces with a growing collection of nuances is exciting. More exciting still is recognizing references to those forces in the media.

But as spring approaches and the College Board examination begins to loom on the horizon, Advanced Placement can seem downright intimidating given the enormous scope and extent of the information that is required to score well. If you are intimidated by the College Board examination, you are certainly not alone.

The best way to deal with an AP examination is to master it, not let it master you. If you manage your time effectively, you will eliminate one major obstacle—learning a considerable amount of material. In addition, if you can think of these tests as a way to show off how your mind works, you have a leg up: attitude *does* help. If you are not one of those students, there is still a lot you can do to sideline your anxiety. This book is designed to put you on a fast track. Focused review and practice time will help you master the examination so that you can walk in with confidence and get a 5.

WHAT'S IN THIS BOOK

This book is keyed to *The American Pageant*, 12th and 11th editions, by David M. Kennedy, Lizabeth Cohen, and Thomas A. Bailey, but because it follows the College Board Topic Outline, it is compatible with all textbooks. It is divided into three sections. Part I offers suggestions for getting yourself ready, from signing up to take the test and sharpening your pencils to organizing a free-response essay. At the end of Part I you will find a Diagnostic Test. This test has all of the elements of the U.S. History examination, but the eighty multiple-choice questions are organized according to the College Board Topic Outline. When you go through the answers at the end of the test, a cluster of wrong answers in one content area will show you where you are weak. Page references at the end of each answer indicate where you will find the discussion on that particular point in both the 11th and

---

12th editions of *The American Pageant*. Scoring is explained, so you will have some idea of how well you can do.

Part II is made up of nineteen chapters organized chronologically by topic. These chapters are not a substitute for your textbook and class discussion; they simply review the U.S. History course. At the end of each chapter you will find ten multiple-choice questions and two free-response questions based on the material in that chapter. Again, you will find page references at the end of each answer directing you to the discussion on that particular point in *The American Pageant*.

Part III has two complete AP U.S. History examinations. At the end of each test you will find the answers, explanations, and references to *The American Pageant* for the eighty multiple-choice questions and comments on what essays for the document-based question (DBQ) and the four free-response questions should cover. Following the answers and explanations is a work sheet that you can fill in to calculate your score and see where you placed compared with students who took the test in 2004.

SETTING UP A REVIEW SCHEDULE

If you have been steadily doing your homework and keeping up with the coursework, you are in good shape. The key to preparing for the examination is to begin as early as possible; do not wait until the exam is just a week or two away to begin your studying. But even if you've done all that—or if it's too late to do all that—there are some more ways to get it all together.

To begin, read Part I of this book. You will be much more comfortable going into the test if you understand how the test questions are designed and how best to approach them. Then take the Diagnostic Test and see where you are right now.

Take out a calendar and set up a schedule for yourself. If you begin studying early, you can chip away at the review chapters in Part II. You'll be surprised—and pleased—by how much material you can cover with half an hour a day of study for a month or so before the test. Look carefully at the sections of the Diagnostic Test; if you missed a number of questions in one particular area, allow more time for the chapters that cover that area of the course. The practice tests in Part III will give you more experience with different kinds of multiple-choice questions and the wide range of free-response questions.

If time is short, skip reading the review chapters. Look at the Key Concepts at the beginning of each chapter to make sure you know the broad concepts, and work on the multiple-choice and free-response questions at the end of each review. This will give you a good idea of your understanding of that particular topic. Then take the tests in Part III.

If time is *really* short, go straight from Part I to Part III. Taking practice tests over and over again is the fastest, most practical way to prepare.

BEFORE THE EXAM

By February, long before the exam, you need to make sure that you are registered to take the test. Many schools take care of the paperwork and handle the fees for their AP students, but check with your teacher or the AP coordinator to make sure that you are on the list. This is especially important if you have a documented disability and need test accommodations. If you are studying AP independently, call AP Services at the College Board for the name of the local AP coordinator, who will help you through the registration process.

The evening before the exam is not a great time for partying. Nor is it a great time for cramming. If you like, look over class notes or drift through your textbook, but concentrate on the broad outlines, not the small details, of the course. You might also want to skim through this book and read the AP tips. However, the evening before the exam *is* a great time to get your things together for the next day. Sharpen a fistful of no. 2 pencils with good erasers for the multiple-choice section of the test; set out several black or dark-blue ballpoint pens for the free-response questions; wind your watch and turn off the alarm if it has one; get a piece of fruit or a snack bar and a bottle of water for the break; make sure you have your Social Security number and whatever photo identification and admission ticket are required. Then relax. And get a good night's sleep. An extra hour of sleep is more valuable than an extra hour of study.

On the day of the examination, make certain to eat breakfast—fuel for the brain. Studies show that students who eat a hot breakfast before testing get higher grades. Be careful not to drink a lot of liquids, necessitating trips to the bathroom during the test. You need energy to power you through the test—and more. You will spend some time waiting while everyone is seated in the right room for the right test. That's before the test has even begun. You will be given a fifteen-minute break between Section I and Section II; the U.S. History exam lasts for over three hours. So be prepared for a long morning. You do not want to be distracted by a growling stomach or hunger pangs.

Be sure to wear comfortable clothes, taking along a sweater in case the heating or air-conditioning is erratic—and by all means wear your lucky socks if you have some.

You have been on the fast track. Now go get a 5.

TAKING THE AP U.S. HISTORY EXAM

The AP U.S. History exam consists of two sections: Section I has eighty multiple-choice questions. Section II, Part A, is a document-based question (DBQ). Section II, Part B and Part C, each have two free-response questions; you will be required to write an essay on one of the two questions in each of those parts. You will have 55 minutes for the multiple-choice portion of the test. Answer sheets for the multiple-choice questions are collected, and you will be given a 15-minute break. You then have 60 minutes for the DBQ—15 minutes for reading the documents and 45 minutes for writing the essay. You are given 70 minutes to write two essays you select from the free-response questions that make up Parts B and C. Keep an eye on your watch. Watch alarms are not allowed.

STRATEGIES FOR THE MULTIPLE-CHOICE SECTION

Here are some rules of thumb to help you work your way through the multiple-choice questions:

- **Guessing penalty** There are five possible answers for each question. Each correct answer is worth 1 point, and there is a 1/4-point guessing penalty for each incorrect answer. If you cannot narrow down the answers at all, it is against the odds to guess, so leave the answer sheet blank. However, if you can narrow down the answers even by eliminating one response, it is advantageous to guess. If you skip a question, be very careful to skip down that line on the answer sheet.
- **Read the question carefully** Pressured for time, many students make the mistake of reading the questions too quickly or merely skim them. By reading a question carefully, you may already have some idea about the correct answer. You can then look for it in the responses. Careful reading is especially important in EXCEPT questions.
- **Eliminate any answer you know is wrong** You can write on the multiple-choice questions in the test book. As you read through the responses, draw a line through any answer you know is wrong.
- **Read all of the possible answers, then choose the most accurate response** AP exams are written to test your precise knowledge of a subject. Sometimes there are a few probable answers but one of them is more specific. For example, a question dealing with the Open Door Policy in 1899 may have an answer that seems correct: "It sought to promote U.S. interests overseas."

However, there may be an even better answer, one that is more specific to the topic: "To provide the U.S. access to trade in Asia."

- **Avoid absolute responses** These answers often include the words "always" or "never." For example, the statement "Jefferson always rejected the Hamiltonian economic program" is an overstatement in that Jefferson never attempted to eliminate one of the key features of Hamilton's economic program, the Bank of the United States.
- **Mark and skip tough questions** If you are hung up on a question, mark it in the margin of the question book. You can come back to it later if you have time. Make sure you skip that question on your answer sheet too.

TYPES OF MULTIPLE-CHOICE QUESTIONS

There are various kinds of multiple-choice questions. Here are some suggestions for how to approach each kind:

CLASSIC/BEST ANSWER QUESTIONS

This is the most common type of multiple-choice question. It simply requires you to read the question and select the most correct answer. For example:

1. All money bills originate in
   (A) the executive branch
   (B) the Senate
   (C) the House of Representatives
   (D) the judicial branch
   (E) the State Department

ANSWER: C. This is a question that has only one correct answer. The Constitution provides for all money bills to originate in the House of Representatives.

EXCEPT QUESTIONS

In the EXCEPT question, all of the answers are correct but one. The best way to approach these questions is as true/false. Mark a T or F in the margin next to each possible answer. There should be only one false answer, and that is the one you should select. For example:

1. All of the following were advantages of the Union in the Civil War EXCEPT
   (A) it needed only to fight a defensive war
   (B) it was more industrialized than the South
   (C) it had a larger population
   (D) it had a more developed railway system than the South
   (E) it had a stronger navy than the South

ANSWER: A. The North had to conquer the Confederacy and therefore could not wage a defensive war. Options B-E are all advantages of the Union.

LIST AND GROUP QUESTIONS

In this type of question, there is a list of possible answers, and you must select the answer that contains the correct group of responses. These questions look hard, but you can simplify them by crossing out items from the list and then eliminating them in the answers below. For example:

1. According to the Constitution, as amended, which of the following is directly elected by the people?

To approach the question, draw a line through choice I, because the president and vice president are not elected directly but are chosen by the Electoral College. Then cross out any response that contains choice I.

~~I. the president and vice-president~~

II. members of the House of Representatives

III. justices of the Supreme Court

IV. senators

~~(A) I and II~~
(B) II and III
~~(C) I, II and III~~
~~(D) I and IV~~
(E) II and IV

Continue to cross out items that are wrong and the responses that contain them. Justices of the Supreme Court are appointed, not elected. Draw a line through III and answer (B), which contains choice III. Now you have narrowed down the possible responses to one.

ANSWER: E. Under the Constitution, including the Seventeenth Amendment, which provides for the direct election of senators, members of the House of Representatives and Senate are elected directly.

CHART/GRAPH QUESTIONS

These questions require you to examine the data on a chart or graph. While these questions are not difficult, spending too much time interpreting a chart or graph may slow you down. To avoid this, first read the question and all of the possible answers so that you know what you are looking for. Before you look at the chart, you may be able to eliminate some obviously incorrect responses. For example:

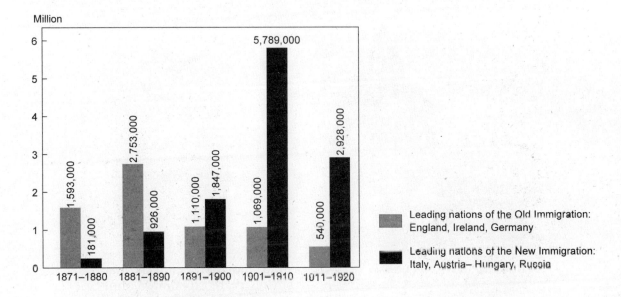

1. Which of the following statements does the table above best support?
   (A) Immigration remained at the same level from 1871 to 1920.
   (B) The period 1871-1880 witnessed the largest immigration of New Immigrants in the late nineteenth century.
   (C) Most immigrants came from Italy and Germany.
   (D) Between 1911 and 1920 approximately 3 million immigrants came from England, Ireland, and Germany.
   (E) The period 1891-1900 was the first decade in the late nineteenth century in which the number of New Immigrants exceeded the number of Old Immigrants.

ANSWER: E. After analyzing the table, option A can be eliminated because the measurement bars are not level in *any* period. Option B is incorrect because the total number of New Immigrants in 1871-1880 is the lowest of any decade represented. Option C is incorrect in that there is no way to tell from the table what percentage of the immigrants came from a specific country. Option D is incorrect because this decade was actually the low point of immigration from England, Ireland, and Germany (540,000 contrasted with over 2,270,000 in the period 1881-1890). Option E therefore is correct because the bar for New Immigrants is higher for the first time than the bar for Old Immigrants.

POLITICAL CARTOON QUESTIONS

These questions require you to interpret a political cartoon. Every political cartoon contains symbolism and a point of view. Examine the cartoon before you read the question and possible responses to determine what each part of the drawing represents and to identify the artist's viewpoint. For example:

1.   What is the viewpoint expressed in the above cartoon?
     (A) The United States rejected the Roosevelt Corollary to the Monroe Doctrine.
     (B) Under Roosevelt the United States allowed European nations to take part in the colonization of South America.
     (C) Roosevelt brought the Caribbean under the control of the United States.
     (D) Roosevelt was protecting the Caribbean nations from U.S. intervention.
     (E) The United States in the early twentieth century began removing its military control of the Caribbean.

ANSWER: **C**. Roosevelt actually strengthened the Monroe Doctrine with his Roosevelt Corollary. Therefore A and B are incorrect because one of the primary purposes of the Monroe Doctrine and the Roosevelt Corollary was to prevent European intervention in the Western Hemisphere. Because the United States consistently intervened in South American affairs, answers D and E are incorrect.

INTERPRETING A MAP

For history students, maps are used to describe not just geography but social and political organization as well. Asked to interpret a map, you can pick up a lot of information just by looking at the key.

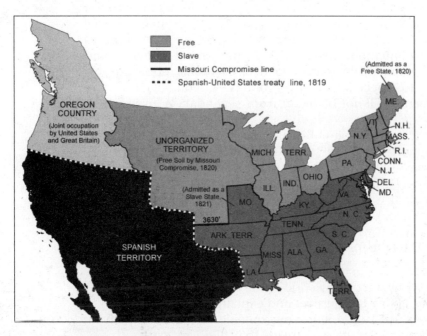

1. The map above shows the United States
   (A) at the end of the Revolutionary War
   (B) following the end of the Mexican-American War
   (C) after all of the Eastern Native American tribes had been moved to reservations in the West
   (D) after the passage of the Missouri Compromise
   (E) at the outbreak of the Civil War

ANSWER: **D**. At the end of the Revolutionary War the United States comprised the thirteen original colonies; therefore answer A is incorrect. B is incorrect for several reasons, foremost being the absence of Texas and the Mexican Cession on the map. There is no information on the map that indicates it has anything to do with Native American removal, thus answer C is incorrect. Answer E is incorrect because, although the map indicates free and slave states, it does not show states, such as California, Arkansas, Texas, and Oregon, that were present in 1861, when the Southern states began to secede.

FREE-RESPONSE QUESTIONS

You are required to write essays for three free-response questions on the United States History examination. Section II, Part A, presents the Document-Based Question. It is mandatory. For the DBQ, you are given 15 minutes for reading the documents and organizing your material and 45 minutes for writing the essay. Section II, Parts B and C, has two standard free-response questions in each. You will be asked to write on one from Part B and one from Part C. You will have a total of 70 minutes for writing these two essays.

THE DOCUMENT-BASED QUESTION

The DBQ is considered by many students to be the most complex and challenging component of the AP examination. As its name implies, the DBQ presents you with a wide variety of primary-source information in the form of ten or more documents. Primary sources are those that are contemporaneous with a time period or event, and they include everything from maps, political cartoons, photographs, and illustrations to speeches, essays, books, documentaries, and editorials. Documents will *not* be taken from secondary sources, such as textbooks.

DBQ questions run the gamut from basic "why" and "explain" questions to "support or refute" and "how and why" questions. All free-response essays require you to utilize your knowledge of the topic, but with the DBQ your essay needs to be grounded on the documents. Your goal is to demonstrate your ability to tease out the thrust and substance of each document, and then combine this information with your own general knowledge in an analytical and evaluative essay. Thus the following are necessary for writing a quality DBQ essay:

- Background—your own knowledge of the topic·
- Analysis—your ability to interpret and explain the documents
- Synthesis—your ability to blend your outside information with the information provided in the documents to explain an issue

Take a look at an abbreviated DBQ, one that contains only four documents for explanation purposes. (Remember, the DBQ for an AP examination includes at least twice as many documents as we are using in this sample. You will have the opportunity practice on full DBQs when you work on the diagnostic and practice tests.)

Question: Using the documents provided and your knowledge of the period, write an answer to the following question:

Analyze the factors that determined the degree of success that labor unions had in securing the goals that American workers desired during the years 1865-1900.

Document A: The Address of the National Labor [Union] Congress to the Working Men of the United States

Andrew C. Cameron, August, 1867

The question of all others which at present engrosses the attention of the American workman, and, in fact, the American people, is the proposed reduction of the hours of daily labor and the substitution of the eight- for the ten-hour system. . . . As might have been expected, the employing capitalists, aided by a venal press, have set up a howl of rage and protested the adoption of such [an] innovation. . . .

There are, probably, no organizations upon the nature of which so much ignorance exists, even among workingmen, or against which such persistent and systematic opposition has been urged, as trades unions. . . . [T]heir establishment has been beneficial to the community in general and the working classes in particular. . . .

Source: excerpted from The Annals of America, *Vol. 10*

Document B: The Preamble to "The Constitution of the Knights of Labor," adopted 3 January 1878

[We] submit to the world the objects sought to be accomplished by our organization . . . .

. . . .

2. To secure to the toilers a proper share of wealth they create. . . .

. . . .

6. . . . the adopting of measures providing for the health and safety of those engaged in mining, manufacturing, or building pursuits.

. . . .

11. The prohibition of the employment of children in workshops, mines, and factories. . . .

. . . .

14. The reduction of the hours of labor to eight per day, so that the laborers may have more time for social enjoyment and intellectual improvement. . . .

Source: excerpted from The Annals of America, *Vol. 10*

Document C: Earnings, Expenses and Conditions of Workingmen and Their Families

No. 51 [Family number], Machinist, American [birthplace]

EARNINGS

Of father	$540
Of mother	255
Of son, aged sixteen	255
Total	$1050

CONDITION

Family numbers 10—parents and eight children, five girls and three boys, aged from two to sixteen. Four of the children attend school. Father only works only 30 weeks in the year, receives $3 per day for his services. They live in a comfortably furnished house, of 7 rooms, have a piano, take an interest in society and domestic affairs, are intelligent, but do not dress very well. Their expenditures are equal, but do not exceed their income. Father belongs to trades union, and is interested and benefited by and in it.

FOOD

Breakfast—Bread, meat and coffee.
Dinner—Bread, meat, vegetables and tea.
Supper—Bread, meat, vegetables and coffee.

COST OF LIVING

Rent	$300
Fuel	50
Meat	100
Groceries	200
Clothing	160
Boots and shoes	50
Dry goods	25
Books, papers, etc.	15
Trades union	10
Sickness [insurance]	50
Sundries	90
Total	$1050

No. 112 [Family number], Coal Miner, American [birthplace]

EARNINGS

Of father	$250

CONDITION

Family numbers 7—husband, wife, and five children, three girls and two boys, aged from three to nineteen years. Three of them go to the public school. Family live in 2 room tenement, in healthy locality, for which they pay $6 per month rent. The house is scantily furnished, without carpets, but is kept neat and clean. They are compelled to live very economically, and every cent they earn is used to the best advantage. Father had only thirty weeks work during the past year. He belongs to trades union. The figures for cost of living are actual and there is no doubt the family lived on the amount specified.

FOOD

Breakfast—Bread, coffee and salt meat.
Dinner—Meat, bread, coffee and butter.
Supper—Sausage, bread and coffee.

COST OF LIVING

Rent	$72
Fuel	20
Meat	20
Groceries	60
Clothing	28
Boots and shoes	15
Dry goods	20
Trades union	3
Sickness [insurance]	10
Sundries	5
Total	$253

Source: 1884, Illinois Bureau of Labor Statistics, Third Biennial Report, 1884 (excerpted from Hollitz, Thinking Through the Past, 2nd ed., Boston: Houghton Mifflin Co.)

Document D: Debs's Claim is Puerile: Violence the Strikers' Main Reliance to Insure Success

President Debs of the American Railway Union, President Gompers of the American Federation of Labor, and other labor leaders who are responsible for strikes, have repeatedly affirmed that during the present [Pullman] strike and in strikes in the past[,] all violent acts were done by men [who were] not strikers. . . . When several persons were shot by the United States troops, he claimed none of them was a member a member of the American Railway Union and instanced this fact to prove that the strikers were not the ones who were committing overt acts [of violence] . . . and are not accountable for the bloodshed, arson, destruction of property in other ways, hindrance to business, and other losses which the [state] always suffers when a big strike is in progress.

That the contrary is true is proved beyond cavil [frivolous objection] by reference to the history of every big strike ever ordered in this country. In a railway strike success can only be achieved by the forcible detention of trains . . . , and the forcible detention of trains means rioting, and perhaps bloodshed.

. . . .

It is because Debs and his ilk cannot, and know they cannot, achieve their communistic ends by the ballot or in any other lawful way that they resort to the use of hurled rocks, blows with clubs, shots fired from ambush, and all the other base acts of a relentless and bloodthirsty guerilla warfare.

Source: New York Times, *11 July 1894 (excerpted from the* Times *through Proquest, an electronic database*

Steps in organizing and structuring the DBQ essay:

Step 1: Brainstorm ideas that relate to the question.

Step 2: Consider a structure for your response.

Step 3: Analyze each document. What is the meaning of the document? What or who is the source—the Supreme Court, a presidential candidate, a labor leader, a capitalist? The source provides important clues to the position being put forth in the document. As you analyze the meaning or significance of the document, jot down margin notes—generalizations that relate to the document. For example:

- **Margin note for Document A** Address to the NLU (National Labor Union) in support of the eight-hour day.
- **Margin note for Document B** Extract from the Knights of Labor constitution regarding higher wages, improved working conditions, and a shortened workday.
- **Margin note for Document C** Bureau of Labor Statistics cost-of-living figures for union members equals the amount paid in salary for the machinist, slightly less for the coal miner.
- **Margin note for Document D** Criticism of claim by Eugene Debs, president of the American Railway Union, that acts of violence were not perpetrated by union members and that Debs's union was interfering with the railroads. Suggestion that Debs is communistic.

When you begin to map out your essay, remember that the DBQ calls for a synthesis of the document information and your own knowledge of the topic. With that in mind, start with your own knowledge that the period 1865-1877 was characterized by tensions between labor and the business owners, or capitalists. You will need to point out the conditions—low pay and dangerous work environments—faced by workers. Documents A, B, and C provide the grist for this point; you might note that the sources for Documents A and B were partisan, while the source for Document C was nonpartisan. To assess the level of success for workers in achieving their objectives, you will need to address factors—in this case, obstacles—such as the role played by government in assisting the capitalist class put down strikes (for example, the Railroad Strike of 1877); the influx of millions of immigrants, which drove down wages; and the methods used by businesses and government to undermine union efforts. As you discuss these features, you should refer to the documents that support your own analysis. For example the degree of success for the American workers in general and unions specifically was in part determined by the attitudes expressed in Document D, which portrays unions as violent. This turned public opinion against labor unions, therefore limiting their success.

AP Tip

Do not wait until you've read the documents to develop your own personal knowledge. Even before reading the documents take a few minutes to brainstorm information that you can recall about the topic. If time permits, organize this information so that you can construct the essay while incorporating the documents into the essay. When the document information is similar to what you have brainstormed, present that knowledge as it is expressed in the documents. Possibly the document material can be used to help you analyze other issues.

STRUCTURE OF A FREE-RESPONSE ESSAY

In writing a free-response essay, whether a DBQ or a general free-response essay, you need the following:
- a well-developed thesis that sums up your perspective

■ an effective analysis and appropriate use of information
■ a lucidly cogent essay that is well-structured and lucidly written
   Below is one model for organizing your thoughts in preparation for writing the free-response and DBQ essays:

Thesis (Opinion)
Supporting Arguments (major reasons, to be developed in the body paragraphs, that defend or support your thesis)
Structured Body Paragraphs
- <u>Topic Sentence</u>
    - supports the thesis
    - introduces the topic of the paragraph
- <u>Historical and Factual Information</u>
    - facts
    - details
    - statistics
    - quotes
- <u>Analysis</u>
    - explains the separate parts of your arguments
    - explains the significance of the information you present as it relates to the thesis

FRAMING THE DEBATE To demonstrate an understanding of the complexity of the issue or question, you need to show that you are aware of both sides of the argument or perspective. This frames the debate for the reader. Thus in the introduction, you want to present the "other" view—the one you are *not* supporting. Make certain, however, that you do not develop the other perspective so fully that the reader is unclear about your thesis. Your objective is to convince the reader that you have a strong thesis and that it is well developed with historical information and analysis.

OUTLINING For each essay in Section II, the AP examination has built in time for you to develop an outline. Time spent on your outlines is important for a number of reasons:
■ It prevents you from writing an essay that is unorganized because you begin writing whatever comes into your head at the moment.
■ It helps you determine your perspective on the issue. If after completing an outline you realize that your information tends to support one view over the other, then this is the perspective you should develop.
■ It provides you with a brief brainstorming opportunity before writing the essay.
   Once you have outlined your essay, it is time to put pen to paper. Remember that examination readers are looking for a clear thesis backed up with specifics. Concentrate on setting out accurate information in straightforward, concise prose. You cannot mask vague information with elegant prose.

A FREE-RESPONSE QUESTION AND THREE SAMPLE ESSAYS

Having established the ingredients of a free-response answer, let us now look at three essays—one excellent (grade: 9), one good (grade: 6), and one poor (grade: 3). Comments following each essay explain ways in which each essay succeeded or failed. All three essays respond to the following free-response question:

Question: Analyze the extent to which compromise was no longer possible between the North and South by the 1850s.

SAMPLE ESSAY 1

By the time Abraham Lincoln was elected president in 1860, the time for compromise between the North and South had passed. Lincoln's election was the spark that ignited secession. Throughout the antebellum period political leaders had attempted to preserve the Union through compromise and by maintaining the political balance in the Senate. As early as the Constitutional Convention there were indications that the conflicting economies and cultures of the regions would ultimately have to be resolved, either through ongoing political compromise or through war. As late as 1858, just two years before secession, Lincoln had said "a house divided against itself cannot stand." The outbreak of the Civil War was the tragic resolution to the sectional differences and the inability to maintain two different economic, political, and cultural systems under one government.

Territorial expansion played a significant role in straining sectional relations because it involved the debate over the expansion or containment of slavery. In 1820 Congress seemed to have resolved this problem when it passed the Missouri Compromise, which prevented the expansion of slavery north of the 36° 30′ line. For a time, Congress was able to balance representation in the Senate by admitting both a slave state and a free state into the Union. For example, Missouri, a slave state, was admitted at the same time as Maine, a free state.

Compromise could only address the symptoms of the problem; it could not resolve the basic economic, moral, and cultural differences, especially because the two regions had completely different economic systems dominated by opposing dominant social, economic, and political classes: the planter-slaveholder in the South and the industrial capitalist in the North. Economically, Northern manufacturers and the Northern economy required a protective tariff, internal improvements, and a national bank to facilitate commerce, whereas the South wanted low tariffs, state banks, and was opposed to internal improvements. The North's economy and culture rested on the wage-labor system, which was, of course, inconsistent with the South's slave economy and culture. Both sought to expand their systems for a variety of reasons: politically the North and South quarreled over the extension of slavery because the addition of a new slave state or free state meant greater political representation in Congress. This in turn meant that either region, if given the political advantage, could pass legislation that affected not only the future expansion of slavery, but other burning political issues as well, such as the tariff.

Furthermore, the North maintained that the Union had been established as a contract between the people of the United States. Southern political leaders responded that the Union was the result of a compact between the states, and that a state had the authority to nullify federal laws and even secede from the Union. These conflicting political theories made compromise even more difficult to achieve because the South claimed to have the authority to reject any federal law it deemed unconstitutional or a threat to states' rights.

Added to this was the role of Northern abolitionists and Southern defenders of slavery whose justifications for or against the peculiar institution added a moral element to the already significant differences. Thus by the time Congress passed the Kansas-Nebraska Act in 1854 and the Supreme Court handed down the Dred Scott decision in 1857, the possibility of maintaining the Union became increasingly tenuous.

Politically, by the 1850s the two major political parties represented, for the most part, different sections: the Democrats articulated the South's objectives, whereas the Republicans represented an adversarial view. Up until the election of Lincoln, the presidency was occupied either by a Southerner or a Northerner who tended to favor the South's position. Lincoln, a Republican and an advocate of the containment of slavery, represented to the South that the executive branch would now become an obstacle to the South's political objectives, and that its political and economic influence would therefore wane over time. Thus, by the 1850s, conditions for secession were already present, and the time for compromise had, for all intents and purposes, passed.

COMMENT This essay effectively outlines the divisions that prevailed between the North and South in the antebellum period. While it by no means completely addresses the issue, given the time constraint (35 minutes) it successfully indicates that while Lincoln's election was the event that finally shattered the Union, deep social, economic, and political divisions had already been festering for decades. The writer articulates the view that the Civil War was the result of irreconcilable differences that could no longer be resolved through compromise. Although listing the features of the Dred Scott case would certainly help, the writer successfully synthesizes selective historical content with effective analysis to support the thesis. Grade: 9 (Excellent)

SAMPLE ESSAY 2

Although there were many disputes, differences, and events that made compromise in the decades before the 1850s very difficult, political leaders such as Clay and Calhoun were able to work out solutions that politically resolved the differences between North and South and therefore prevented secession and war. Unfortunately the nation's political leaders were not up to the task in the 1850s. As early as the Constitutional Convention the Framers developed solutions to sectional problems such as the Three-fifths Compromise and the Assumption Bill. In the early nineteenth century, with tensions high over the attempt to expand or limit the spread of slavery, congressional leaders were able to work out the Missouri Compromise, which defined where slavery could and could not expand. In 1850 the United States could have experienced civil war had not political leaders worked out the Compromise of 1850, which strengthened the Fugitive Slave Act in the South's favor but allowed California to enter as a free state. True, the Dred Scott decision effectively eliminated the Missouri Compromise, but political leaders such as Senator Stephen Douglas could not create compromises that would reduce tensions. Instead, they offered the controversial Kansas-Nebraska Act.

The idea of popular sovereignty made compromise almost impossible because Congress could no longer establish areas where slavery could expand and where it could not. Besides, the Kansas-Nebraska Act further enforced the Fugitive Slave Act, which angered Northerners immensely. The only thing holding the Union together at this point was the hope on the part of the South that it could in the future continue to expand slavery. Lincoln, who was opposed to the expansion of slavery, concerned the South so much that no one in 1860 could find any way to compromise. With Lincoln's election the South seceded. But it didn't have to come to that. The nation's political leaders had failed to do what their predecessors in Congress had been able to achieve: effective compromises.

COMMENT This essay has a clear thesis: the nation's political leaders in the 1850s were responsible for failing to reduce or resolve the sectional tensions through effective compromises that earlier political leaders had accomplished. The writer cites several important political compromises. The scope of this essay could be broader, however, in that the author does not incorporate the role of territorial expansion into the discussion. Further, the discussion is limited in that no clear differences between the sections are established. Thus the essay focuses only on the controversy over the expansion of slavery and not on its economic and political consequences for the sections. It also depicts the Compromise of 1850 as a workable solution that had no subsequent repercussions. In fact the North was outraged by the Fugitive Slave component of the act. There is also a factual error: the Kansas-Nebraska Act did not strengthen the Fugitive Slave Act. An explanation of popular sovereignty would also add to the quality of this essay. Nevertheless, the writer exhibits a good understanding of the topic and uses information that sustains the thesis throughout the essay. Grade: 6 (Good)

SAMPLE ESSAY 3

Compromise in the 1850s was impossible because the North and South no longer wanted to negotiate. They believed that only through war would their differences be settled. The Missouri Compromise was more effective than the Kansas-Nebraska Act. It prevented war, whereas the Kansas-Nebraska Act made war more possible. Popular sovereignty was not an effective solution either. Now slavery could spread anywhere and the North would be opposed to this. Lincoln was opposed to the spread of slavery, but he was not willing to break up the Union for it. Therefore a better solution to the problem could not be found. If Lincoln opposed the spread of slavery, what other option did the South have but to leave the Union? Also, the North and South viewed slavery differently. The North opposed it as inhumane, but the South claimed it was an institution that benefited both Southern whites and slaves. Had the Framers at the Constitutional Convention addressed the issue of slavery, future generations would not have to find solutions and compromises to this problem. But even if Congress did work out compromises, such as the Missouri Compromise, no one could determine what the Supreme Court would do, such as the <u>Dred Scott</u> case. Lincoln's election was not the cause of the war. True, he was a Northerner, but so were other presidents. Put simply, neither the North nor the South favored compromise by the 1850s because they could not resolve their political differences.

COMMENT This essay is weak in a number of areas. While it has a thesis, it is rudimentary; the thesis is not developed in the essay effectively. The writer strings together generalizations that have little connection to one another. Important issues are not explained. For instance the writer contends that the Missouri Compromise was more effective than the Kansas-Nebraska Act but does not explain how or why the former prevented war. This essay lacks focus, analysis, and sufficient historical information to defend the thesis. Grade: 3 (Poor)

A HISTORIOGRAPHICAL APPROACH

One misconception about historical study is that it is merely a string of facts, meaningless dates, and the names of often long-dead individuals, with little relevance to our lives and the times. Nothing could be further from the truth. Historians study the nature of change. To be sure, facts are an integral component of historical study and discourse, but equally important is the meaning we give to historical information. One interesting approach to the study of history is historiography—the interpretation of information. There are two dominant schools of historiography. One historiographic perspective argues that change is the result of consensus among groups, classes, ethnicities, races, and genders that change is needed; strains, divisions, and class interests exist, but they are not fundamental and have not interfered with the process of consensual change. Those who subscribe to this view are called consensus or traditional historians. Other historians, referred to as revisionist or conflict historians, view conflict among groups, classes, ethnicities, races, and genders as fundamental to change, its wellspring. As you become immersed in the study of U.S. history at the

Advanced Placement level, filtering the information you learn through the lens of historiographic analysis can make for a richer experience and provide you with the analytical tools to interpret the nature of change. Analyzing, synthesizing, and evaluating the forces that shaped this nation are important aspects of any student's intellectual growth, and they are essential tools for achieving a 5 on the Advanced Placement U.S. History examination.

A DIAGNOSTIC TEST

The purpose of this diagnostic test is to provide you with an indication of how well you will perform on the AP U.S. History examination. Keep in mind that the exam changes every year, so it is not possible to predict your score with certainty. While the test is *not* organized chronologically, the questions are organized by historical periods, with each represented by two or more questions. For example, the first four questions are associated with the pre-American Revolution era, whereas the next two questions test one's knowledge of the Second Great Awakening in the early nineteenth century. You can thus identify which periods to concentrate on when preparing for the AP exam.

AP UNITED STATES HISTORY EXAMINATION
Section I: Multiple-Choice Questions
Time—55 minutes
Number of questions—80

Directions Each question or incomplete statement below has five possible answers. For each question, select the best response.

1. The colonists who ultimately embraced the vision of America as an independent nation had in common all of the following characteristics EXCEPT
   (A) the desire to create an agricultural society
   (B) learning to live lives unfettered by the tyrannies of royal authority
   (C) learning to live lives unfettered by the tyrannies of official religion
   (D) an unwillingness to subjugate others
   (E) learning to live lives unfettered by the tyrannies of social hierarchies

Estimated Slave Imports to the New World, 1601–1810

	17th Century	18th Century	Total	Percent
Spanish America	292,500	578,600	871,100	11.7
Brazil	560,000	1,891,400	2,451,400	33
British Caribbean	263,700	1,401,000	1,664,700	22.5
Dutch Caribbean	40,000	460,000	500,000	6.7
French Caribbean	155,800	1,348,400	1,504,200	20.3
Danish Caribbean	4,000	24,000	28,000	.4
British North America and future United States	10,000	390,000	400,000	5.4
TOTAL			7,419,400	100

2. Which of the following conclusions can be drawn from the table above?
   (A) By the nineteenth century, slave importation had significantly declined.
   (B) Brazil imported more slaves in the seventeenth century than the other areas in the New World combined.
   (C) No other New World area experienced a greater increase in slave imports from the seventeenth to the eighteenth century than the Danish Caribbean.
   (D) British North America and the United States represented the smallest percentage of slave imports from the seventeenth to the eighteenth century.
   (E) The Caribbean represented the most significant percentage of slave imports in the seventeenth and eighteenth centuries.

3. By the 1770s which of the following issues helped bring about a crisis of imperial authority?
   (A) trade restrictions
   (B) slavery
   (C) few colonists clung to any hope of accommodation with Great Britain
   (D) the coronation of a new king
   (E) the rise to power of radical patriots in the American colonies

4. The settlement founded in the early 1600s that was the most important for the future United States was
   (A) Santa Fe
   (B) Quebec
   (C) Jamestown
   (D) Massachusetts Bay
   (E) Saint Augustine

5. Religious revivals of the Second Great Awakening resulted in
   (A) little increase in church membership
   (B) a strong religious influence in many areas of American life
   (C) surprisingly few humanitarian reforms
   (D) greater attention to church history and doctrine
   (E) improved conditions for indentured servants

6. The greatest of the revival preachers of the Second Great Awakening was
   (A) Joseph Smith
   (B) Horace Greeley
   (C) Carl Schurz
   (D) Charles G. Finney
   (E) Angelina Grimké

7. New England reformer Dorothea Dix is most notable for her efforts on behalf of
   (A) prison and asylum reform
   (B) the peace movement
   (C) the temperance movement
   (D) abolitionism
   (E) women's education

8. By the 1850s the crusade for women's rights was eclipsed by
   (A) the temperance movement
   (B) the "Lucy Stoners"
   (C) abolitionism
   (D) prison reform advocates
   (E) evangelical revivalism

9. The Oneida Community declined due to
   (A) widespread criticism of its sexual practices
   (B) the loss of the colony's property to the government
   (C) their adoption of communism
   (D) its inability to pay state and federal taxes
   (E) its move from New York to California

10. The Hudson River School excelled in the art of painting
    (A) portraits
    (B) classical frescoes
    (C) still life
    (D) daguerreotypes
    (E) landscapes

11. *Civil Disobedience,* an essay that later influenced both Mahatma Gandhi and Martin Luther King, Jr., was written by the transcendentalist
    (A) Louisa May Alcott
    (B) Ralph Waldo Emerson
    (C) James Fenimore Cooper
    (D) Margaret Fuller
    (E) Henry David Thoreau

12. One of the major tests the new nation passed was when
    (A) we elected our first president
    (B) we avoided being drawn into the wars in Europe
    (C) we dealt fairly with the Native Americans
    (D) an alliance was formed with Britain
    (E) power was transferred peacefully from the Federalists to the Jeffersonians

13. As part of the egalitarian movement of the American Revolution,
    (A) several northern states abolished slavery
    (B) most states outlawed the overseas trade in indentured servants
    (C) many states repealed laws against interracial marriage
    (D) some southern states passed legislation providing for the gradual abolition of slavery
    (E) laws against interracial marriage were eliminated

14. As a result of the Revolution's emphasis on equality, all of the following were achieved EXCEPT
    (A) the reduction of property qualifications for voting by most states
    (B) the growth of trade organizations for artisans and laborers
    (C) the establishment of the world's first antislavery society
    (D) full equality between white women and men
    (E) abolishing medieval inheritance laws

15. The Articles of Confederation were finally approved when
    (A) agreement was reached on who would be president
    (B) states gave up their right to coin money
    (C) all states claiming western lands surrendered them to the national government
    (D) the states gave up their power to establish tariffs
    (E) a two-house national legislature was added

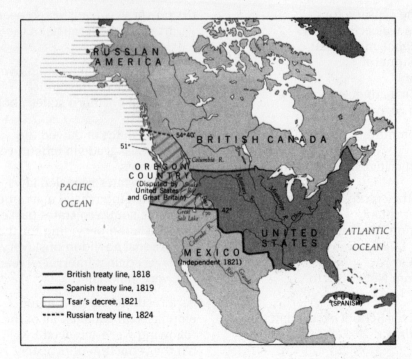

The West and Northwest, 1819–1824

— British treaty line, 1818
— Spanish treaty line, 1819
▨ Tsar's decree, 1821
- - - - Russian treaty line, 1824

16. The map above shows that in the period 1819 to 1824
    (A) the British controlled nearly all of North America except Mexico
    (B) Russia, Britain, and the United States all laid claim to the Oregon Country
    (C) Mexico won its independence
    (D) Spain lost all of its colonial possessions in the New World
    (E) U.S. territorial possessions ended at the Mississippi River

17. Shays's Rebellion was provoked by
    (A) fears that the Articles of Confederation had created too strong a national government for the United States
    (B) efforts by wealthy merchants to replace the Articles of Confederation with a new constitution
    (C) a quarrel over the boundary between Massachusetts and Vermont
    (D) foreclosures on the mortgages of backcountry farmers
    (E) the government's failure to pay bonuses to Revolutionary War veterans

18. The Great Compromise at the Constitutional Convention worked out an acceptable scheme for
    (A) regulating commerce
    (B) levying taxes
    (C) apportioning congressional representation
    (D) electing the president
    (E) choosing senators

19. The Constitutional Convention addressed the North-South controversy over slavery through the
    (A) "large-state plan"
    (B) "small-state plan"
    (C) "three-fifths" compromise
    (D) closing of the slave trade until 1808
    (E) Northwest Ordinance

20. In 1932 Franklin Roosevelt campaigned on the promise that as president he would attack the Great Depression by
    (A) nationalizing all banks and major industries
    (B) mobilizing America's youth as in wartime
    (C) returning to the traditional policies of laissez-faire capitalism
    (D) continuing the policies already undertaken by President Hoover
    (E) experimenting with bold new programs for economic and social reform

21. The Glass-Steagall Act
    (A) took the United States off the gold standard
    (B) empowered President Roosevelt to close all banks temporarily
    (C) created the Securities and Exchange Commission to regulate the stock exchange
    (D) permitted commercial banks to engage in Wall Street financial dealings
    (E) created the Federal Deposit Insurance Corporation to insure individual bank deposits

22. In order to persuade the Border States to remain in the Union, President Lincoln
    (A) relied solely on moral appeal
    (B) used only totally legal methods
    (C) guaranteed that they could keep slavery permanently
    (D) never had to use troops
    (E) declared martial law where needed

23. As the Civil War began, the South seemed to have the advantage of
    (A) greater ability to wage offensive warfare
    (B) more talented military leaders
    (C) superior industrial capabilities
    (D) superior transportation facilities
    (E) a more united public opinion

24. A supposed asset for the South at the beginning of the Civil War that never materialized to its real advantage was
    (A) effective military leadership
    (B) intervention from Britain and France
    (C) the fighting skill of Southern males
    (D) its ability to fight on its own soil
    (E) its belief that it was defending its way of life

25. Match each early-twentieth-century muckraker below with the target of his or her exposé.
    a. David G. Phillips
    b. Ida Tarbell
    c. Lincoln Steffens
    d. Ray Stannard Baker
    1. the United States Senate
    2. the Standard Oil Company
    3. city governments
    4. the condition of blacks

    (A) a-1, b-2, c-3, d-4
    (B) a-4, b-2, c-3, d-1
    (C) a-3, b-1, c-2, d-4
    (D) a-3, b-2, c-4, d-1
    (E) a-1, b-4, c-2, d-3

26. In *Muller v. Oregon,* the Supreme Court upheld the principle promoted by progressives like Florence Kelley and Louis Brandeis that
    (A) child labor under the age of fourteen should be prohibited
    (B) the federal government should regulate occupational safety and health
    (C) factory labor should be limited to ten hours a day five days a week
    (D) female workers should receive equal pay for equal work
    (E) female workers required special rules and protection on the job

27. Teddy Roosevelt helped to end the 1902 strike in the anthracite coal mines by
    (A) using the military to force the miners back to work
    (B) passing legislation making the miners' union illegal
    (C) helping the mine owners to import strike-breakers
    (D) appealing to mine owners' and workers' sense of the public interest
    (E) threatening to seize the mines and to operate them with federal troops

28. Japanese-Americans were placed in concentration camps during World War II
    (A) due to numerous acts of sabotage
    (B) in retaliation for the placement of Americans in concentration camps by the Japanese
    (C) as a result of anti-Japanese prejudice and fear
    (D) because many were loyal to Japan
    (E) to prevent them from leaving the United States to help Japan in the war

29. President Roosevelt and Prime Minister Churchill announced at their wartime conference in Casablanca that their principal war aim was to
    (A) destroy the last remnants of European imperialism
    (B) promote the national independence of all European nations
    (C) contain the postwar power of the Soviet Union
    (D) force the unconditional surrender of both Germany and Japan
    (E) create an effective postwar Atlantic alliance

30. African-Americans did all of the following during World War II EXCEPT
    (A) fight in integrated combat units
    (B) rally behind the slogan "Double V" (victory over dictators abroad and racism at home)
    (C) move to the North and West in large numbers
    (D) form a militant organization called the Congress of Racial Equality
    (E) serve in the Army Air Corps

31. The "New Right" movement that helped to elect Ronald Reagan was spearheaded by
    (A) fiscal conservatives
    (B) evangelical Christians
    (C) gold-standard advocates
    (D) midwesterners
    (E) neoconservatives

32. The Democrats' hopes for the 1988 election rose sharply because of major scandals in the Reagan administration involving
    (A) bribes involving business deals in the Soviet Union
    (B) election fraud
    (C) the Iran-Contra affair and savings-and-loan banks
    (D) kickbacks for oil leases on federal lands
    (E) payoffs for U.S. hostages and campaign contributions from foreign corporations

33. Nativists in the 1850s were known for their
    (A) support of Native Americans
    (B) support of slavery
    (C) opposition to old-stock Protestants
    (D) anti-Catholic and antiforeign attitudes
    (E) opposition to alcohol and Sabbath-breaking

34. The panic of 1857 resulted in
    (A) a demand to end the government policy of giving away farmland
    (B) the extension of slavery to the territories
    (C) price supports for farmers
    (D) calls for restrictions on land and stock speculation
    (E) clamor for a higher tariff

35. The long-range purpose of the Albany Congress in 1754 was to
    (A) achieve colonial unity and common defense against the French threat
    (B) propose independence of the colonies from Britain
    (C) declare war on the Iroquois tribe
    (D) prohibit New England and New York from trading with the French West Indies
    (E) gain peace with France

36. In the wake of the Proclamation of 1763
    (A) American colonists obeyed the law they hated
    (B) relations with France improved
    (C) relations between the American colonies and the British government improved
    (D) the American colonies believed their destiny had been destroyed
    (E) American colonists moved west, defying the Proclamation

37. Teddy Roosevelt's New Nationalism
    (A) pinned its economic faith on competition
    (B) opposed consolidation of labor unions
    (C) favored the free functioning of unregulated and unmonopolized markets
    (D) supported a broad program of social welfare
    (E) favored state rather than federal government activism

38. Woodrow Wilson's political philosophy included all of the following EXCEPT
    (A) faith in the masses
    (B) scorn for the ideal of self-determination for minority peoples in other countries
    (C) a belief that the president should provide leadership for Congress
    (D) a belief that the president should appeal over the heads of legislators to the sovereign people
    (E) a belief in the moral essence of politics

39. One weapon that was used to put Boss Tweed, leader of New York City's infamous Tweed Ring, in jail was
    (A) the cartoons of the political satirist Thomas Nast
    (B) federal income tax evasion charges
    (C) the RICO racketeering act
    (D) New York City's ethics laws
    (E) granting immunity to Tweed's cronies in exchange for testimony

40. During the Gilded Age, the Democrats and the Republicans
    (A) had few significant economic differences
    (B) agreed on currency policy but not on the tariff
    (C) were separated by substantial differences in economic policy
    (D) held similar views on all economic issues except for civil-service reform
    (E) were divided over silver versus gold currency

41. The Compromise of 1877 resulted in
    (A) a renewal of the Republican commitment to protect black civil rights in the South
    (B) the withdrawal of federal troops from the South
    (C) the election of a Democrat to the presidency
    (D) passage of the Bland-Allison Silver Purchase Act
    (E) a plan to build the first transcontinental railroad

42. In the 1896 case of *Plessy v. Ferguson,* the Supreme Court ruled that
    (A) African-Americans could be denied the right to vote
    (B) segregation was unconstitutional
    (C) "separate but equal" facilities were constitutional
    (D) the Fourteenth Amendment did not apply to African-Americans
    (E) literacy tests for voting were constitutional

43. The House of Representatives decided the 1824 presidential election when
    (A) no candidate received a majority of the vote in the Electoral College
    (B) William Crawford suffered a stroke and was forced to drop out of the race
    (C) the House was forced to do so by "King Caucus"
    (D) Henry Clay, as Speaker of the House, made the request
    (E) widespread voter fraud was discovered

44. The purpose behind the spoils system was
    (A) to press those with experience into governmental service
    (B) to make politics a sideline and not a full-time business
    (C) to reward political supporters with public office
    (D) to reverse the trend of rotation in office
    (E) the widespread encouragement of a bureaucratic office-holding class

45. The Force Bill of 1833 provided that
    (A) the Congress could use the military for Indian removal
    (B) the Congress could employ the navy to stop smuggling
    (C) the president could use the army to collect excise taxes
    (D) the military could force citizens to track down runaway slaves
    (E) the president could use the army and navy to collect federal tariff duties

46. The political cartoon above
    (A) expresses the view that U.S. colonies such as Cuba were angered by U.S. territorial expansion in the early nineteenth century
    (B) indicates that President McKinley was more than willing to engage in territorial expansion
    (C) is an attempt to provide justification for U.S. imperialism following World War I
    (D) shows President McKinley's displeasure in establishing a U.S. international empire.
    (E) provides evidence that the U.S. repudiated imperialism in the late nineteenth century.

47. U.S. naval captain Alfred Thayer Mahan argued that
    (A) free trade was essential to a nation's economic health
    (B) control of the sea was the key to world domination by the United States
    (C) the United States should continue its policy of isolationism
    (D) an isthmian canal between the Atlantic and the Pacific was impossible
    (E) the United States should construct a fleet of battleships

48. The Teller Amendment
    (A) guaranteed the independence of Cuba
    (B) made Cuba an American possession
    (C) directed President McKinley to order American troops into Cuba
    (D) appropriated funds to combat yellow fever in Cuba
    (E) granted the United States a base at Guantanamo Bay

49. American military forces entered Vietnam in order to
    (A) gain eventual control of North Vietnam
    (B) help to stage a coup against Ngo Dinh Diem
    (C) prevent Ngo Dinh Diem's regime from falling to the communists
    (D) keep South Vietnam from falling to the communists until after the 1964 election
    (E) promote democratic reforms in South Vietnam

50. When the Soviet Union attempted to install nuclear weapons in Cuba, President Kennedy ordered
    (A) the installation of nuclear weapons in Turkey
    (B) surgical air strikes against the missile sites
    (C) the invasion of Cuba at the Bay of Pigs
    (D) resumption of atmospheric testing of nuclear weapons
    (E) a naval quarantine of that island

51. The landmark Civil Rights Act of 1964 accomplished all of the following EXCEPT
    (A) creation of the Equal Employment Opportunity Commission
    (B) prohibiting discrimination based on gender
    (C) banning sexual as well as racial discrimination
    (D) banning racial discrimination in most private facilities open to the public
    (E) requiring "affirmative action" against discrimination

52. The influx of immigrants to the United States tripled, then quadrupled, in the
    (A) 1810s and 1820s
    (B) 1820s and 1830s
    (C) 1830s and 1840s
    (D) 1840s and 1850s
    (E) 1860s and 1870s

53. As a result of the development of the cotton gin,
    (A) slavery revived and expanded
    (B) American industry bought more southern cotton than did British manufacturers
    (C) a nationwide depression ensued
    (D) the South diversified its economy
    (E) the textile industry moved to the South

54. In the case of *Commonwealth v. Hunt,* the supreme court of Massachusetts ruled that
    (A) corporations were unconstitutional
    (B) labor unions were legal
    (C) labor strikes were illegal
    (D) the Boston Associates' employment of young women in their factories was inhumane
    (E) the state could regulate factory wages and working conditions

55. The "cult of domesticity"
    (A) gave women more opportunity to seek employment outside the home
    (B) resulted in more pregnancies for women
    (C) restricted women's moral influence on the family
    (D) glorified the traditional role of women as homemakers
    (E) was especially strong among rural women

56. One argument against annexing Texas to the United States was that the annexation
    (A) could involve the country in a series of ruinous wars in America and Europe
    (B) might give more power to the supporters of slavery
    (C) was not supported by the people of Texas
    (D) offered little of value to America
    (E) would lead to tensions and possible war with Mexico

57. The nomination of James K. Polk as the Democrats' 1844 presidential candidate was secured by
    (A) expansionists
    (B) anti-Texas southerners
    (C) Henry Clay
    (D) eastern business interests
    (E) proslavery forces

58. Passage of the Neutrality Acts of 1935, 1936, and 1937 by the United States resulted in all of the following EXCEPT
    (A) abandonment of the traditional policy of freedom of the seas
    (B) a decline in the navy and other armed forces
    (C) making no distinction whatever between aggressors and victims
    (D) spurring aggressors along their path of conquest
    (E) balancing the scales between dictators and U.S. allies by trading with neither

59. Which of the following does NOT accurately reflect a U.S. foreign policy position in the twentieth century?
    (A) The United States attempted to maintain a policy of neutrality on the eve of World War I.
    (B) The United States embarked on a policy of isolationism in the post-World War II period.
    (C) The United States sought to contain the spread of communism in the post-World War II period.
    (D) The United States was concerned that European nations might attempt to colonize the Caribbean in the 1930s.
    (E) The United States quarantined Cuba to prevent the Soviets from delivering nuclear missiles to that nation.

60. Republican economic policies under Warren G. Harding
    (A) sought to continue the same laissez-faire doctrine as had been the practice under William McKinley
    (B) hoped to encourage the government to guide business along the path to profits
    (C) worked to get standpatters out of administration bureaus
    (D) aimed at supporting increased competition in business
    (E) aided small business at the expense of big business

61. The 1928 Kellogg-Briand Pact
    (A) formally ended World War I for the United States, which had refused to sign the Treaty of Versailles
    (B) set a schedule for German payment of war reparations
    (C) established a battleship ratio for the leading naval powers
    (D) condemned Japan for its unprovoked attack on Manchuria
    (E) outlawed war as a solution to international rivalry

62. One of the major problems facing farmers in the 1920s was
    (A) overproduction
    (B) the inability to purchase modern farm equipment
    (C) passage of the McNary-Haugen Bill
    (D) the prosecution of cooperatives under antitrust laws
    (E) drought and insects like the boll weevil

63. The Progressive party did not do well in the 1924 election because
    (A) it could not win the farm vote
    (B) too many people shared in prosperity to care about reform
    (C) it was too caught up in internal discord
    (D) the liberal vote was split between it and the Democratic party
    (E) La Follette could not win the Socialists' endorsement

64. As a result of the Hawley-Smoot Tariff of 1930,
    (A) American industry grew more secure
    (B) duties on agricultural products decreased
    (C) American economic isolationism ended
    (D) campaign promises to labor were fulfilled
    (E) the worldwide depression deepened

65. The controversy surrounding the Wade-Davis Bill and the readmission of the Confederate states to the Union demonstrated
    (A) the deep differences between President Lincoln and Congress
    (B) the close ties that were developing between President Lincoln and the Democrats
    (C) President Lincoln's desire for a harsh Reconstruction plan
    (D) that a congressional majority believed that the South had never legally left the Union
    (E) the Republicans' fear of re-admitting Confederate leaders to Congress

66. For congressional Republicans, one of the most troubling aspects of the Southern states' restoration to the Union was that
    (A) the South would be stronger than ever in national politics
    (B) inexperienced Southern politicians would be elected
    (C) blacks might actually gain election to the U.S. Congress
    (D) a high tariff might be reinstituted
    (E) slavery might be reestablished

67. Black leader Dr. W. E. B. Du Bois
    (A) demanded complete equality for African-Americans
    (B) established an industrial school at Tuskegee, Alabama
    (C) supported the goals of Booker T. Washington
    (D) was an ex-slave who rose to fame
    (E) sought to resettle blacks in Africa and the Caribbean

68. Labor unions favored immigration restriction because most immigrants were all of the following EXCEPT
    (A) opposed to factory labor
    (B) used as strikebreakers
    (C) willing to work for lower wages
    (D) difficult to unionize
    (E) non-English speaking

69. Disillusioned by war and peace, Americans in the 1920s did all of the following EXCEPT
    (A) denounce "radical" foreign ideas
    (B) condemn "un-American" life-styles
    (C) enter a decade of economic difficulties
    (D) shun diplomatic commitments to foreign countries
    (E) restrict immigration

70. The Ku Klux Klan of the 1920s was a reaction against
    (A) capitalism
    (B) new immigration laws passed in 1924
    (C) the nativist movements that had their origins in the 1850s
    (D) race riots
    (E) the forces of diversity and modernity that were transforming American culture

71. The 1920 census revealed that for the first time most
    (A) men worked in manufacturing
    (B) adult women were employed outside the home
    (C) Americans lived in cities
    (D) Americans lived in the trans-Mississippi West
    (E) families had fewer than four children

72. The Taft-Hartley Act delivered a major blow to labor by
    (A) outlawing strikes by public employees
    (B) creating a serious inflationary spiral
    (C) banning labor's political action committees
    (D) outlawing the "closed" (all-union) shops
    (E) forbidding union organizers to enter workplaces

73. In an effort to forestall an economic downturn, the Truman administration did all of the following EXCEPT
    (A) create the President's Council of Economic Advisers
    (B) sell war factories and other government installations to private businesses at very low prices
    (C) pass the Employment Act, which made it government policy to promote maximum employment, production, and purchasing power
    (D) pass the Servicemen's Readjustment Act, known as the GI Bill of Rights
    (E) continue wartime wage and price controls

74. In the 1950s, the work force began to change when
    (A) white-collar workers outnumbered blue-collar workers
    (B) unskilled workers outnumbered any other group
    (C) union membership exceeded fifty percent of all workers
    (D) women held more than sixty percent of all jobs
    (E) the average age of workers dropped under forty

75. Soviet specialist George F. Kennan framed a coherent approach for America in the Cold War by advising a policy of
    (A) détente
    (B) appeasement
    (C) containment
    (D) limited war
    (E) negotiation

76. President Truman's Marshall Plan called for
    (A) military aid for Europe
    (B) substantial financial assistance to rebuild Western Europe
    (C) economic aid for Japan
    (D) foreign aid for Third World countries to resist communism
    (E) an alliance to contain the Soviet Union

77. At the peace conference at Ghent, the British began to withdraw many of its earlier demands for all of the following reasons EXCEPT
    (A) reverses in upper New York
    (B) a loss at Baltimore
    (C) increasing war weariness in Britain
    (D) concern about the still-dangerous France
    (E) the American victory at New Orleans

78. The resolutions from the Hartford Convention
    (A) helped to cause the death of the Federalist party
    (B) resulted in the resurgence of states' rights
    (C) called for southern secession from the union
    (D) supported use of state militias against the British
    (E) called for the West to join the War of 1812

79. All of the following were results of the Missouri Compromise EXCEPT
    (A) extremists in both the North and South were not satisfied
    (B) Missouri entered the Union as a slave state
    (C) Maine entered the Union as a free state
    (D) sectionalism was reduced
    (E) the balance between the North and South was kept even

80. In interpreting the Constitution, John Marshall
    (A) favored "loose construction"
    (B) supported "strict construction"
    (C) supported an unchanging document
    (D) advocated state control of interstate commerce
    (E) set few precedents

STOP
END OF SECTION I

IF YOU FINISH BEFORE TIME IS CALLED, YOU MAY CHECK YOUR WORK ON THIS SECTION. DO NOT GO ON TO SECTION II UNTIL YOU ARE TOLD TO DO SO.

Section II: Free-Response Essays

Section II of the examination has two kinds of questions. Part A is the Document-Based Question, which you must answer. Part B and Part C each have two general free-response essay questions. You are to answer *one essay question from Part B* and *one essay question from Part C*. You will have a total of 130 minutes to complete the document-based essay and two free-response essays.

Part A: Document-Based Question (DBQ)
Mandatory reading time—15 minutes
Writing time—45 minutes

Directions The question below asks you to develop a coherent, well-structured essay that integrates information from ten documents with your own knowledge of the topic. You are not required to use information from all of the documents.

1. Was U.S. imperialism at the turn of the twentieth century based on arrogance and superiority or did it reflect a humanitarian concern for the nations of South America and the Pacific?

Document A: American Anti-Imperialist League Program, 1899

We hold that the policy known as imperialism is hostile to liberty and tends toward militarism, an evil from which it has been our glory to be free. We regret that it has become necessary in the land of Washington and Lincoln to reaffirm that all men, of whatever race or color, are entitled to life, liberty, and the pursuit of happiness. We maintain that governments derive their just powers from the consent of the governed. We insist that the subjugation of any people is "criminal aggression" and open disloyalty to the distinctive principles of our government.

   We earnestly condemn the policy of the present national administration in the Philippines. It seeks to extinguish the spirit of 1776 in those islands. We deplore the sacrifice of our soldiers and sailors, whose bravery deserves admiration even in an unjust war. We denounce the slaughter of the Filipinos as a needless horror. We protest against the extension of American sovereignty by Spanish methods.

Document B

WELL, I HARDLY KNOW WHICH TO TAKE FIRST!

Document C

"CIVILIZATION BEGINS AT HOME."

Document D

Uncle Sam Gets Cocky

European chickens: "You're not the only rooster in South America."

Uncle Sam rooster: "I was aware of that when I cooped you up."

Document E

Document F

Document G: Alfred Taylor Mahan Defines Security in Terms of Sea Power, 1897

. . . The interesting and significant feature of this changing attitude is the turning of the eyes outward, instead of inward only, to seek the welfare of the country. To affirm the importance of distant markets, and the relation to them of our own immense powers of production, implies logically the recognition of the link that joins the products and the markets,--that is, the carrying trade; the three together constituting that chain of maritime power to which Great Britain owes her wealth and greatness. Further, is it too much to say that, as two of these links, the shipping and the markets, are exterior to our own borders, the acknowledgment of them carries with it a view of the relations of the United States to the world radically distinct from the simple idea of self-sufficingness? We shall not follow far this line of thought before there will dawn the realization of America's unique position, facing the older worlds of the East and West, her shores washed by the oceans which touch the one or the other, but which are common to her alone. . . .

Document H: Platt Amendment

U.S. Government
1901

Article III. The Government of Cuba consents that the United States may exercise the right to intervene for the preservation of Cuban independence, the maintenance of a government adequate for the protection of life, property, and individual liberty, and for discharging the obligations with respect to Cuba imposed by the Treaty of Paris on the United States, now to be assumed and undertaken by the Government of Cuba. . . .

Article V. The government of Cuba will execute, and, as far as necessary, extend the plans already devised, or other plans to be mutually agreed upon, for the sanitation of the cities of the island, to the end that a recurrence of epidemic and infectious diseases may be prevented, thereby assuring protection to the people and commerce of Cuba, as well as to the commerce of Southern ports of the United States and the people residing therein. . . .

Article VII. To enable the United States to maintain the independence of Cuba, and to protect the people thereof, as well as for its own defense, the Government of Cuba will sell or lease to the United States lands necessary for coaling or naval stations, at certain specified points, to be agreed upon with the President of the United States.

Document I

Document J: Roosevelt Corollary to the Monroe Doctrine

Roosevelt, Theodore
1904

It is not true that the United States feels any land hunger or entertains any projects as regards the other nations of the Western Hemisphere save such as are for their welfare. All that this country desires is to see the neighboring countries stable, orderly, and prosperous. Any country whose people conduct themselves well can count upon our hearty friendship. If a nation shows that it knows how to act with reasonable efficiency and decency in social and political matters, if it keeps order and pays its obligations, it need fear no interference from the United States. Chronic wrongdoing, or an impotence which results in a general loosening of the ties of civilized society, may in America, as elsewhere, ultimately require intervention by some civilized nation, and in the Western Hemisphere the adherence of the United States to the Monroe doctrine may force the United States, however reluctantly, in flagrant cases of such wrongdoing or impotence, to the exercise of an international police power. . . .

End of documents for Question 1
Go on to the next page.

Part B and Part C: Free-Response Essay Questions
Writing time—70 minutes

Directions Answer TWO of the following questions, one question from Part B and one from Part C. It is recommended that you spend 5 minutes planning each essay and 30 minutes for writing. Write a well-structured, clearly written essay that provides sufficient evidence to support your thesis. Make certain to identify in the test booklet which essay questions you have selected.

Part B Select ONE question from Part B.

1. Compare and contrast the political features of the Articles of Confederation and the U.S. Constitution.

2. To what extent were the Jeffersonian Democrats and the Jacksonian Democrats similar in their political views and goals?

Part C Select ONE question from Part C.

4. Analyze the relationship between government, business, and labor from the end of the Civil War to the end of the nineteenth century.

5. Discuss whether U.S. presidents in the postwar years up to 1963 were successful in containing communism. Select TWO of the following:
    President Truman
    President Eisenhower
    President Kennedy

END OF EXAMINATION

ANSWERS FOR SECTION I

MULTIPLE-CHOICE ANSWER KEY

1. D	17. D	33. D	49. C	65. A
2. E	18. C	34. E	50. E	66. A
3. C	19. C	35. A	51. E	67. A
4. C	20. E	36. E	52. D	68. A
5. B	21. E	37. D	53. A	69. C
6. D	22. E	38. B	54. B	70. E
7. A	23. B	39. E	55. D	71. C
8. C	24. B	40. A	56. B	72. D
9. A	25. A	41. B	57. A	73. E
10. E	26. E	42. C	58. E	74. A
11. E	27. E	43. A	59. B	75. C
12. E	28. C	44. C	60. B	76. B
13. A	29. D	45. E	61. E	77. E
14. D	30. A	46. B	62. A	78. A
15. C	31. B	47. B	63. B	79. D
16. C	32. C	48. A	64. E	80. A

Scoring The multiple-choice section counts for 50 percent of your examination grade.

EXPLANATIONS FOR THE MULTIPLE-CHOICE ANSWERS

Questions 1-4 cover the early colonial period (The American Pageant. 12th and 11th eds., Chapters 1-2).

1. ANSWER: **D**. Although the colonists came to America to improve their own lives, they soon subjugated others, first Native Americans and then Africans who were brought to the colonies as slaves (*The American Pageant,* 12th and 11th eds., p. 3).

2. ANSWER: **E**. The Caribbean represented almost 50 percent of the total percentage of slaves imported to the New World in the seventeenth and eighteenth centuries (*The American Pageant,* 12th ed., p. 70/11th ed., p. 67).

3. ANSWER: **C**. By 1770, issues such as trade restrictions, taxes, and a desire for self-rule diminished significantly any hope that British-American relations could be repaired (*The American Pageant,* 12th and 11th eds., p. 3).

4. ANSWER: **C**. Jamestown was the first permanent colony in America (1607). It was started after the Virginia Company received a charter from King James I of England (*The American Pageant,* 12th and 11th eds., p. 25).

Questions 5-11 cover the early-nineteenth-century religious experience known as the Second Great Awakening and early-nineteenth-century reform (The American Pageant, 12th ed., Chapter 15/11th ed., Chapter 16).

5. **ANSWER: B.** The Second Great Awakening transformed American life by instilling a religious fervor in those who participated in the revivals. It also represented a challenge to that aspect of Protestantism that espoused predestination (*The American Pageant,* 12th ed., pp. 321-322/11th ed., pp. 329-330).

6. **ANSWER: D.** Finney led massive revival meetings in New England and the mid-Atlantic states in the 1820s (*The American Pageant,* 12th ed., p. 322/11th ed., p. 331).

7. **ANSWER: A.** Dix was a social reformer who advocated for the humane and scientific treatment of mental illness and the treatment of prisoners (*The American Pageant,* 12th ed., p. 329/11th ed., p. 337).

8. **ANSWER: C.** The passions that erupted over the expansion or abolition of slavery in the 1850s eclipsed other social issues, including the women's rights movement (*The American Pageant,* 12th ed., pp. 333, 336-337/11th ed., pp. 341, 344-345).

9. **ANSWER: A.** The Oneida Community challenged the sexual standards and traditions of the era. Selective breeding and arranged marriages shocked the colony's New York neighbors (*The American Pageant,* 12th ed., p. 337/11th ed., p. 345).

10. **ANSWER: E.** The Hudson River School included artists such as Thomas Cole and Asher Durand who created large romantic landscapes of America's wilderness (*The American Pageant,* 12th ed., pp. 338-339/11th ed., pp. 346-347).

11. **ANSWER: E.** Thoreau articulated the view that one should challenge injustice not through violence but through civil nonviolent passive resistance (*The American Pageant,* 12th ed., p. 341/11th ed., p. 349).

Questions 12-19 cover the post-Revolutionary War era, including the struggles to create a new government under the Articles of Confederation (AOC) and the Constitution (The American Pageant, 12th and 11th eds., Chapter 9).

12. **ANSWER: E.** Often referred to as the "Revolution of 1800," the election of Thomas Jefferson represented the first peaceful transfer of political power in U.S. history from one political party (the Federalists) to another (the Democratic-Republicans) (*The American Pageant,* 12th and 11th eds., p. 165).

13. **ANSWER: A.** The American Revolution unleashed an egalitarian spirit that convinced states in the North to either abolish slavery or provide for the gradual emancipation of slaves. No southern state, however, abolished slavery, though some southern slaveowners did manumit their slaves. Unfortunately conditions for freed slaves were usually dreadful (*The American Pageant,* 12th and 11th eds., p. 167).

14. **ANSWER: D.** In nearly all spheres of life women were relegated to a second-class status, though they were expected to instill in their

children a sense of civic responsibility referred to as "republican motherhood." It would take well over one hundred years for women to have the right to vote in all elections in the United States (*The American Pageant,* 12th and 11th eds., pp. 167-168).

15. ANSWER: **C**. One of the chief reasons for discord in ratifying the AOC had to do with western land claims. Some states such New York and Virginia had huge western land claims, whereas others such as Maryland and Pennsylvania had none. Not until New York dropped its claim and Virginia appeared ready to do the same did the last holdout, Maryland, ratify the AOC (*The American Pageant,* 12th and 11th eds., pp. 171-172).

16. ANSWER: **C**. Mexico won its independence from Spain in 1821, though Spain still controlled Cuba. Only Britain and the United States laid claim to the Oregon Country (*The American Pageant,* 12th ed., p. 254/11th ed., p. 253).

17. ANSWER: **D**. Shays's Rebellion (1786-1787) was a protest by Massachusetts farmers, led by a former officer in the Continental army named Daniel Shays, against the state legislature for refusing to issue paper currency that would make it easier for them to pay their mortgages and therefore prevent foreclosures on the homes and farms (*The American Pageant,* 12th and 11th eds., p. 176).

18. ANSWER: **C**. Drafted by Roger Sherman of Connecticut, the plan that ultimately became the Great Compromise was based on a bicameral legislature: representation in the House of Representatives would be based on population; representation in the Senate would be equal for all states (*The American Pageant,* 12th and 11th eds., p. 180).

19. ANSWER: **C**. The three-fifths compromise allowed southern states to count their slaves as part of their total population for purposes of representation and taxation. Each slave would count as three-fifths of a free person (*The American Pageant,* 12th and 11th eds., p. 180).

*Questions 20-21 cover the New Deal era (*The American Pageant, *12th ed., Chapter 34/11th ed., Chapter 36).*

20. ANSWER: **E**. Many of Roosevelt's programs and policies were purely experimental and generally pragmatic. He engaged in deficit spending, for example, in order to create programs that would put money in people's pockets and thus stimulate consumer demand, which in turn would increase employment levels (*The American Pageant,* 12th ed., p. 779/11th ed., p. 797).

21. ANSWER: **E**. The Glass-Steagall Act (also known as the Banking Act of 1933) was instituted during the Hundred Days and was designed to restore the public's trust in the stability of the nation's banks by insuring individual deposits (*The American Pageant,* 12th ed., p. 783/11th ed., p. 801).

*Questions 22-24 cover the Civil War era (*The American Pageant, *12th ed., Chapter 20/11th ed., Chapter 21).*

22. ANSWER: **E**. Lincoln even (illegally) suspended the writ of habeas corpus (whereby a person cannot be held in detention unless there

are legal grounds to do so), declared martial law, and sent in troops in order to guarantee that Border States would stay in the Union (*The American Pageant*, 12th ed., p. 437/11th ed., p. 447).

23. ANSWER: **B**. The South's early successes can in part be attributed to its excellent officer corps. Generals such as Lee, Jackson, and Longstreet compensated for the South's military disadvantages in manpower and industry. Lincoln, on the other hand, appointed and fired generals in rapid succession until he found generals such as Grant and Sherman who understood how to defeat the Confederacy (*The American Pageant*, 12th ed., pp. 438-439/11th ed., pp. 448-449).

24. ANSWER: **B**. The Confederacy hoped that Britain's need for cotton would compel it to intervene. The enormous prewar production of cotton, however, had created huge surpluses in Britain. After Lincoln issued the Emancipation Proclamation and made abolition an objective of the war, France and Britain thought twice about siding with the slave-holding South (*The American Pageant*, 12th ed., p. 441/11th ed., p. 451).

*Questions 25-27 cover the progressive era (*The American Pageant, *12th ed., Chapter 29/11th ed., Chapter 31).*

25. ANSWER: **A**. Muckrakers, a term of derision coined by Theodore Roosevelt, were reform-minded writers who investigated aspects of American business and politics that were riddled with corruption and greed. Their exposés were enormously popular with the public and in some cases helped to bring about much-needed reforms (*The American Pageant*, 12th ed., pp. 666-667/11th ed., pp. 684-685).

26. ANSWER: **E**. The case limited women's work hours on the grounds that women were the "weaker sex" and therefore needed the protection of the government (*The American Pageant*, 12th ed., p. 670/11th ed., p.688).

27. ANSWER: **E**. President Roosevelt intervened after coal supplies dwindled as a result of a strike by thousands of coal miners in Pennsylvania who were seeking higher wages and a reduction in the workday from ten to nine hours. Angered by the owners' refusal to negotiate with the strikers, Roosevelt threatened to seize and operate the mines using federal troops. This was an unprecedented measure in that the federal government had not intervened exclusively on the side of business. Finally, a compromise was reached (*The American Pageant*, 12th ed., p. 673/11th ed., p. 689).

*Questions 28-30 cover the role of the United States in World War II (*The American Pageant, *12th ed., Chapter 36/11th ed., Chapter 38).*

28. ANSWER: **C**. Fearing that Japanese-Americans might engage in acts of sabotage, thousands were sent to concentration camps despite no real evidence that this would occur. Meanwhile, Japanese-Americans contributed to the war effort by fighting against the Nazis in Europe (*The American Pageant*, 12th ed., p. 829/11th ed., p. 689).

29. ANSWER: **D**. The Casablanca conference was designed in part to shore up the Allied war effort by convincing the Soviets that Britain and the United States would not seek a separate peace treaty with Germany (*The American Pageant,* 12th ed., p. 842/11th ed., p. 864).

30. ANSWER: **A**. The U.S. armed forces were not integrated until 1948 (*The American Pageant,* 12th ed., pp. 835-836/11th ed., p. 855).

Questions 31-32 cover the Reagan era and the resurgence of conservatism (The American Pageant, *12th ed., Chapter 41/11th ed., Chapter 43).*

31. ANSWER: **B**. The rise of the New Right in the 1970s and 1980s was partly in response to the counterculture protests of the 1960s. Most of those who identified with the New Right and who voted for Reagan lived in the West and South, the bastion of the Old Right. At the center of this constituency were evangelical Christians who believed that core values and traditions were being eroded (*The American Pageant,* 12th ed., pp. 976-977/11th ed., pp. 990-991).

32. ANSWER: **C**. In the Iran-Contra affair, members of Reagan's National Security Council, with tacit approval from the president, sold weapons to a hostile nation, Iran, and diverted those funds to the Contras, who were attempting to overthrow a leftist government in Nicaragua. This was in violation of the Boland Amendment prohibiting such an act. The Savings-and-Loan debacle was another serious scandal. The Reagan administration had deregulated the savings-and-loan (S&L) industry, which proceeded to offer loans to impetuous investors, many of whom wanted to take advantage of lucrative real estate investments in the Southwest. When the bottom fell out of the real estate market, the S&Ls were devastated. The federal government then bailed out these banks, using billions in taxpayer dollars (*The American Pageant,* 12th ed., pp. 985-987/11th ed., pp. 1001-1002).

Questions 33-34 cover the antebellum (pre-Civil War) era (The American Pageant, *12th ed., Chapter 19/11th ed., Chapter 20).*

33. ANSWER: **D**. A significant influx of German and Irish in the 1850s worried Protestants, who organized a secret anti-Catholic and antiforeign organization known as the Know-Nothings (*The American Pageant,* 12th ed., pp. 415-417/11th ed., pp. 425-426).

34. ANSWER: **E**. The panic of 1857 primarily affected the North. Congress lowered the tariff rate just six months prior to the panic, and northern manufacturers now wanted higher tariffs to protect their businesses from overseas competition (*The American Pageant,* 12th ed., pp. 418-419/11th ed., pp. 428-429).

Questions 35-36 cover the French and Indian War era (The American Pageant, *12th and 11th eds., Chapter 6).*

35. ANSWER: **A**. The Albany Congress sought to conciliate the Iroquois and establish greater colonial unity in the war against the French (*The American Pageant,* 12th ed., p. 114/11th ed., p. 112).

36. **ANSWER: E.** The purpose of the Proclamation of 1763 was to prevent colonists from moving beyond the Appalachian Mountains in order to avoid conflict with Native Americans. The Americans viewed it as a way to control them and defied the Proclamation (*The American Pageant,* 12th ed., p. 121/11th ed., p. 119).

Questions 37-38 cover progressivism under Theodore Roosevelt and Woodrow Wilson (The American Pageant, 12th ed., Chapters 29-30/11th ed., Chapters 31–32).

37. **ANSWER: D.** Roosevelt's New Nationalism (part of his "Bull Moose" campaign of 1912) comprised a broad program of social reforms that included a minimum wage law and women's suffrage (*The American Pageant,* 12th ed., pp. 688-689/11th ed., pp. 704-705).

38. **ANSWER: B.** Wilson, a Virginian, sympathized with the Confederacy's failed attempt at self-determination, an ideal he favored for people in other countries (*The American Pageant,* 12th ed., p. 690/11th ed., p. 706).

Questions 39-42 cover the Gilded Age (The American Pageant, 12th ed., Chapter 23/11th ed., Chapter 24).

39. **ANSWER: E.** Nast's powerful political cartoons illustrated the extent of Tweed's corruption in a manner that was accessible to most Americans (*The American Pageant,* 12th ed., pp. 504-505/11th ed., pp. 515-516).

40. **ANSWER: A.** The two major parties agreed on many of the most important issues of the day, such as civil-service reform, the tariff, and the currency question (*The American Pageant,* 12th ed., pp. 507-508/11th ed., pp. 517-518).

41. **ANSWER: B.** In return for not contesting the presidential election of Republican Hayes, despite considerable voting irregularities, the Republicans agreed to withdraw federal troops from the South, effectively ending Reconstruction (*The American Pageant,* 12th ed., p. 509/11th ed., p. 520).

42. **ANSWER: C.** In an 8-1 decision, the Supreme Court ruled that as long as facilities and treatment of the races was equal, separation was constitutional and did not imply inferiority. The case sustained the subordination of black Americans (*The American Pageant,* 12th ed., p. 511/11th ed., p. 522).

Questions 43-45 cover the Jacksonian era (The American Pageant, 12th ed., Chapter 13/11th ed., Chapters 13-14).

43. **ANSWER: A.** Of the four presidential candidates, Andrew Jackson received the most popular votes but failed to gain the necessary electoral votes for a victory. The House of Representatives was given the responsibility of selecting the three top candidates (as authorized by the Twelfth Amendment). Henry Clay was eliminated but threw his support to John Quincy Adams, who was elected president (*The American Pageant,* 12th ed., p. 258/11th ed., p. 260).

44. ANSWER: **C**. The term "spoils system" is synonymous with patronage. Although a common practice dating to the Jackson administration, by the late nineteenth century reformers wanted the patronage system replaced with one based on merit, not political connections. The Pendleton Civil Service Act (1883) is one example of the federal government's attempt to eliminate the spoils system (*The American Pageant,* 12th ed., p. 262/11th ed., p. 268).

45. ANSWER: **E**. The bill authorized the president to use military force against a state if necessary to enforce federal law. South Carolina's nullification of the tariff led President Jackson to ask Congress for the authority to use military force to enforce the tariff (*The American Pageant,* 12th ed., p. 265/11th ed., p. 274).

Questions 46-48 cover late-nineteenth-century U.S. imperialism (The American Pageant, 12th ed., Chapter 27/11th ed., Chapter 29).

46. ANSWER: **B**. President McKinley asked Congress to declare war on Spain in 1898. The U.S. victory provided the United States with an international empire that included Cuba, Puerto Rico, and the Philippines (*The American Pageant,* 12th ed., p. 624/11th ed., p. 642).

47. ANSWER: **B**. Mahan's *The Influence of Sea Power upon History* influenced, among others, President Theodore Roosevelt, that in order to establish an international empire the United States would have to first build a modern navy in order to control the seas (*The American Pageant,* 12th ed., p. 624/11th ed., p. 642).

48. ANSWER: **A**. Passed by Congress in 1898 as part of a pre-Spanish-American War resolution, the U.S. government declared it had no intention of denying the Cubans their autonomy. The Platt Amendment of 1901 allowed for U.S. intervention, however, to ensure that Cuba would not fall under the control of a foreign power (*The American Pageant,* 12th ed., p. 631/11th ed., p. 649).

Questions 49-51 cover early 1960s foreign and domestic affairs under John F. Kennedy and Lyndon B. Johnson (The American Pageant, 12th ed., Chapter 39/11th ed., Chapter 41).

49. ANSWER: **C**. The Diem regime, notoriously corrupt, repressive, and unpopular, was bolstered by President Kennedy's decision to send U.S. troops to South Vietnam in 1961 (*The American Pageant,* 12th ed., p. 920/11th ed., p. 940).

50. ANSWER: **E**. Kennedy took the United States and the Soviet Union to the brink of a nuclear confrontation when he placed a naval quarantine around Cuba in 1962 in order to prevent the Soviets from delivering nuclear weapons to Cuba (*The American Pageant,* 12th ed., pp. 922-923/11th ed., pp. 941-942).

51. ANSWER: **E.** This landmark legislation provided the federal government with increased powers to enforce school integration and combat discrimination; however, it did not compel the southern states to eliminate discriminatory voting practices such as the literacy test. The following year, Congress addressed this abuse by passing the Voting Rights Act of 1965 (*The American Pageant,* 12th ed., p. 931/11th ed., pp. 950-951).

Questions 52-55 cover the expanding U.S. economy in the antebellum era (The American Pageant, *12th ed., Chapter 14/11th ed., Chapter 15).*

52. ANSWER: **D.** Most of the immigrants in this period came from Ireland and Germany. For example, in the decade 1831-1840, approximately 207,000 Irish emigrated to the United States, whereas in the next decade, 1841-1850, approximately 780,000 emigrated to the United States (*The American Pageant,* 12th ed., p. 291/11th ed., p. 301).

53. ANSWER: **A.** Picking cotton was very labor-intensive and therefore expensive. Not until Eli Whitney's cotton gin was introduced in 1793 did cotton production become profitable (*The American Pageant,* 12th ed., p. 302/11th ed., pp. 310-311).

54. ANSWER: **B.** The supreme court of Massachusetts ruled that labor unions were not unlawful arrangements, provided their methods were legal and peaceful. This was a major gain for unions, but it would be another hundred years before labor was on equal terms with management (*The American Pageant,* 12th ed., p. 305/11th ed., p. 313).

55. ANSWER: **D.** In the antebellum period, attitudes about women, especially in middle-class families, were built around the following "ideals": purity, piety, domesticity, and submissiveness (*The American Pageant,* 12th ed., p. 307/11th ed., p. 315).

Questions 56-57 cover antebellum U.S. territorial expansion (The American Pageant, *12th ed., Chapter 17/11th ed., Chapter 18).*

56. ANSWER: **B.** Northerners were concerned that annexing Texas would ultimately lead to statehood, thus upsetting the balance of power in the Senate between free and slave states (*The American Pageant,* 12th ed., p. 375/11th ed., p. 385).

57. ANSWER: **A.** Many Americans were supportive of the notion of Manifest Destiny, that it was the nation's fate to dominate the Western Hemisphere. Democratic party candidate Polk, an expansionist who favored the annexation of Texas and resolving the feud with Britain over Oregon Territory, defeated the Whig party candidate Henry Clay (*The American Pageant,* 12th ed., p. 377/11th ed., p. 387).

Questions 58-59 cover FDR and the road to World War II (The American Pageant, *12th ed., Chapter 35/11th ed., Chapter 37).*

58. ANSWER: **E.** The Neutrality Acts, which forbade the sale of supplies to belligerents, actually favored the militarist dictators such as Hitler and Mussolini by preventing the United States from selling supplies and armaments needed more by the democratic nations

such as Britain and France than by Germany and Italy, which already had substantial military stockpiles (*The American Pageant,* 12th ed., pp. 810-811/11th ed., pp. 829-830).

59. **ANSWER: B.** The United States was actively engaged in all forms of foreign policy after World War II. It emerged from the war a superpower seeking to contain the spread of communism in the postwar era. To this end it used utilized various options: economic, political, and military (*The American Pageant,* 12th ed., p. 645/11th ed., p. 663).

Questions 60-64 cover the post-World War I era to the eve of the Great Depression (The American Pageant, *12th ed., Chapter 33/11th ed., Chapter 35).*

60. **ANSWER: B.** Harding, representing the interests of "Old Guard" Republicans, favored government intervention to assist businesses in realizing greater profits. This was a variation of their earlier laissez-faire approach, which favored limiting government regulations of businesses (*The American Pageant,* 12th ed., pp. 754-755/11th ed., pp. 772-773).

61. **ANSWER: E.** Profoundly affected by the devastation of World War I, world leaders sought to outlaw wars of aggression but not defensive wars. An excuse for the latter could always be found, thus devaluing the effectiveness of the Kellogg-Briand Pact (*The American Pageant,* 12th ed., p. 758/11th ed., p. 776).

62. **ANSWER: A.** With the increased use of technology by farmers, crop yields rose dramatically in the early twentieth century. Consequently, with overproduction, prices for crops declined precipitously, which caused a depression in the agrarian sector of the economy in the 1920s (*The American Pageant,* 12th ed., p. 761/11th ed., p. 779).

63. **ANSWER: B.** For many Americans the 1920s was a period of unprecedented prosperity. Thus the cries of the progressives to reform the capitalist system did not have the public appeal it once did (*The American Pageant,* 12th ed., p. 762/11th ed., p. 780).

64. **ANSWER: E.** The Hawley-Smoot Tariff was the highest peacetime protective tariff in the nation's history. Foreign nations responded in kind, thus limiting the sale of U.S.-made commodities overseas. All nations suffered, adding to the already seriously weakened international economies (*The American Pageant,* 12th ed., p. 767/11th ed., p. 785).

*Questions 65-66 cover Reconstruction (*The American Pageant, *12th ed., Chapter 22/11th ed., Chapter 23).*

65. **ANSWER: A.** President Lincoln favored the "10 percent" plan, which would allow for an easy readmission of seceded states, whereas many in Congress, especially under the Radical Republicans, sought a more punitive and harder readmission process for the conquered former Confederate states (*The American Pageant,* 12th ed., p. 483/11th ed., p. 493).

66. ANSWER: **A**. With the abolition of slavery the three-fifths compromise, whereby a black person counted for partial Southern representation in Congress, would no longer be in effect. Consequently the South would receive greater representation in Congress because blacks were to be counted as full persons (*The American Pageant,* 12th ed., p. 485/11th ed., p. 495).

Questions 67-68 cover the black civil rights movement and immigration in the late nineteenth century (The American Pageant, *12th ed., Chapter 25/11th ed., Chapter 26).*

67. ANSWER: **A**. Du Bois, cofounder of the NAACP, opposed gradual equality for blacks, as articulated by Booker T. Washington, and was in favor of immediate and complete equality (*The American Pageant,* 12th ed., p. 574/11th ed., p. 581).

68. ANSWER: **A**. In fact, immigrants who resided in urban areas found that their employment opportunities were limited to factory work, often at lower wages (*The American Pageant,* 12th ed., pp. 568-569/11th ed., p. 575).

Questions 69-71 cover life in the United States in the 1920s (The American Pageant, *12th ed., Chapter 32/11th ed., Chapter 34).*

69. ANSWER: **C**. The 1920s was a period of prosperity for many Americans during the interwar years (*The American Pageant,* 12th ed., pp. 728-730/11th ed., pp. 746-748).

70. ANSWER: **E**. The reactionary KKK grew profoundly in the 1920s, in large part because of the wave of immigration that brought many non-Protestant foreigners to the United States in this period. Further, those who rejected the transformation of the United States to a more modern and cosmopolitan culture often joined the KKK, whose membership rose to approximately 5 million in the 1920s (*The American Pageant,* 12th ed., p. 730/11th ed., pp. 748).

71. ANSWER: **C**. The influx of immigrants in the early twentieth century, combined with the expansion of the U.S. economy, expressed itself in the 1920 census, which revealed that the U.S. urban population had expanded enormously and now contained most of the nation's population (*The American Pageant,* 12th ed., p. 745/11th ed., p. 763).

Questions 72-76 cover the post-World War II era to the 1950s (The American Pageant, *12th ed., Chapter 37/11th ed., Chapter 39).*

72. ANSWER: **D**. Passed over President Truman's veto by a probusiness Republican Congress, the Taft-Hartley Act undermined unions— for example, by eliminating the closed shop, whereby a business owner can employ only union workers (*The American Pageant,* 12th ed., p. 859/11th ed., p. 881).

73. ANSWER: **E**. Following the end of World War II, as the government sought ways to incorporate millions of servicemen and servicewomen back into the nation's work force, inflation, which had been kept in check by wage and price controls, was a real concern. As the economy expanded, there was no longer a need to maintain these restraints, which had been established by the

government during the war. Both labor and management favored a lifting of these controls (*The American Pageant,* 12th ed., p. 859/11th ed., p. 881).

74. **ANSWER: A.** This transformation was largely the result of the transition from an industrial to a postindustrial economy. Consequently there were fewer blue-collar jobs and more employment opportunities in the service and technology sectors of the economy (*The American Pageant,* 12th ed., pp. 908-909/11th ed., pp. 927-928).

75. **ANSWER: C.** Kennan's influential analysis maintained that the Soviets would spread communism throughout the world if given the opportunity. U.S. political leaders subsequently decided to use whatever means were necessary to contain this expansion of Soviet influence (*The American Pageant,* 12th ed., p. 874/11th ed., pp. 894-895).

76. **ANSWER: B.** The Marshall Plan had two objectives: provide the United States with valuable trading partners, and prevent Soviet-backed communism from penetrating an economically vulnerable Western Europe (*The American Pageant,* 12th ed., p. 875/11th ed., p. 895).

Questions 77-80 cover the War of 1812 and the rise of American nationalism (The American Pageant, 12th and 11th eds., Chapter 12).

77. **ANSWER: E.** The American victory at the Battle of New Orleans occurred after both sides agreed to the terms of the Treaty of Ghent. Due to the slowness of sea travel, the battle was fought three weeks after the treaty was signed (*The American Pageant,* 12th and 11th eds., p. 237).

78. **ANSWER: A.** The resolutions adopted at the Hartford Convention by antiwar Federalists occurred at the same time the news of the Treaty of Ghent reached Washington, D.C. Many thus came to associate the Federalists with treason. Consequently their presidential candidate in the next election (1816) was trounced by Democratic-Republican James Monroe (*The American Pageant,* 12th ed., p. 239/11th ed., p. 238).

79. **ANSWER: D.** Although neither North nor South strongly favored or opposed the Missouri Compromise, it merely set aside the issue of the expansion or containment of slavery for a later generation to resolve. Sectionalism continued to undermine the unity of the nation (*The American Pageant,* 12th ed., p. 245/11th ed., p. 244).

80. **ANSWER: A.** Marshall, a loose constructionist, expanded the role of the judicial branch by establishing the principle of judicial review and the power of the federal government in relation to the states. In his decision on the Bank of the United States, he articulated the idea of implied powers—in other words, powers granted to the government that were not specifically identified in the Constitution (*The American Pageant,* 12th ed., p. 247/11th ed., p. 248).

SECTION II, PART A: DOCUMENT-BASED QUESTION (DBQ)

Below are short analyses of the documents. The italicized words suggest what your margin notes might include:

DOCUMENT A This statement by the American Anti-Imperialist League harshly *criticizes U.S. imperialism* as an affront to the principle of self-determination as well as *contradicts American political and cultural values.*

DOCUMENT B This political cartoon depicts Uncle Sam's *voracious appetite for colonial possessions.* President McKinley, the waiter, is obviously intent on satiating the nation's hunger for an *international empire.*

DOCUMENT C This document is a scathing *indictment* of the *U.S. goal of "civilizing"* the inhabitants of its *colonies* at a time when its *own black population* is denied justice and is *brutalized.*

DOCUMENT D Although this political cartoon shows the *aggressive nature of U.S. foreign policy* at the turn of the twentieth century, it *also represents the United States* as a *protector of South American nations* from the imperialistic European powers. The "cooped-up" chickens represent European powers whose designs on the Western Hemisphere are contained by the *Roosevelt Corollary to the Monroe Doctrine.*

DOCUMENT E In this political cartoon the artist shows a heavily armed Uncle Sam (the United States) *blindly stepping into a militarist and imperialist foreign policy* in which he (and the nation) will soon plunge to *catastrophe.*

DOCUMENT F The artist depicts the extravagantly dressed European leaders (or their symbols, as in the case of Britain's version of Uncle Sam, called John Bull) being thwarted by *Uncle Sam, who is protecting the obviously needy South American countries* from the exploitative intentions of the European powers.

DOCUMENT G In this passage, *Mahan* articulates the *need for international markets,* the protection of which would be the responsibility of the *U.S. Navy.* The navy, in turn, would require access to colonies, which would serve as *coaling and supply stations,* as well as *markets for U.S. commodities.*

DOCUMENT H Article III of the Platt Amendment reveals how *Cuba's autonomy was sacrificed to U.S. interests.* The passage points out the *justifications for U.S. intervention* in Cuba's affairs—in other words, when the United States deemed it necessary to do so.

DOCUMENT I This political cartoon depicts an athletic and robust Theodore Roosevelt flexing his muscles in a *demonstration of U.S. hegemony in South America.*

DOCUMENT J *Roosevelt* portrays *U.S. hegemony in the Western Hemisphere* as *benevolent* and paved with good intentions. *Yet,* the passage *implies a sense of moral, political, and cultural superiority* in that "wrongdoing" on the part of the South Americans is tantamount to being uncivilized.

Documents that reflect arrogance or superiority on the part of the United States in its relationship with South America and the Pacific are grouped as negative; those documents that suggest a humanitarian concern on the part of the United States are grouped as positive. Documents that are not necessarily identified with one perspective or another can nonetheless be used them to defend your perspective. The following is a categorization of the documents:

Negative Documents	Positive Documents	Neutral Documents
A	D	E
B	F	G
C		J (also negative)
H		
I		

In developing the essay, you should incorporate the following historical information:

- The "New Imperialism" paved the way for the adoption of expansionist policy by the United States with the intention of establishing international markets for domestically produced commodities as well as providing raw materials necessary for industrialization. Furthermore, colonies could ostensibly provide a "safety valve" for those discontented with domestic conditions in the United States.
- Social Darwinism was used as a justification for imperialism. Social Darwinists claimed that certain civilizations had evolved faster than others. In other words, some societies were civilized and others were "barbaric." The implication was that Western cultures, being more advanced than other generally non-Western cultures, had the right and duty to expand and "uplift" other "less developed" people.
- President Roosevelt's "Big Stick" policy in South America called for U.S. military and political intervention in Venezuela and other South American nations that could default on loans to European nations and therefore risked European intervention in violation of the Monroe Doctrine. This convinced Roosevelt to extend the authority of the United States under the Monroe Doctrine. By this Roosevelt Corollary, the United States claimed the right to intervene in South American countries whenever the United States deemed it necessary to do so.
- The United States supported Panamanian independence as part of an arrangement to build the Panama Canal and ultimately to provide the United States with long-term control of the canal.

The causes and effects of the Spanish-American War played an important role. Make certain to include the following:

- Teller Amendment
- Platt Amendment
- *Insular Cases*

A SAMPLE ESSAY

An essay that takes the position that the United States was arrogant and felt superior to those in South America and the Pacific might look something like this:

By the late nineteenth century the United States had embarked on a policy of international territorial expansion. Having expanded to the Pacific Ocean, it now looked to establish a world empire, first by gaining new colonies, and second by preventing the European imperial powers from colonizing the Western hemisphere. The United States, like other imperial powers, had certain assumptions regarding those nations in which it had either direct or indirect control. For example, in 1823 the United States adopted a hegemonic policy in the Western Hemisphere, warning Europe not to take steps to recolonize South America. This pivotal foreign policy statement, the Monroe Doctrine, has been the cornerstone of U.S. foreign policy, not only in the Western Hemisphere, but as applied to Asia, Europe, and Africa as well. For, though the initial document applied to the Western Hemisphere, the United States has used it to justify its intervention in other areas of the world to protect U.S. interests. In other words, in the Cold War period the United States claimed it was defending itself from communist penetration in South America and the Caribbean by attempting to eliminate communism in, say, Asia.

At the turn of the twentieth century, the United States was arrogant and condescending in its treatment of South American nations. In order to justify its feeling of superiority, U.S. political leaders rationalized that the application of the Monroe Doctrine by means of periodic U.S. interventions in the internal affairs of these nations was based in large part on the ideas associated with Social Darwinism. Those who advocated this perspective claimed that nonmodern or less developed nations were simply less evolved than, for example, the United States, which had over time developed into a modern nation. This perspective was held by many political leaders such as President Theodore Roosevelt, who maintained that U.S. hegemony was beneficial to less developed cultures. For example, in his Corollary to the Monroe Doctrine he claimed the United States had the right to intervene when South American nations acted "irresponsibly." We see this attitude conveyed in the political cartoon "His Foresight," in which the United States (Roosevelt) is depicted as the protector of South American nations, which could fall prey to the European powers were it not for the United States. In the Corollary President Roosevelt further articulated the view that the United States would intervene in South American nations if "it became evident that their inability or unwillingness to do justice at home and abroad had violated the rights of the United States or had invited foreign aggression to the detriment of the entire body of American nations" (Document J). This view of superiority was expressed in the Platt Amendment following the Spanish American War, which legitimized U.S. intervention in order to maintain political stability in Cuba, as well as to establish a U.S. military presence in Cuba (the naval base at Guantanamo) and restricted Cuba's diplomatic autonomy. By establishing a strategic naval base in Cuba, the U.S. was fulfilling the recommendation of Captain Alfred Thayer Mahan (whose The Influence of Sea Power upon History had a profound influence on Roosevelt). In Document G Mahan articulates the view that the United States needed to protect its international trade and markets by establishing a powerful navy, as well as by obtaining naval bases and coaling stations to supply the navy's ships. No thought was given to the idea of Cuban self-determination, which had been one reason why the U.S. claimed it fought against Spain in the war.

COMMENT This essay synthesizes outside information—the reader's knowledge and use of the Social Darwinism, the Roosevelt Corollary to the Monroe Doctrine, the Platt Amendment, and Mahan's thesis—with information gleaned from the documents—a political cartoon, two quotes from the Roosevelt Corollary, and Mahan's view on sea power. Together, the information from the documents and the outside information sustain a defense of the thesis.

SCORING The DBQ essay counts for 45 percent of the *total free response grade,* or 22.5 percent of the total examination grade.

SECTION II, PART B AND PART C

QUESTION 2 Your essay should point out the rationale behind the differences that defined the two governments. The AOC was established during the Revolutionary War, when most colonists who fought for independence had a fear of a strong central government, preferring to place political and economic of power with the states. To this end, discuss the compact theory of government and then provide features of the AOC that indicate these preferences. In a discussion of the Constitution point out how the deficiencies of the AOC were addressed by the creation of a strong central government with powers reserved to the states. For example, the AOC lacked an executive branch, whereas the Constitution provided for an executive branch with significant powers. Discuss the Constitution as a reflection of the contract theory of government.

A strong essay identifies the weaknesses of the AOC in addressing foreign and domestic problems facing the nation following the Revolutionary War. Including a discussion of the specific features of the government, such as the absence of a national court system as an obstacle to interstate trade and the requirement of unanimity as a hindrance to the development of nationalism, is an integral part of an excellent essay on this topic. Further, an exceptional essay would include the inability of the legislative branch to impose taxes and the difficulties in approving legislation and amending the AOC. To complete the essay, discuss the differing features of the Constitution that provided the government with the authority to address the nation's domestic and foreign affairs concerns, such as establishing an executive branch to carry out and enforce laws passed by Congress and to make treaties with other nations.

QUESTION 3 At the heart of a discussion on Jeffersonian democracy and Jacksonian democracy is the nature of reform—the democratization of the nation's socioeconomic and political institutions and rights. Pointing out that some historians refer to Jefferson's election as the "Revolution of 1800" sets the tone of this part of the answer. Thus an explanation of the ways in which Jefferson's election promoted the interests of the common man over the interests of bankers and manufacturers is needed. You should also take up Jefferson's attempt to implement the ideals of limited government and strict constructionism. Like Jefferson, Jackson claimed to represent the common man. He too claimed to attack the expansive nature of government. Thus a discussion of the Bank War is essential, as is an analysis of Jackson's political responses, such as the spoils system and the Kitchen Cabinet, to entrenched elitism.

An effective essay is one that addresses how the two administrations viewed the nature of reform and liberalism. However, a fuller discussion should indicate that reform did not emanate exclusively from the federal government; state governments also sought to address abuses in government, society, and the economy that were not democratic. Also, a discussion of grassroots movements—that is, citizens at the local level engaged in improving and democratizing American institutions and social life, such as urban decay, abolition of slavery, education, and women's rights—is essential to an excellent essay on this topic. A first-rate essay might also incorporate the inconsistencies and contradictions of Jeffersonian and Jacksonian reform—for example, the treatment of Native Americans under both governments, the fact that both presidents were slave owners, and the territorial expansion that sought to expand American democracy at the expense of Native Americans.

QUESTION 4 An excellent essay establishes the close relationship between government and big business, often at the expense of labor, in the decades following the Civil War. The Railroad Strike of 1877 is a very good initial example and shows the role and power of the executive branch in ending the strike. Including the government's loose immigration policy—in part at the behest of businesses, which wanted an expanded labor pool—led to lower wages and more competition for jobs. The extent to which government provided railway companies with land while playing, at best, a limited role in social welfare points out the close relationship government had with big business.

The rise of monopoly capitalism in this era is an indication that government and big business had an intimate relationship that not only hurt wage laborers but limited economic opportunities for other capitalists, investors, and entrepreneurs who wanted to compete in the marketplace. A discussion of the government's selective laissez-faire policy demonstrates a more complete understanding of the question. To this end an excellent essay would identify those areas in which government refused to side with labor (on wages, working conditions, and the right to collective bargaining) yet intervened on behalf of big business (protective tariffs, failure to address child labor, and unwillingness to establish maximum working hours).

QUESTION 5 A discussion of the containment policy should precede an elaboration on whether these presidents were effective in containing communism in the approximately fifteen years following World War II. For all intents and purposes, the containment policy went into effect under Truman. For that reason, it is advisable to select Truman as one of your two presidents. Under Truman the United States established the Truman Doctrine, the Marshall Plan, the Berlin airlift, and NATO. A discussion of the success in containing the spread of communism in the Korean War and the failure—despite economic and military assistance to the Chinese Nationalists—to contain communism in China is essential if you do decide to select Truman. In discussing Eisenhower, the end of the Korean War is an excellent starting point. An effective discussion of Eisenhower's attempt to implement the containment policy would include both the massive military buildup that occurred under his administration and the Eisenhower Doctrine. For Kennedy you should point out that he followed his predecessors in maintaining the containment policy. His handling of the Bay of Pigs invasion, the Cuban missile crisis, the response to the construction of the Berlin Wall, and U.S. military intervention in Vietnam would be included in an effective essay.

Scoring for this essay would depend on whether you identified the key foreign policy elements of the Truman, Eisenhower, and Kennedy administrations as they attempted to contain communism. Although this is an analytical question, it also asks you to evaluate whether the presidents in question applied the containment policy effectively. However, an essay of this nature, which asks for an analysis of their individual policies, can point out the limitations of the containment policy, such as the decision not to use U.S. military troops in the Chinese Civil War or the French-Indochina War and the inability of the United States to assist nations like Hungary in their effort to break free from communist control.

SCORING Together, the two free-response essays from Part B and Part C count for 55 percent of the free-response essay grade, or 27.5 percent of your total examination grade.

Grade your essays on a scale of 0-9.

8-9: EXCELLENT   The essay has a clear thesis, is well written and organized, covers all aspects of the topic in depth, analyzes the question effectively, and supports the thesis with sufficient and relevant historical information. It may contain minor errors.

5-7: GOOD   The essay has a clear thesis, though it is not as well developed as in an 8-9 essay. It has clear though not excellent organization. The essay covers only one aspect of the question in depth and does not fully indicate an understanding of the complexity of the question or topic. The analysis is not as well developed as in an 8-9 essay and makes limited use of relevant historical information. The essay may contain errors that do not affect the overall quality of the essay.

2-4: FAIR The essay either lacks a clear thesis or the thesis is confused or even missing. It is not well organized and exhibits weak writing. It does not indicate an understanding of the complexity of the question or topic, and it fails to support a thesis with sufficient historical information and/or analysis. It may contain significant errors.

0-1: POOR The essay has no thesis, poor structure and organization, is poorly written, lacks historical information and analysis, and tends to offer rhetorical comments. It contains both major and minor errors.

It is important that you be as objective as possible when evaluating your essays. You might ask a teacher, parent, fellow student, or friend to evaluate your essays for you.

CALCULATING YOUR SCORE ON THE DIAGNOSTIC TEST

SCORING THE MULTIPLE-CHOICE SECTION

Use the following formula to calculate your raw score on the multiple-choice section of the exam:

$$\underset{\substack{\text{number} \\ \text{correct}}}{\underline{\hspace{2cm}}} - (\underset{\substack{\text{number} \\ \text{incorrect}}}{\underline{\hspace{2cm}}} \times 1/4) = \underset{\substack{\text{raw} \\ \text{score}}}{\underline{\hspace{2cm}}} \text{ (round to nearest whole number)}$$

SCORING THE FREE-RESPONSE SECTION

Use the formula below to calculate your raw score on the free-response section of the exam:

$$(\underset{\text{DBQ}}{\underline{\hspace{1cm}}} \times 4) + (\underset{\substack{\text{essay} \\ \#1}}{\underline{\hspace{1cm}}} \times 2.44) + (\underset{\substack{\text{essay} \\ \#2}}{\underline{\hspace{1cm}}} \times 2.44) = \underset{\substack{\text{raw} \\ \text{score}}}{\underline{\hspace{1cm}}} \text{ (round to nearest whole number)}$$

YOUR COMPOSITE SCORE

$$1.13 \times \underset{\substack{\text{multiple-} \\ \text{choice}}}{\underline{\hspace{2cm}}} = \underset{\substack{\text{raw} \\ \text{score}}}{\underline{\hspace{2cm}}} \text{ (weighted multiple-choice score: NOT rounded)}$$

$$2.73 \times \underset{\substack{\text{free-} \\ \text{response}}}{\underline{\hspace{2cm}}} = \underset{\substack{\text{raw} \\ \text{score}}}{\underline{\hspace{2cm}}} \text{ (weighted free-response score: NOT rounded)}$$

Once you have completed your calculations, add the two weighted sections (and round to the nearest whole number). You now have your composite score. Now see where your score falls in the Composite Score Range below. Remember that this score is an estimate of your performance on the College Board exam.

AP GRADES BY SCORE RANGE

AP Grade	Composite Score Range
5	114–180
4	91–113
3	74–90
2	49–73
1	0–48

Part II

A Review of AP U.S. History

EUROPEAN COLONIZATION: 1492–1700

Thirty to forty thousand years before Christopher Columbus—or any Western European, for that matter—found his way to the New World (the Western Hemisphere), the continent had already been settled by migrants who had crossed a land bridge that once connected Alaska with Russia. Much later, in the early eleventh century, Viking ships entered the Western Hemisphere intent on establishing colonies in North America, but the Norse venture failed. In the latter stages of the feudal era, powerful Western European nations such as Spain and Portugal were emerging, and they too were bent on expanding their political and economic advantages through colonization. As Europe emerged from its feudal period around the fifteenth to sixteenth century, commerce and exploration increased in intensity, stimulated by new navigational developments such as the compass and better shipbuilding techniques, as well as nonmaritime discoveries and advancements such as the printing press. In the feudal age, power had been diffused and often decentralized, but with the rise of the modern nation-state, powerful monarchs and wealthy merchants were willing to finance explorations of discovery. Colonization ultimately followed these explorations, and it was not long before France, Holland, and England set covetous eyes on the New World as well. In fact, the expansion of commerce was an essential element in the explorations that took place in the fifteenth and sixteenth centuries. Leading the way were Spain and Portugal, but England, the latecomer, would gain the upper hand in North America and set the stage for the unfolding of United States history.

KEY CONCEPTS

- The rise of nation-states in Europe was a factor in stimulating explorations to the New World.
- Spain and Portugal initially colonized the Western Hemisphere.
- The Dutch colonized the Hudson River Valley, the French settled in parts of Canada and the Ohio River Valley, and the English ultimately established a strong foothold on the eastern seaboard.
- The origins of the English colonies varied, as did their social and political systems.

The exploration of the New World and colonial life in North America are discussed in depth in *The American Pageant,* 12th and 11th eds., Chapters 1–5.

SPAIN COLONIZES THE NEW WORLD

At the time of Columbus's arrival in 1492, hundreds of generally small Native American tribes occupied North and South America and the Caribbean, which questions whether the New World was "discovered" by European explorers. In fact, by the time Europeans arrived, Native Americans had introduced agricultural crops—among them corn, potatoes, tomatoes, and tobacco—that would someday play important roles in Western diet and commerce. Some inhabitants of the Americas such as the Aztecs and Incas had established flourishing civilizations that would, by the sixteenth century, be eliminated by Spain, victims of its quest for gold and other precious materials. Using more powerful military technology—for instance the gun—and playing one indigenous people off another, the Spaniards were able to defeat the native tribes, which had already been weakened by exposure to European diseases like smallpox.

The Treaty of Tordesillas, drafted in 1494 with influence from the pope, had drawn a line of demarcation to divide the world between Catholic Spain and Portugal. All of the Western Hemisphere except Brazil was assigned to Spain; Portugal was permitted to colonize Asia. Although other nations did not take this agreement seriously, Spain and Portugal were in the forefront of exploration.

Initially, the Spanish journeyed to North and South America in search of precious metals and gave little thought to colonizing the areas they explored. Only when other European powers such as France took an interest in North America did Spain make a concerted effort to establish permanent settlements, first at St. Augustine, Florida (1565), later in South America, the American Southwest, and as far west as California. On the heels of the early explorers and settlers came Catholic missionaries, who viewed the Western Hemisphere as fertile ground for proselytizing their religious views. The goal of the Spanish monarchy, however, was to establish and defend a mercantilist policy that would reserve to Spain all the rewards the New World had to offer. In North and South America, the authority of the king and his representatives was supreme. By the 1640s the economic benefits accrued by Spain in the New World began to seriously decline. There were many causes: increased pressure from the other imperial nations, especially from the Dutch; domestic problems in Spain itself; declining profits because of the expense of maintaining its colonies; enormous military expenditures for the protection of its colonies; and a fleet to defend its trade ships. Spain was left a second-rate power.

> ## AP Tip
>
> Information in this chapter can be used in a free-response question that deals with the causes of imperialism, inter-imperialist competition, and the clash of cultures.

DUTCH SETTLEMENTS AND A FRENCH EMPIRE IN NORTH AMERICA

The Dutch entered the race for colonies in the late sixteenth century, exploring what later became known as the Hudson River, where they established a colony, New Netherland. Shortly thereafter another major colony, New Amsterdam, was founded on Manhattan Island. The Dutch, like the French, sought to exploit the lucrative fur trade. And like the French colony in Quebec, New Amsterdam did not receive support from the government at home. Despite enticing settlers with patroonships (large tracts of land given in return for settling an area), few Dutch emigrants arrived, and the colony suffered incessant attacks by Native Americans and incursions by other European nations.

While the Spanish settled colonies in warmer climates, the French established their first permanent settlement in the less hospitable climate of Quebec (1542) and Nova Scotia, collectively referred to as New France in the seventeenth century. Not surprisingly, the colony was at first sparsely settled. The French government provided little incentive for its citizens to resettle in the frigid areas in and around Quebec, and it forbade French citizens who were looking for a way out of France, the Huguenots (Protestant reformers persecuted for their break from the Catholic Church), from emigrating. Not surprisingly, the vast majority of French citizens who settled in Canada returned home. Not until 1608 would the French make inroads into acquiring lucrative North American resources such as beaver pelts. Much later in the century (1682), the French laid claim to the Mississippi Valley, calling it Louisiana after their king, Louis XIV. Thirty years later the city of New Orleans was established; it would eventually become an important military and economic strategic location. By the second decade of the eighteenth century, the French had settled as far west as present-day New Mexico and South Dakota.

As a consequence, the English colonies that had been settled in the early seventeenth century along the east coast were restricted to territory east of the Appalachian Mountains by French control of the area from the Ohio River Valley to Louisiana. The turning point, however, for French expansion in North America came with the Treaty of Utrecht (1713). Having been on the losing side in the War of Spanish Succession, France lost Newfoundland, Hudson Bay, and Acadia (Nova Scotia) to Britain. While France could ostensibly afford to lose territory—though of course it preferred not to, especially to its rival Britain—it was the lack of French inhabitants there that hampered the development of its empire in the New World; British settlers outnumbered French settlers in the mid-eighteenth century 3:1. Both Britain and France had Native American allies to swell their numbers as far as defense was concerned, but in 1763, when France was defeated by Britain and its American colonists in the French and Indian War, France temporarily had no major territorial possessions in North America. The Louisiana territory had been ceded to Spain in 1762, and while Napoleon Bonaparte regained it in 1800, this vast territory was sold to the United States in 1803. By the middle of the eighteenth century Great Britain controlled nearly all of North America from the eastern seaboard to the Mississippi River as well as Canada.

THE BRITISH EMPIRE IN THE NEW WORLD

England had established a colony, the doomed Roanoke, in Virginia, as early as 1585, but grander forays into the New World had been slowed by the need to resolve religious division between Catholics and Protestants, a result of King Henry VIII's decision to separate from the Catholic Church. With that settled, and buoyed by the defeat, under Queen Elizabeth I, of the invading Spanish Armada, in 1588, the English caught up with the other European imperial powers in exploring and settling the New World. As with the Dutch and French, the English sailed to North America in search of a Northwest Passage to Asia. But the English had other motives as well: exploration could yield lucrative benefits for investors who bought into joint-stock companies in the hopes of realizing a profit. The lure of raw materials was an important incentive as well, especially as these resources were vital to England's expanding manufacturing sector. At the heart of the government's desire for colonies was mercantilism; the need to accumulate gold, silver, and other precious resources; the establishment of a favorable balance of trade between the mother country and its colonies; and the establishment of colonies to act as a counterbalance to the influence of other imperial nations. The major early English colonies included the following:

- **Jamestown** England's first permanent colony in North America, Jamestown was established by the Virginia Company after receiving a charter from King James I in 1606. The original settlers suffered from disease (especially malaria because the colony was established near swampland), internal strife, and starvation, and they were heavily dependent on supplies from the mother country and assistance from Native Americans. The colony's economy finally stabilized when tobacco was successfully cultivated. In 1676 Jamestown was burned to the ground during Bacon's Rebellion. Rebuilt a number of years later, it was again destroyed by a fire in 1698.
- **Plymouth** Whereas the settlers who established Jamestown did so for predominantly economic reasons, Plymouth Colony was established by religious separatists seeking autonomy from the Church of England (Anglican Church). In 1620 these "Pilgrims" sailed on the *Mayflower* to New England after receiving a charter

from the Virginia Company. By the end of the century, Plymouth, where the Pilgrims settled first, had become part of the colony of Massachusetts.

■ **Massachusetts Bay Colony** Started as a commercial adventure in 1630, the Massachusetts Bay Colony became home to many Puritans, who left England because of the persecution they faced from the Crown and the Anglican Church. Under Calvinist religious leaders such as John Winthrop, the colony almost immediately developed into a theocracy in which the church was paramount in all decisions, political as well as religious. Though far from democratic, it became the first English colony to establish the basis of a representative government when residents demanded representation if they were to be taxed.

■ **Other New England colonies** Major colonies were also established in Connecticut, Rhode Island, New Hampshire, and Maine. In the former, a productive fur trade operated in the Connecticut River Valley. Unlike the Massachusetts Bay Colony, religion was less important than commerce in Connecticut. Importantly, Connecticut colonists were the first in America to write a constitution. The New Hampshire and Maine colonies originated when two Englishmen, given a government grant to the areas north of Massachusetts, divided the land. Both colonies eventually were absorbed into the Massachusetts Bay Colony, but New Hampshire became an independent royal colony in 1679. Maine remained a part of Massachusetts until 1820. Rhode Island's colonial history is very much tied to the trials and tribulations of Roger Williams, whose advocacy of separation of church and state and complete individual religious freedom convinced Boston's Puritan leaders to banish him from the Massachusetts Bay Colony. Undeterred, Williams went on to establish the colony of Providence. Other religious refugees, among them Anne Hutchinson, soon found their way to Rhode Island, and in 1663, Parliament granted the colony a new charter that guaranteed religious freedom.

■ **The middle colonies** New York became an English colony through conquest. In the seventeenth century, England and Holland had engaged in a series of commercial wars in which the North American fur trade became increasingly important. To eliminate Dutch competition, the Duke of York was provided a fleet by his brother, King Charles II, to capture New Netherland, which he did in 1664. Under the duke, democracy was, at best, limited in the colony now named for him—New York. New Jersey originally belonged to the duke as well, but he transferred parts of it to other nobles. Quakers inhabited parts of east and west New Jersey, but in 1702 the colony was unified and granted a royal charter. Its neighbor to the west, Pennsylvania, was founded as a sanctuary for Quakers when William Penn was provided a grant to establish a settlement. It would be home to Germans, Quakers, and a wide variety of settlers who wanted good farmland in a colony that was, by and large, democratic for the time. Delaware—once Sweden's colony, then taken by the Dutch, and finally lost to the English—was also owned by the Duke of York. Concerned that Pennsylvania was landlocked, Penn purchased Delaware to provide his settlers access to the sea.

■ **The southern colonies** Maryland was conceived as a refuge for Catholics by Lord Baltimore, a recent convert to Catholicism and a London Company stockholder. After his death, the English Crown granted his son, the second Lord Baltimore, a charter to administer the colony. For all intents and purposes, Lord Baltimore ran Maryland as if it was a fiefdom, giving vassals land in return for their loyalty and assistance. Over time, republican features seeped into Maryland's political system and a bicameral legislature was established. Religious problems ensued, however, between Protestants, who settled the area in increasing numbers, and Catholics, for whom the colony was originally established. In 1649 the Maryland Toleration Act guaranteed freedom of worship for Christians while punishing those who made blasphemous remarks and committed other religious transgressions. In the Carolinas, land was granted as a reward for those who had helped in the restoration of the monarchy, following the English Civil War and parliamentary rule. The Carolinas were similar to the middle colonies, which had for the most part been founded by proprietors, not (stock) companies. However, like Maryland, they were initially reminiscent of feudal kingdoms. Over time the Carolinas came to be identified with religious and political freedom, but, paradoxically, slavery was introduced almost immediately because the proprietors also had investments in the slave trade. Thus while indentured servants were represented in the labor force of other colonies, the Carolinas embraced slavery. Not until 1729 was the huge colony divided into North and South Carolina. Georgia, as already mentioned, began its history as a penal colony (where originally rum, Catholics, and blacks were prohibited) and as a first line of defense against Spanish-held Florida. When the number of convicts was found to be insufficient to sustain a viable colony, Georgia welcomed Protestants and skilled craftsmen from England, Scotland, and Germany.

By the eighteenth century the American colonies were on the way to developing their own unique cultures while maintaining the essence of their Old World customs. Some colonies were more theocratic and politically elitist than others; a few had some of the political rights found in a democracy—or anywhere in Europe, for that matter—such as freedom of religion and political expression. For their part, typical English colonists came to the New World in the hopes of improving their economic status or to seek greater political and religious autonomy—the goal of Quakers, Puritans, and Catholics. Once in North America, some sought to convert the Native American population to Christianity. Some arrived as indentured servants, others as refugees from persecution, some as slaves, and still others as castoffs because of criminal records or, more often, indebtedness. Some found success and freedom in the New World; others sank into poverty and despair. As in Europe, the wealthy colonists were generally politically powerful, their interests and concerns not necessarily consistent with those of their less fortunate fellow colonists. Over time, deeper economic, political, class, and racial divisions would emerge, but in the short term by the middle of the eighteenth century some American colonists began to envision a future for their colonies that would entail the right to self-determination that could only come with independence.

Multiple-Choice Questions

1. Which of the following best describes the impact European colonization had on the Western Hemisphere's native population?
    (A) The native population was highly respected in terms of territorial possessions and religious beliefs.
    (B) The Europeans for the most part did not interact with the native population.
    (C) Spain was the only European country to successfully create an alliance with the native population.
    (D) Spain worked in conjunction with the Aztecs and Incas to harvest South America's resources.
    (E) Native populations were often killed off or driven away by the Europeans.

ANSWER: E. The impact of European colonization on the native populations of both North and South America and the Caribbean was devastating (*The American Pageant*, 12th ed., p. 15/11th ed., pp. 14-15).

2. Which of the following imperial powers originally settled the Hudson River Valley?
    (A) Holland
    (B) England
    (C) France
    (D) Sweden
    (E) Portugal

ANSWER: A. The Dutch established New Netherland and later New Amsterdam (*The American Pageant*, 12th ed., p. 57/11th ed., p. 55).

3. The colony of Georgia was
    (A) comparatively the most democratic English colony
    (B) established by Spain in order to protect its colony of Florida
    (C) established by England as a penal colony
    (D) organized by English Catholics who had been persecuted by the Anglican Church
    (E) eventually ceded to Spain in return for Florida

ANSWER: C. Another reason the English established the Georgia colony was to act as a barrier to potential incursion by the Spaniards in Florida (*The American Pageant*, 12th ed., p. 39 /11th ed., p. 37).

4. Which English colony was established by proprietors that also had investments in the slave trade and therefore introduced slavery to their colony?
    (A) New York
    (B) Pennsylvania
    (C) Virginia
    (D) The Carolinas
    (E) Maryland

ANSWER: **C**. The tobacco rush that swept over Virginia spurred the creation of large tobacco plantations—and the need for slave labor (*The American Pageant,* 12th ed., p. 33 /11th ed., pp. 31-32).

5. The Duke of Baltimore established the colony of Maryland
    (A) as an opportunity to invest in that colony's maritime industry
    (B) in order to prevent France from seizing that territory
    (C) as a haven for persecuted English Catholics
    (D) for Quakers who had been evicted from Pennsylvania
    (E) after failing to colonize the Carolinas

ANSWER: **C**. The duke was a recent convert to Catholicism and wanted to establish a colony for English colonists who were mistreated by the Anglican Church (*The American Pageant,* 12th ed., p. 33 /11th ed., p. 32).

6. French immigrants to the New World tended to inhabit
    (A) Canada
    (B) Florida
    (C) territory east of the Appalachian Mountains
    (D) southern colonies
    (E) the Middle Atlantic colonies

ANSWER: **A**. The French settled mainly in Canada. After the French and Indian War Canada became part of Britain's North American empire (*The American Pageant,* 12th ed., pp. 106–108 /11th ed., pp. 105-107).

7. As the founder of Rhode Island, Roger Williams
    (A) established religious freedom for Jews and Catholics
    (B) supported freedom of religion for the Huguenots
    (C) established complete religious freedom for all of the colony's settlers
    (D) established mandatory church attendance
    (E) abolished religious practices throughout the colony

ANSWER: **C**. Williams established totals religious freedom, even for Jews and Catholics (*The American Pageant,* 12th ed., p. 48 /11th ed., p. 47).

8. Which of the following stunted the physical growth of the English colony of New York?
    (A) Most settlers refused to recognize the Anglican Church.
    (B) Native Americans laid claim to all of New York.
    (C) New York relied almost exclusively on imports from Britain.
    (D) Few colonists wanted to settle in the western part of the colony.
    (E) Aristocrats controlled vast tracts of land.

ANSWER: **E**. For example, along the Hudson River, aristocrats owned immense landholdings (*The American Pageant,* 12th ed., p. 59 /11th ed., p. 58).

9. Which of the following sought to exploit the lucrative fur trade in North America?
    (A) the French
    (B) the British
    (C) the French and Dutch
    (D) the Portuguese

(E) the Spanish and the French

ANSWER: **C**. New Netherland was established as the base for the Dutch fur trade, and the French traveled across North America in search of beaver pelts (*The American Pageant,* 12th ed., pp. 57, 108–109 /11th ed., pp. 56, 107-108).

10. John Winthrop is associated with which colony?
   (A) New Amsterdam
   (B) Massachusetts Bay Colony
   (C) Jamestown
   (D) Quebec
   (E) Pennsylvania

ANSWER: **B**. A Calvinist, Winthrop helped to establish a theocracy in the Massachusetts Bay Colony (*The American Pageant,* 12th ed., p. 46 /11th ed., p. 45).

Free-Response Questions

1. Explain how English colonies in the New World were different from one another in terms of government, population, and origin.

RESPONSE You should address the differences by explaining that some colonies were started for religious reasons, others as economic ventures, some as grants from the monarch, and Georgia as a penal colony. Some were more democratic than others, and some were more religiously tolerant that others. Massachusetts and the mid-Atlantic colonies tended to have a higher population density than those in the south.

2. What role did religion play in the establishment of English colonies in North America?

RESPONSE You should point out that religion was one of several important motives for colonization. Explain the role religion played in the establishment of colonies such as Plymouth and Maryland. Discuss the theocracy that was established in the Massachusetts Bay Colony, and contrast this with the freedom of religion that prevailed in Rhode Island. Important to this question is the establishment of Pennsylvania by the Quaker William Penn, whose colony tolerated religious freedom.

2

CAUSES OF THE AMERICAN REVOLUTION: 1650–1774

When thinking about the causes of American colonial independence, many people often give little thought to factors other than the desire for liberty. All agree that the Revolution began because the colonists wanted independence, but they don't always trace this desire back to the imperialistic foreign policy adopted by the British long before the struggle for independence began. There are essentially two types of revolution: anti-imperialist and social or domestic. The objective of the first is self-determination, or autonomy. Profound social change, as in democratization, is the goal of the second type. Ultimately, when you study the causes of the American Revolution, you will need to interpret whether there were one or two revolutionary impulses.

KEY CONCEPTS

- Prior to 1763, the British subordinated American capital to British capital.
- The British success in the French and Indian War transformed the relationship between Britain and the American colonies.
- British policies after 1763 were designed to raise revenue to pay for the cost of the empire.
- The American colonists were divided over what course of action to take in response to British policies.
- The Americans created a government, the Continental Congress, to address the deteriorating relationship between Britain and the colonies.

The causes of the American Revolution are discussed in depth in *The American Pageant,* 12th and 11th eds., Chapters 6 and 7.

EUROPEAN COLONIES IN THE NEW WORLD

Great Britain was not the only European imperial power to establish colonies in the Western Hemisphere. Think about all the Dutch names in New York, listen to Brazilians speak Portuguese, Canadians living in Quebec speak French, and Mexicans in North America speak Spanish. Holland (today called the Netherlands), Portugal, France, and Spain also laid claim to the riches of the New World.

But by the middle of the eighteenth century, mainly two powerful competitors, Britain and France, continued to vie for dominance in North America. In the seventeenth and early eighteenth centuries, Great Britain dominated the eastern seaboard of what would become the United States. The French were in control of Canada and also laid claim to an enormous swath of land that stretched west well beyond the Mississippi River and south to present-day Texas. Actually, both Britain and France had been fighting intermittently for centuries before they engaged each other militarily and diplomatically over the potential rewards of the North American continent. The French (like the Spaniards) had experienced some success in the New World because of the alliances they established with various Native American tribes. In fact, the French had earlier joined with two tribes, the Algonquian and the Huron, in a fight with the powerful Iroquois. Unfortunately for all Native Americans, regardless of their tribe, the Europeans brought with them diseases for which the Native Americans had no immunity. The mortality rate was staggering.

French and British interimperialist rivalry was most intense between 1689 and 1763, when the French were finally defeated. Before this, however, Great Britain and France fought a series of wars. The final and most famous of which that was fought in North America (before spreading to Europe) was the French and Indian War, commonly referred to in Europe as the Seven Years' War. The focal point of the struggle in North America was the Ohio Valley, where the French began constructing forts to stop the westward expansion into what they called New France by British colonists. Eventually, British and colonial forces, under the leadership of a youthful governor of Virginia named George Washington, engaged the French in the Ohio Valley. They were defeated. It was apparent that the war would last a bit longer than the British and their colonists had anticipated. In order to prepare for the ensuing warfare, the colonists, with encouragement from Britain, organized the Albany Congress. The immediate objective of this meeting was to keep the Iroquois tribes loyal to Britain. This would be accomplished by involving the Iroquois in discussions about issues affecting both the Iroquois and the American colonists and their British government officials. Under the leadership of Benjamin Franklin, the delegates drew up an American colonial response to the French, which became known as the Albany Plan of Union. This coalition would have provided for an American Congress, which would in turn have the authority to

- carry out diplomatic relations with the Native American tribes
- control public territory
- raise an army
- tax colonial citizens

Unfortunately, the colonists were too concerned about their own interests and unwilling to relinquish control to a provincial congress, so the Albany plan was not accepted. Still, it created a foundation for future colonial cooperation, especially when it mattered even more, in the war against Britain.

Early on in the French and Indian War, the British suffered serious setbacks—for example, General Braddock's defeat at the hands of the French and their Native American allies near Ft. Duquesne, the worst British defeat in North America up to that time. But many French colonists were suffering hardships as well, despite their countrymen's military successes. French-Canadians living in Acadia (present-day Nova Scotia) were driven out, ultimately settling in New Orleans (where their culture is commonly called Cajun). In 1756 the two imperialist rivals took their war global, each attacking its enemy's colonies in the Caribbean, the Pacific, and in India. Not until 1758 did British fortunes improve. Under a new British secretary of state, William Pitt, the British and Americans found common ground to address the military and economic demands of the war. Successes followed on the battlefield. The capture of the major French stronghold, Ft. Duquesne, by troops under the command of George Washington along with major British victories in New York drove the French out of most of the area they previously controlled. Retreating to Quebec, the French commander, General Montcalm, was decisively defeated by Britain's General Wolfe on the Plains of Abraham, outside of Quebec. Militarily and financially exhausted, the French sued for peace.

The Peace of Paris brought hostilities to a close, and with it French control of North America. The parts of the treaty that relate to North America include the following:

- Britain received all of French Canada and all territory south of Canada and east of the Mississippi River.
- France and its ally, Spain, lost their West Indian colonies.
- Britain received Florida from Spain.
- Spain received from France its territory west of the Mississippi, including control of the port city of New Orleans, as compensation for its loss of Florida.

PROBLEMS INHERITED BY BRITAIN FOLLOWING THE WAR

With military victory came political and economic problems for the British. While they defeated their long-time rival in a pivotal campaign for territorial expansion and colonization, the British government had incurred a large debt. Prosecuting the war had been expensive. That and the huge cost of maintaining and controlling its expanded empire created a fiscal crisis, forcing the British to address important political and economic concerns that came with empire building:

- The newly won land, which doubled the size of Britain's North American territory, must be governed.
- Revenue must be raised to help absorb the costs of maintaining and controlling this vast territory. To make matters worse, citizens in Great Britain were already heavily taxed.

- Hostile Native Americans in the Appalachian region, who felt threatened by American westward expansion into the Ohio River Valley, needed to be controlled. (In 1763, under the leadership of Chief Pontiac, Native Americans in the Ohio Valley responded to these encroachments on what they considered to be their land by destroying forts and homes. The British, wary of their colonists' fighting capabilities, sent their own redcoats, not the colonial militias, to put down Pontiac's rebellion.) That year, the British government imposed restrictions on westward settlement.
- French Canadians needed to be assimilated into the British Empire.
- Opening new trade channels posed difficulties.
- Intractable American colonists were not about to accept restrictions on their activities. Some colonists, in fact, were beginning to compete effectively with British capitalists and refused to subordinate their economic interests to those of British manufacturers.

So extensive were these problems, so aggravating to colonial-British relations, that it can be rightly stated that Britain's eventual loss of its American colonies paradoxically began with its interimperialist victory in the French and Indian War.

Not surprisingly, with the defeat of the French, American colonists no longer felt threatened by French attacks, but an unanticipated consequence of the war soon became apparent. The British and Americans had taken away from the conflict contrary views of their relationship during the course of the conflict. For its part, Britain was highly critical of the American military contribution to the war effort. The American militia, they claimed, had fared poorly—in fact, not all colonies had sent troops to help. To the British, it was obvious that the Americans would be incapable or unwilling to defend the mother country's newly acquired territories. Further, throughout the war the Americans had continued to engage in illegal smuggling, which was harmful to the British economy. The American colonists, however, were equally disappointed with the British. Convinced they had indeed fought well, they were highly critical of Britain's military, which seemed more suited for European-style warfare than for warfare in the dense woodlands of North America. Politically and economically, the outcome of the war was to forever change the relationship between the center, Britain, and its periphery, the colonies. Eventually that outcome took both to a point hardly imaginable at the end of the French and Indian War, a fight for colonial independence.

PRE-REVOLUTIONARY WAR BRITISH POLICY IN THE COLONIES

Many historians view the British-colonial relationship before the French and Indian War as benign. In other words, while the British sought to regulate trade and influence the colonial governments overall, it generally limited its intervention and management. During what is often referred to as a period of "salutary neglect," the years from about 1650 to the end of the French and Indian War, the Americans were largely left alone to develop their economy without serious British intervention. But some historians question this view, especially given that mercantilism was the prevailing economic system, one that emphasizes that a nation's economic power expands by maintaining a favorable balance of trade and controlling hard currency—specie. As with other imperial powers, Britain viewed the American colonies as a reliable source of raw materials and a viable market for British goods, as well as a place for profitable investment opportunities. For example, by the eighteenth century large swaths of Britain had been deforested, a serious concern for a nation that relied heavily on its wooden naval ships to control the seas. North America, on the other hand, had millions of acres of forest that could be harvested for British use.

British mercantilist policies were generally not challenged by the colonists, in part because they were difficult to implement and often infrequently enforced. As long as competition from the Americans wasn't significant and Britain wasn't experiencing an economic or fiscal crisis, there was little need or incentive to abandon the policy of salutary neglect. The major British mercantilist policies in the pre-1760 period include the following:

- **The Navigation Laws** These were a series of strict British trade policies designed to promote English shipping and control colonial trade in regard to important crops (such as tobacco) and resources, which had to be shipped exclusively in British ships. In order for the Americans to trade certain enumerated items with other nations, their ships had to stop in England first. The Navigation Law of 1660 would have had a devastating effect on the American economy had the British enforced the law. The British added further requirements in subsequent Navigation Laws in 1663, 1673, and in 1696, the latter allowed British customs officials using writs of assistance—search warrants—to search for and seize smuggled commodities.

- **The Wool (1699), Hat (1732), and Iron (1750) Acts** These acts were intended to subordinate American capital to British capital by preventing American businessmen from turning raw materials into finished commodities. For example, the fashion fad of the eighteenth century was beaver hats. The Hat Act prevented Americans from turning the beaver pelts into hats and selling them on the open market. Instead, as with many raw materials, the pelts were to be sold to English manufacturers, who then used them to make hats, which in turn were sold on the international market, including to the Americans. This type of legislation helps you see why some members of the colonial merchant class, those who had the most to lose financially, took up arms against Great Britain.

- **The Molasses Act (1733)** Molasses, an important sweetener—and an important component of the triangle trade—was used primarily in this era as an essential ingredient in the making of rum, an enormously popular beverage in the colonial period. In an attempt to control the lucrative sale of sugar cane to the colonies, the British government established regulations and restrictions, again not well enforced. Besides, the Americans often purchased sugar from the non-British sugar-producing Caribbean islands.

Overseeing trade in American colonies was the British Board of Trade, which had the authority to recommend legislation and enforce mercantilist policies.

While annoying to some Americans, British policy before the French and Indian War was not as irritating to them as what was to follow. The year 1763, while not as indelible as, say, 1776, is no less as fateful for two significant events that would profoundly shape the American colonists' relationship with Britain. In some ways, 1763 can be considered a turning point in the association between Britain and its American colonies. 1. That year King George III appointed George Grenville as prime minister. Under Grenville, the British devised a solution to their economic woes by fundamentally transforming their political, economic, and trade relationship with the American colonies. 2. The policy of salutary neglect was abandoned. From then on, the British government would play a considerably enlarged (and, to some colonists, exploitative) role in the colonies. The first major controversial measure was the Proclamation of 1763.

One especially undesirable consequence of sustaining an imperialist policy is the cost of empire exceeding its benefits. Britain in the mid-eighteenth century was sensitive to this. Given the limited military resources the Crown had in the colonies and the large size of its territory after the French and Indian War, the British were already stretched thin. Allowing colonists to move farther west beyond British control (though Parliament would use the word "protection" instead) would only aggravate their already evident difficulties in governing the American colonies. Having to constantly fight Native Americans out West (for example, Pontiac's rebellion) would be a further drain on Britain's military and financial resources. Out of this concern came the Proclamation of 1763, which prohibited colonial migration and settlement west of the Appalachian Mountains. Americans were incensed by the act, but it didn't prevent them from streaming across the Appalachian Mountains—and the proclamation line. The colonists believed that the Proclamation had little to do with preventing colonial-Native American hostilities and almost everything to do with political, military, and economic control of them. The Proclamation effectively closed the area to Americans who wished to invest in the economic opportunities—fur and timber, land speculation—that the West offered.

Discontent on the Frontier

That same year, 1763, a band of western Pennsylvania frontiersmen, the Paxton Boys, attacked Native Americans whom they believed had been part of Pontiac's rebellion. When the Native Americans took refuge in Philadelphia, the Paxton Boys, numbering in the hundreds, descended on the city to demand funding to support their defensive needs on the frontier. It was not until Benjamin Franklin convinced the belligerent frontiersmen that financial aid would be forthcoming that the Paxton Boys returned home. This event, however, was not the first occasion in which settlers living on the frontier of their colonies took up arms to address grievances they claimed were being ignored by the colonial government. Nearly a hundred years before the Paxton Boys marched on Philadelphia, discontent on Virginia's frontier erupted into armed insurrection. In 1676 the royal governor of Virginia, William Berkeley, became the focus of discontent for those Virginians on the colony's frontier. It had become obvious to them that Berkeley was concerned more with the wealthy planters on Virginia's eastern seaboard (called the Tidewater region) than with those in western Virginia whose lives were considerably more tenuous on account of constant fighting with Native Americans. Taking matters into their own hands, the Virginians, led by Nathaniel Bacon, attacked the Native Americans, whereby Governor Berkeley, after promising some needed reforms, organized an attack on Bacon's forces. Bacon and his men retaliated by marching on Jamestown and burning it. Then, unexpectedly and fortuitously for Berkeley, Bacon died. The revolt came to an end, and many of Bacon's followers were hanged. Nevertheless, the event was a harbinger of what would happen a century later. Further, many Americans saw that they had a common perception: colonial governments favored the aristocracy over the needs of the masses.

Yet another example of class tensions in the colonies occurred a few years before the American Revolution. In 1771, Carolinians calling themselves Regulators revolted against what they believed were unfair taxes and a lack of representation in their state legislature. Although the rebellion was put down, it personalized the assertion that taxation without representation is tyranny. Some historians believe that the Revolution was needed to not only win independence but to democratize American society and government.

Over the two years following the Proclamation of 1763, Parliament would enact a series of revenue-raising acts that infuriated many American colonists, especially as the British began to enforce their colonial laws. The following controversial legislation was passed:

- **Sugar (or Revenue) Act of 1764** With the first Navigation Law passed by Parliament in the previous century, Britain established its authority to regulate colonial trade. In 1733 it attempted to control the lucrative sugar trade between the colonies and the Spanish and French West Indies. The Sugar Act of 1764, which replaced the ineffective Molasses Act of 1733, actually reduced the duties on imported sugar (possibly as an enticement to colonial importers to stay within the law), but the British made a concerted effort to enforce the act and punish smugglers.
- **The Currency Act of 1764** Superseding the Currency Act of 1751 (which applied only to New England), this act forbade the colonists from printing their own currency and instead required them to use hard currency (gold and silver), which was in short supply in the colonies. All taxes had to be paid in hard currency as well.

- **The Quartering Act** Instituted in 1765, this required Americans to provide food and supplies to British troops stationed in the colonies.
- **Stamp Act (1765)** Few acts of Parliament angered the American colonists as much as this attempt to raise revenue by taxing virtually all printed material, from newspapers and wills to marriage licenses and even playing cards. American opposition to this direct, or internal, tax was vociferous. Many colonists did not challenge Parliament's right to tax its citizens (and most Americans at this point believed themselves to be British citizens). What they wanted, as Virginia's Patrick Henry so passionately declared, was the right accorded other British subjects—namely, no taxation without representation. Many colonists were directly affected by the act, especially those who relied on the use of legal documents, such as attorneys and businessmen. It is not surprising, then, that the colonial middle class was so actively involved in organizing resistance to this act and subsequent legislation. In the case of the Stamp Act, they organized almost immediately. In the fall of 1765, delegates from nine colonies met in New York City for what was referred to as the Stamp Act Congress. They issued a Declaration of Rights, the essence of which was the contention that Britain could not tax the colonists because they lacked representation in Parliament. Recalcitrant Americans responded to the Stamp Act with noncompliance—not using items that were affected by the tax (a boycott). Some used force and coercion. For example, the Sons (and Daughters) of Liberty and the Loyal Nine organized to attack and intimidate tax agents as well as fellow colonists who used the stamps. By the following year the British government realized that the act was a political and economic debacle—made abundantly clear when they could find no one willing to risk his life collecting the tax—and repealed it. But the act had allowed individuals and organizations—for example, Sam Adams's the Loyal Nine and the Sons of Liberty—to suggest that a complete break with Britain was essential to the colonies' future.
- **Declaratory Act (1766)** Britain professed the right to tax the colonists without challenge (or, in the language of the document, "in all cases whatsoever") even as it repealed the Stamp Act. Britain's response to the cry of no taxation without representation was that in fact the Americans possessed *virtual representation*. That is, members of Parliament were representatives of all British subjects wherever they lived.

Many British elites criticized Parliament for appeasing the colonies and expected the government to compel the colonists to pay their share of taxes. Under the new prime minister, Charles Townshend (called Champagne Charley for his ability to make speeches in Parliament while drunk), the British looked for new ways to address their revenue problem. The result was the Townshend Acts (1767).

In order to bring revenue into the Exchequer (British treasury), Townshend proposed that items produced in Britain and sold in America—such as paper, glass, lead, paint, and tea—be taxed. But this was not a direct levy in that it did not immediately come out of the individual consumer's pocket; it was to be paid at American ports. One way or another, however, the price of these commodities would be inflated. Further, Townshend suspended the New York Assembly for refusing to provide British troops with supplies, as required by the Quartering Act. The suspension was also meant as a warning to other disobedient colonies. To prevent further smuggling, Townshend established an American Board of Customs and admiralty courts to hear such cases. Writs of assistance were again issued to prevent smuggling. To make matters worse, some of the revenue raised from the act would go to pay for the salaries of the colonial royal governors, those very same individuals who were charged with the responsibility of governing the colonists and therefore enforcing the Townshend Acts.

The colonial response was immediate: boycott. In Massachusetts, the legislature condemned the Townshend Acts in a circular letter—that is, a letter disseminated in all the colonies. It stated that "a taxation of their constituents, even without their consent, grievous as it is, would be preferable to any representation that could be admitted for them there." The British maintained that the circular letter was treasonous, but it was not long before other colonies had adopted their own circular letters. Dissent was spreading, and even individual citizens took quill to paper to express their concerns. In Pennsylvania, John Dickinson published his *Letters from a Pennsylvania Farmer* (1767) in which he attacked Britain's assertion of the right to tax the colonists to raise revenue—Dickinson, like most Americans, had no argument with Britain's right to regulate colonial trade. Other colonial leaders such as Benjamin Franklin and Sam Adams weighed in as well, Franklin through the use of reasoned oratory and Adams via intimidation and belligerence. One coercive and humiliating tactic designed to send a message to officials in the colonies and in Britain was to tar and feather customs officers. Still, many colonists were not terribly affected by this indirect tax, especially because they could purchase smuggled items, such as tea, at a lower, nontaxed price. From the British perspective, these actions could not be tolerated. In haste, more British troops were sent to the center of discontent, Boston. It was there on a winter's day in March 1770, that one of the most famous and incendiary events in our story took place, the Boston "Massacre."

THE BOSTON "MASSACRE"

For enlisted men, serving in the British army was often an act of desperation. They were paid subsistence wages, and discipline was maintained through the use of physical punishment and intimidation. In the American colonies, most notably in Boston, these lobsterbacks (as they were derisively referred to because of their scarlet coats) sometimes took spare jobs when they were off-duty for a fee lower than colonial workers would accept. This only added to the tension that prevailed in Boston—already a tinderbox in 1770. On March 5, a crowd of Bostonians attacked a squadron of British troops. The redcoats opened fire, killing and wounding about eleven of the provocateurs, including a black or mulatto mob leader, Crispus Attucks. John Adams defended the British soldiers, winning an acquittal for most of them. But American propagandists wasted little time in presenting the event as an unprovoked attack on Americans. A

Boston silversmith named Paul Revere created a powerful and widely distributed engraving whose imagery left no doubts as to the nature of the event. Long after the deadly volley had ceased, it would be referred to as the Boston Massacre. And it took the colonies one step closer to a formal separation with Britain, five more years in the future.

In the months following the Boston Massacre, the colonies settled into a period of comparative calm after Parliament agreed with the new prime minister, Lord North, that the Townshend duties, except the tax on tea, should be repealed. Although this was a significant victory for the colonies, activists and radicals such as Sam Adams nurtured the revolutionary spirit by creating committees of correspondence. The committees acted as a conduit for the exchange of ideas and for disseminating the goal of a unified response by the colonial governments.

THE TEA TAX

In the midst of this period of calm, two incidents revealed that the tranquility was deceptive. On a summer night in 1772, a British customs schooner, *Gaspee*, ran aground near Providence, Rhode Island. Residents in the area led by a merchant named John Brown wasted no time in burning the *Gaspee* to the waterline, but not before putting its crew ashore and looting the ship. Although a board of inquiry was established, the British never were able to establish guilt, in large part because of uncooperative Rhode Islanders. The looting of the *Gaspee*, while serious, pales in comparison with the plundering of a British commercial ship by Bostonians the following year. That ship carried tea in its holds.

In some areas, many colonists continued to boycott British tea. Yet by 1773 most Americans had begun once again to purchase tea from British merchants. In fact the opposition to paying the tea tax had withered, mainly because of the abundance of tea for sale, which made British tea cheaper than smuggled tea. The supply of tea became so great that the powerful British East India Company had an enormous surplus, which brought it to the brink of bankruptcy. But the company had powerful friends in high places in the British government, and they too were not eager to see the lucrative tea tax dry up should the company go under. The British government's solution to the problem was to grant the company a monopoly of the colonial tea trade. New England merchants who sold non-British tea believed this legislation placed them at a competitive disadvantage. Then tea prices came down even more as the company sought to unload its surplus. But most colonists would have none of it. True, they could purchase tea at a cost lower than ever, but the Americans believed the British government was duplicitous, getting the Americans to pay the tea tax by enticing them with lower prices. Incensed, individual consumers, merchants, and even colonial assemblies throughout the colonies responded, in some cases with violence, in others with noncompliance. Some of the tea was in fact confiscated and sold, the money eventually—and ironically—going to fund the Continental Army.

THE BOSTON TEA PARTY AND THE BRITISH RESPONSE

Our story returns to Boston, where residents by this point had had considerable experience with acts of civil disobedience, protest, and violence. One victim was the royal governor of Massachusetts, Thomas Hutchinson. After he confronted the mob in the Stamp Act crisis of 1765, his home was burned by the protestors. Hutchinson was resolute: he would enforce the letter of the law. Bostonians, however, were resolved not to pay the tea tax. The British government was determined to unload the tea in Boston despite strong opposition; they even considered suspending some civil liberties, which further enraged some Bostonian radicals such as Sam Adams. In response, Bostonians disguised to look like Native Americans boarded the tea ships on the evening of December 16, 1773, and proceeded to throw the cargo into Boston Harbor as citizens of the city looked on silently and, more often than not, sympathetically. Governor Hutchinson returned to England in disgust. He had had enough of Boston.

The British government now faced an important question. A strong response might only exacerbate the situation; no response was tantamount to appeasement and tolerance of the destruction of private property. By spring the British had decided on their answer. They would punish not just those who destroyed the tea, and not the city of Boston alone, but the entire state of Massachusetts, to show other colonies the consequences of challenging British authority. Collectively the British response is referred to as the Intolerable Acts (or Coercive Acts) of 1774, which included

- **The Boston Port Bill**, which closed the port of Boston and relocated the customs house so that some important supplies could enter Massachusetts.
- **The Administration of Justice Act**, which required that trials of royal officials accused of serious crimes in the colonies while carrying out their duties be held in Britain.
- **The Massachusetts Government Act**, which greatly limited citizens' rights to organize freely. It also replaced the election of Massachusetts judiciary and council members with Crown appointees.

In addition, the Quartering Act was expanded to require all colonists to house British troops when ordered.

To make matters even worse, in 1774 the British passed another act that was considered nothing short of contemptible by the Americans. The Quebec Act was designed to facilitate the incorporation of French Canadians and their land into Britain's colonial American empire. Quebec's boundary was extended to the Ohio River, Catholicism was recognized as Quebec's official religion, and a nonrepresentative government was established for its citizens. The Quebec Act was roundly condemned by the American colonists because they

- feared a precedent had been established in regards to the type of government (nonrepresentative) that was created in Quebec
- resented the expansion of Quebec's (French Canadian) colonial territory, to which they had been denied access by the Proclamation of 1763

■ were offended by the Crown's recognition of Catholicism, given that most American colonials were Protestants

Little did Parliament know when it passed the Intolerable Acts in 1774 that in just one year its troops and its colonists would exchange gunfire that would open the floodgates to a full-scale war for independence.

THE FIRST CONTINENTAL CONGRESS

In September 1774 delegates from twelve of the colonies sent representatives to Philadelphia to discuss a response to the Intolerable Acts. The eventual rejoinder from this body, later known as the First Continental Congress, ultimately took the form of a series of radical resolutions.

The vast majority of delegates reflected the views of those in their home colonies—namely, that conditions did not yet warrant a complete break with Great Britain. A distinct minority, however, did see this as the only viable alternative to what they viewed as a long series of British abuses. Others looked back, hoping to find a solution to the crisis in the pre-French and Indian War relationship. The delegates then fell into three distinct groups:

■ **Radicals** (such as Virginia's Patrick Henry, Massachusetts's Sam and John Adams, and Pennsylvania's Charles Thomson) believed that the colonies' relationship with Britain had already passed a point of no return. For them there were only two alternatives: force Britain to accede to their demands or declare independence.
■ **Moderates** (such as Pennsylvania's John Dickinson and Virginia's George Washington) believed that the relationship between the colonies and Great Britain could be repaired.
■ **Conservatives** (such as New York's John Jay and Pennsylvania's Joseph Galloway) were not prepared to make an aggressive response but did favor a mild rebuke of the British. In fact, Galloway proposed a union of colonies under British authority similar to that proposed in the ill-fated Albany plan of the French and Indian War. If adopted, the relationship would return Britain and the colonies essentially to what had been the situation before the dramatic changes that took place in 1763 and the years since. There was one substantial addition, however: a colonial "grand council" would have the power to veto British acts. The Galloway plan was narrowly defeated, setting the stage for the radicals to guide the direction of events and actions.

Using as their philosophical inspiration the ideas set forth by Thomas Jefferson in his pamphlet, *A Summary View of the Rights of British America*, the more radical delegates applied the following ideas to their response:

■ Parliament possessed no inherent authority to tax the colonists.
■ The British Empire was a compact (or loose union) between the center (the mother country) and its colonies, not one unit dominated by Britain.
■ Each colony possessed its own legislature independent of Britain's legislative authority.

■ Holding together this loose-knit union was a collective allegiance to the king.

The delegates adopted a statement of rights, the Declaration and Resolves, which had originally been enacted in Massachusetts as the Suffolk Resolves. In it the delegates took the following actions:

■ They declared the Intolerable Acts null and void.
■ They recommended that colonists arm themselves and that militias be formed. (In fact, Massachusetts residents had already taken this step, forming militia units ready to respond at a moment's notice—the Minute Men.)
■ They recommended a boycott of British imports. ("Associations" were established in every colony to make sure the boycott was enforced.)

After a month of deliberations and squabbling, the delegates adjourned in late October, agreeing to reconvene in the spring. As they made their way home from Philadelphia, few delegates could have anticipated that in April 1775, events in a small Massachusetts town would take the Americans and the British to a crossroad in their rocky relationship.

Multiple-Choice Questions

1. A major goal of the French in wanting to maintain control over the Ohio Valley was to
   (A) prevent attacks by Native Americans on their forts and outposts
   (B) eventually expand into Canada
   (C) merge its landholdings from Canada to the Mississippi Valley
   (D) exploit the lumber trade
   (E) prevent Spain from taking control of the Mississippi River

ANSWER: **C**. The French sought to control territory west of the Appalachian Mountains, which would counterbalance Britain's landholdings along the eastern seaboard (*The American Pageant,* 12th ed., pp. 108–110 /11th ed., pp. 105-108).

2. The most immediate objective of the Albany Congress was to
   (A) bring to an end the French and Indian War
   (B) unite French and American settlers in order to defeat hostile Native American tribes
   (C) convince American colonists to boycott British-made goods
   (D) end hostilities between Native Americans and French settlers in the Ohio Valley
   (E) improve relations with the Iroquois tribes

ANSWER: **E**. Though the Albany Congress addressed other concerns, such as coordinating a united response to the French, its most immediate objective was keeping the powerful Iroquois Nation loyal to Great Britain (*The American Pageant,* 12th ed., pp. 113-114/11th ed., pp. 112-113).

3. As a result of the British victory in the French and Indian War
   (A) relations between French and Americans colonists improved dramatically
   (B) France was able to hold on to Canada but lost the rest of its North American empire
   (C) the Americans and British developed a mutual respect for each other's military abilities
   (D) Britain returned the lower Mississippi Valley to Spain
   (E) none of the above

ANSWER: **E**. France lost its entire North American empire to Britain, but the war strained British-American relations (*The American Pageant,* 12ᵗʰ ed., pp. 115–116 /11th ed., pp. 113-114).

4. Which of the following is the correct chronological order?
   The Peace of Paris (1)
   The Tea Act (3)
   The Albany Congress (5)
   Navigation Law of 1660 (2)
   The Molasses Act (4)
   (A) 1, 2, 3, 4, 5
   (B) 2, 5, 1, 4, 3
   (C) 5, 4, 1, 3, 2
   (D) 1, 2, 5, 4, 3
   (E) 5, 1, 3, 4, 2

ANSWER: **B**.

5. Under Britain's mercantilist policy
   (A) Britain and the other imperialist powers worked out a trade agreement that would prevent conflict
   (B) the colonies were expected to export more finished goods than they imported
   (C) trade restrictions on the colonies were forbidden
   (D) the colonies were expected to supply Great Britain with raw materials
   (E) the colonies enjoyed considerable political and economic growth

ANSWER: **D**. Under mercantilism, the colonies supplied the center (or mother country) with raw materials and became a market for finished goods (*The American Pageant,* 12ᵗʰ ed., pp. 124–125 /11th ed., pp. 122-123).

6. Prior to the 1760s, Britain's Navigation Acts
   (A) were effective in raising enormous revenue for the Crown
   (B) prevented the American colonies from shipping raw materials to Great Britain
   (C) were only loosely enforced in the American colonies
   (D) successfully ended smuggling in the American colonies
   (E) none of the above

ANSWER: **C**. Prior to the 1760s Americans avoided the Navigation Laws through such illegal activities as smuggling. The British did not yet have a financial need to enforce the acts (*The American Pageant,* 12ᵗʰ ed., pp. 123-124 /11th ed., p. 122).

7. The primary goal of the Hat Act, Iron Act, and Wool Act was to
   (A) subordinate American capitalism to British capitalism
   (B) increase production levels of these items in the colonies
   (C) prevent British manufacturers from shipping raw materials to America
   (D) raise revenue to pay for the salaries of British officials serving in the American colonies
   (E) raise enough money for American militias to effectively fight the French

ANSWER: A. The acts prevented American businessmen from turning raw materials into finished commodities. British manufacturers made considerably larger profits by producing finished goods and selling them on the open market.

8. The Declaration of Rights (adapted from the Suffolk Resolves by the delegates to the First Continental Congress) declared the _____ null and void.
   (A) Tea tax
   (B) Declaratory Acts
   (C) Intolerable Acts
   (D) Quartering Act
   (E) Navigation Laws

ANSWER: C. (*The American Pageant,* 12th ed., p. 134 /11th ed., pp. 133-134).

9. All of the following are correct regarding the Quebec Act EXCEPT
   (A) it was warmly accepted by American colonists as a way of building a closer relationship with French colonists
   (B) Catholicism was accepted as the official religion of French Quebec
   (C) Americans were suspicious that the nonrepresentative assembly established in Quebec would set a precedent for British rule in the American colonies
   (D) Americans were angry that Quebec's territory was extended to the Ohio River
   (E) it was an attempt to incorporate the French Canadians into the British North American Empire

ANSWER: A. Most American colonists rejected the Quebec Act for the reasons expressed in answers B-D. E is the primary reason the Quebec Act was passed (*The American Pageant,* 12th and 11th eds., p. 133).

10. Conservative delegates to the First Continental Congress
    (A) sought immediate independence from British control
    (B) favored using violence and intimidation to convince the British to grant the Americans their independence
    (C) generally were from the New England states
    (D) supported the Galloway plan
    (E) argued that the colonies had no legal right to representation

ANSWER: D. The Galloway plan, with some modifications, sought to return British-American relations to their pre-1763 status. It was rejected by the delegates.

Free-Response Questions

1. Analyze the following statement:

    Those Americans who fought as patriots were influenced by two revolutionary impulses: independence from Britain and the desire to democratize American society and government.

RESPONSE A discussion of the causes of the American Revolution must focus on the desire for independence, but another dimension can be added depending on your perspective: the war was also fought to democratize American society by removing the British, who were content to maintain the status quo in the colonies. For the first revolutionary impulse, you should address pre- and post-1763 policies. For the second, discuss the features of colonial America that were not particularly democratic.

2. The First and Second Continental Congresses were shaped by disputes between moderates, radicals, and conservatives. Discuss the positions of the three factions and explain which was the most persuasive and effective in achieving its goals.

RESPONSE Be sure to point out that twice as many Americans were opposed or indifferent to independence as favored liberty. This is reflected in the First and Second Continental Congresses: conservatives favored a return to the relationship that existed before the French and Indian War. Moderates maintained that events had not yet necessitated a break from Britain, and radicals favored immediate independence. Later events would satisfy the radicals' goals.

3

THE AMERICAN REVOLUTION: 1774–1783

When the First Continental Congress's appeal to King George III, the Declaration of Rights, reached Britain in 1774, it was, to put it mildly, poorly received. Massachusetts was now considered to be in open rebellion, and soon fresh troops began arriving to enforce British laws and policies.

KEY CONCEPTS

- Both the British and the Americans had military, political, and economic advantages and disadvantages in the war.
- The Battle of Saratoga was the turning point in the war, for it persuaded the French to give what proved to be significant help to the Americans in the war for independence.
- Black Americans played an important role in the war.
- The American victory did not fundamentally change the condition or status of blacks or women.

The American Revolution is discussed in depth in *The American Pageant*, 12th ed. and 11th ed., Chapters 7 and 8.

Massachusetts met this escalation of hostilities with its own call to arms. In April 1775, General Thomas Gage, who had replaced Hutchinson as royal governor of Massachusetts, dispatched troops to seize military supplies that militiamen had stored in Lexington. Upon meeting the Minute Men (militiamen who could be mobilized at a moment's notice) in Lexington, shots were exchanged between the two forces, killing eight of the Massachusetts combatants. The British then proceeded to Concord to continue their futile search for gunpowder and weapons. On their return from Concord, the British were ambushed time and again as they attempted to make their way back to

Boston. Their losses were staggering, almost three hundred casualties. Even more damaging, however, was that the events at Lexington and Concord had a lightning-rod effect. Soon colonists were organizing to confront the British. As planned, the following month the Second Continental Congress assembled in Philadelphia. This time there were but two conflicting groups: those who sought immediate independence and those who still hoped for a negotiated settlement. Both sides had their say. The Congress then drew up military plans, in the Declaration of the Causes and Necessities for Taking Up Arms, which called for

- an American army to be organized and led by George Washington
- an American navy to be created to disrupt British shipping
- a military expedition to be led by Benedict Arnold to wrest Canada from the British Empire

By this time, Ethan Allen and his Green Mountain Boys had already seized Fort Ticonderoga in New York. But the center of hostilities continued to be Massachusetts, specifically Boston, the hotbed of radical dissent.

THE WAR BEGINS IN EARNEST: BUNKER HILL

For weeks after Lexington and Concord, both British and American troops poured into the Boston area, anticipating a major conflict. The Americans, under General Israel Putnam, occupied two strategic areas overlooking Boston, Breed's Hill and Bunker Hill, in advance of the British, who also wanted to control the high ground around Boston. On June 13, 1775, British troops, in their distinctive, conspicuous scarlet uniforms and weighed down with heavy supplies, attacked. After launching several assaults in which over one thousand British and some four hundred Americans were killed, the redcoats drove the Americans, who were nearly out of supplies, from their positions. Importantly, the colonists had stood their ground against what was considered the best European fighting force at that time. But even then there were still some colonial leaders who firmly believed that a peaceful solution could be found. The month after the Battle of Bunker Hill, Congress sent the Olive Branch Petition to King George III. Reaffirming their loyalty to him, they implored him to intercede on their behalf. Their appeal fell on deaf ears; the king would not negotiate with his own subjects, especially those who had taken up arms and clashed with his forces. In August, Parliament issued the Prohibitory Act, declaring all of the colonies in open rebellion and suspending all trade between Britain and the American colonies.

THE DECLARATION OF INDEPENDENCE

In early June of 1776, Virginia's representative to the Second Continental Congress, Richard Henry Lee, introduced a resolution in Congress that declared the colonies free and independent states. A committee that included John Adams and Benjamin Franklin was established to write a draft declaring this sentiment and the

---

Tom Paine's *Common Sense* (January 1776)

Whereas some colonists viewed the king's response to the Olive Branch Petition with dismay and foreboding, a recent English immigrant to Philadelphia, Thomas Paine, was resolute in his demands for independence. Considered incendiary and radical, Paine's forty-seven-page pamphlet, *Common Sense,* made some bold assertions. Foremost among them was his condemnation of monarchy and aristocracy. Moreover, Paine viewed the American cause as one that had historical impact for all people under the thumb of foreign domination. Obviously the themes of the pamphlet resonated with those who advocated a republican form of government, one deriving its power from the people. Over 150,000 copies were sold, an astounding number for its day. But the pamphlet, like the revolution it espoused, has lived on as a political inspiration ever since.

---

justifications for it. Thomas Jefferson, a gifted writer and brilliant thinker, was given the task of writing the document, which was then to be edited by the committee. Jefferson was influenced by the Enlightenment philosophers of his day, whose ideas can be found in the document he presented. By early July, all of the colonies except New York, which had a large percentage of its population still loyal to the king, adopted Lee's call for independence as articulated in Jefferson's draft. On July 4, 1776, the Declaration of Independence was formally approved by Congress.

In the first part, which includes the Preamble (an introduction), Jefferson explains the necessity of independence for the preservation of basic natural laws and rights. These were John Locke's thoughts about the social contract, articulated in his *Two Treatises of Government,* and Jean-Jacques Rousseau's *Social Contract.*

> We hold these truths to be self-evident: That all men are created equal; that they are endowed by their Creator with certain unalienable rights; that among these are life, liberty, and the pursuit of happiness.

The second part of the Declaration of Independence lists a series of "abuses and usurpations" by the king and his government. This maltreatment, claimed Jefferson, violated the social contract the British monarch had with his colonies, thereby justifying the actions his American subjects felt compelled to take. The document ends with what is tantamount to a formal declaration of war. Even before signing the Declaration of Independence, the Second Continental Congress appointed a committee to draft the first constitution of the United States—the Articles of Confederation.

THE MILITARY PHASE OF THE REVOLUTIONARY WAR

For upstart colonists to challenge the formidable British army and the even more potent Royal Navy in the late eighteenth century was an intimidating task. But as in all wars, both sides had their strengths and weaknesses.

■ British Advantages

- The British had a considerably larger population from which to draw for troops. However, they relied on volunteers and mercenaries (such as hired Germans called Hessians).
- The British possessed considerable financial resources.
- Britain had a highly trained and experienced professional fighting force.
- Britain's Royal Navy controlled the seas, and therefore trade.
- Native American tribes, eager to see an end to colonial westward expansion, generally allied themselves to the British.
- Many Americans opposed to independence, called Tories or Loyalists, fought against the Continental Army.
- Black American slaves were offered freedom if they helped the British and some served in the British army.

- British Disadvantages
  - Britain needed a substantial part of its military to maintain its global empire. In fighting the Americans it eventually battled Holland, Spain, and France, nations all eager to see Britain defeated.
  - The European style of fighting practiced by the British army was not suitable for the North American wilderness.
  - The British had considerable logistical problems as their lines of communication and supplies stretched across the Atlantic Ocean.
  - The British army had to crush the rebellion by destroying Washington's army.

- Colonial (Patriot) Advantages
  - Americans were fighting for a lofty ideal—liberty—as well as for their homes and way of life.
  - By and large, the Americans had excellent officers, such as George Washington, as well as foreigners who came to assist the Americans, such as Thaddeus Kosciusko and Casimir Pulaski of Poland, Germany's Baron von Steuben, and, most famously, the Marquis de Lafayette from France.
  - The Americans were able to utilize guerrilla warfare, which often effectively counteracted Britain's disciplined troops and greater firepower.
  - The Americans received financial support from France and greatly benefited from direct French military intervention after 1778.
  - The Americans hoped that a protracted war would convince the British public and allies of the American cause in Parliament that continuing the war was senseless.

- Colonial Disadvantages
  - George Washington's army was considerably smaller than Britain's military forces in North America.
  - The Continental Congress had no real political authority. It had no power to tax or to create a sound currency.

- Most Americans were loyalists or were indifferent or neutral about the war and so did not support it. Many Tories actually took up arms to crush the rebellion.
- The Continental Army frequently suffered from supply shortages.
- As with their foe, the Americans were vulnerable to war weariness and a sense of futility, possible consequences of a long war.

MAJOR MILITARY EVENTS OF THE WAR

Though they suffered significant losses at the Battle of Bunker Hill, the Americans, under the command of George Washington, forced the British out of Boston in 1776. The British commander, Lord Howe, relocated his center of operations to New York. Washington's forces attempted to drive the British out of New York in 1776, but they were decisively defeated at the battles of Long Island and Washington Heights. Retreating to New Jersey, the Continental Army launched successful attacks on Hessian troops at Trenton and on the British at Princeton. The British then devised a plan that, if successful, would strategically divide the New England colonies from the rest. It called for a coordinated pincer movement requiring British Generals Burgoyne in Canada, St. Leger in the Great Lakes region, and Howe in the South to unite their forces in central New York, near Albany. Unfortunately for the British, Howe inexplicably moved south to Philadelphia instead of north, and St. Leger was forced to retreat to Canada. Howe did manage to capture Philadelphia and defeat Washington's army at the battles of Brandywine and Germantown in Pennsylvania, but these actions left Burgoyne isolated north of Albany. Washington's troops then retreated to Valley Forge, Pennsylvania, where, despite a serious shortage of supplies and in critical condition, they bravely endured a miserable winter. ("These are the times that try men's souls," declared Thomas Paine.)

But despair was soon to turn to victory for the Continental Army. Upon reaching Albany, Burgoyne's army was surrounded and defeated at the Battle of Saratoga (1777) by American forces under General Horatio Gates. More than just a decisive military victory, Saratoga was the turning point in the war. It convinced the French, still bitter about their defeat in the French and Indian War, to help the Americans. There is considerable speculation among historians as to the likelihood of American military success had the French not provided military and economic aid.

Following the debacle at Saratoga, British morale improved when Howe's replacement, Sir Henry Clinton, launched a major military campaign in the southern states. But in 1781, the sixth year of the war, fortunes in the South again changed as American forces began to win a series of military engagements. A British army under General Cornwallis's command marched to Yorktown, on the coast of Virginia, so that it could be protected by the Royal Navy. By this time, the British controlled only New York City and several southern ports. Their future success was tied to Cornwallis's army in Virginia.

Unfortunately for Cornwallis, Washington's army was closing in on him from the north, General Lafayette's combined French and

American force was on the move in Virginia, and French Admiral DeGrasse's flotilla of warships cut Cornwallis off from supplies, reinforcements, and finally even retreat. There was only one option left to the British general. On October 17, 1781, with the British band playing "The World Turned Upside Down," Cornwallis's army surrendered. Upon hearing of the defeat, the British public demanded an end to the war, Lord North resigned as prime minister, and before long the British and Americans convened peace negotiations in Paris.

THE TREATY OF PARIS

The three principal American diplomats—Benjamin Franklin, John Jay, and John Adams—were directed to work closely with the French to bring about a suitable resolution. Whereas the Americans and French had been effective military allies, their diplomatic relationship soon revealed weaknesses. Both had been unified in their effort to defeat the British, but it became apparent that the French had further objectives; for instance, they stipulated that Britain return Gibraltar to its ally, Spain, as a prerequisite to an agreement. The Americans were also concerned that France might negotiate an independent settlement with Britain that would exclude American independence. Thus the three American delegates chose to carry out their negotiations independent of the French. In September 1783, the British and American delegates reached an agreement that effectively ended all hostilities between the two. On January 14, 1783, Congress ratified the Treaty of Paris. Two weeks later, Britain, France, and Spain agreed to their own provisional peace treaty.

The Terms of the Treaty of Paris were as follows:

- Britain formally and unconditionally recognized the independence of the United States.
- The boundaries of the new nation were established: north at the Canadian border and along the Great Lakes, west to the Mississippi River, and south to Florida (which in a separate treaty had been returned by Britain to Spain).
- American fishing ships were given unlimited access to the waters off Newfoundland.
- The government of the United States agreed it would not interfere legally with British creditors and merchants seeking to collect debts owed to them by Americans.
- The United States would compensate loyalists whose property had been confiscated during the war.

WOMEN AND THE REVOLUTION Women's rights would not be addressed by a major reform movement until the mid-nineteenth century, and even then, women would have to wait until 1919 just for the right to vote. (Though New Jersey did enfranchise women after the American Revolution, this right was repealed early in the nineteenth century.) American women were certainly conscious of the revolutionary goals their male family members were fighting for: liberty and the "rights of man." But some women wondered whether their own rights could be enhanced as well. Abigail Adams counseled her husband that when writing the "new code of laws...I desire you would remember the ladies [and] do not put such unlimited power in the hands of husbands." Some enlightened leaders such as Benjamin Franklin were even supportive of female education; however, women at the end of the American Revolution were no better off than before—this despite the fact that women played a major role in maintaining the colonial economy. They had run the family farms and businesses while their husbands, sons, and brothers were away fighting the war. Women also contributed to the war effort by providing essential supplies, serving as nurses, and, in rare cases, even as soldiers. Yet, in nearly every sense of the word, they continued to be subordinated to men. The patriarchal society that defined gender roles in the colonial period would survive for many more decades.

BLACKS AND THE REVOLUTION In the first draft of the Declaration of Independence, Thomas Jefferson actually blamed King George III for the existence of slavery in the colonies. Thankfully, Benjamin Franklin and the other editors of the document removed that allegation. Still, it is one of the tragic ironies of U.S. history that some of the most famous leaders of the war for independence—among them Washington and Jefferson—owned slaves. This did not go unnoticed by Dr. Samuel Johnson, the famous British author and contemporary of the American Revolution. "How is it that the loudest yelps for liberty," he asked, "come from the drivers of slaves?" Even more ironic is that black Americans contributed to both sides during the war, and for basically the same reason: their own independence. Some black colonists actually fought as redcoats because they were promised their freedom if they joined the British. As for the American side, blacks had actually been in northern militia units before the war and could rightly be called Minute Men. Some were even veterans of the French and Indian War. At the outbreak of hostilities in 1775, due in large part to pressure from the southern colonies (who feared that blacks would seek their own freedom), the Continental Congress prohibited blacks from serving in the Continental Army, whether they were free men or slaves. As the war dragged on, however, blacks began to enter the Continental Army from both northern and some southern colonies. By the end of the war, approximately 5,500 black colonists fought for the American side, though frequently they were segregated from white troops. They had hoped that their contribution to American independence would entitle them to their own freedom, but many black soldiers were returned to slavery at the end of the war. They had been considered patriots in name only.

TWO REVOLUTIONS?

The primary goal of those who took up arms against Britain was to end British control of their colonies. To this end, the war was an anti-imperialist revolutionary struggle. But did the war have another dimension, one that also sought to democratize America socially and politically? Some historians contend that this is not the case, that the war was in fact a conservative revolution. In their view, America was qualitatively and comparatively democratic already and the revolutionaries of all classes consequently were seeking to preserve the social, economic, and political order, not transform it. These historians point to the democratic features already in place in the colonies in the eighteenth century, such as basic political, economic, and religious freedoms. For example, they argue, there were few obstacles to white male enfranchisement. Given the vast amount of land, most Americans had the ability to purchase inexpensive property and therefore meet any land-ownership requirements for voting. What is more, social mobility was indeed open to nearly all white males; thus social conflict in colonial society was minimal.

Other historians see a dual impulse: win independence in order to further democratize society, government, and the economy. Independence was the precondition for this goal because it was in Britain's interest to preserve the status quo in the colonies. This in turn permitted the colonial elites to maintain their dominance and control over the rest of colonial society through, for example, voting qualifications based on property ownership (substantial in some colonies, especially New York, where thirty families controlled three-quarters of the land), and the merchant class's monopoly of the retail trade. The outbreak of violence against entrenched elites—for example, the hostility expressed in the Regulator Movement in the late eighteenth century and Bacon's Rebellion in the mid-seventeenth century—demonstrate class tensions in pre-Revolutionary America. There are other examples as well; in Boston, over 40 percent of the city's wealth was controlled by just 1 percent of the population. There are many points to support both perspectives. As you reflect on the causes and impact of the American Revolution, it is important to remember that there were members of society who, even after independence had been won, were just as concerned about the effects of too much democracy as there were those who believed the war had in part been fought to expand it. The creation of a permanent government in the postwar years would reveal the nature of this debate as well as concerns over the constitutional powers and limitations that should be accorded the new government of the United States.

Multiple-Choice Questions

1. The Declaration of Rights
   (A) was issued by Parliament to grant greater autonomy for colonial governments
   (B) was a formal declaration of war issued by the First Continental Congress
   (C) was written by George Washington
   (D) was viewed by King George III as a positive effort by the First Continental Congress to prevent an outbreak of hostilities
   (E) was rejected by the British Parliament

ANSWER: E. The king's government rejected the appeal, which led to an intensification of hostilities (*The American Pageant,* 12th and 11th eds., p. 134).

2. The opening shots of the American Revolution occurred at
   (A) the Battles of Lexington and Concord
   (B) the Battle of Bunker Hill
   (C) the Boston Massacre
   (D) the Battle of Saratoga
   (E) Valley Forge

ANSWER: **A**. British redcoats and Massachusetts Minute Men fired the first shots at Lexington and later at Concord. They have been called "the shots heard 'round the world" (*The American Pageant,* 12th and 11th eds., pp.134-135).

3. Which one of the following was NOT an advantage the British had in their war effort to suppress the American rebellion?
   (A) a larger military
   (B) shorter supply lines
   (C) any colonists, either supporting the British or indifferent
   (D) a larger and stronger navy
   (E) greater financial resources

ANSWER: **B**. Great Britain had to wage war and therefore supply its troops from three thousand miles away (*The American Pageant,* 12th and 11th eds., p. 136).

4. The Olive Branch Petition
   (A) was an attempt by the British to reach a political settlement after their defeat at the Battle of Saratoga
   (B) was offered by radicals in the First Continental Congress to more moderate delegates in an attempt to unify colonial opposition to British policies
   (C) was issued by France in an attempt to bring hostilities between the British and Americans to an end
   (D) was offered to Native American tribes by the First Continental Congress to gain their support in the war against the British
   (E) was an attempt by the First Continental Congress to prevent further hostilities after the Battle of Bunker Hill

ANSWER: **E**. Even after a major battle, Bunker Hill, had been fought, the First Continental Congress appealed to King George III to end hostilities. The petition was summarily rejected (*The American Pageant,* 12th ed., p. 143/11th ed., p. 144).

5. Which of the following British measures declared that because the American colonies were in open rebellion against the British Crown, all trade would be suspended?
   (A) the Intolerable Acts
   (B) the Quartering Act
   (C) the Declaration of Rights
   (D) the Prohibitory Act
   (E) the Declaratory Act

ANSWER: **D**. The Prohibitory Act (1775) was an attempt to stop the rebellion by crippling the American economy.

6. Thomas Paine
   (A) was Britain's prime minister during the early stage of the American Revolution
   (B) was president of the First Continental Congress
   (C) wrote *Common Sense*, an appeal to the colonists to resist the British and establish a republican form of government
   (D) was the leader of the radicals in the Second Continental Congress
   (E) was the British general who surrendered his army at Yorktown

ANSWER: **C**. Thomas Paine's widely read pamphlet *Common Sense* was influential in generating support for the American war effort. Paine rejected monarchy and favored its replacement with a republican—representative—form of government (*The American Pageant,* 12th ed., pp. 144-145/11th ed., pp. 145-146).

7. The Battle of Saratoga was the turning point of the American Revolution because
   (A) the French entered the war on the American side
   (B) the last major British army in North America surrendered to Washington's army
   (C) most Americans who had been Tories decided to switch sides and fight for independence
   (D) the British issued the Olive Branch Petition, in which they agreed to open peace negotiations with the Americans
   (E) American public opinion began to turn against the war

ANSWER: **A**. Not only was the Battle of Saratoga a major American victory; it convinced the French to provide financial and military assistance to the Americans (*The American Pageant,* 12th and 11th eds., p. 171).

8. The argument that "abuses and usurpations" by King George and his government violated the social contract that had existed between Britain and its American colonies was articulated in
   (A) the Declaratory Act
   (B) the Treaty of Paris
   (C) the Declaration of Rights
   (D) the Declaration of the Causes and Necessities for Taking Up Arms
   (E) the Declaration of Independence

ANSWER: **E**. Borrowing from Locke's social contract theory, Jefferson asserted in the Declaration of Independence that British violations of American rights had voided the contract between the king and his American subjects (*The American Pageant,* 12th and 11th eds., p. 148).

9. The Regulator Movement, Bacon's Rebellion, and the Paxton Boys
   (A) were the names of Tory militia units who fought against the American revolutionaries in the war
   (B) indicate to some historians the undemocratic nature of pre-Revolutionary American society
   (C) were Massachusetts radicals who participated in the Boston Tea Party
   (D) were black American military units who fought for American independence
   (E) organized committees of correspondence to unite American colonial opposition to the tea tax

ANSWER: **B**. The Regulators, Bacon's supporters, and the Paxton Boys rose up against their colonial governments to protest the lack of representation and the claim that these governments served the interests of colonial America's elites (*The American Pageant*, 12th ed., pp. 68, 86/11th ed., pp. 66, 84).

10. The Treaty of Paris included the following terms EXCEPT
    (A) Britain formally recognized American independence
    (B) Britain was allowed to maintain several forts in the area west of the Appalachian Mountains in order to protect its trading posts
    (C) American fishing ships were given permission to fish off the coast of Newfoundland
    (D) the Americans promised to compensate loyalists whose property had been confiscated during the war
    (E) the American government promised not to legally interfere with British creditors who were seeking payment on debts owed to them by Americans

ANSWER: **B**. Great Britain removed all of its troops from the area south of Canada. However Britain still held political and military control of Canada (*The American Pageant*, 12th ed., pp. 161-162/11th ed., pp. 160-161).

Free-Response Questions

1. How justified were the Americans in initiating a revolution against Great Britain after nearly 150 years of British administration? In your answer, make certain to address the political relationship between Britain and the American colonies.

RESPONSE You should incorporate in your essay the idea of taxation without representation versus the British policy of virtual representation. Also, royal governors were appointed to oversee the colonies, which diluted the colonial governments. As for the economic relationship, you should discuss the reasons for specific British economic acts and whether the American responses to these acts were based on moderation or inspired by radicals.

2. How prepared were the American colonists to face the economic and military power of Great Britain when war broke out in 1775?

RESPONSE You should discuss the fact that American colonists were divided. Many on the frontier and more remote areas were unaffected by the British government's acts and policies. Point out that the Americans faced serious economic, political, and military disadvantages. On the other hand, point out the political and military advantages on the American side, and be sure to include French intervention.

4

CREATION OF THE U.S. CONSTITUTION: 1781–1791

When Virginia's Richard Henry Lee introduced a resolution in the Second Continental Congress on June 7, 1776, in favor of American independence, he also proposed that a government be established based on an accord of confederated states—an association of sovereign states. Within a month, under the direction of John Dickinson, a committee established by the Congress had devised a plan of government called the Articles of Confederation and Perpetual Union.

The Articles of Confederation were adopted by the Congress the next year and were finally approved by all the states in 1781. But by 1787, it was clear that the Articles were insufficient for the young nation. A convention charged with revising the Articles concluded that an entirely new structure was needed. The Constitution was the result. In this chapter we will take a closer look at the Founding Fathers and how they came to write the Constitution.

KEY CONCEPTS

- The Articles of Confederation were unable to address the economic and political problems facing the new nation.
- The Constitution was completed only because the delegates to the Constitutional Convention were able to reach a number of major compromises.
- Opposition to ratification of the Constitution came from antifederalists, who feared a strong central government.
- Promise of a bill of rights was important to ratification of the Constitution.

The Articles of Confederation and the Constitution are discussed in depth in *The American Pageant,* 12th and 11th eds., Chapter 9.

CREATING THE NATION'S FIRST GOVERNMENT: ISSUES AND CONCERNS

Not unexpectedly, problems developed as the committee drawing up the Articles of Confederation worked out the details of this newly independent political system. One critical concern was the issue of where, in this new government, power should reside. Would the states be autonomous and more powerful than the central government? Would the central government be paramount in its dealings with the states? Or would there be a sharing of powers and responsibilities? Keep in mind that Americans were then fighting a war against what they perceived to be a tyrannical government, autocratic and seemingly insensitive to the rights of American colonists. As a consequence, Americans were deeply suspicious about placing too much authority in the hands of a central power. But if the central government had little authority compared with the states, then what was the purpose of even having one? Other questions soon arose as well. Would this new government be bicameral (a two-house legislature) or unicameral (a one-house legislature)? How would representation be apportioned? Would larger states with larger populations have more representation than smaller states? Would larger states pay more in taxes? What about the relationship between the powers of the government and the rights of citizens? These were questions that could be answered only if the delegates were able to agree on what was arguably the most pivotal question: What did they actually intend when they created a *United States* of America?

In most cases, these questions were adequately addressed by the delegates in their deliberations and in the ultimate ratification of the Articles of Confederation. Other key issues, however, would go unresolved for decades. In fact, it took the Civil War and not the first U.S. government to conclusively determine the relationship between the states and federal government. But what delayed ratification of the Articles for nearly four years had little to do with issues relating to the nature of the government or the powers of the states, but rather disputes over western land claims. Some states—Rhode Island, for one—insisted that jurisdiction over disputed western lands should be a responsibility of the central government. But settling land claims was an especially difficult task because western state boundaries were often not clearly delineated. This led to claims by more than one state for the same territory. In fact, some states insisted that their western boundaries stretched to the Mississippi River and even as far as the Pacific Ocean. Some land claims were seemingly arbitrary, such as Virginia's claim to land in what is present-day Wisconsin. Only when the two states that had been obstacles to a compromise, New York and Virginia, agreed to relinquish their western land claims was the new government, embodied in the Articles of Confederation, ratified by the Continental Congress, in March 1781.

The Major Features of the Articles of Confederation (AOC)

Under the AOC, the central government was extremely ineffective and impotent; most authority remained with the individual states. To many, the decentralization of authority was important to the maintenance of democracy. Further, it protected against potential tyrannical abuses by a strong central government. The Articles of Confederation had the following features, many of which were considered weaknesses by those favoring a stronger central government:

- a unicameral legislature
- no authority for Congress to impose taxes
- one vote in Congress for each state
- no national court system
- no provision for a uniform national currency
- no chief executive
- a requirement that nine of the thirteen states approve passage of certain legislation
- unanimity for amendment of the AOC
- no authority for Congress to regulate either interstate or foreign commerce

AP Tip

Many of the problems and abuses that occurred in the years immediately following the end of the American Revolution can be traced to the weaknesses of the AOC in addressing these concerns. Making this connection is important in understanding why the AOC were inadequate for the new nation and why early on some questioned the new government's usefulness.

As the United States emerged from the turmoil of war, it was immediately faced with serious economic concerns. These were some of the problems afflicting American society in the 1780s:

- The infant manufacturing sector of the economy was adversely affected by Great Britain's practice of flooding the American market with British goods. The consequent unfavorable balance of trade had a negative effect on the nation's economy in general and on many of the new American industries and businesses that emerged in the postwar years.
- Infrastructure (roads, bridges, highways) had been neglected, so the transportation system was inadequate for commerce and trade.
- Inflation was rampant because of the absence of a uniform currency and also because notes were often given an arbitrary value by private banks and state governments. This had a direct impact on business transactions within a state and between states.
- Interstate trade was adversely affected by state trade barriers and a vast assortment of currencies.

- The government could do little to address the effects of a depression that struck following the war.

Because the new government could not address the economic needs of the nation and the individual states, the AOC could do nothing to remedy the maladies of inflation and depression. Individual states had to solve their economic problems. Some states imposed heavy taxes on their citizens to tackle inflation and address their infrastructural needs. For example, Massachusetts imposed a thirty percent tax on the average farmer. Overburdened by the weight of this levy, many farmers lost their farms or went to debtor's prison. It was not long before farmers in Massachusetts organized and petitioned their state legislature to enact stay laws (which would stay, or keep, them from prison for indebtedness). They also wanted their state government to issue more money in order to inflate the economy, thereby expanding the credit system and inflating prices. The Massachusetts state legislature rejected their demands in favor of a deflationary policy (less money in the system), which they expected would strengthen the economy and therefore enhance the public's confidence; this in turn would allow for a more viable credit system. As it turned out, that approach did not work. The depression intensified, and deflation replaced inflation as more and more money was taken out of the system. Believing their government was insensitive to their economic predicament, some farmers engaged in open revolt.

ACHIEVEMENTS OF THE ARTICLES OF CONFEDERATION

In its short life as the government of the United States (1777-1789), the AOC did achieve some noteworthy successes. The AOC was, after all, the government during the American Revolution and negotiated peace terms with the British at the end of the war. In addition, two very important land policies that would shape the future of the nation, the Land Ordinance of 1785 and the Northwest Ordinance of 1787, came about in this period. Both were significant achievements in that they facilitated the settlement of western territories and made expansion systematic.

- **Land Ordinance of 1785** In 1784 Congress decided that western lands would be organized into states roughly the size of the each of the original thirteen states. This area would first be divided into sovereign districts, which in due course would become states. However, the plan was not instituted, in large part because of the political clout of land speculators, who wanted to increase the amount of acreage that an individual or company could purchase. Instead, a new plan was enacted, the Land Ordinance of 1785, which had the following provisions:

Shays's Rebellion

The most famous example of agrarian discontent in the postwar years occurred in Massachusetts in 1786. An armed band of farmers numbering in the hundreds and led by Daniel Shays, a former officer in the Continental Army, sought to shut down the courts as a form of protest and to prevent the continued foreclosure of their farms and the collection of taxes. The farmers were met by an equally large state militia force, but they still managed to close the courts. However, when Shays and his men marched on the Springfield arsenal, they were routed. In the end, Shays and his men were pardoned and the state of Massachusetts did modify its tax laws. But the rebellion made an indelible impression on the minds of some Americans and their political leaders: civil disobedience could spread easily from county to county and state to state.

As delegates began arriving in Philadelphia in the late spring of 1787 to amend the AOC, the events in Massachusetts weighed heavily on their minds, particularly the nation's conservative political leaders, who believed that a strong central government with the authority to suppress domestic disturbances was necessary. When the delegates wrote a new constitution for the nation, they had the symbolic importance of Shays's Rebellion in mind when they gave to the national government the authority to "protect each of them [states] against invasion; and … against domestic violence" (Article IV, Section IV). For others, the strengthening of the national government would lead to tyranny; it would allow those in power to maintain the status quo by preventing fundamental changes to society, the economy, and government. No wonder, then, that in refusing to attend the Constitutional Convention, the famous patriot Patrick Henry exclaimed, "I smelt a rat."

- Townships six miles square would be surveyed. These in turn would again be divided into sections equaling one square mile.
- The sections were to be sold in lots of 640 acres at no less than $1 an acre. Land speculators found this agreeable; they had large amounts of ready cash. The average buyer did not have $640 in disposable wealth, nor was credit made available as part of the plan.
- The revenue from the sale of one section for each township would be used to develop public education.

The Land Ordinance of 1785 established a precedent for subsequent surveys of public land and federal support for public education.

- **The Northwest Ordinance** (also known as the Land Ordinance of 1787) embodied two of the nation's guiding political principles: federalism and republicanism. It provided for the following:
  - The Northwest Territory would be divided into three to five separate territories.
  - A methodical process would advance each territory to statehood.
  - Unorganized territories would be overseen by officials appointed by Congress.
  - Once the population of the territory reached 5,000 it could be organized as a territory. Residents would then elect members to a state legislature and send a delegate to Congress.

■ Once the population reached 60,000 a constitution would be written and the territory would apply to Congress for statehood.

From the region that was the Northwest Territory, five states emerged between 1803 and 1848: Ohio, Indiana, Illinois, Michigan, and Wisconsin.

THE AOC ATTEMPT TO CONFRONT FOREIGN AFFAIRS PROBLEMS

Problems for the new government were not limited to domestic issues and concerns. Difficulties with foreign affairs were another burden. After the war, relations with European powers quickly deteriorated, especially with the new nation's former nemesis, Great Britain. In some cases the United States brought the problems on itself, as it failed to abide by the Treaty of Paris. Remember that the U.S. government had promised to compensate loyalists whose property was confiscated during the war and to pay foreign debts. Both promises were not met. But the British violated the treaty as well. King George III, who was never impressed with American military power (and now especially since the AOC had to rely on the states to provide troops to protect the nation), broke Britain's treaty obligations by maintaining forts in the Northwest Territory. The United States could do nothing about the forts except vehemently protest. The British also placed various trade restrictions on the United States, which further damaged its already weak economy. To make matters worse, the disunity that plagued the nation under the AOC raised eyebrows in Europe's political circles and threatened the reputation of the United States. European nations reasoned that since the individual states were themselves embroiled in trade disputes, commercial agreements with the United States would certainly be questionable.

Even a former wartime ally, Spain, saw an opportunity to exploit the new nation. The monarchical government of Spain, always wary of the potential for the United States to expand its power, was perhaps even more wary of the democratic ideals emanating from the United States. The two countries quarreled over the undefined northern boundary of Florida (which Britain had ceded back to Spain in 1783), called the Yazoo Strip. There was friction, too, over navigation rights to the Mississippi River—the Spanish controlled the lower river, which was vital to American commerce. Still another problem was Spain's relationship with Native American tribes in the West. Both wanted to contain American western expansion, especially in the South, which interfered with Georgia's desire to expand. In 1785 war broke out between the state of Georgia and the Creeks. Despite the enmity of the Native Americans and Spanish, Americans flooded into what would eventually become Tennessee and Kentucky. Some of these settlers did not hold deeds to this land, which often was owned by eastern speculators. In eastern Tennessee, a group of settlers organized a new state, which they named Franklin in honor of their celebrated compatriot Benjamin Franklin. They then petitioned Congress to admit Franklin into the United States but were rejected. Spain saw its chance. Secret agents were employed to bring Franklin under Spain's

Early Attempts to Revise the AOC

By the time the delegates met in Philadelphia, two attempts had already been made to revise the AOC.

- **Alexandria Conference (1785)** Delegates from Virginia and Maryland met to discuss ways to improve navigation and commerce on the Potomac River. They decided to invite delegates from the other states to a meeting in Annapolis, Maryland, to discuss commerce on a national level.
- **Annapolis Conference (1786)** Eight states sent delegates to this conference, but only five arrived on time. Nevertheless, while attendance was poor, there was obviously strong sentiment across the nation that the AOC had to be revised. Important leaders such as James Madison of Virginia and Alexander Hamilton of New York took it upon themselves to invite states to send delegates to a national convention in Philadelphia.

control. (It seems that Daniel Boone was one of the agents, but he did nothing to help the project, even though he was paid by Spain.) The effort ultimately collapsed, but not because of any response by the United States. Given the inability of the AOC to address troublesome domestic and foreign affairs problems, it is not surprising that some of the nation's foremost political leaders wanted to revise the AOC. In 1787, delegates met in Philadelphia to do just that. Before they were through, however, they had in fact created an entirely new government.

THE CONSTITUTIONAL CONVENTION

By May 1787, fifty-five delegates from twelve states (Rhode Island chose not to participate) had arrived in Philadelphia to begin work on revising the government of the United States. The list of delegates was a veritable "who's who" in America at that time, among them George Washington and James Madison (both future presidents), Benjamin Franklin, George Mason, and Roger Sherman. Those who were absent were just as formidable: radical leaders Patrick Henry, Sam Adams, and Thomas Paine chose not to attend, for they were wary of any attempt to increase the power of the central government. Future presidents Thomas Jefferson and John Adams were serving overseas as U.S. ambassadors. Generally, the delegates to the Constitutional Convention were men of wealth and property. To a large extent, their motives were twofold: to create a government that would protect the nation and at the same time to protect their investments. The difficulty they faced was in designing a strong central government while safeguarding individual liberties. They knew that a new government would not be ratified by the people unless it balanced authoritarian rule and democratic rule. Rest assured that both extremes concerned them.

Historians Interpret the Intent of the Framers

Which concerns, issues, and hopes motivated the delegates as they left the comfort of their homes in late spring 1787, headed for Philadelphia to revise the AOC? Historians have contemplated this question for over a century. One of the earliest views held that the Framers did what was necessary and appropriate given the domestic and foreign affairs problems that were plaguing the nation under the AOC.

Not until the early decades of the twentieth century was this view challenged. Most significantly, historian Charles Beard powerfully rejected this view in his highly influential book *An Economic Interpretation of the Constitution of the United States.* Beard's thesis was simple and devastating: the Framers had their own self-interest at heart when they met in Philadelphia. As men of property and wealth, they wanted a government that would stimulate trade and industrial growth, protect private property against "mob rule," and recover loans owed to them in the form of public debts. According to Beard, the AOC government, had it been given a chance to develop, could have become a perfectly suitable system of government. Forty years later, Beard's thesis was in turn refuted by other historians who claimed that there was no correlation between support for the Constitution and one's financial status. Instead, a delegate's regional interests and concerns were the key to their support. Beard's thesis has so eroded that many historians have serious reservations about it. But other historians, with Beard's view in mind, have added to the debate by claiming, for example, that the delegates' views on ratifying the new Constitution were certainly based on their economic outlook. On the one hand, agrarian interests were cautious about creating a centralized government, whereas more commercially minded delegates considered centralization necessary for the sustained economic growth of the nation. Regardless of one's view, the debate over the Framers' rationale continues to be a lively and vital part of any debate on the Constitution.

To be sure, most delegates concluded that the old form of government was no longer suitable. In retrospect, the Framers had four general goals in mind when they deliberated on how best to revise the government. It must be able to

- prevent a tyranny of the majority
- prevent a tyranny of the minority
- have sufficient powers to create conditions for both short- and long-term economic development
- formulate and conduct a more effective foreign policy

AP Tip

The Constitution is at the heart of American history. You must be able to identify the ways in which the Constitution was designed to allow the government to meet changing conditions and attitudes.

It was not long, however, before core conflicts emerged between different interest groups:

Two Proposals for Representation

Large states, which favored a bicameral legislature with representation based on population, put forward the Virginia Plan. It called for a lower house of Congress elected by the people, which in turn would elect members to an upper house. Both houses would then elect an executive—president—who could serve only one term. A judiciary system would also be established. This plan granted more power to the central government while maintaining some features of the AOC. The smaller states favored a unicameral legislature with each state receiving one vote (as it was with the AOC), an executive with no veto power, and a judiciary that could arbitrate cases that had originated in state courts. The smaller states would support the New Jersey Plan.

- bankers (hard money advocates) versus debtors (cheap money advocates)
- northern (commercial) versus southern (rural slave) economic interests
- economic competition between states
- conflicts between states over western land ownership
- large states (representation by population) versus small states (equal representation for each state)
- supporters of a strong central government versus supporters of individual and states' rights
- those with democratic ideals versus those with aristocratic leanings
- slave states, which wanted to include slaves in the population count (for purposes of representation in Congress) versus nonslave states, which sought to omit them from the count (thereby reducing the South's representation in Congress)

Despite the enormous chasm between advocates of the differing approaches, a number of important compromises were worked out:

- The Commerce Compromise (regulating trade and commerce)
  - The South agreed to federal control over foreign and interstate trade.
  - The importation of slaves would be permitted for twenty years, until 1808.
  - The federal government was given the authority to collect import taxes, but there would be no duties on exports.
- The Great (or Connecticut) Compromise (dealing with representation in Congress)
  - A state's representation in the House of Representatives was to be based on population.
  - The states' representation in the Senate would be equal (two senators for each state).
  - All money bills would originate in the House.
  - Direct taxes on states were to be assessed according to population.
- The Three-fifths Compromise (counting slaves for representation in Congress)
  - Three-fifths of a state's slave population would be counted for purposes of taxation and representation.

■ A fugitive slave law required that runaway slaves who escaped to a free state must be returned to their owners.

The delegates also divided power within the national government, creating three branches: the legislative (Congress), the executive (the president), and the judicial (the courts). There was considerable disagreement about the powers of the executive branch, which was given a good deal of power; the AOC had had no executive. Much less discussion was devoted to the judiciary. There was no mention of judicial review, an essential part of the system of checks and balances. That would be established under Chief Justice John Marshall, who served on the court from 1801 to 1835.

- Powers of the legislative branch
  - Congress has the power of the purse—power to set and collect taxes, borrow money, regulate trade, coin money.
  - Congress was to set up a postal service and issue patents and copyrights.
  - War must be authorized by Congress.
  - Congress is responsible for raising and maintaining an army and a navy.
- Powers of the executive branch
  - The president carries out and enforces laws passed by Congress.
  - The president can veto congressional bills (though Congress can override an executive veto with a two-thirds vote, considerably more difficult than the majority need to pass a bill).
  - The president makes treaties (though the Senate has the authority to accept or reject treaties).
  - The president is commander in chief of the U.S. military.
  - The president appoints federal officials, such as federal judges; however, the Senate must consent to the appointments.
- Powers of the judicial branch
  - Congress was to establish a Supreme Court and lower courts.
  - The kind of cases that could be heard in federal courts was specified.
  - The Supreme Court's jurisdiction was outlined.
  - Treason was defined; requirements for conviction were set; and punishment was to be in the hands of Congress.

THE RATIFICATION DEBATE: FEDERALISTS VERSUS ANTIFEDERALISTS

Ratifying the new government was not easy. For nine months heated exchanges flew back and forth between supporters and opponents of the new constitution. Those who advocated for the new government were known as federalists; opponents were called Antifederalists.

Federalists	Antifederalists
Support came mainly from coastal and urban areas and from the upper classes—merchants, financiers, shippers, planters, though not all upperclass citizens were Federalists.	Support came mainly from backcountry and agricultural areas, debtors, and people philosophically opposed to a strong central government.
Prominent leaders included Washington, Hamilton, Madison, and Franklin.	Prominent leaders included Patrick Henry, John Hancock, and George Mason.
They favored a strong central government to maintain peace and stability and to strengthen the Union in ways that the AOC could not.	They opposed a central government that did not guarantee protection of individual rights. They believed the Constitution subordinated states' rights.

In order to convince the voting public in the crucial state of New York to support ratification, key advocates of the Constitution composed a series of essays for publication in a New York newspaper. Written by James Madison, Alexander Hamilton, and John Jay, the *Federalist Papers* went beyond merely pointing out the inadequacies of the AOC. The underlying premise of their argument was that because man is corruptible he cannot always be trusted to govern himself. What is needed, therefore, is an elaborate constitutional system to prevent rulers from acting in an arbitrary and abusive manner, as well as to control the passions of the masses. One of the most famous of the essays was *Federalist* No. 10, which argues that a republican form of government can effectively and fairly operate in a large and heterogeneous nation in which there are many factions and power is diffused. The authors also addressed claims that too much power would be concentrated in the executive branch, that there would not be enough powers reserved to the states, and that power would be diffused in the federal government as well so that both a "tyranny of the majority" and a "tyranny of the minority" would be prevented. In other words, the delegates were as concerned with a faction of elites (for example, commercial interests or agrarian interests) dominating the government as they were about the masses gaining too much influence.

THE BILL OF RIGHTS AND RATIFICATION OF THE UNITED STATES CONSTITUTION

Many citizens opposed ratification unless a list of rights was added to the Constitution. Federalists argued that this was unnecessary because members of Congress would be elected by the people. Further, they argued that by defining the delegated powers of government, they had drastically limited the potential for abuse of

The Intellectual Influences on the Framers

The Framers did not write the Constitution in a political or intellectual vacuum. They were very much shaped by the ideas of the previous two centuries, most especially the Scientific Revolution of the seventeenth century and the Enlightenment of the eighteenth century. Profoundly important scientific inventions such as Galileo's astronomical telescope and Leeuwenhoek's microscope allowed thinkers to view the functioning of planetary and human bodies. Their empirical evidence led them to conclude that everything in the universe—for example, the planets revolving around the sun—operated according to certain natural laws. Human anatomy also functions according to anatomical laws. Consider the chambers of the heart, each with a separate function that is necessary for the entire organ to function. Eighteenth-century thinkers such as Jefferson and Franklin believed that God created the universe but left it to man to identify the laws of the universe. They concluded that since God defined perfection, everything he created would be in a state of equilibrium. Therefore, since humans were created in God's image, everything they created, such as a political system, should also reflect this equilibrium.

Enlightenment thinkers added to the Framers' understanding of natural law and human behavior. Take, for instance, Newton's laws of motion: for every action there is an equal and opposite reaction. Or John Calvin's contention (based in large part on Protestantism) that human nature could not be trusted because men were selfish, greedy, and evil, supplemented by Thomas Hobbes's argument that since man was basically evil, he required a strong and powerful government to control his inclinations. Consequently, we see here a direct correlation between these ideas and the principles and mechanisms of the Constitution that reflect bicameralism, separation of powers and checks and balances, and federalism.

- **Bicameralism** A two-house legislature allows for the upper and lower houses to check each other's authority.
- **Separation of powers and checks and balances** Each branch has its own powers and responsibilities, but the three branches of government are compelled to interact. For example, Congress passes a bill, which then goes to the president, who may veto it or sign it into law. In turn, the law may be ruled unconstitutional by the judicial branch. These principles were seen as a safeguard against tyranny—by which was meant one branch, especially the executive, gaining too much power.
- **Federalism** Power is divided between the central government and the states. Although federal law is paramount, states have reserved, or enumerated, powers under the Tenth Amendment—for example, overseeing elections and driving ages. The powers of the federal government, which are delegated powers, include declaring war, borrowing money, and establishing a post office, as well as making all laws "necessary and proper." Yet it took the Civil War to determine conclusively the relationship between the central government's powers and the states' rights.

power. But if the rights of citizens were enumerated, that would in effect place limitations on their rights. Opponents, the antifederalists, contended that only a list of basic civil rights could protect citizens from a tyrannical government. The deadlock was resolved when the federalists promised to add a bill of rights once the Constitution was ratified. (Honoring that promise, the first congressmen elected under the Constitution proposed twelve amendments, ten of which were ratified and adopted in 1791 and make up what we know as the Bill of

Rights. They provide for various protections, among them freedom of religion, speech, and the press. There are also protections for the rights of the accused. The Ninth Amendment affirms that citizens have rights that, even if not mentioned, are protected. The Tenth Amendment reserves to the states and the people rights not delegated or prohibited by the Constitution.)

Despite strong opposition, by various states, classes, and regions, the supporters of the new government were able to win over nine of the thirteen states necessary for ratification by July 1788. North Carolina eventually ratified the Constitution once the Bill of Rights was added. As for the last state, Rhode Island, coercion was needed. Congress threatened to boycott the state if it didn't follow the other twelve in ratifying the new government. The following year, 1789, George Washington became the first president of the United States under the new form of government. Though the Framers had put together a document and system of government that was certainly more formidable than the AOC, fissures and divisions that had been present during the Constitutional Convention would soon emerge. Subsequent political leaders in all branches of the government, as well as emerging political parties, would transform the nation's political system, and therefore its economy and society. What is certain, however, is that the U.S. Constitution, despite its inadequacies and limitations, has stood the test of time. It is the world's oldest living written constitution.

Multiple-Choice Questions

1. Which one of the following was a major success of the Articles of Confederation?
   (A) They ended the French and Indian War.
   (B) They led to the creation of a powerful U.S. military.
   (C) They paved the way for closer economic ties with Great Britain.
   (D) They devised land policies that would allow for the systematic incorporation of new states.
   (E) They resolved the dispute over the powers of the central government and the powers of the states.

ANSWER: **D**. The Land Ordinance of 1785 and the Northwest Ordinance were considerable achievements of the AOC (*The American Pageant,* 12th ed., p 174/11th ed., p. 173).

2. Of the following list of political leaders, which one was strongly opposed to the plan of government created by the delegates at the Philadelphia convention?
   (A) Patrick Henry
   (B) George Washington
   (C) James Madison
   (D) Benjamin Franklin
   (E) Alexander Hamilton

ANSWER: **A**. Wary that the delegates might create a tyrannical government, Patrick Henry refused to attend the Constitutional Convention and later opposed ratification (*The American Pageant,* 12th ed., p. 185/11th ed., p. 184).

3. Which of the following was NOT a feature of the Articles of Confederation?
   (A) They called for a bicameral legislature.
   (B) Unanimity was required to amend the AOC.
   (C) Nine of thirteen states were required to pass legislation.
   (D) There was no national court system.
   (E) Each state had one vote in Congress.

ANSWER: **A**. The AOC had a unicameral legislature, which critics claimed did not allot sufficient power to states that had large populations (*The American Pageant,* 12th and 11th eds., p. 179).

4. Shays's Rebellion
   (A) convinced many political leaders of the destructive consequences of a strong central government
   (B) was eventually suppressed when the federal government sent troops to Massachusetts
   (C) convinced some political leaders of the necessity of giving more power to the central government
   (D) came about when American settlers clashed with the British over western land claims
   (E) was organized by the antifederalists who sought to prevent ratification of the Constitution

ANSWER: **C**. Some delegates were alarmed that the federal government possessed no authority to raise an army to defend the nation or suppress domestic violence (*The American Pageant,* 12th and 11th eds., p. 176).

5. Which important controversy was resolved by the Great (or Connecticut) Compromise?
   (A) western land claims
   (B) representation in Congress
   (C) no national currency
   (D) no national military
   (E) weak judicial branch

ANSWER: **B**. The Great Compromise created a bicameral legislature. In the Senate, representation would be equal. Representation in the House of Representatives would be based on population (*The American Pageant,* 12th ed., p. 180/11th ed., p. 179).

6. Powers granted to the federal government under the U.S. Constitution are expressed as
   (A) enumerated powers
   (B) checks and balances
   (C) reserved powers
   (D) executive powers
   (E) unicameral legislature

ANSWER: A. Enumerated powers include making treaties, raising an army, and creating a postal service, among many others (*The American Pageant*, 12th ed., p. A38/11th ed., p. A8).

7. All of the following are true regarding the antifederalists EXCEPT
   (A) their important leaders included John Hancock and Patrick Henry
   (B) their political support came mostly from backcountry and agricultural areas
   (C) debtors were supporters of the antifederalists
   (D) they were opposed to a strong central government
   (E) they maintained there was no need for a bill of rights

ANSWER: E. The potential for tyrannical abuses by the central government under the Constitution was always on the minds of the antifederalists. They therefore insisted that a bill of rights be included that would protect citizens from the possible abuses of government (*The American Pageant*, 12th ed., p. 183/11th ed., p. 182).

8. The Federalist Papers
   (A) were written by opponents of the Constitution, who feared that a tyrannical government would be a consequence of ratification
   (B) were the intellectual ideas that shaped the creation of the AOC
   (C) were written by those who advocated maintaining the AOC
   (D) claimed that under the AOC the states had too much power compared with the central government
   (E) attempted to calm the anxieties many had about the powers granted to the central government under the Constitution

ANSWER: E. The *Federalist Papers* attempted to convince critics and doubters that the Constitution had in place various checks on the concentration of power (*The American Pageant*, 12th ed., p. 185/11th ed., p. 184).

9. North Carolina refused to ratify the Constitution
   (A) because the government under the AOC had not yet determined the status of its western land claims
   (B) until Congress imposed a boycott on the state
   (C) until the government removed British forts from its western frontier
   (D) unless a bill of rights would eventually be added
   (E) until it was ratified by the other southern states

ANSWER: D. Concerned that the Constitution deposited too much power in the executive branch, voters in North Carolina were adamant about the inclusion of a bill of rights.

10. Which part of government was not as fully developed as the others by the delegates to the Constitutional Convention?
    (A) judicial branch
    (B) State Department
    (C) House of Representatives
    (D) Senate
    (E) executive branch

ANSWER: **A**. Not until the Marshall court in the first few decades of the nineteenth century would the Supreme Court's powers be articulated.

Free-Response Questions

1. To what extent were the Articles of Confederation an inadequate form of government? In your answer include discussions on the following topics:
   foreign affairs problems
   domestic affairs problems
   features of the government under the AOC

RESPONSE You should first point out that the very nature of a confederation government is one that has a weak central government and that most power resides in the states. This ultimately became a problem for the new nation under the AOC. In foreign affairs the AOC government had to request troops from the states, and it had no chief executive or state department to conduct foreign affairs. Domestically, the government did not have the authority to tax, establish a uniform currency, or regulate trade (domestic and international). Your essay should address the impact this had on the nation's economy at the end of the Revolutionary War.

2. Analyze the differences of opinion between supporters and opponents on whether to ratify the U.S. Constitution

RESPONSE You can begin by pointing out that both sides of the debate were wary of tyranny. For the antifederalists tyranny meant a powerful central government that could potentially deny certain basic rights to the individual and autonomy to the states. This is why the Bill of Rights, which stated certain basic rights of citizens as well as powers reserved to the states, was later added to the Constitution. Federalists believed that, for example, checks and balances and a bicameral legislature would prevent tyranny of the majority and tyranny of the minority. These proponents of the Constitution believed that the AOC was inadequate to address the problems facing the nation after the war. Further, you should address some of the forces that shaped this view, such as Shays's Rebellion, which convinced some of the need for a strong central government that would have the power to defend the nation, but also be prepared to suppress domestic uprisings.

5

THE NEW NATION: 1789–1800

In March 1789 the first Congress to serve under the new Constitution assembled in what was then the nation's capital, New York City. They immediately set to work counting the presidential electors' ballots and declared that George Washington and John Adams had been unanimously elected. One month later, Washington and Adams were sworn in as the nation's first president and vice president. Thomas Jefferson, Alexander Hamilton, and Henry Knox were appointed to newly created departments in the executive branch: secretary of state, secretary of the treasury, and secretary of war. These appointments gave birth to the cabinet system, whereby the president appoints individuals to head the different departments of the executive branch of government. For its part, the Congress made good on its promise to incorporate a Bill of Rights into the Constitution. Also, believing it had a mandate to address the nation's pressing economic needs and, in the process, facilitate capital accumulation, the Congress also passed a protective tariff to raise revenue and protect the nation's infant manufacturing. In order to give greater definition to the judicial branch, they passed the Judiciary Act of 1789, which created the Supreme Court, with John Jay as chief justice, and a lower federal court system. Obviously, Congress was taking steps to make certain that the federal government would be, if anything, more active than the previous one. But the political disputes that shaped the constitutional ratification debate would soon spill over into the federal government and ultimately lead to the rise of political parties.

KEY CONCEPTS

- Hamilton's economic plan promoted manufacturing and enlarged the role of government.
- The Bank of the United States and the tariff were opposed in rural areas and southern states.
- There were both differences and similarities between the Hamiltonian and Jeffersonian movements.
- The election of Jefferson is referred to as the "Revolution of 1800."
- The Marshall Court defined the role and powers of the judicial branch.
- Relations with France and Britain were strained under Adams and Jefferson.

These topics are discussed in depth in *The American Pageant,* 12th and 11th eds., Chapters 10 and 11.

THE HAMILTONIAN VISION VERSUS THE JEFFERSONIAN VISION

Alexander Hamilton was one of the most influential members of the new government. As a strong supporter of ratification and as an author of the *Federalist Papers,* he had advocated a commercial and manufacturing vision for the nation that was at odds with the vision of those, such as Jefferson, who saw an agrarian future for the nation. Under Secretary Hamilton's guidance, the federal government became increasingly involved in the promotion of capital accumulation and economic growth and expansion. In a strong attempt to address the impediments to commerce and trade inherent in the AOC, Hamilton created a mercantilist plan that would facilitate economic expansion by, in part, protecting and nurturing the nation's manufacturing sector. Rather than being an obstacle to capital growth, the new government would become a catalyst to an ever-expanding economy and a midwife for economic development. Hamilton's program had four major features:

- **The Tariff of 1789** Designed to protect domestic manufacturing, this tariff discouraged competition from abroad and compelled foreign competitors to raise prices on their commodities. At the same time, it would provide the government with much-needed revenue.
- **Report on Public Credit** At the time, the United States owed an enormous amount of money to creditors: $20 million to individual states, $11 million to foreigners, and $40 million to private individuals. Hamilton used this report to suggest that the United States pay off its domestic and foreign debts. Paying off its debts would improve the credit rating of the nation; then additional loans could be obtained, and the economy could be expanded by offering credit (loans) to start new businesses and expand others.

  Southern states were opposed to having the central government pay off the debts at face value, because most of it had been incurred by the northern states. The latter's rejoinder was that all states must share the burden of debt, because all would

The Elastic Clause: Loose versus Strict Interpretations of the Constitution

The creation of a Bank of the United States raised a serious constitutional question. Because the Constitution did not explicitly state that the federal government had in its enumerated powers the authority to create such an institution, was the Bank constitutional? Although the defenders of the Bank cited the elastic clause as their "loose" constitutional justification ("necessary and proper") for creating this financial institution, opponents, such as Jefferson, claimed in their "strict" interpretation of the Constitution that there was nothing "necessary" about the creation of the Bank. To which Hamilton responded that the enumerated powers of the federal government gave to it the authority to coin and borrow money. The Bank, he argued, was certainly necessary for maintaining the nation's financial stability and so was indeed constitutional. To this day, political leaders and jurists are divided over how best to interpret the Constitution: strictly ("original intent" of the Framers) or loosely (necessary and proper).

enjoy the fruits of an improved economy; further, the North had sustained considerably more damage in the American Revolution. Yet other critics saw this aspect of Hamilton's plan as an opportunity to transfer money to self-centered speculators. In the end, an agreement was worked out, the Assumption Bill: Southerners agreed to support Hamilton's proposal if the capitol of the United States was relocated to the South.

- **Report on Manufactures** Hamilton envisioned a government program that had as its precise objective the growth and development of manufacturing. This would be accomplished through
  - tariffs, loans, and grants for businesses.
  - excise taxes (taxes on certain manufactured goods) to raise revenue to finance the government and to aid businesses and manufacturing.
  - infrastructural development—aid in the construction of those facilities that are necessary for economic development, such as transportation and communication networks. Public taxes would help finance many of these programs.

- **Creation of a national bank (the Bank of the United States)** A national bank, reasoned Hamilton, would aid the capitalist class by extending credit to them. This credit would allow for expanded employment opportunities, which in turn would further stimulate economic growth. The government could also address economic problems, such as reckless speculation, by controlling the amount of credit available at any one time and by issuing sound currency. This would contribute to a steady and balanced growth of the economy. The Bank of the United States, though chartered by the United States, would be controlled by the following:

  - the U.S. government: 20 percent
  - private U.S. citizens: 60 percent

■ private foreign citizens: 20 percent (although many Americans were opposed to any foreign control of the bank)

After considerable squabbling, Congress adopted Hamilton's economic program.

FOREIGN AND DOMESTIC AFFAIRS

In his two terms as president, Washington's administration faced international and domestic tribulations. In his first term, revolution broke out in France and Washington was faced with a crucial decision whether to provide assistance to the French monarchy or to the revolutionaries who were attempting to overthrow King Louis XVI. After all, the revolutionaries were attempting to establish what the Americans in their revolution had recently achieved: a republic. Many Americans, including Thomas Jefferson, therefore sympathized with the revolutionaries, especially because France was at war with Britain, which had been interfering with American merchant ships sailing to French ports. To put the matter to rest, President Washington issued the Neutrality Proclamation, claiming that the new American republic was in no position to confront European powers such as Great Britain. In protest, Jefferson resigned as secretary of state. But the issue did not end there. The French minister to the United States, Edmond Genêt, broke all diplomatic protocol by appealing directly to the American public to persuade their government to intervene on France's behalf in its war against Britain. Washington demanded that the minister be recalled, but the incident hurt the pro-French faction in the American government. In other aspects of foreign affairs, the United States agreed to two major treaties during Washington's second term:

■ **The Jay Treaty (1794)** Chief Justice John Jay was sent by Washington to negotiate with the British an end to their practice of seizing American ships and impressing American sailors into the British navy. The British did agree to remove their forts on America's western frontier, but made no guarantees that seizures and impressments would end. The U.S. Senate narrowly ratified the treaty, but the American public was so incensed by Britain's disdain for American neutral rights that support for the French cause in the United States swelled. Nevertheless, the United States was able to maintain its neutrality in the Anglo-French war.

■ **The Pinckney Treaty (1795)** Concerned that the animosity between Britain and the United States was thawing, Spain made a series of concessions in negotiations with the U.S. ambassador to Spain, Thomas Pinckney. The treaty opened up the lower Mississippi and the important port city of New Orleans to American trade and shipping. It also granted Americans the right of deposit—a transfer of goods—in New Orleans without having to pay a tax to the Spanish. Spain further agreed to accept the 31st parallel as Florida's northern border, and to stop inciting Native American tribes.

In 1794 farmers in western Pennsylvania tested the new powers of the federal government under the Constitution. As you will recall, one of the weaknesses of the central government under the AOC was its inability to confront domestic challenges. When the farmers refused to pay a federal excise tax, part of Hamilton's economic program, on whiskey and even attacked federal tax collectors, Washington called on the states to assist the government in putting down the uprising, the Whiskey Rebellion. With the collapse of the revolt, the federal government had demonstrated its newfound strength in dealing with domestic challenges to its authority. As for the farmers, who were generally destitute and saw little value in Hamilton's programs, the suppression of the uprising drove them further into the antifederalist camp.

When his second term expired, Washington chose not to seek reelection, a precedent that would stand for over a century until Franklin D. Roosevelt was elected to four terms. (The Twenty-second Amendment, adopted in 1951, limits the president to two terms.) Prior to leaving office, Washington provided the nation with advice in the form of a Farewell Address. In it the first president counseled the American people about

■ maintaining national unity despite the discord that prevailed between divergent regions, groups, and classes
■ obeying and supporting the principles and authority of the Constitution
■ the dangers inherent in creating political parties
■ creating permanent alliances with foreign nations and not becoming embroiled in European affairs

The division between the federalists and antifederalists and between Jefferson and Hamilton had made Washington wary of intense political allegiances. But by the time he left office, Washington had become identified with Hamilton's Federalist faction. He was not alone in his political party affiliations. By 1796, despite his warnings about creating political parties, his vice president and successor to the presidency, John Adams, and his former secretary of state, Thomas Jefferson, had rapidly identified themselves as either Federalists (the Federalist party, later to become the present-day Republican party) or anti-Federalists (later the Democratic-Republicans and then the present-day Democratic party). The presidential election of 1796 was particularly vitriolic. Adams emerged with a very narrow Electoral College victory, and peculiarly enough Jefferson, the second-place winner, became his vice president. (This unlikely and awkward situation was rectified in 1804 with the passage of the Twelfth Amendment, which requires that presidential and vice presidential candidates be from the same party.) Upon assuming the office of president, Adams faced foreign and domestic problems and even discord in his own party ranks, as many Federalists looked to Hamilton, not Adams, for their ideological inspiration. Shortly into Adams's only term as president, U.S.-French relations began unraveling as it became abundantly clear to the French, from a reading of the Jay Treaty, that the Federalists were pro-British. Disregarding American neutrality, the French attacked American shipping. In an attempt to reduce tensions, Adams sent a special mission to France in 1794. Upon arriving in France the three U.S.

commissioners, John Marshall, Elbridge Gerry, and Charles Cotesworth Pinckney, were asked by the French Minister Talleyrand (through his agents, who became known as X, Y, and Z) for a bribe of $250,000 and millions in loans even before negotiations could begin. Pinckney purportedly declared: "No, no, not a sixpence." Later, the outraged American public and government memorialized the U.S. response with the slogan "Millions for defense, but not a cent for tribute." Again, the nation geared up for war. Hamilton, never far from the center of the action, pressed Adams to arm American merchant ships and raise an army. His rationale was that the further the United States moved away from France the closer it moved to a more lucrative commercial relationship with Britain. But Adams refused to declare war on France.

Two years later, Adams sent another mission to France, despite being admonished from members of his own party. This time an agreement was worked out, mainly because Emperor Napoleon wanted to focus on European domination. In the Convention of 1800, the 1778 treaty between the two nations was canceled and relations between the two nations improved.

The Federalists, in the meantime, had sought to silence opposition to their policies from the Democratic-Republicans. Inspired by the ideas of Hamilton, the Federalists drafted a series of acts, the Alien and Sedition Acts, designed to neutralize any challenges to their dominance.

- **The Naturalization Act** An attempt to curb criticism emanating from immigrants—especially the French and Irish—whom Federalists assumed were identified more closely with the Democratic-Republicans, the act raised the residency requirement for citizenship from five to fourteen years. As expected, the act limited the growth of the Democratic-Republicans because of the residency requirement.
- **The Alien (Friends) Act** This gave the president the authority to deport individuals whom he considered a threat to the United States.
- **The Alien Enemies Act** This provided for the deportation or imprisonment of any individuals in a time of declared war.
- **The Sedition Act** Probably the most insidious of the acts, this legislation stated that speaking, writing, or publishing criticisms of the government were at the very least misdemeanors and possibly treasonous.

Without question, the four acts violated the First Amendment and established a precedent more consistent with authoritarian governments than with a democratic republic. Unfortunately, President Adams signed the Alien and Sedition Acts into law. Though they temporarily silenced political opposition, the acts backfired on the Federalists as disgusted Americans gravitated to the Democratic-Republicans. This crisis in constitutional rights, however, would not end until the Federalists lost the White House in the election of 1800. Judicial review would ultimately decide the fate of controversial laws, but that would have to wait for the Marshall Court. Nevertheless, the Alien and Sedition Acts did not go unchallenged. The same year the acts were passed, 1798, the Kentucky legislature adopted a resolution by Thomas Jefferson questioning the federal government's authority to pass such legislation. The Virginia legislature, guided by James Madison, went even further and articulated what has become known as the "compact" theory of government (or states' rights). The logic of the argument is as follows:

The federal government was created by the states.

There are instances when conflicts arise between the rights and laws of the states and the authority of the federal government.

When such conflicts arise, the interests of the states take precedence over the laws and actions of the federal government.

Therefore, a state has the right to declare national laws null and void.

After the 1800 election, the new Democratic-Republican congressional majority repealed the laws or allowed them to expire. Despite the stain on their reputation that came with the Alien and Sedition Acts, the Federalists had

- strengthened the federal government
- established a sound fiscal system
- formulated policies and programs that stimulated capital accumulation and therefore diversification of the economy

As for John Adams, his presidency was limited to one term. The 1800 election ended the supremacy of the Federalists and led to the nation's first peaceful transition from one political party to its adversary, which is one reason why some historians refer to the election of Jefferson as a political revolution.

"THE REVOLUTION OF 1800"

In the election of 1800, Democratic-Republicans Thomas Jefferson and Aaron Burr tied. The election eventually went to the House of Representatives, where, oddly enough, Hamilton's support for Jefferson made the Virginian president. Hamilton apparently considered Jefferson less objectionable than Burr. Yet the divisions between the philosophies of Hamilton and Jefferson remained. Many historians see the following distinctions inherent in the outlook of their respective movements:

- The Jeffersonian Movement
  - The spirit of the movement was embodied in the Democratic-Republican party, which represented the interests of the common man, the farmer, and was

therefore a movement that further democratized the United States.

■ It was anticapitalistic (favoring the subsistence farmer).

■ It favored limitations on the power of the federal government and a strict interpretation of the Constitution.

■ It maintained that the future of the nation was dependent on maintaining an agrarian society.

■ Following Jefferson, a Francophile, the party favored support of France.

■ The Hamiltonian Movement

■ The spirit of the movement was embodied in the Federalist party, which represented the interests of the capitalist class.

■ It favored the expansion of the federal government's power and a loose interpretation of the Constitution.

■ It maintained that the future of the nation was dependent on developing manufacturing and industry.

■ Following Hamilton, an Anglophile, the party favored Great Britain.

AP Tip

A free-response question that relates to the Jeffersonian movement, presidency, or the "Revolution of 1800" may in part ask you to relate the meaning of these terms in relation to the alternative perspective, the Hamiltonian movement. Historians have debated the two perspectives for decades, and their observations will help you make a thorough analysis. The contrasts between the Jeffersonian and Hamiltonian movements listed above represent one way of looking at the issue. Historians who see these distinctions go on to contend that the Jeffersonian movement was one that advanced democracy in the United States. Further, it was the first example of political liberalism—reforming the political and economic system—in the nineteenth century: under Jefferson, the government was viewed as the guardian of the people against the abuses of the upper classes. Conversely, Hamilton is often seen as wanting to further the privileges and objectives of the northern commercial/capitalist interests. Consequently, Hamilton and Jefferson inhabit opposite ends of the political spectrum.

Other historians do not see it this way. To them, there are basically no substantial differences between Hamilton and Jefferson or between the Federalists and Democratic-Republicans, because both represented the interests of the upper classes, whether northern capitalists or southern planters. What is more, Jefferson was a pragmatist who was not tied to any particular philosophical approach to government but adjusted to what was expedient, as expressed in his first inaugural address: "We are all Republicans, we are all Federalists." Some would argue that he was attempting to provide a smooth transition from one political party to another. Other historians point to two important examples that show Jefferson was not consistent with the ideals he preached. The first was an abandonment of his strict interpretation of the Constitution when he purchased the Louisiana Territory from France. No clause in the Constitution gave him the authority to do so; he did what was "necessary and proper," the argument of those holding a loose interpretation. The second example is that despite his opposition to the Bank of the United States, upon becoming president he did not seek to eliminate it but simply allowed its charter to expire. Taking into account these conflicting opinions will make for a more compelling free-response essay.

KEY EVENTS IN JEFFERSON'S PRESIDENCY

In his first term, Jefferson generally carried out the domestic and foreign policies of his predecessors. He maintained the Bank of the United States and continued Hamilton's debt repayment plan. Following Washington's advice, he sought to steer clear of international alliances and maintain the nation's neutrality. The latter allowed him to reaffirm his party's philosophy by reducing the size of the government. In this case, the military saw its funding reduced. Also, the hated excise tax was eliminated while the government's budget was simultaneously cut.

The Louisiana Purchase (1803) was the most notable achievement of Jefferson's first term. The French emperor, Napoleon, strapped for cash, needed more money to fight Britain. His decision to sell France's last major territorial possession in North America was made more palatable by a successful slave revolt against the French on the Caribbean island of Santo Domingo. Napoleon reasoned that if he could not hold on to a small island in the Caribbean, there was little chance he would be able to control an enormous swath of land west of the Mississippi River. France's quandary was America's gain. In return for the enormous Louisiana Territory including New Orleans (which France had reacquired from Spain at the turn of the century), the United States paid only $15 million. Despite reservations about the constitutionality of the president's treaty, the purchase of this land was too good to reject. Almost overnight, the territory of the United States doubled in size.

Having purchased the land from France, Jefferson decided it was time to find out more about the vast territory. As soon as the Senate ratified the treaty, Jefferson organized an expedition led by Meriwether Lewis and William Clark. Jefferson instructed the men to find out as much as possible about the territory's topographical features and resources as well as to gain scientific evidence about the climate and flora and fauna of this western land. Two years after departing, Lewis and Clark reached the Pacific Ocean. Upon returning east their journals were published. Extremely helpful to the U.S. government, their work also caught the imagination of the American public and consequently paved the way for future westward exploration and development.

Jefferson's first term had been comparatively smooth; the second was anything but. Far away in North Africa, coastal nations collectively known as the Barbary States were seizing international ships and holding their crews for ransom. Because the United States had no navy to speak of, its merchant ships were vulnerable. The U.S. government decided to pay tribute to protect its ships, but not until the United States defeated the Barbary pirates, in 1815, did the depredations cease.

Tensions with France and Britain also worsened. Near the end of Jefferson's first term, the two European powers had intensified their conflict, which in turn again threatened to interrupt American shipping. By 1805 Napoleon's forces had gained control of much of the European continent, though the British navy continued to dominate the seas. Supplying both sides of the conflict was initially beneficial for American merchants and shippers. But when Britain sought to stop the lucrative trade between the United States and France, the situation quickly spiraled out of control, as is obvious from the following sequence of events:

- **Essex decision (1805)** The British ruled that trade closed during peacetime could not be opened during wartime. For U.S. shippers, this meant that they would be prohibited from trading with the French West Indies.
- *Leopard-Chesapeake* **Incident (1807)** Although it was powerful, the British navy was short on sailors. To remedy this problem it began the highly questionable tactic of stopping American ships on the high seas and impressing—forcing—its sailors, whether they were British or not, into their navy. In one egregious case, the British warship *Leopard* fired on an American warship, the *Chesapeake,* and removed several sailors, a few of whom were deserters.
- **Orders in Council (1806 and 1807)** Britain blockaded the ports of France and its allies, thereby preventing neutral nations from trading with these nations.
- **Berlin Decree (1806)** France responded in kind to the Orders in Council.
- **Milan Decree (1807)** France announced it would seize any ships that had obeyed Britain's Orders in Council.

As a result of these decrees, Britain and France frequently seized American ships. Rather than go to war with one or both powerful European nations, Jefferson—and his successor, James Madison—sought to punish British and French commercial interests through a series of trade acts:

- **Nonintercourse Act (1806)** This halted the importation of many British commodities but failed to influence the British.
- **Embargo Act (1807)** This prohibited all foreign trade. It had a devastating effect on the New England economy and ultimately hurt more than helped the United States. Many New Englanders denounced Jefferson and Madison and gave their support to Charles Pinckney, the Federalist candidate in the 1808 election.
- **Nonintercourse Act (1809)** Trade was opened with all nations except the belligerents, Britain and France. Jefferson agreed to trade with either nation so long as it repealed its trade restrictions against American shipping.
- **Macon's Bill No. 2 (1810)** Madison replaced the Nonintercourse Act with his own plan to open trade with both Britain and France. He promised to suspend trade with the enemy of the nation that first agreed to cease its violations of American shipping rights. Napoleon deceived the American president by claiming to revoke the Berlin and Milan decrees so long as Britain repealed its Orders in Council. Madison accepted France's terms and agreed to a policy of nonintercourse with Britain. In the meantime, pressured by its own merchants and traders, the British had every intention of ending their trade dispute with the United States. Unfortunately, by the time Britain's concession had reached the United States it had declared war on Great Britain.

While the executive and legislatives branches were agonizing over all these problems with foreign affairs, the judicial branch was evolving—in large part because of the efforts of Supreme Court Justice John Marshall.

THE MARSHALL COURT

The appointment of Federalist John Marshall, a distant cousin of President Jefferson, to the Supreme Court in 1801 coincided with his party's decline. A political chasm opened between the two as Marshall forged a role for the judicial branch that expanded the powers of the federal government. When he assumed his duties, the Supreme Court lacked both power and prestige. The Court met only six weeks each year—the first Supreme Court Justice, John Jay, resigned due to inactivity! Although he was not a legal scholar, in his thirty-five years on the bench, Marshall wrote nearly half of its decisions and in the process transformed the court. The Marshall Court became strongly identified with

- vested rights in contract clauses
- expanding the Court's jurisdiction
- judicial nationalism over states' rights
- blocking state regulations that limited property rights
- freeing American commerce from restraints placed on it by the states

The most significant decisions made by the Marshall Court include the following:

- *Marbury v. Madison* **(1803)** This decision established the concept of judicial review—that is, the implied power of the judicial branch to determine the constitutionality of state and federal legislation.
- *Fletcher v. Peck* **(1810)** The Court ruled that a state could not pass laws that invalidated a contract.
- *Martin v. Hunter's Lessee* **(1816)** Established the supremacy of federal courts over state courts.
- *Dartmouth College v. Woodward* **(1819)** Reaffirming the *Fletcher* decision, the Court ruled that a state cannot alter or invalidate a contract.
- *McCulloch v. Maryland* **(1819)** The Court ruled that the government possessed the implied power to create a national bank; that the bank could not be taxed by a state because this would give the "power to destroy" to the bank; and that federal law is absolute over state law.
- *Gibbons v. Ogden* **(1821)** The Court recognized the federal government's authority over interstate trade.
- *Cohens v. Virginia* **(1821)** Much to the dismay of states' rightists, the Court asserted the right of the Supreme Court to review the decisions of state supreme courts in issues dealing with the authority of the federal government.

The period from 1788 to 1808 was problematic for the new nation. Washington's administration had experienced infighting between various political leaders and their followers. Jefferson's second term witnessed serious foreign challenges to the sovereignty of the United

States. Yet the nation was developing, physically—just think of the Louisiana Purchase—and politically—consider the emergence of the judicial branch. Early in the nineteenth century, the United States would fight another war with Britain, and despite serious regional and economic rifts caused by the war, the United States would emerge, for the most part, with its sense of nationalism intact. The Federalist party would weaken, linger, then fade from the scene. Still, in less than two decades the Americans had established a government, elected a president for the first time, been challenged from abroad, and seen a peaceful transition of power from one political party to another.

Multiple-Choice Questions

1. Which one of the following did NOT serve in George Washington's administration?
    (A) Thomas Jefferson
    (B) Alexander Hamilton
    (C) John Adams
    (D) John Marshall
    (E) Henry Knox

ANSWER: **D**. Jefferson was secretary of state, Hamilton, secretary of the treasury, Knox, secretary of war, and Adams was vice president. Marshall was first appointed to the Supreme Court by Adams (*The American Pageant*, 12th ed., p. 218/11th ed., p. 216).

2. In the Report on Manufactures
    (A) Hamilton sought to promote the agrarian sector of the economy
    (B) Hamilton and Jefferson promoted an excise tax
    (C) Jefferson argued that the nation should develop its infrastructure
    (D) Hamilton maintained that a small government would be more efficient
    (E) Hamilton supported policies that would protect American industry from foreign competition

ANSWER: **E**. Hamilton wanted government to assist in the development of American industry and manufacturing. Jefferson was strongly opposed to Hamilton's economic agenda (*The American Pageant*, 12th ed., p. 195/11th ed. p. 194).

3. The first chief justice of the U.S. Supreme Court was
    (A) John Marshall
    (B) John Jay
    (C) Thomas Paine
    (D) Edmond Genet
    (E) Thomas Pinckney

ANSWER: **B**. Jay was the first, but it was only under John Marshall, who became chief justice in 1801, that the role and powers of the judicial branch were defined (*The American Pageant*, 12th ed., p. 193/11th ed., p.192).

4. The compromise that led to the Assumption Bill involved southerners accepting Hamilton's economic program in return for
   (A) an end to the protective tariff
   (B) legalizing the slave trade
   (C) relocating the nation's capitol to the South
   (D) purchasing the Louisiana Territory
   (E) shrinking the military budget

ANSWER: **C**. The location of the capitol in the South was considered quite prestigious to that section (*The American Pageant*, 12th ed., p. 194/11th ed., p. 193).

5. The Twelfth Amendment to the Constitution
   (A) abolished slavery
   (B) led to the creation of the judicial branch
   (C) gave to the federal government the authority to create a national bank
   (D) prevented a president from seeking a third term
   (E) required that presidential and vice presidential candidates be from the same party

ANSWER: **E**. After the election of 1796 in which the Federalist John Adams was elected president and the Democratic-Republican Jefferson was elected vice president, the Twelfth Amendment was drafted. It was ratified in 1804 (*The American Pageant*, 12th ed., p. 202/11th ed., p. 201).

6. Which one of the following represents an improvement in French-American relations?
   (A) the Milan Decree
   (B) the Orders in Council
   (C) the XYZ affair
   (D) the Convention of 1800
   (E) the Berlin Decree

ANSWER: **D**. The Convention of 1800 thawed hostile American-French relations. Answers A, B, and E were actions taken by France and Britain that violated American neutrality. The XYZ affair was a French demand for a bribe as a prerequisite to opening negotiations with American delegates (*The American Pageant*, 12th ed., p. 205/11th ed. pp. 203-204).

7. In his more than thirty years as a Supreme Court justice, John Marshall
   (A) strengthened the powers of the states in relation to the federal government
   (B) ruled time and again in support of the compact theory of government
   (C) ruled that the Supreme Court could not overturn a decision handed down by a state Supreme Court
   (D) blocked state regulations that limited property rights
   (E) upheld the constitutionality of monopolies

ANSWER: **D**. Marshall strengthened the federal judiciary, especially in relation to the states and the legislative branch (*The American Pageant*, 12th ed., p. 218/11th ed. p., 216).

8. In which Supreme Court case was the concept of judicial review established?
   (A) *Marbury v. Madison*
   (B) *Dartmouth College v. Woodward*
   (C) *McCulloch v. Maryland*
   (D) *Gibbons v. Odgen*
   (E) *Fletcher v. Peck*

ANSWER: **A**. (*The American Pageant*, 12th ed., pp. 218-219/11th ed., pp. 216-217).

9. The concept of judicial review means that
   (A) the executive branch can veto legislation
   (B) the president has the final say in all decisions of the judicial branch
   (C) the courts have the power to determine the constitutionality of laws
   (D) the Supreme Court is required to review all bills passed by Congress
   (E) a state court can overturn a decision by the Supreme Court if it believes doing so would be in the state's best interest

ANSWER: **C**. This is an essential power of the federal court system in that it provides a check against unconstitutional legislation (*The American Pageant*, 12th ed., p. 219/11th ed., p. 217).

10. Pinckney's Treaty resulted in all of the following EXCEPT
    (A) it improved Spanish-American relations
    (B) it gave the Americans the right of deposit in New Orleans
    (C) it gave to the United States Spain's Caribbean islands in return for American aid
    (D) it settled the Florida boundary dispute
    (E) Spain agreed to cease inciting Native American tribes against the Americans

ANSWER: **C**. This was never an issue between the United States and Spain, which maintained its important colonial possessions in the Caribbean (*The American Pageant*, 12th ed., p. 201/11th ed., p. 217).

Free-Response Questions

1. Evaluate the presidency of Thomas Jefferson. Include in your answer discussion of
   Jefferson's foreign affairs policies and actions
   Jefferson's domestic policies and actions

RESPONSE You should incorporate in your essay Jefferson's purchase of the Louisiana Territory, his undeclared war with the Barbary pirates, and the acts he sponsored—for example, the Nonintercourse Act—to deal with British and French actions.

2. Compare and contrast the Hamiltonian and Jeffersonian movements in regard to
   political philosophy
   long-term social and economic outlook
   interpretations of the Constitution
   federal versus state power

RESPONSE Your essay should compare Hamilton's support for an extensive role for the federal government and his loose-constructionist view—for example, the Bank of the United States—with Jefferson's strict-constructionist view. Also include a description of Hamilton's economic program and compare it to Jefferson's support for the yeoman farmer.

6

U.S. FOREIGN AFFAIRS FROM 1812 TO THE 1850S

The United States has been consistent in its foreign policy in that it has always had expansionist tendencies, or, as one historian has phrased it, "Empire as a way of life."

KEY CONCEPTS

- Territorial expansion was an objective of the U.S. government from its inception, as witnessed by the removal of Native Americans and by the Mexican-American War.
- Various groups and ideologies supported territorial expansion for economic, political, and cultural reasons.
- Controversial British actions and American policies aggravated relations between the two nations, leading to the War of 1812.
- New England and the Federalists strongly opposed the war and floated the idea of secession.
- Under the Monroe Doctrine, the U.S. established a policy of hegemony—dominance—in the Western Hemisphere.

Early nineteenth-century foreign affairs are discussed in depth in *The American Pageant*, 12th ed., Chapters 12-14/11th ed., Chapters 12-15.

THE IMPULSE FOR EXPANSION

In the two centuries since the ratification of the Constitution, the size of the United States has more than quadrupled. As one of our most important historians, Arthur Schlesinger, Jr., has pointed out, "The drive across the continent does not call for complicated analysis. An energetic, acquisitive people were propelled by their traits and technologies to push restlessly into contiguous spaces sparsely inhabited by wandering aborigines." But there may be more to it than that. Even before independence was won, Americans lusted after the lands west of the Appalachian Mountains—so much so that the British imposed the Proclamation of 1763 to keep the colonists closer to the eastern seaboard. Our first four presidents gave voice to this expansionist impulse:

- Washington called the new nation a "rising empire."
- John Adams remarked that the United States was "destined to occupy all of the northern part of this quarter of the globe and that when accomplished, would be a significant achievement for mankind."
- Jefferson referred to a "vast territory that would provide room enough for the descendants to the thousandth and ten thousandth generation."
- Madison urged that the United States "extend the sphere, extend the republic as one great respectable and flourishing empire."

Two of the most important events of the early nineteenth century were the purchase of the Louisiana Territory, in 1803 and the War of 1812. Both reflect the driving force—territorial expansion—behind U.S. foreign policy in this period. As in the previous century, Americans continued their drive westward, acquiring new territories and conquering indigenous Native American tribes. By the 1840s the United States would again be at war, this time with Mexico, ultimately taking by conquest that nation's northern territory. By the eve of the Civil War, the United States had expanded well beyond the Mississippi River. As the nation continued to enlarge, Americans would cite a number of economic, political, cultural, and historical arguments to justify U.S. territorial expansion. Politicians, literary figures, educators, newspapermen, and religious leaders, all contributed to a set of ideas that collectively became known as Manifest Destiny. The term was coined by a newspaper editor, John O'Sullivan, in the 1840s as Americans began rapidly crossing the Mississippi River and beyond the Rocky Mountains to reach California and Oregon. Manifest Destiny implied that it was a God-given right and inevitability for the United States to spread its Protestant religion, capitalist economy, and democratic-republican political system across the continental United States. Religious leaders claimed that God wanted Americans—"God's chosen people"—to expand and dominate other peoples in order to convert these "heathens" to the Christian religion. More sophisticated proponents of empire provided a more comprehensive argument by integrating the economic, political, and cultural rationalizations. The ideology of Manifest Destiny was useful in its own right, serving

- to rationalize U.S. foreign policy—it was often cited to ease what may have been guilty consciences at taking someone else's land
- to create national unity and to inspire citizens to rally around the government
- to counter criticisms raised by other nations

Interest in territorial expansion and the quest for empire cut across many segments of the American population:

- farmers and those wishing to become landowners

- manufacturers seeking a source of abundant and inexpensive natural resources
- investors and industrialists seeking profitable investment opportunities in the areas of mining, agriculture, land speculation, and the like
- those who believed that American civilization was biologically and culturally superior
- politicians and military men searching for ways to enhance the nation's political and geographic situation relative to other nations

AP Tip

Take note that internal political factors sometimes inhibited territorial aggrandizement—for example, the internal debate that ensued over Cuba and the Ostend Manifesto.

Major Territorial Acquisitions: 1783-1853

Territory (Date Acquired)	Circumstances of Acquisition
Original Thirteen States (1783)	Treaty of Paris—all land east of the Mississippi River
Louisiana Purchase (1803)	Purchased from France for $15 million—825,000 square miles
Florida (1819)	Adams-Onis Treaty; U.S. pays $5 million
Texas (1845)	Initially declared itself independent from Mexico; eventually enters the Union as a slave state
Oregon Country (1846)	Forty-ninth parallel established by the U.S. and Britain as the boundary for Oregon
Mexican Cession (1848)	Treaty of Guadalupe Hidalgo—Mexican defeat leads to the loss of its northern territory, for which U.S. pays $15 million
Gadsden Purchase (1853)	U.S. purchase of a strip of land from Mexico for $10 million to complete a southern transcontinental railroad

The Federalists, New England, and the War: The Hartford Convention

The Federalists and those they represented, mainly in the New England states, deeply opposed the war against Britain for personal as well as commercial reasons. From their perspective, the Jefferson and Madison administrations (both Democratic-Republicans) were to blame for unwisely forcing a war against the British. Rest assured, New England Federalists were vocal in their opposition. However, some of their actions were highly questionable, and others were clearly treasonous. For example, while many New Englanders refused to buy war bonds, others actually sold provisions to enemy forces in Canada. Some states even refused to send their militias to fight in Canada. Federalist hostility to the war peaked in 1814 when New England delegates were sent by their states to a convention in Hartford, Connecticut, to organize resistance to what they perceived were highly questionable measures by the Democratic-Republicans. Using the compact theory of government as their guide, they proceeded to draft resolutions that would reduce the influence of the South and of the Democratic-Republicans. Their proposals included

- eliminating the three-fifths clause because it inflated the South's representation in the House
- requiring a two-thirds vote in Congress to admit new states, impose embargoes, and declare war
- limiting a president to one term so as to prevent two consecutive terms from the same state (four of the first five presidents were referred to as the "Virginia Dynasty")
- holding a future conference to discuss the possibility of secession (not convened because the war ended first)

Attempts at expansion would not always meet with success. For example, the United States failed in its effort to wrest Canada away from Britain in its second and final war against its old Revolutionary War enemy.

THE WAR OF 1812

As the United States entered the second decade of the nineteenth century, tensions with Britain were exacerbated by the Napoleonic Wars in Europe. As you recall, both Britain and France had violated America's neutral shipping and commercial rights. The British were no more or less at fault than the French, but Americans were already blaming them and British Canadians for inciting Native American uprisings in the West. (In truth, Americans, in their hunger for more land, incited the unrest.) A famous example of conflict between white Americans and Native Americans that was blamed on the British was Shawnee Chief Tecumseh's raids on settlements in the Indiana Territory. Tecumseh's attempt to unite all the tribes in the Mississippi Valley ended when future president William Henry Harrison's force defeated him at the Battle of Tippecanoe in 1811.

THE WAR HAWKS

The defeat of Tecumseh coincided with the convening of Congress. Many of those who came to Washington for the 1811-1812 session were newly elected, mostly western and southern Democratic-Republican congressmen who also happened to be highly nationalistic. They were soon labeled "war hawks" and their hostility to Britain was a large reason why they were given this moniker. Led by Henry Clay of Kentucky and John C. Calhoun of South Carolina, the war hawks favored punishing Britain militarily for seizing merchant ships and impressing American sailors, violations of American neutrality. But they also wanted to seize land from the Native Americans in the West, drive the British from Canada, and even annex Spanish Florida. Opposition to such endeavors came from the Federalists and their region of influence, New England; they tended to be Anglophiles, and they also believed—correctly—that war with Britain would damage their commercial interests. Nevertheless, an unprepared United States declared war on Britain on June 18, 1812.

THE WAR: MILITARY OPERATIONS

Unfortunately for the United States, it declared war with an army numbering fewer than ten thousand soldiers and a navy numbering fewer than twenty ships—this when it was challenging the mightiest fleet in the world and a formidable British army as well. But fortunately for the Americans, Great Britain was yet again involved in another phase of its ongoing conflict with France and so could not apply the full weight of its military might against the United States. This did little to alter the results on the battlefield, however, as three separate American invasions of Canada failed. Surprisingly the Americans experienced considerably more success against the British navy in the Great Lakes and as far south as Bolivian waters. Two of the most famous and successful naval engagements in U.S. history took place between the American warship *Constitution* and HMS *Guerriere*, in 1812, and at the Battle of Lake Erie, in 1813. Although the United States experienced initial success using privateers to attack British shipping and sustain American commerce, by the second year of the war the British had effectively paralyzed American trade and commerce. The region most affected was of course New England.

On land U.S. forces fared better against the Native Americans than they did against the British. William Henry Harrison's troops were victorious against Tecumseh's force at the Battle of the Thames, killing the tribal leader in the process. To the south, another future president, Andrew Jackson, and his militia troops defeated the Creeks at the Battle of Horseshoe Bend (then proceeded to slaughter Creek women and children as retribution for Native American attacks). The two defeats, for all intents and purposes, neutralized the Native Americans as British allies. The British, however, continued on with their own military strategy. Utilizing a three-pronged attack, they invaded the United States, marched on Washington, D.C., in the summer of 1814, and burned the White House and other public buildings. They then turned north and marched on Baltimore, but they were unable to capture the strategically placed Fort McHenry—this was the battle that inspired Francis Scott Key to write "The Star Spangled Banner." At the same time, the British were decisively defeated in upstate New York. By winter 1814 both sides had had enough. In December they signed a peace treaty in Ghent, Belgium, ending all hostilities, except one. Because of the slowness of travel in the early nineteenth century, the peace terms had not reached the United States before the most famous engagement of the war had taken place, the Battle of New Orleans. Although the war had already ended, the lopsided U.S. victory added luster to the military reputation of the Americans and their commanding general, Andrew Jackson.

EFFECTS OF THE WAR

The Treaty of Ghent brought about no significant concessions. For the most part, relations and conditions between the two warring nations returned to their prewar status. In fact, none of the issues that caused the war were resolved, though both sides returned conquered territory to its original owner. The consequences of the war for the United States were mixed:

- The U.S. economy was devastated.
- Large areas of the nation's capitol were destroyed.
- American nationalism intensified.
- The nation won foreign respect for its military capabilities, which allowed the United States to hold its own against the mighty British Empire.
- The Federalists and New England were discredited by their antipathy to the war and the actions they took to impede the war effort. This temporarily reduced the importance of sectionalism as the nation prepared to enter the "Era of Good Feelings," a newspaper term used to describe the two terms of President James Monroe. During this period, there was only one major political party, the Democratic-Republicans; it was therefore assumed that political discord had evaporated.
- Military careers were launched or enhanced by the war, most noticeably those of Jackson and Harrison, who would use their new-won popularity to propel them into the Oval Office.

Two years after the treaty was signed the United States and Britain agreed to demilitarize the Great Lakes in the Rush-Bagot Treaty. As for the attempt to annex Florida, Secretary of State John Quincy Adams and Spanish Minister Luis de Onis concluded an agreement, the Adams-Onis Treaty (1819), which revealed the weakened state of Spain in the early nineteenth century; for $5 million the United States received Florida. The southwestern boundary now extended as far as the Mexican territory of Tejas (Texas). Seizing on Spain's obvious weakness, all of Spain's South American colonies gained their independence by the early 1820s. It was not long, however, before the United States would become the hegemonic power in both North America and South America.

THE MONROE DOCTRINE

Following the end of the Napoleonic Wars in 1815, the victorious nations met in Vienna to discuss postwar goals. One of the decisions made by the European powers was to restore monarchies and governments that had collapsed or had been overthrown by Napoleon's Grand Army. This concerned the United States because it suspected that the reactionary powers would attempt to restore Spain's control over South America. For their own reasons, the British were opposed to such a development, though they and the Russians sought to control the Pacific coast of North America. Secretary of State John Quincy Adams informed both nations not to interfere in territory that he claimed belonged naturally to the United States. Leery of Europeans' intentions of acquiring territory in the Americas or even colonizing South America, the Monroe administration decided to act. At the behest of his cabinet, President Monroe issued a stern foreign policy statement that became known as the Monroe Doctrine. Monroe admonished the Europeans from colonizing the Western Hemisphere. To do so, warned the president, would be deemed a threat to U.S. national security. In short, Europe should stay out of the Western Hemisphere and the United States would stay out of Europe.

Traditionally, historians have viewed the Monroe Doctrine as a defensive strategic policy. It has often been cited as an example of American altruism and anti-imperialist tradition. Recently, historians have questioned this perspective. They argue that the Monroe Doctrine was an expression of Manifest Destiny: in order for the United States to dominate the Western Hemisphere, it would have to prevent European nations from doing so. Subsequent presidents have added to the Monroe Doctrine, and it even played a role in U.S. foreign policy following World War II.

THE TRAIL OF TEARS: THE PLIGHT OF THE CHEROKEE

As the nation kept a wary eye on Europe, it focused the other eye on the one major Native American tribe in the area southeast of the Mississippi, the Cherokees. Having earlier pacified the Cherokees, the next objective was to move them to the West. The Cherokees inhabited several states—Alabama, Tennessee, Georgia, and Mississippi. In 1827 a tribal council established a constitutional representative government, not unlike the U.S. political system, and proceeded to declare independence. The Georgia legislature maintained that to declare a separate government and nation within its borders was unconstitutional. Georgia then requested assistance from the federal government in removing the Cherokees from its borders. The discovery of gold in the Cherokees' land certainly played a role in the state legislature's wish to relocate them. Later, the Cherokees, insulted by President Andrew Jackson's lack of sympathy for Native Americans and by the passage in 1830 of the Indian Removal Act, sued to stop their resettlement. The Marshall Supreme Court, while sympathetic to their plight, ruled in *Cherokee Nation v. Georgia* (1831) that because they were not a foreign nation, the Cherokees could not bring suit in federal court. The following year, however, the Court ruled in *Worcester v. Georgia* that state law had no authority within Cherokee territory. An advocate of states' rights when it was expedient and an opponent of Native American rights, Jackson exclaimed, "John Marshall has made his decision, now let him enforce it." The chief executive would not use his constitutional authority to enforce federal law when it came to Native Americans. Before the decade was out, most of the Cherokees were driven west in a grueling trek known as the "Trail of Tears."

TEXAN INDEPENDENCE

In 1821 Mexico had gained its independence from Spain. Hoping to draw settlers to its sparsely inhabited northern province, the Mexican government enticed large numbers of immigrants by introducing a system of landownership that was considerably more favorable than what was available in the United States. Before long, southerners by the thousands began streaming into Texas in northern Mexico. Stephen Austin, for example, brought hundreds of families to settle in the area, starting a migration that soon found the Mexican inhabitants far outnumbered by the American settlers and their slaves. Americans continued to resettle in northern Mexico despite the Mexican government's new stipulations: in 1829 it required all settlers to convert to Catholicism, and it abolished slavery. Most settlers were not willing to obey these laws so the Mexican government halted immigration. Unfazed, the Americans ignored Mexican law and poured in, many from the South. In 1834 the dispute came to a head when General Antonio de Santa Anna proclaimed himself dictator of Mexico. Santa Anna was determined to enforce the laws of his nation as it applied to the American settlers in the northern province. In response, the settlers declared their independence from Mexico in 1836, created a government, and selected Sam Houston as commander of the Texas military. Santa Anna moved in to stop the Texans. Initial conflicts between the two sides favored the Mexican army, despite money, supplies, and volunteers from American citizens. The most famous Texan defeat occurred in 1836 at the Alamo, a fortified mission held by the Texans. Despite holding out against enormous odds, the Texas garrison was annihilated by Santa Anna's forces. Shortly thereafter, another Texas army surrendered to Santa Anna. On orders from the Mexican general, they were massacred. But the Texans soon had their revenge. Sam Houston's small army inflicted a mortal blow on the Mexicans at the Battle of San Jacinto, in the process capturing Santa Anna. This battle effectively ended hostilities and guaranteed Texas independence. Most Texans supported U.S. statehood, but they would have to wait; for more than a decade, Texas was to remain an independent republic.

PRESIDENT JAMES K. POLK AND TERRITORIAL EXPANSION

When James K. Polk was inaugurated president in March 1845, he had several foreign policy objectives in mind: the settlement of the Oregon boundary dispute with Britain, which had almost led to military hostilities in the 1839 Aroostook War; the acquisition of California; and the incorporation of Texas into the Union. He achieved all of these goals. John Tyler had already paved the way for Texas statehood, and despite strong opposition from antislavery forces, Texas was admitted on December 29, 1845. As for the Oregon question, it was resolved at the same time relations with Mexico were unraveling. In the Webster-

Ashburton Treaty (1842), the United States and Britain had settled the boundary dispute between Maine and Canada and also agreed to suppress the slave trade. Soon, however, they were again bickering over the Oregon Territory's northern border. Initially the Americans offered the 49th parallel as the dividing line; that was rejected by the British. Despite bellicose outbursts by the Americans such as "Fifty-four forty or fight," Britain was in no mood for another war with the United States. In the Oregon Treaty (1846), the nations agreed to settle the dispute peacefully by extending the Oregon Territory-Canadian border along the 49th parallel

THE MEXICAN-AMERICAN WAR

The fragile relationship between the United States and Mexico deteriorated even further when the United States formally annexed Texas in 1845. Not satisfied with acquiring this enormous territory, Polk also wanted to acquire the California-New Mexico region as well. After the failure of the Slidell mission, an attempt to purchase the territory from Mexico, Polk resorted to a decidedly more aggressive and controversial posture; he sent troops into the disputed area near the Nueces River and the Rio Grande. Many Americans and their political representatives believed the area belonged to the Mexicans, but when hostilities erupted, the United States declared war on Mexico. Polk claimed that Mexican forces had crossed the border to attack Americans, but this was never verified. Regardless, Polk had his war. Although the U.S. army was supported by poorly trained and ill-disciplined volunteer troops, some of whom committed atrocities in the course of the war, U.S. forces had taken control of the entire southwest by 1847. Several other American military successes followed before General Zachary Taylor's army defeated Santa Anna's force near Buena Vista. Taylor then proceeded to take Monterrey but was replaced by President Polk for disobeying orders. (Taylor returned home a hero and later became president.) The new U.S. commander, General Winfield Scott, captured Vera Cruz followed a short time later with a victory in the Battle of Cerro Gordo. More victories followed before the Americans launched their final attack on Mexico City. After first taking the mountain fortress of Chapultepec, the Americans captured the Mexican capital. Santa Anna fled and the war ended. The Treaty of Guadalupe-Hidalgo (1848) included the following provisions:

- Mexico recognized the American claims to the area north of the Rio Grande.
- Mexico ceded California and New Mexico to the United States in return for $15 million.
- The United States agreed to assume approximately $3 million in debts Mexico owed to American citizens.

President Polk was not satisfied with the terms of the treaty. He believed the United States should have received even more territory from the defeated Mexicans. But he would have to settle for the one-half million square miles of territory (one million if Texas is included in the tally) taken from the Mexicans. In his one term as president, Polk had given meaning to Washington's reference to the United States as a "rising empire."

Multiple-Choice Questions

1. Which of the following was NOT in favor of U.S. territorial expansion in the first half of the nineteenth century?
   (A) farmers
   (B) manufacturers
   (C) investors
   (D) abolitionists
   (E) religious leaders

ANSWER: **D**. Abolitionists feared that with the expansion of U.S. territory, slavery would spread (*The American Pageant,* 12th ed., pp. 362-366/11th ed., pp. 371-374).

2. The term Manifest Destiny implies
   (A) a desire to limit the territorial expansion of the United States
   (B) that the cost of expansion is greater than its benefits
   (C) that it was America's God-given right to expand
   (D) that nations should share newly discovered resources rather than fight over them
   (E) that taking land from others was a violation of God's will

ANSWER: **C**. Manifest Destiny implied that Americans were God's "chosen people" and therefore had a right to expand (*The American Pageant,* 12th ed., p. 377/11th ed., p. 387).

3. The United States purchased the Louisiana Territory from
   (A) Mexico
   (B) Britain
   (C) Spain
   (D) Russia
   (E) France

ANSWER: **E**. The region had been ceded to France in 1800 (*The American Pageant,* 12th ed., p. 220/11th ed., p. 218).

4. The Gadsden Purchase
   (A) allowed the United States to build a southern transcontinental railroad
   (B) was territory in the West where the Cherokee were relocated
   (C) allowed the United States to extend its northern border with Canada to the Pacific Ocean
   (D) was vetoed by President Polk
   (E) gave the United States access to the Oregon Territory

ANSWER: **A**. The purchase of this thin strip of land south of the Rocky Mountains allowed the United States to build a southern transcontinental railroad (*The American Pageant,* 12th ed., p. 405/11th ed., pp. 414-415).

5. The war hawks
   (A) were led by John Adams
   (B) were opponents of territorial expansion
   (C) were U.S. congressmen who represented the New England states
   (D) supported going to war against Britain in the early nineteenth century
   (E) was a Native American tribe who fought against U.S. territorial expansion

ANSWER: D. Incensed by British violations of American neutrality and supportive of territorial expansion, war hawks strongly supported war against Britain (*The American Pageant*, 12th ed., p. 229/11th ed., p. 227).

6. The Hartford Convention
   (A) ended the War of 1812
   (B) was organized by the Federalist opposition to the war with Britain
   (C) included some of the most important leaders of the Democratic-Republican party
   (D) was organized to oppose territorial expansion
   (E) made way for Texas's admission into the Union

ANSWER: B. The Federalists were strongly opposed to the War of 1812. They met in Hartford, Connecticut, to discuss strategies for reducing the power of the southern and western Democratic-Republicans (*The American Pageant*, 12th ed., p. 239/11th ed., p. 238).

7. The Battle of New Orleans
   (A) was a major U.S. victory over Mexico
   (B) convinced the British to agree to peace terms that ended the War of 1812
   (C) was fought after the peace treaty ending the War of 1812 was signed
   (D) was a major Mexican victory over the Texans
   (E) was a major U.S. naval victory in the War of 1812

ANSWER: C. Although it was a major American victory, the battle was fought several weeks after the Treaty of Ghent (*The American Pageant*, 12th ed., p. 239/11th ed., p. 238).

8. "Fifty-four forty or fight" refers to
   (A) the Federalists' opposition to the war with Britain
   (B) the amount of money Mexico demanded from the United States in return for allowing it to annex Texas
   (C) the boundary dispute between the United States and Mexico
   (D) the war hawks' demand for concessions from the British for violating American neutrality rights
   (E) the dispute between Britain and the United States over the Oregon Territory.

ANSWER: E. Eventually the United States and Britain compromised on the 49th parallel (*The American Pageant*, 12th ed., pp. 379-380/11th ed., pp. 389-390).

9. Which of the following decisions by the Mexican government angered Americans who settled in Texas?
   (A) The Americans were required to pay enormous taxes to the Mexican government.
   (B) The Mexicans forbade the Americans from farming on the most fertile land.
   (C) The Mexicans forbade the American settlers from trading with the United States.
   (D) The American settlers were prohibited from becoming citizens of Mexico.
   (E) The Mexicans abolished slavery.

ANSWER: **E**. The Mexican government established two laws in 1829: settlers must convert to Catholicism, and slavery was prohibited. Both angered the settlers, who were mostly southern Protestant supporters of slavery (*The American Pageant,* 12th ed., pp. 275-276/11th ed., p. 282).

10. The Supreme Court ruled in *Worcester v. Georgia* that
    (A) Native American tribal land could not be purchased by the state of Georgia
    (B) Georgia must grant citizenship rights to the Cherokees living within its borders
    (C) the Cherokees could not sue the state of Georgia in federal court
    (D) Georgia's state laws had no authority within Cherokee territory
    (E) Georgia had a responsibility for the care of the Cherokees living within its borders

ANSWER: **D**. Though previously the Supreme Court ruled against the Cherokees, this decision provided them some autonomy (*The American Pageant,* 12th ed., pp. 266–267/11th ed., pp.280-281).

Free-Response Questions

1. To what extent did nationalism play a role in the formulation and application of U.S. foreign policy in the early nineteenth century?

RESPONSE You should address the ideologies that supported territorial expansion—for example, the Mexican-American War—the goals and attitudes of the war hawks on the War of 1812, the significance of the Monroe Doctrine in extending U.S. influence to the entire Western Hemisphere, and the relocation of Native Americans so that their land could be used by white Americans.

2. Support or refute this statement:

In going to war against Mexico, President Polk was taking into account the best interests of the United States.

RESPONSE To support this statement, you can point out that Polk was an advocate of territorial expansion, shown by his work to settle the Oregon border question and the acquisition of California. Bringing Texas into the Union was a key part of his territorial ambitions. All of these acquisitions would benefit the U.S. economically.

To oppose the statement, point out that by adding new southern territory, Polk had reopened the slave state/free state controversy. Would Texas's admission set off heated exchanges between the regions and their politicians? Also point out that there was no justification for the U.S. invasion of Mexico and that many Americans, especially in the north, were morally opposed to the war. Others were opposed to an imperialist policy.

7

JACKSONIAN DEMOCRACY AND THE AGE OF REFORM: 1820s–1850s

Paradoxically, at the same time the United States was acquiring land, often through conquest, it was engaged in democratizing its own institutions. This era, the 1820s to the 1850s, has been referred to as the age of reform. Some historians, however, choose to title the period after its most celebrated president, Andrew Jackson, and refer to it as Jacksonian democracy. It is important to note, however, that this designation is challenged by historians who maintain that Jackson was actually indifferent, opposed to, or unaware of some of the reforms. Those critical of the term see obvious contradictory impulses present during this period: slavery, expansion and imperialism, and the marginalization of blacks, women, Native Americans, and laborers. Yet over the years, the terms have come to mean the same thing—an unprecedented expansion of egalitarian ideas that transformed America socially, politically, and economically, if only for white men.

KEY CONCEPTS

- Social, economic, and political conditions and attitudes led to the reform spirit in the mid-nineteenth century.
- As the Federalist party faded, an "Era of Good Feelings" set in.
- The second party system took shape as the National Republicans challenged the Democrats.
- Grassroots movements and government reforms attempted to address the social and economic problems confronting the nation.
- The intellectual roots of reform shaped perceptions of the individual's role in society.

■ This period witnessed important economic and political reforms, but women, blacks, and Native Americans remained subordinated.

Jacksonian democracy and the age of reform are discussed in depth in *The American Pageant,* 12th and 11th eds., Chapters 13-15.

SETTING THE STAGE FOR REFORM

There are two sources of reform: the first is the government, which can draw up policies and legislation that further democratize society; the second is grassroots movements. In the case of the latter, individual citizens and private groups, classes, organizations, and movements take it upon themselves to address the maladies that plague their society. In the period following the end of the War of 1812 until the eve of the American Civil War, both the government and grassroots movements had a role in reforming American society, although, more often than not, grassroots movements have influenced the government to initiate programs and policies needed to address society's problems.

There are various origins of the age of reform:

■ Democratic impulses were the basis of the American Revolution, which sought to address the inequalities inherent in colonial American society and to free Americans from their subordinate relationship with Britain.

■ The antifederalists of the 1780s and 1790s were determined not to sacrifice civil and democratic liberties in creating a new constitutional government.

■ The Jeffersonian Democratic-Republicans professed to represent the ideals and aspirations of the common farmer.

■ Profound social and economic changes occurred in the early nineteenth century—for example, the influence of what many historians refer to as the market revolution on the U.S. economy.

The Northeast and Old Northwest experienced rapid improvements in transportation (railroads; canals, such as the Erie Canal; and the National, or Cumberland, Road). Concurrently, the nation was experiencing an immense wave of immigration. These factors hastened the collapse of the older yeoman and artisan economy and stimulated the further development of a cash-crop agrarian system and capitalist manufacturing. For instance, in the South, a cotton boom revived a flagging plantation slave economy, which then continued to expand.

Additional tensions developed as the economy expanded. Some farmers could not keep up with the changing economy and experienced farm foreclosures. In the Northeast, an emerging laboring class was dogged by abject working conditions and subsistence-level wages. In the South, strained relations existed between non-slaveholders and the planter class. In the West, tensions between would-be yeoman farmers and land speculators and banks prevailed. Farmers and laborers had every reason to believe that the free-market system would bring them not boundless opportunities but new forms of dependence. Jacksonianism grew directly from the tensions it generated within white society. Even expectant capitalists (those with surplus capital searching for investment opportunities in this growing market economy) suspected that entrenched capitalists would block their way and shape the nation's economic development to suit only themselves.

Henry Clay's American System (a tariff to protect industry and manufacturing, a national bank to facilitate credit and provide sound currency, and federally funded infrastructural development), which became the center of his 1824 presidential campaign, confirmed the suspicions of the opponents of an ever-expanding central government that the powerful and wealthy would be best served by this design. Clay's program became the core of the National Republicans' platform, which explains why some Americans saw the Jacksonian Democrats as representing the masses, whereas the National Republicans represented the elites.

THE ERA OF GOOD FEELINGS, THE SECOND PARTY SYSTEM, AND EMERGENCE OF JACKSON

Following the War of 1812, the Federalist party for all intents and purposes imploded. Its unpopular position on the war as well as a number of questionable actions by the Federalists, not least of which was the Hartford Convention, destroyed the party. Since ostensibly only one party, the Democratic-Republicans, was left standing, the decade or so following the war is often referred to as the "Era of Good Feelings"; the assumption being that because there was no political party strife, most Americans tended to have a common outlook. In other words, the term suggests that social relations in the United States were characterized by consensus and relative social harmony. True or not, sectionalism and the slavery issue were always under the surface, ready to disturb the tranquility. It was not long before these differences manifested themselves in opposing political parties—the second American political party system. For the time being, however, the nation had only one party to speak of.

In 1824 all four candidates—John Quincy Adams, Andrew Jackson, Henry Clay, and William Crawford—ran as Democratic-Republicans. In the election Adams defeated his fellow party member in what Jackson's supporters claimed was the result of a "corrupt bargain." Jackson had received more popular votes but Adams had more electoral votes, though not enough to give him the presidency. The Twelfth Amendment required that the issue be resolved in the House of Representatives, with each state having one vote. When the vote was tallied, Adams had received more than half. Jackson's backers accused Clay of manipulating the voting to benefit Adams. Although this was obviously denied by Clay, eyebrows were raised when President Adams made Clay his secretary of state, a position viewed at the time as heir to the presidency. In the next election, 1828, Jackson, running as the Democratic candidate (the Republican suffix was dropped) had his revenge, defeating Adams (who ran on the new National Republican ticket) handily in both the popular and electoral votes. In a sense, the National Republicans, who were strong in the Northeast, rose out of the ashes of the old Federalist party in that they advocated for the Bank of the United States and the tariff (especially

Dorr's Rebellion

In Rhode Island voting was restricted to those who held property worth at least $150. Consequently, unequal representation prevailed within the state. For example, although Providence had a larger population than Newport, the latter had more representatives in the state legislature because it had more landowners. In the 1842 gubernatorial election, the reform candidate, Thomas Dorr, was elected; however, the opposition refused to recognize his victory. The two sides then armed themselves and prepared to settle the dispute violently, if necessary. Dorr's arrest defused the situation, but several years later his reform party was reelected. Sentiments outside the state were mixed. Some Americans viewed it as a threat to law and order while others viewed Dorr's rebellion as an effort to correct an undemocratic system.

after the Panic of 1819 damaged the Northeast's economy). The National Republicans ran Clay for the presidency in 1832, but he too was defeated by Jackson. (The National Republicans would, over the next couple of decades, become the Whig party, and eventually the Republican party.) For our purposes, the man at the center of this reform period, Jackson, would be elected to two terms. His eight years in office and those of his successor, Martin Van Buren, are considered the heart of the Age of Reform.

In analyzing American society in the antebellum period it is important to identify those problems—political, economic, and social—that reformers sought to address:

- Unfavorable Political Conditions
  - In general, many American citizens were excluded from the political process. They had little impact, if any, on how and what decisions were made.
  - Women were disenfranchised (denied the right to vote and participate in the political process).
  - Free black Americans were disenfranchised as well. Of course, slaves had no citizenship rights.
  - In some states, property ownership was a requirement for voting.
  - The process associated with how political parties chose their presidential candidates, called "King Caucus," was exclusive and closed to most. There was no primary system to provide rank-and-file party members the opportunity to select candidates. Instead, political party leaders selected candidates.
  - Disproportionate representation still existed.
- Unfavorable Economic Conditions
  - There were no stay laws (which prevented a person from going to prison for indebtedness).
  - Oppressed urban workers were attempting to protect themselves by forming unions.

The Anti-Renters Movement

In upstate New York, property ownership resembled that of a feudal society. Wealthy and powerful landowners held old leases to enormous tracts of land. Their tenants were often compelled to provide feudal obligations, such as working on the landlord's manor for a set number of days per year. Following the American Revolution, many tenants were convinced that the terms of the leases had long since expired, that the leases were highly exploitative, and that, at the very least, feudal relationships had been swept away by the American Revolution. By 1839 a grassroots organization of tenant farmers was organized to prevent the collection of rents. Sure enough, when authorities attempted to collect the rents, violence erupted. It was not until the early 1850s that new legislation was passed to limit leases of farmland to twelve years. Still the farmers refused to pay "back rents," and they formed the Anti-Renters Association.

- The existence of unfair tax laws discriminated against small farmers and members of the urban working class, many of whom were mired in debt.
- Land was not attainable for many inhabitants of the United States.
- Many farmers could not afford to own their own farm. Instead, they hired themselves out or rented land.
- The market economy was susceptible to the fluctuations and problems inherent in the business cycle (recession, depression, inflation, and deflation).
- There were limited opportunities for small and expectant capitalists because of monopolies and the political and economic power and influence of the entrenched capitalists.
- Unfavorable Social Conditions
- Because of discrimination, women were second-class citizens.
- Racial discrimination was pervasive.
- Slavery was becoming intolerable. There were a number of slave revolts during this period, such as Denmark Vesey's insurrection in 1822 and Nat Turner's rebellion in 1831.
- Treatment of the mentally ill was inhumane, as were the conditions prevalent in prisons.
- Urban decay and problems such as poor housing and sanitation, crime, and disease were rampant.
- Working conditions were both unsafe and unhealthy.
- Because there was no public education system, learning was available only to those who could afford it.
- The Native American population was being systematically decimated by the Indian Removal Act and other actions and policies of the states and the federal government.

Cures for these maladies were proposed. The first, put simply, was to expand democratic rights, beginning with the abolition of property qualifications for voting in those states that retained this prerequisite. Also, the economy could be redirected to include the interests of the nonentrenched capitalist class. And by making available more and cheaper land in the West, those seeking relief from creditors, speculators, and bankers (especially the despised Second Bank of the United States) would be helped.

Why then did disenchanted, alienated, and exploited white males coalesce behind Jackson, a one-time land speculator and opponent of debtor relief, and the Democrats? Born into poverty, Jackson entered business at a relatively young age. By the 1820s, his own ill-fated business experiences soured him on speculation and paper money and left him permanently suspicious of the credit system in particular, and banks in general. To many, then, Jackson represented a healthy contempt for the old hierarchical, preferential system. His position on a number of key issues reflects this perspective:

- **The spoils system** For decades, individuals holding positions in the federal government were not replaced when their presidential appointee left office. Jackson changed this tradition. For him and the Democratic party, the expression "To the victor belong the spoils" described the way federal jobs were distributed. Jackson replaced those loyal to the previous administration with supporters of his own party. Critics referred to this method as the spoils system. (Defenders had a more democratic-sounding term: rotation in office.) Like Jackson, they detested experts and deemed the common man more than capable to fill any government post.

- **The Indian Removal Act** Discussed in the previous chapter, Jackson's attitudes regarding Native Americans often reflected those of the average citizen. When he spoke of the common man, Jackson was simply not referring to Native Americans.

- **Veto power** Claiming he was the representative of the people, protecting them against governmental abuses and policies that enhanced the standing of the politically and economically entrenched, Jackson vetoed more bills than all of his predecessors combined.

- **Unofficial advisers** Rather than limit himself to the views of professional politicians, such as cabinet members—who, with the exception of Martin Van Buren, were mediocre men selected to appease sectional interests and the Democratic party—Jackson came to rely on a group of informal advisers (mostly newspaper editors) known as the "kitchen cabinet."

- **The bank war** Although it was successful in regulating interest rates and adopting policies conducive to economic stability and growth, the Bank of the United States was not rechartered by Congress in 1811 because of the resentment of smaller state chartered banks. Five years later Congress chose to recharter the (Second) Bank of the United States despite continued opposition by state banks. And again, the bank was successful. It provided credit, which allowed for economic development in the East and West. Despite the Supreme Court's ruling in *McCulloch v. Maryland,* in 1819, which made the bank paramount in relation to state banks, Jackson strongly opposed it. To him, the bank represented preference and monopoly; it violated states' rights and was partially controlled by foreigners. Besides, he reasoned, as did Jefferson, that the bank was unconstitutional because the Constitution did not explicitly provide for such an institution. Jackson's personality clash with the president of the bank, Nicholas Biddle, only increased his contempt for the institution. (At one point Jackson told Biddle, "I do not like your Bank any more than all banks.") Jackson's opponents, foremost among them Senator Henry Clay, were able to convince Congress to pass a bill to again recharter the bank. Jackson vetoed the bill. If the election of 1832 was any indication of the public's position on the Bank of the United States, which the president made the central issue of his campaign, Jackson's landslide defeat of Clay put any doubts to rest. During the campaign, Jackson had declared, "The Bank is trying to kill me, but I will kill it." And he did. But the impact on the economy was devastating. His vetoing of the bank set off a chain of events that ultimately intensified the downward spiral the economy would experience. Unfortunately for Martin Van Buren, Jackson's demolition of the bank would have dire consequences when he became president.

After vetoing the rechartering of the Second Bank, Jackson withdrew federal funds from the bank and distributed it to state banks, referred to as "pet banks." This action had the long-range effect of contributing to wild speculation:

The additional money the pet banks possessed made it possible for them to expand and extend credit.

This had the effect of increasing demand for land. Prices for land skyrocketed.

Many banks found that they were overextended.

Because the one force that could have controlled wild speculation and overextension—the Bank of the United States—had been destroyed by Jackson, he was thus forced to issue the Specie Circular:

Banks and all types of lenders were forced to call in their loans and specie.

This resulted in panic selling.

Consequently, prices plummeted, and many borrowers defaulted on their debts.

As a result, many banks went bankrupt.

From 1837 to 1843 the economy spiraled downward. The Specie Circular served only to aggravate the economic decline the nation was soon to experience when a depression hit during Van Buren's term. The following are causes of that depression:

- the domestic and international decline in the demand for cotton
- uncontrolled land and financial speculation
- the withdrawal of capital by British investors
- the normal workings of the business cycle—expansions and contractions common in the capitalist system

JACKSON'S POSITION ON FEDERAL VERSUS STATES' RIGHTS

There has been considerable debate among historians as to whether Jackson was an advocate of states' rights or a firm believer in the supremacy of the federal government.

Others maintain that constitutional questions had little to do with his support or opposition to specific issues. Below are a number of events in Jackson's presidency that correlate to this debate:

- **The Maysville Road veto** In 1830 Congress passed a bill that would authorize the government to invest in the construction of a road from Maysville, Kentucky, to Lexington, the hometown of Henry Clay. Jackson's veto of the bill provided him the opportunity to weigh in on federal funding for internal improvements and strike a blow at Clay, his political enemy. Jackson argued that since the road lay within one state (regardless that the road was to become a section of the National Road), the bill was unconstitutional. His veto of the Maysville Road Bill established a precedent that would go unchanged until the twentieth century. Until then, individual states and private capital, not the federal government, would be responsible for the construction of roads.
- **Cherokee Nation** Jackson refused to intervene on behalf of the Cherokees after John Marshall's favorable ruling toward them in the *Worcester v. Georgia* Supreme Court case. As chief executive it was his constitutional responsibility to uphold federal laws.
- **Nullification** In 1828 Congress passed what became known in the South as the "Tariff of Abominations," a very protective tax that was very high on some imports and lower on others. The bill was actually a political ploy by Jackson supporters to embroil President Adams in a political controversy. Never one to tolerate legislation that he believed violated states' rights (especially those of his home state, South Carolina), Senator John C. Calhoun cited the argument (known as *interposition*) that if a state believed the federal government had exceeded its authority, it could object to the government's acts and actions. Although at one time Jackson's vice president, Calhoun and Jackson were soon at odds over the tariff and other issues relating to states' rights. At an 1830 dinner celebrating the anniversary of the birth of President Jefferson and attended by leaders of the Democratic party, including Jackson and Calhoun, President Jackson toasted, "Our Federal Union—it must be preserved." To which Calhoun responded, "The Union—next to our liberty the most dear..." One of Calhoun's more radical solutions to the prevailing political animosities between the North and South was the antiquated notion of a *concurrent majority* to secure and maintain a balance between the political rights of the less populated (and therefore minority) South with those of the more populated North, even going so far as to consider a dual

presidency. As if this was not enough, Calhoun declared in his *South Carolina Exposition* (1828) that state legislatures had the right to rule federal laws unconstitutional and to nullify those laws, which is exactly how the South Carolina legislature responded to the Tariff of 1828. Calhoun further reasoned that, if necessary, a state had the right to secede. When Jackson became president, the tariff and nullification were still hot issues. Faced with South Carolina's refusal to abide by federal law and threatened secession, Jackson warned that he would use the U.S. army to invade the state. Not until Henry Clay worked out a compromise tariff, in 1833, did South Carolina rescind its nullification, thus preventing a showdown between Calhoun and the federal government. Jackson had shown that he would use all means at his disposal to enforce national law.

While President Jackson was redefining the role of the presidency, individuals in the North and West took it upon themselves to address the ills of the nation and reconstruct society according to their principles and ideas. Because of the rigid nature of southern society in the antebellum period, most of the reform movements that sprung up between the 1820s and 1850s did not find fertile ground in the South.

GRASSROOTS MOVEMENTS IN THE AGE OF REFORM

One of the ideological inspirations behind this desire to reform was the religious revivals that became popular at the turn of the century. Often women were at the center of these revivals, which were among the few opportunities they had to operate outside their clearly defined roles as wives and mothers. This was not the first time religious fervor of this magnitude erupted on the national scene. In the 1730s and 1740s, a New England reverend named Jonathan Edwards had preached that personal repentance and faith in Christ could lead to salvation. George Whitefield, an English preacher, traveled extensively throughout the colonies advocating personal repentance. In powerful and dramatic religious meetings throughout the colonies, "sinners" confessed their guilty ways and then repented in emotional outpourings of devotion. The impact of this, called the First Great Awakening, was a reduction in the influence of church leaders, for the individual could find salvation on his own, and it led to a schism within the Protestant Church. Newer sects such as Baptists and Methodists (the "New Lights") emerged, only to be challenged by the older, more established ("Old Light") churches such as the Anglicans.

The Second Great Awakening represented an individualistic and emotional reaction to the Enlightenment's reliance on reason over faith, a decline in church attendance, and what many perceived as a decline in piety. Unlike its predecessor in the eighteenth century, religious camp meetings did not take firm hold in the South because the revivals included many women, and even some blacks, and because individualism was being promoted in a section of the country that had no tolerance for such ideas. Beginning around the turn of the century and peaking in the 1830s and 1840s, ministers preached "hellfire and brimstone" sermons (in areas that became known as "burned over districts"). Participants were swept into powerful and emotional states in which they hoped to find repentance and salvation. Leading the way in this religious revival was Charles Grandison Finney. An abolitionist, Finney preached that through good works and deeds, individuals could find salvation, not only for themselves, but also for the nation. In this way then there is a connection between the influence of the Second Great Awakening and the fervent of reform in the antebellum period.

The secular intellectual foundation of the reform spirit had its origins in large part in the ideas of Immanuel Kant. In his *Critique of Pure Reason* (1781), the German scholar raised doubts about the power of reason. Those who accepted this view, the romanticists, believed that while science can test hypotheses, individuals know their own reality through faith. The most significant expression of romanticism was the transcendentalist movement of New England. Advocates believed that one could "transcend" the limits of the intellect and strive for emotional understanding and unity with God without the assistance of organized religion. The transcendentalist movement provided intellectuals with a secular ideology that compelled individuals to scrutinize their own views and then to follow one's conscience.

AP Tip

In constructing an essay, how does one make connections between events, movements, and effects and the intellectual origins that shaped them? Often students will write about the philosophical or ideological influences of a period separate from what was actually happening at that time. A more effective and analytical approach is to use the ideas to explain motivations and causation. For example, in making a connection between the Second Great Awakening, transcendentalism, and romanticism, and the reform spirit of the antebellum period, you might assert that these movements asked individuals to get in touch with their own emotions rather than their sense of reason. Thus, while an individual in the antebellum era might present a reasonable economic and social justification for the existence of slavery, one responding to emotional visions of enslavement and degradation might very well come to the conclusion that the institution of slavery was simply barbaric.

Around the same time, American artists who were popularizing landscape painting, known as the Hudson River School, sought to evoke emotional responses to the beauty of the United States as a "chosen nation." Literary figures also spread the transcendentalist message across the nation in such important works as Henry David Thoreau's *Walden* and Ralph Waldo Emerson's *Nature*. Speaking for those attempting to better their society, Emerson asked: "What is man born for but to be a reformer, a remaker of what man has made?"

The following were major reform movements:

- **Women's rights** The women's rights movement emerged as a result of shared discontent by those who no longer tolerated subjugation—their own and that of the slave. Led by Elizabeth Cady Stanton and Lucretia Mott, among others, women's rights advocates met at Seneca Falls, New York, in 1848. There they expressed in the "Declaration of Rights Sentiments" their demand to be enfranchised. Later their agenda included attaining women's property rights. Throughout the antebellum period women's rights activists were also intimately involved in the abolitionist movement. Unfortunately, women would have to wait until 1919 to vote in federal elections. Even the Fourteenth Amendment provided for universal male suffrage.

- **Abolitionist movement** Major abolitionist leaders included Theodore Weld, Frederick Douglass, Harriet Tubman, John Brown, and William Lloyd Garrison. The latter's newspaper, *The Liberator*, was influential in abolitionist circles.

- **Education reform** One of the most outspoken advocates of education reform was Horace Mann. His Massachusetts model was the basis of a tax-supported public school system.

- **Mental health** Outraged at the barbaric treatment of patients in mental health facilities, Dorothea Dix led the way to better treatment of those afflicted with mental illnesses.

- **Prison reform** Humiliation, physical abuse, and neglect were common practices used to maintain order and discipline in prisons (as they were in mental health institutions). Reformers sought more humane measures through discipline and the moral improvement of inmates, a sort of nineteenth-century attempt at rehabilitation.

- **Social welfare** These reformers attempted to confront the adverse effects of urbanization and industrialization on the working class.

- **Trade unionism** Supporters attempted to organize workers in order to combat exploitative conditions and wages.

- **Reform of the U.S. policy toward Native Americans** Some favored assimilation, others supported autonomy for Native American tribes.

- **Utopian societies** By establishing experimental societies, supporters of utopianism believed they could further their own moral and spiritual development through cooperative communities. Some utopian societies were religious and economic in nature (The Harmonists, Amana Colony, and Brook Farm). Others followed a particular leader (Robert Owens's New Harmony). A third type was based purely on a religious model (Shakers, Oneida Community).

- **The temperance movement** This movement was led by those who believed that alcohol was interfering with the political and social development of the nation.

- **Anti-immigration movements** While reformers were finding ways to expand democracy for the citizens of the United States, the nativist movement was organized to keep foreigners out. Nativists believed that the customs, traditions, and values of American society were being compromised by the arrival in large numbers of Irish and German immigrants. The nativists reached their political zenith in the 1850s when they formed the Know-Nothing, or American, party. It was able to gain control in several states but died out by the late 1850s. Nativist sentiment towards immigrants, however, would continue to be an ongoing feature of U.S. history.

POLITICAL AND ECONOMIC ACCOMPLISHMENTS IN THE AGE OF REFORM

The political accomplishments in this period were significant. In many states, especially in the new western states, property qualifications for voting and holding office were abolished. The method of selecting presidential candidates was democratized in various states; the people were given the power to select the candidates, effectively doing away with "King Caucus," which was a major issue in the 1828 campaign. Many more public offices were elective rather than appointive, making public officials more accountable to the electorate. The spoils system and rotation in office were adopted.

There were economic accomplishments too. One of the primary economic objectives was to break the bonds between entrenched capitalists and certain members of the political hierarchy, thereby putting an end to privilege and monopoly. In other words, there was an effort to create a competitive economy based on equal opportunity. These ideas especially represented the wishes of expectant and small capitalists. One way to accomplish this was to enact incorporation laws. In the past, a corporation charter had to be granted before one could start a business. If the business posed a threat to entrenched capitalists, the charter application was often refused. With incorporation laws, a person needed only to fulfill the criteria for a charter to be granted. One case in particular expresses the change in governmental attitude in this period. The Charles River Bridge case shows the change in governmental attitude in this period. In the late eighteenth century, Massachusetts chartered the Charles River Bridge Company to construct a bridge connecting Boston and Charlestown. The state gave permission to the bridge company to collect tolls for seventy years. In 1828 the state legislature chartered a second company to build a bridge adjacent to the original one. The use of this second bridge was free. The Charles River Bridge Company sued on the grounds that the construction of the new bridge was a contract violation the company had with the state. Earlier, in the *Dartmouth College* case, the Marshall court had ruled in favor of the sanctity of contracts. In the *Charles River Bridge* case, Chief Justice Taney ruled against the Charles River Bridge Company for two reasons: the old charter stunted future infrastructural development, and it represented a monopoly. Yet another accomplishment was the enactment in many states of stay laws.

In some areas, accomplishments were more limited. For example, low-priced federal land was not always available. A national bankruptcy law was not enacted; it would be realized at a later date. And while trade unions were formed, raising the consciousness of laborers to their plight, real gains would not occur until much later in the nation's history.

As the Age of Reform shaped the West and North, the South remained for the most part traditional and unindustrialized. After visiting the United States, Alexis de Tocqueville contrasted the North and South in his major work, *Democracy in America*. One was vibrant with business and activity, the other, considerably less so. In some ways, the period of reform that shaped the nation in the antebellum years served to widen the chasm between the South and the rest of the nation. Ultimately, it would take a war to transform the South.

Multiple-Choice Questions

1. The spoils system
   (A) was condemned by Jackson and his supporters for being undemocratic
   (B) prevented women, Native Americans, and blacks from voting
   (C) was a derisive term used by opponents of the Tariff of 1828
   (D) is a term that is synonymous with rotation in office
   (E) was a corrupt bargain made by the opponents of Jackson that prevented him from winning the presidency in 1824.

ANSWER: **D.** Jackson saw the spoils system as a way of increasing participation in government and rewarding party loyalists (*The American Pageant*, 12th ed., pp. 262-263/11th ed., pp. 268-269).

2. The origins of the Age of Reform can be found in all of the following EXCEPT
   (A) the defeat of the South and slavery in the Civil War
   (B) the democratic influences of the American Revolution
   (C) the Jeffersonian Democratic-Republicans
   (D) the antifederalists of the 1780s and 1790s
   (E) the profound social and economic changes and conditions of the early nineteenth century

ANSWER: **A.** The Civil War occurred after the Age of Reform (*The American Pageant*, 12th ed., p. 256/11th ed., p. 241).

3. The "kitchen cabinet"
   (A) was the name given to Jackson's political opponents
   (B) was a derisive term for men who advocated for women's rights
   (C) was a term used to attack critics of Jackson's position on the Bank
   (D) were those who settled on land for which they no longer held a lease
   (E) was the nickname of Jackson's unofficial advisors

ANSWER: **E.** Jackson was suspicious of "experts" and professionals and relied on editors of pro-Democratic newspapers for political advice.

4. Jackson's Maysville Road veto was an opportunity for him to
   (A) challenge federal infrastructural development
   (B) attack opponents of his policy to relocate Native Americans
   (C) disregard John Marshall's ruling on contracts
   (D) advocate for the construction of a National Road
   (E) undermine financial support for the Bank of the United States

ANSWER: **A.** Jackson claimed that since the Maysville Road lay within one state, the federal government should not be responsible for the cost of its construction. This provided him an opportunity to challenge federally funded infrastructural development.

5. The leader of South Carolina's opposition to the "Tariff of Abominations" was
    (A) Martin Van Buren
    (B) Henry Clay
    (C) William Lloyd Garrison
    (D) John C. Calhoun
    (E) John Marshall

ANSWER: **D**. Calhoun, a gifted politician, protested the "Tariff of Abominations" in *The South Carolina Exposition* (*The American Pageant*, 12th ed., p. 264/11th ed., p. 262).

6. Jackson was embroiled in a controversy with Nicholas Biddle over the
    (A) construction of the Maysville Road
    (B) construction of the Charles River Bridge
    (C) resettlement of Native Americans
    (D) abolition of slavery
    (E) Bank of the United States

ANSWER: **E**. Biddle was the president of the bank, the institution that Jackson destroyed (*The American Pageant*, 12th ed., p. 269/11th ed., pp. 277-278).

7. The Specie Circular
    (A) sought to address the problems associated with the Panic of 1819
    (B) was a primary factor in the development of the New Market economy
    (C) was nullified by the South Carolina legislature
    (D) was an attempt by Jackson to remedy the problems associated with the destruction of the bank
    (E) was used by the Charles River Bridge Company to raise funds to build a bridge over the Charles River in Massachusetts

ANSWER: **D**. Jackson's Specie Circular attempted to address the economic problems caused by his destruction of the bank, but it only aggravated the situation (*The American Pageant*, 12th ed., p. 272/11th ed., p. 279).

8. William Lloyd Garrison is most associated with which of the following reform movements?
    (A) prison reform
    (B) reforming mental health facilities
    (C) abolition of slavery
    (D) education reform
    (E) the plight of Native Americans

ANSWER: **C**. Garrison was the publisher of *The Liberator*, an abolitionist newspaper and one of the leading proponents of the abolition of slavery (*The American Pageant*, 12th ed., p. 364/11th ed., pp. 372-373).

9. The Seneca Falls Convention is associated with which of the following reform movements?
   (A) women's rights
   (B) abolition
   (C) education reform
   (D) opposition to Jackson's policies toward Native Americans
   (E) urban reform

ANSWER: **A**. At the Seneca Falls Convention in 1848, the delegates issued the "Declaration of Sentiments," a call for enfranchisement and other rights accorded to white men (*The American Pageant*, 12th ed., pp. 332, 968/11th ed., p. 340).

10. Which of the following is FALSE regarding the Second Great Awakening?
   (A) It promoted individualism.
   (B) It was not experienced by southerners.
   (C) It placed reason over faith.
   (D) It challenged the Enlightenment's reliance on reason.
   (E) It came about in response to the perception that piety was declining.

ANSWER: **C**. The Second Great Awakening placed faith over reason, which was the cornerstone of Enlightenment ideas (*The American Pageant*, 12th ed., pp. 321-322/11th ed., pp. 330-331).

Free-Response Questions

1. Support or refute this statement:
   An accurate title for the period from the 1820s to the 1850s is Jacksonian democracy.

RESPONSE You should address the nature of reform that emanated from both the federal government and grassroots movements. To support the claim that Jackson was the inspiration for this reform period, point out that he represented the common man, favored states' rights over the power of the federal government, and freed up Native American land to be used by whites.

To refute the claim, you can point out that Jackson was a member of the planter-slaveholding class whose interests were not with the common man at all. He was not supportive of some reforms, such as the women's rights movement; opposed others, such as abolition; or was unaware of a number of reforms. His spoils system/rotation in office approach to government had its supporters and detractors.

2. Were the grassroots movements in the Age of Reform successful in achieving their goals? In your answer cite THREE of the following:
   a. women's rights
   b. abolition
   c. public education
   d. prison reform

RESPONSE Your essay should first take up the objective conditions—how things were—that existed in the antebellum period, such as abolition and women's rights, then explain the accomplishments or failures of the three reform movements you have selected. For example, while women organized at the Seneca Falls Conference to create a list of demands and expectations, the Cult of Domesticity was merely replaced with Republican Motherhood in this period. Women were still relegated to second-class status.

8

THE AMERICAN CIVIL WAR: 1860–1865

To understand this nation's history, you must understand the causes and effects of the American Civil War (1861-1865). One historian even referred to the Civil War as the "crossroads of our being." A study of U.S. history that minimizes the impact of that conflict would be similar to a study of human anatomy that downplays the role of the heart, making our knowledge of human anatomy, well, heartless.

KEY CONCEPTS

- Various tensions within and between regions came together to cause the Civil War.
- A fundamental disagreement between Northerners and Southerners about the Constitution contributed to the Civil War.
- Slavery became a crisis in the context of western expansion.
- Compromise on slavery, dating from the writing of the Constitution, became harder and eventually impossible by 1860.

The Civil War is discussed in depth in *The American Pageant*, 12th ed., Chapters 16, 18, and 19/11th ed., Chapters 17, 19, and 20.

Many social scientists view the Civil War as a watershed in American historical development, for it shaped the future of the nation in a number of ways:

- The war was a catalyst in the industrialization of the United States, and the industrial capitalist class became dominant.
- The federal government was deemed paramount in relation to the states.
- Race and class relations were profoundly affected by the war.
- The war further stimulated and accelerated industrialization.

- The war forever ended the institution of slavery.
- Asked about the causes of the Civil War, everyone talks about slavery. Of course, slavery was the fundamental cause, but there were other causes too. A deeper understanding of the Civil War reveals other tensions in this nation prior to the war, though all were in one way or another affected by the slavery issue. Some of these tensions came from regional differences, some from political differences.

AP Tip

There are usually numerous causes that explain why an event happened. Some are more important than others, but an understanding of the many causes will allow you to write a fuller free-response or DBQ essay, in addition to scoring well on the multiple-choice section of the AP exam. If you are explaining why the Civil War occurred, a response such as "To free the slaves" would be seriously inadequate.

REGIONAL ECONOMIC DIFFERENCES

The types of economies that developed in the three regions of the United States in the first half of the nineteenth century had a powerful impact on political goals and decisions. The South grew important cash crops such as cotton, tobacco, sugar, and rice. The North was far more industrialized than the South or West, having shifted from mercantile capitalism. At the same time the West shifted from subsistence farming to commercial agriculture and produced more foodstuffs, such as corn and wheat, than the other two regions. The North came to rely more and more on western foodstuffs. In return, westerners became consumers of northern industrial and commercial products. By the 1850s the North and West were economically joined, and the North's economy was rapidly evolving into a modern-day industrial and commercial system.

- Characteristics of the North's Economy
  - banking
  - shipping
  - insurance
  - small and large business ownership—creating a middle, or bourgeois, class
  - some agriculture—both commercial and subsistence farming
  - availability of wage laborers
- Political Objectives of the North
  - a tariff, a tax on imports to protect the North's growing industries
  - federal aid in the development of infrastructure—those things necessary for business to flourish, such as roads, canals, bridges, and railroads

■ a loose immigration policy, which would provide cheap labor

■ availability of free or cheap land in the West for settlement and investment opportunities, creating new markets for Northern manufactured goods

■ the containment of slavery

In the South, cash crops such as rice and tobacco were grown extensively. Yet no commodity was more important to the South than cotton. One southern political leader was so certain that the rest of the nation depended on the South's cotton production that he declared, "Cotton is King!"

Cotton was one of the most important commodities in the world in the nineteenth century. Factories in the Northern states as well as European countries such as Britain and France needed cotton for their important textile industries. The most powerful producers of cotton in the South were the planter-slaveholders (owners of a hundred slaves or more, sometimes thousands). This class, a fraction of the entire Southern population, was politically, economically, and socially important. Some slaveholders owned only a few slaves. The majority of the Southern population was either subsistence farmers, who grew just enough food to sustain themselves, or yeoman farmers, who grew and sold surplus crops. As much as 25 percent of the South's white population owned slaves on the eve of the Civil War.

Many of the whites who owned no slaves resented the planter-slaveholding class. However, their fear of economic loss if slavery was abolished as well as their belief that whites are superior to blacks were powerful forces in maintaining the status quo. The planters made all of the political and economic decisions. Many nonslaveholders, with dreams of improving their lot and owning slaves, supported what many began calling the "peculiar institution." For most, however, preserving the planter slaveholder's dominance of the South was not a reason to wage war.

■ Characteristics of the South's Economy
  ■ dependent on the plantation system, the center of economic, political, cultural, and social life in the South
  ■ slave labor, the dominant labor force in the South producing the greatest value in the region
  ■ a majority of the white population engaged in subsistence farming
  ■ yeoman farmers, who owned small- or medium-sized commercial farms, a small proportion of the white population
  ■ a small urban bourgeois (or middle) class
■ Political Objectives of the South
  ■ low tariffs because of the planter class's dependence on trade with Britain—cotton in return for consumer goods
  ■ the expansion of slavery for political, economic, and ideological reasons
  ■ opposition to a cheap public land policy, which would force the planter-slaveholder to compete politically,

economically, and ideologically with the independent farmer in the West

■ make it far more difficult for the planter-slaveholder class to exert control over new territories

■ expose poor whites and even slaves to the capitalist and democratic views expressed by Northern emigrants to the new territories

TENSIONS OVER POLITICAL THEORIES

Northerners believed in the *contract theory* of government, whereas Southerners believed in the *compact theory*. This explains why Southerners believed they had the right to secede from the Union and why Northerners were willing to prevent them from doing so. Here are the basic features of each theory:

THE COMPACT THEORY

■ The states, not the people, created the national government.

■ The laws of the states are supreme when in conflict with the laws and actions of the federal government. For example, in the antebellum North, personal liberty laws were passed to counteract federal fugitive slave laws.

■ The states can declare the laws of the federal government null and void if they deem it necessary and appropriate.

■ The logical conclusion of this theory if taken to its extreme is secession.

Examples of the compact theory include

■ the Virginia and Kentucky Resolutions (1798)
■ the Hartford Convention (1815)
■ *the South Carolina Exposition and Protest* (1828)
■ the Ordinance of Nullification (1832)

THE CONTRACT THEORY

■ The people, not the states, created the Union.
■ The federal government is supreme.
■ Thus, federal laws and actions take precedence over state laws and actions.

Examples of the contract theory include

■ the various decisions made by the Marshall Court
■ John Locke's *Second Treatise on Government*
■ *Texas v. White* (1869)

ATTITUDES IN THE NORTH AND SOUTH

In the first half of the nineteenth century, many Northerners were content to allow slavery to reside in the Southern states. Only when Southern leaders sought to expand slavery did many Northerners become concerned. Most Northerners, however, were not necessarily morally opposed to slavery. After all, the ancient Greeks and Romans owned slaves. Even the Bible seemed to justify its existence. Politically and economically, however, the expansion of slavery worried many Northern citizens and their political leaders. Did it matter if it spread to Kansas, Oregon, or California? Absolutely! Slavery was at the root of a social, economic, political, and cultural system that many Northerners disdained, partly because it was antithetical to the values of a vibrant, expanding capitalist system. Many Northerners tended to see the South as static. There was little social or economic mobility, little industry, and therefore few opportunities for wage laborers. For these reasons and because land was available out West, many immigrants avoided the South and settled in one of the other two regions.

Southern political leaders, on the other hand, ironically referred to Northern wage earners as "wage slaves." To them, the North was a mess. Northern cities were congested, and workers earned poverty wages and worked and lived in dismal conditions. Southerners saw slavery as a paternalistic system that provided slaves with the basic needs of life. Furthermore, they argued, a slave was an investment; a Northern wage earner could be replaced. Although their owners often horribly mistreated slaves, Southern apologists claimed the opposite was true. Slaves, they maintained, were too valuable to mistreat. On the eve of the Civil War, a prime field slave could cost upward of $2,000, a substantial sum of money in the mid-nineteenth century.

Containing slavery became important to Northerners, who believed that as slavery expanded, Northern industrial capitalism would be limited. In fact, a new political party emerged in the 1850s, the Republicans, whose political goals were "free labor, free soil, free men." The industrial capitalists, owners of the North's factories and workshops, had the most to gain by containing the spread of slavery and expanding capitalism. For example, as capitalism expanded, they hoped to expand the labor pool (by supporting a loose immigration policy), which in turn would drive down the wages they would have to pay to workers. Just as the planters dominated the South, the industrial capitalists profoundly influenced the North's political, economic, and cultural system. What is more, their political and economic objectives often clashed with those of the South's planter class. In the South, militant political leaders, referred to as fire-eaters, chafed at the notion of containing slavery, let alone abolishing it entirely.

Helping to shape the debate on the containment of slavery were the abolitionists, whose ranks were made up of whites and blacks. Unlike many who supported the containment of slavery—some of them racists—abolitionists sought to eliminate slavery. Some would simply free the slaves. Others, like Abraham Lincoln in the 1850s, sought to send freed slaves to Africa (the American Colonization Society). Whereas some abolitionists sought the gradual abolition of slavery, others (among them Frederick Douglass, William Lloyd Garrison, Harriet Tubman, John Brown, and Sojourner Truth) favored an immediate end—peaceful or violent—to the institution.

> **AP Tip**
>
> A good way to organize your understanding of the causes of the war is to consider if the war was reconcilable <u>or</u> irreconcilable. In other words, could it have been prevented? The fact that it did happen does not mean that it had to happen. For example, some historians claim that a generation of bumbling politicians in the 1850s could not match the compromises reached by Clay, Calhoun, and Webster prior to 1850. Other historians contend that fire-eaters in the South and radical abolitionists in the North exacerbated the relationship between more moderate politicians, making compromise impossible. Still others argue that a dual civilization—the South based on a culture of slavery, the North on a culture of wage labor—could no longer be sustained under the same government. Lincoln may have had something like this in mind when he declared, "A house divided against itself cannot stand. I believe this government cannot endure permanently half slave and half free. It will become all one thing or all the other."

THE BREAKDOWN OF COMPROMISE

Throughout the first half of the nineteenth century, various differences between the North and South were resolved. But the relationship deteriorated over the issue of territorial expansion. By 1860 all attempts at compromise failed, and within a year the nation was in the midst of the bloody Civil War that would cost over 600,000 Americans their lives. You need to understand the important decisions that shaped the political debate over such issues as the tariff and the expansion and containment of slavery. These include

- **The compromises at the Constitutional Convention** (See *The American Pageant*, 12th ed., Chapter 9.)
- **The Missouri Compromise (1820)** This was an attempt to maintain the balance in the Senate between slave and free states. In a compromise worked out by Senator Henry Clay, Maine entered the Union as a free state while Missouri came in as a slave state. Slavery north of latitude 36°30′ was prohibited. War was averted for forty years and thus for a later generation to fight, but the damage to American nationalism helped to erode the so-called Era of Good Feelings.
- **The Nullification Crisis and the Compromise of 1833** In 1828 Congress passed a tariff that protected Northern industries but consequently drove up domestic prices. This new bill outraged Southerners, who began calling it the Tariff of Abominations. In particular, South Carolina, citing the doctrine of nullification, sought to challenge the new bill. The issue of nullification was eventually taken up in the Senate in the famous Webster-Hayne debate. When a new protective tariff was added in 1832, South Carolina, under the leadership of John C. Calhoun, its primary spokesperson and, at the time, vice president, voted to nullify the

new tariff. President Jackson, though an advocate of states' rights, threatened to invade South Carolina if its leaders refused to participate in the collection of tariff duties. He even threatened to "hang the first man of them I can get my hands on to the first tree I can find." (Jackson just may have done it.) After Calhoun's resignation, the crisis ended when Congress passed a bill that reduced the protective tariff the following year. No one was hanged, but South Carolina became the hotbed of southern dissent.

- **The Compromise of 1850** This crisis might never have occurred had, say, coal and not gold been discovered in California. By 1850 over 100,000 hoping-to-get-rich-quick settlers had poured into California, and it was not long before they asked that California be admitted into the Union as a free state. Though he was a slaveholder, President Taylor supported California's admission. Not surprisingly, southern fire-eaters threatened to pull their states out of the Union. Enter Henry Clay. His compromise, which was eventually signed into law by the new president, Millard Fillmore, included the following features:

  - California would enter the Union as a free state.
  - The more stringent Fugitive Slave Law of 1850 had guarantees that the law would be rigidly enforced.
  - The slave trade, but not the ownership of slaves, was banned in Washington, D.C.
  - The land taken from Mexico (Mexican Cession) would be divided into two new territories, New Mexico and Utah. Both territories would determine the status of slavery in their areas by *popular sovereignty*.

- **The Kansas-Nebraska Act (1854)** Senator Stephen A. Douglas (Illinois's "Little Giant") favored the passage of a bill that would route a major railroad line through Illinois (and consequently drive up the value of his own landholdings in the region). Even though this would stimulate the further settlement of the West, not everyone was convinced that the plan had merit. In order to get the bill passed, Douglas sought out Southern allies in Congress, and a deal was struck. Little did they know that their compromise, the Kansas-Nebraska Act, would touch off intense sectional hostilities. The features of the bill included the following:

  - The Nebraska Territory would be divided into the Kansas and Nebraska territories.
  - Settlers in those areas would determine the status of slavery—popular sovereignty.

Although the bill sounded reasonable to Southerners, it was the North's turn to be outraged. Both territories were located north of the 36°30' line, which the Missouri Compromise had closed to slavery. Still, the bill passed both houses of Congress and was signed by President Pierce. So angered were Northerners and Westerners by the passage of the Kansas-Nebraska Act that they began forming a political party that they hoped would take a stronger stand against the South's "slavocracy." Before long the Republican party was a major player in American politics.

- **The *Dred Scott* decision (1857)** The U.S. Supreme Court did not play a significant role in the conflict over slavery until Dred Scott compelled it to act. Scott was a slave who had been taken from

Missouri, a slave state, to Wisconsin, a free territory, by his owner. He resided there for two years until he was returned to Missouri. Scott sued for his freedom, contending that his residence in a free state made him a free citizen. Unfortunately for Scott, the chief justice of the Supreme Court was Roger Taney, a pro-Southern Democrat. Under Taney, the Court's ruling went well beyond the underlying principle of the case:

- Because Congress did not have the power to deny a citizen the right to his or her property without due process—and Scott, as a slave, was considered property—Congress could not prevent a slaveholder from taking his property to a free state. Thus the Missouri Compromise was invalid. There were now no limits to the potential expansion of slavery. Not satisfied with this decision, the court went further.

- The Constitution had not provided citizenship rights for blacks. Therefore, Scott had no constitutional right to sue his master in federal court.

The South was overjoyed by the Supreme Court's ruling. The North was outraged, again. Northern Democrats like Stephen Douglas found it increasingly difficult to reconcile their support of popular sovereignty with the *Dred Scott* decision. To more and more Northerners, the Republican party seemed to represent their views best. The Republicans were a coalition of:

- Free-Soilers, a political party formed in 1848 to represent western farmers by advocating a Homestead Law (cheap federal land for sale out West), internal improvements, and the containment of slavery
- Northern capitalists, who favored a high protective tariff, internal improvements, liberal immigration laws, and a sound money and banking system
- social reformers
- abolitionists
- Northern Democrats who felt betrayed by their party's support for the Kansas-Nebraska Act
- members of the Whig party who sought the containment of slavery
- various labor groups in the North

Democrat James Buchanan defeated the first Republican presidential candidate, John C. Frémont, in the 1856 election. In the 1860 presidential race, the Republican candidate, a tall, lanky former Illinois congressman called Abe by his friends, would fare much better, though his election would convince the South to secede.

THE ROAD TO WAR

A series of events in the late-1850s seemed to propel the nation to war:

- **"Bleeding Kansas"** This hostility in 1856 was a prelude to the full-scale war that would begin five years later. The conflict arose over whether Kansas would enter the Union as a free or slave state. (Keep in mind that the majority of antislavery forces in Kansas wanted to contain the spread of slavery, not end it.) Since popular sovereignty would decide the issue, it seemed that the majority of Kansas's antislavery farmers would align Kansas with free states. Proslavery sympathizers in neighboring Missouri were not about to stand by while their neighbor cast its lot with the free states. Soon "border ruffians" crossed into Kansas with the intention of making it a slave state. In response, Northern opponents of slavery like the New England Emigrant Society began sending supporters to Kansas. Fighting soon erupted as advocates of slavery created a government in Lecompton, Kansas, and their opponents established an antislavery government in Topeka. Shortly thereafter, proslavery forces massacred citizens of the antislavery town of Lawrence. In retaliation, a violent abolitionist named John Brown organized his own massacre of proslavery advocates at Pottawatomie Creek. Democratic President Pierce's decision to remain aloof from the events in Kansas further damaged what was left of his party's cohesion. In the ensuing months it seemed as if Kansas would enter as a free state—that is, until the new president, James Buchanan, accepted the proslavery Lecompton Constitution, which would admit Kansas as a slave state. Some Democrats, Stephen Douglas among them, joined forces with Republicans in 1858 to oppose the Lecompton Constitution, and Kansas ultimately became a free state.

- **Lincoln-Douglas Debates (1858)** Having served only one term in the House, Lincoln challenged the nationally recognized Illinois senator Stephen Douglas in his campaign for reelection. Despite the fact that Lincoln lost the election, the debates thrust him into the national spotlight, for Lincoln had found a responsive chord with opponents of slavery. Although no abolitionist himself, Lincoln's rhetoric matched the sentiments of those who were opposed to the expansion of slavery as well as those who morally condemned it.

- **John Brown's Harpers Ferry Raid (1859)** John Brown's crusade to eradicate slavery was indeed noble, but his methods were violent. He believed that the planter-slaveholders who maintained a violent system of human ownership could be compelled to end slavery only through violent means. In what many consider a misguided attempt to start a slave rebellion, Brown and his supporters seized the federal arsenal at Harpers Ferry, Virginia (now West Virginia). Hoping that slaves would flock to his cause and take up arms, Brown was instead met by U.S. Army troops under the command of Colonel Robert E. Lee. Captured and ultimately hanged, Brown became a martyr to many Northerners, which in turn made Southerners suspect that Northerners were involved in or at least supportive of violent slave rebellions.

Though many did not know it then, one more significant event would shatter the Union. A slave revolt? Another bloody conflict like the one in Kansas? No. It was a presidential election that led to secession and civil war. The election of 1860 showed just how divided the nation was. Four candidates sought the presidency:

- The Republican candidate was Abraham Lincoln, whose major political platform was the containment of slavery.
- The Democrats split between a Northern candidate and a Southern candidate. The former, Stephen A. Douglas, continued to advocate

popular sovereignty. The latter, John C. Breckinridge, opposed the containment of slavery.

- ■ The Constitutional Unionists ran John Bell. His position was generally ambiguous, though preserving the Union seemed to be his primary goal.

Lincoln was elected despite the fact the he received only about 39 percent of the popular vote. In most Southern states his name did not even appear on the ballot. Because Lincoln was determined to stop the spread of slavery, South Carolina believed its future in the federal Union was threatened: more and more new free states would dramatically tip the balance in Congress in the North's favor. Shortly after Lincoln's election, South Carolina seceded from the United States, followed by six other Deep South states.

The new Southern government, called the Confederate States of America, elected Jefferson Davis, a former secretary of war and U.S. senator, as its president, with former U.S. Senator Alexander Stephens as vice president. The other Southern states waited to see if Lincoln would use force against South Carolina when he entered the White House in March 1861. In the meantime, the incumbent, James Buchanan, fretted and frowned, and did nothing.

Lincoln had to wait nearly half a year after his election to become president. During that time, Kentucky Senator John Crittenden proposed a compromise that would essentially return the nation to 1820 and the Missouri Compromise. This last-ditch attempt to prevent war failed as many Republicans, including Lincoln, believed the proposal would allow slavery to spread to the territories.

THE WAR

- ■ The opening shots occurred on April 12, 1861, when Confederate shore batteries fired on Fort Sumter off the coast of Charleston, South Carolina, compelling the fort's commander to surrender. Although seen as a military victory in the South, it was a political victory for the Lincoln administration because the South had opened hostilities.
- ■ Lincoln immediately called for 75,000 volunteers to suppress the rebellion, whereby four more Southern states seceded. The capital of the Confederacy was moved from Alabama to Richmond, Virginia.
- ■ In what became known as the Trent Affair, a Union warship stopped and seized a British ship carrying Mason and Slidell, Confederate diplomats to Britain and France, and arrested the two. Lincoln was forced to release them for fear that Britain would declare war on the United States.

At the outbreak of hostilities, Lincoln had Confederate sympathizers arrested and in the process suspended the writ of habeas corpus, a fundamental legal right that requires the government to bring specific charges against the accused and prevents it from jailing an individual indefinitely. Justice Taney ruled that Lincoln had violated their civil rights and ordered them released.

Comparison of Union and Confederate Strengths and *Weaknesses*

Union	Confederate
Population: 22 million	*Population: 6 million whites*
Had to conquer the South (offensive war)	Defensive war
Considerably more factories, wealth; a much more diverse economy than the South's	*Economy is backward and under-developed; relies on overseas demand for cotton*
Strong central government (including A. Lincoln)	*New and weak central government*
Generals who understood the nature of "total war," such as Grant and Sherman	Initially better generals, such as Lee and Jackson

Initially the South was successful in waging war against the Union, in part because of the type of war—defensive—that the South was fighting. The Union military had the considerably more difficult task of capturing and holding major strategic areas. It had to conquer the South, whereas the Confederacy hoped that if the war dragged on, the Northern public would soon grow tired of "Lincoln's war" and sue for peace. The result of the war, however, was in large part ordained by the enormous population and industrial and transportation advantages of the North. To be sure, historians refer to other important factors such as better political leadership (Lincoln versus Davis). But as one Civil War historian put it, the North fought the war "with one hand tied behind its back." Below is a list of major military engagements. In general, the Union named battles after the nearest body of water (in italics) and the Confederates named them after the nearest town (roman).

- *First Bull Run*, 1861 (Manassas): Confederate victory
- Peninsula Campaign, 1862 (Seven Days): Confederate victory made possible by the brilliant leadership of Robert E. Lee
- *Second Bull Run*, 1862 (Manassas): Confederate victory
- *Antietam*, 1862 (Sharpsburg): Union victory. After a string of Union defeats, this victory, which turned back a Confederate invasion of the North, allowed Lincoln to issue the Emancipation Proclamation several months after the battle. This decreed that slaves living in those states that were in open rebellion against the United States would be forever free. The Emancipation Proclamation did not apply to the four Border States (Maryland, Missouri, Kentucky, and Delaware); for though they were slave states, they had not seceded. Lincoln had enough on his hands without inviting more states to take up arms against his government.
- Fredericksburg, 1862: Confederate victory
- *Monitor* and *Merrimac*, 1862: In order to break the Union blockade of Southern ports, which was designed to prevent the South from

exporting cotton and importing needed supplies (the Anaconda Plan), the Confederacy launched the *Merrimac*, an ironclad ship. The *Merrimac* proceeded to wreak havoc on the wooden Union blockade ships. But the North had not been idle in its development of an ironclad vessel. The North's ironclad, the *Monitor*, fought the *Merrimac* to a draw. The consequences of this famous naval battle were twofold: it rendered wooden fleets obsolete, and the Union, given its vast resources, began to build a fleet of ironclad warships, which it used to gain control of important waterways and defeat Confederate forts that guarded such important rivers as the Mississippi.

- Gettysburg, 1863: Union victory. Considered the most famous battle fought on North American soil, the defeat of the second and last major Confederate invasion of the North was the turning point of the war. The Confederates had reached their high-water mark, a point from which their fortunes steadily declined.
- Vicksburg, 1863: Union victory. This gave control of the Mississippi River to the North, effectively cutting the Confederacy in half.
- Sherman's "March to the Sea," 1864: Union victory. The Confederacy was again cut in half.
- Petersburg Campaign, 1864-1865: Union victory. Grant closed in on the Confederate capital.
- Appomattox Court House, 1865: Confederate General Lee surrendered to General Grant, effectively ending the war. Five days later, Lincoln was assassinated by a Confederate sympathizer, John Wilkes Booth.

IMPACT OF THE WAR

Both the North and the South were transformed dramatically by the war. Slavery was of course abolished (Thirteenth Amendment), the planter class was defeated, and the South quickly came under military rule. The war also marked the emergence of the United States as a nation-state. It was no longer a confederation of states—when his state seceded in 1861, Robert E. Lee resigned his commission in the U.S. Army because he could not take up arms against his "country," Virginia. The United States had become a federal union.

Even as it fought a major civil war, the North was changing. During the war it had passed a number of important acts, such as

- the Morrill Tariff of 1861, a high protective tariff
- the Homestead Act of 1862, leading to further development of the West
- the Morrill Land Grant Act of 1862, stimulating the growth and development of higher education
- a banking act that created (in 1863) the National Banking System
- a loose immigration law

The U.S. government also continued to develop the transcontinental railroad, further linking East and West, and it provided black Americans the opportunity to fight for their freedom as soldiers in the Union Army, which they did in considerable numbers—180,000.

Because of the application of industry and technology to warfare in the period 1861-1865, the Civil War is sometimes seen as the first modern war. The use of submarines, aerial reconnaissance, repeating rifles (an early form of machine gun), and ironclad ships is a short list of new technologies applied to waging that war. War also became considerably more personal and shocking with the extensive use of early photography in the Civil War. (The Crimean War, 1854-1856, was the first military conflict to be photographed, but it produced nowhere near the volume and graphic nature of pictures taken during the American Civil War.)

Extraordinarily, the North also held a democratic presidential election in the midst of the Civil War, despite the fact that the incumbent, Lincoln, seemed certain to lose. But he didn't. By late spring 1865, the American Civil War was over. But a new battle was looming, one that would attempt to combat racial injustice and shape the way Americans viewed their newly reunited nation.

Multiple-Choice Questions

1. Which of the following is NOT an accurate statement regarding the North in the antebellum period?
   (A) Its industrial development was greater than the other two regions.
   (B) The textile industry was important to several of the states in this region.
   (C) The planter class was dominant in most of the states in the region.
   (D) Northerners favored a high protective tariff.
   (E) Much of the nation's banking industry was located in the North.

ANSWER: **C**. The planter class was the dominant social, economic, and political class in the antebellum South (*The American Pageant,* 12th ed., pp. 302-306, 351/11th ed., pp. 311-314, 360).

2. The turning point of the American Civil War occurred at the battle of
   (A) First Bull Run
   (B) Second Bull Run
   (C) *Monitor* and *Merrimac*
   (D) Antietam
   (E) Gettysburg

ANSWER: **E**. Gettysburg. From this point on, though the South did win several important battles, it was greatly weakened (*The American Pageant,* 12th ed., p. 462/11th ed., p. 472).

3. Which of the following is consistent with the contract theory?
   (A) *South Carolina Exposition*
   (B) the political views of John C. Calhoun
   (C) the states, not the federal government, are supreme
   (D) the Kentucky and Virginia Resolutions
   (E) the decisions handed down by the Marshall Court

ANSWER: E. Answers A-D all support the alternative compact theory. In a number of important decisions, the Marshall Court strengthened the role of the federal government in relation to the states (*The American Pageant*, 12th ed., pp. 218-219/11th ed., pp. 216-218).

4. The Compromise of 1850
   (A) banned slavery in Washington, D.C.
   (B) allowed Kansas to enter as a slave state
   (C) ended the Fugitive Slave law
   (D) gave all of the land taken from Mexico to Texas
   (E) allowed California to enter as a free state

ANSWER: E. California's entrance into the Union as a free state was a major concession of the South. The slave trade, not slavery, was banned in Washington, D.C. Kansas entered the Union as a free state. The Fugitive Slave Law was strengthened, not ended. The territory acquired from Mexico was divided into two territories, Utah and New Mexico (*The American Pageant*, 12th ed., pp. 397-401/11th ed., pp. 407-410).

5. Popular sovereignty was the idea that
   (A) the government of each new territory should be elected by the people
   (B) the American public should vote on whether to admit states with or without slavery
   (C) it was for the citizens of a territory to decide if their territory would enter the Union as a slave state or a free state
   (D) the United States should assume popular control of the territory acquired from Mexico
   (E) slavery should be prohibited from any territory acquired by the United States

ANSWER: C. Popular sovereignty, an idea put forth by Lewis Cass as a means to compromise, gave citizens of a territory the right to decide on the status of slavery when joining the Union (*The American Pageant*, 12th ed., pp. 390-391/11th ed., pp. 400-401).

6. In the *Dred Scott* decision, the Supreme Court
   (A) avoided controversy by ruling that Dred Scott had no right to sue in federal court
   (B) ruled that the Kansas-Nebraska Act was unconstitutional
   (C) ruled that Congress could not prohibit slavery in the territories because slaves were private property
   (D) ruled that slaves could sue in federal court only if their masters allowed them to do so
   (E) ruled that a slave that had been transported to a free state or territory was a free citizen of the United States

ANSWER: **C.** The Taney Supreme Court ruled that Scott, as a slave, was property that could be transported wherever his master decided to take him. The decision, highly controversial, invalidated the Missouri Compromise, not the Kansas-Nebraska Act (*The American Pageant*, 12th ed., pp. 417-418/11th ed., pp. 427-428).

7. The Crittenden Proposal
   (A) forbade slavery west of the Mississippi River
   (B) would have granted the Southern states their independence if they abolished slavery
   (C) would have lowered the protective tariff in return for abolishing the Fugitive Slave Act
   (D) ended the slave trade but not slavery in Washington, D.C.
   (E) would have guaranteed slaveholders the right to own slaves south of the 36°30′ line

ANSWER: **E.** This last-ditch attempt to forestall civil war would have, for all intents and purposes, returned the United States to 1820 and the Missouri Compromise (*The American Pageant*, 12th ed., pp. 429-430/11th ed., pp. 438-439).

8. In the election of 1860
   (A) most Southerners refused to vote in protest against Lincoln's candidacy
   (B) the majority of citizens living in the three sections voted for the Republican candidate
   (C) the tariff was the most controversial issue
   (D) the vast majority of southerners voted for the compromise candidate, John Bell
   (E) the Republicans gained control of the executive branch for the first time

ANSWER: **E.** Lincoln, the first Republican to win the presidency, was elected with only 39 percent of the popular vote. Southerners did indeed vote, but primarily for Breckinridge. The tariff was not the most controversial issue in 1860, though it was still a point of tension between the North and South (*The American Pageant*, 12th ed., pp. 429-430/11th ed., pp. 438-439).

9. The Emancipation Proclamation
   (A) abolished slavery in all states that were in open rebellion
   (B) abolished slavery in the Border States
   (C) ended the slave trade but not slavery
   (D) was ruled unconstitutional by the Taney Supreme Court
   (E) allowed for popular sovereignty in those states that willingly returned to the Union

ANSWER: **A.** Although controversial, the proclamation added another important moral and legal dimension to the Union cause by undermining slavery in those states that had seceded. It also made it morally difficult for France and Britain to provide aid to the Confederacy (*The American Pageant,* 12ᵗʰ ed., pp. 458-460/11ᵗʰ ed., pp. 468-470).

10. Which of the following is NOT associated with the North during the war?
    (A) continued industrialization
    (B) the Morrill Tariff of 1861
    (C) the Homestead Act of 1862
    (D) the use of blacks in the Union military
    (E) the ratification of the Fifteenth Amendment guaranteeing voting rights to male U.S. citizens

ANSWER: **E.** The Fifteenth Amendment was not ratified until 1870, fully five years after the end of the Civil War (*The American Pageant,* 12ᵗʰ ed., pp. 447-449, 488-489/11ᵗʰ ed., pp. 457-459, 497-498).

Free-Response Questions

1. Analyze the conflict between the industrial capitalist class and the Southern planter-slaveholding class. Discuss the following topics in your essay:
      economic differences
      the expansion of slavery

RESPONSE When you are asked to analyze a topic or issue, you need to break it down into its fundamental aspects. In this question, the topics are selected for you. Identify and discuss economic differences—for example, the tariff—between the two classes. A discussion of the political objectives—in favor of the expansion or containment of slavery—as it relates to the interests of the industrial and capitalist class of the North and the planter-slaveholder class of the South should be your focus for the second part of the essay.

2. Analyze the following statement:
      The Civil War was the result of irreconcilable differences between the North and West on the one hand and the South on the other.

RESPONSE Keep in mind that this question is not asking you to support or refute the statement but to break down the various components of this particular perspective whether the differences leading to the Civil

War could have been reconciled. You may wish to discuss the divergent political and economic differences and disputes between the sections, as well as the ideological justifications each side utilized to defend its way of life. Another aspect of your discussion may include the view held by some historians that the North and the South had two incompatible civilizations that could not be sustained under one government, and thus they resorted to war to settle their economic and political differences.

9

RECONSTRUCTION: 1863–1877

A pivotal movement in recent U.S. history has been the struggle by blacks to achieve racial equality. Many remember or are at least aware of the leaders, organizations, and demonstrations that shaped the 1950s and 1960s over the question of the rights of African-Americans. But the plight of black Americans did not begin thirty or forty years ago. In fact, it can be said that this struggle is as old as the nation. Yet, two decades in the nineteenth century, the 1860s and 1870s, stand out as much as any, including the 1950s and 1960s, as essential to the goal of redefining race relations in the United States. Beginning in the middle of the Civil War and ending in the late 1870s, the Reconstruction era was in some ways a success and in others a failure. In fact, one historian has called it an "unfinished revolution," while another has referred to it as a "splendid failure." Whatever one's view, it is important to understand that Reconstruction was more than a civil rights movement.   It also redefined and re-created the South, expanded capitalism, and temporarily led to the rise and division of one political party, the breakdown of another, and set in motion forces that would have long-term consequences for the nation. What is more, it helped determine the nature of the American nation-state.

KEY CONCEPTS

- Attitudes and economic and political forces influenced the dimensions of Reconstruction.
- Lincoln's and Johnson's lenient Reconstruction plans clashed with the radical Republicans' Reconstruction methods and objectives.
- The Republican party sought to contain blacks in the South in order to establish the nucleus of their party in that section of the country.

- Southern "redeemers" temporarily reinstated the South's prewar political and social system, leading to the more punitive radical Republican Reconstruction.
- Congress ratified three important civil rights amendments—the Thirteenth, Fourteenth, and Fifteenth Amendments.
- Reactionaries regained control of the South, and blacks were relegated to sharecropping and social and political subordination.
- A political deal between Southern Democrats and the Republican party ended Reconstruction.

Reconstruction is discussed in depth in *The American Pageant,* 12th and 11th eds., Chapters 22 and 23.

AP Tip

As much as any period in U.S. history, historians hold widely divergent views about the causes, ramifications, successes, and failures of Reconstruction. You should attempt to read as widely as possible on the interpretive nature of the debate over this topic. Should the College Board offer a free-response question or a DBQ on Reconstruction, an understanding of various historians' interpretations will provide you with a broader grasp of its significance as well as relevant interpretations around which you can develop your own view. If your AP teacher does not infuse class discussions and notes as well as assigned readings with evaluative essays, ask for suggestions regarding analytical literature on the subject.

THE WAR, THE EXPANSION OF THE FEDERAL GOVERNMENT, AND THE IMPACT ON RECONSTRUCTION

Before we explore the dimensions and dynamics of Reconstruction, it is important to understand how the war transformed the U.S. government, for in the end, it was the government that was center stage in the debate over reconstructing the South and addressing the problems of integrating blacks into the nation's social, political, and economic fabric. In March 1865, just one month before the end of the war, Congress passed the Bureau of Refugees, Freedmen, and Abandoned Lands Act (more commonly known as the Freedmen's Bureau). Under the leadership of General O. O. Howard, it assisted both freed slaves and poor whites who were destitute and in need of food and medical care. It also provided them farmland that had earlier been owned by slaveholders; President Johnson undermined this effort when he returned most of the confiscated land to previous owners. But the most well-known legacy of the Freedman's Bureau was its success in constructing schools that educated thousands of Southern blacks and poor whites, often under the tutelage of Northern whites, many of whom were women. Despite the achievements of the Northerners who worked for the Freedmen's Bureau, many Southerners referred to them derisively as "carpetbaggers," implying that they were opportunists who, for their own self-interest rather than altruistic reasons, rushed down South after the war. This transformation of governmental power was taking place as war was being waged, for the war expanded the role of the federal government in unprecedented ways. A short list would include the following:

- In an unprecedented decision, the government instituted conscription—the draft.
- For the first time in U.S. history, the national government assumed responsibility for guaranteeing and protecting the constitutional rights of a segment of U.S. society.
- The government had to raise millions of dollars to fight the war. To do this, the government issued greenbacks (paper currency) in record amounts.
- Lincoln used the power of the government to suspend basic constitutional rights such as habeas corpus.

AP Tip

Students sometimes ask whether they should incorporate contemporary ideas and issues into their free-response and DBQ essays. Believing that history is a continuum in which the forces that shape our contemporary world have their historical antecedents, you can make connections between past and present events. For example, Lincoln's suspension of habeas corpus rights is relevant to a discussion of the PATRIOT Act. *Make certain, however, that you maintain your focus on the specific question that is asked of you.* A question on Lincoln, the Civil War, and habeas corpus should not get lost in a political discussion on governmental powers in combating terrorism since 9/11. Also, *do not incorporate an issue into your discussion if you know little or nothing about it.* College Board readers can identify these. Ask what your teacher advises.

Reconstruction continued this trend of governmental intervention and influence in all regions of the United States. In the North a powerful relationship was fostered between government and capital. And in the South, the government was instrumental in creating a new mode of production, capitalism, to replace the collapsed slave-based economy. In short, the federal government took on the responsibility of reconstructing the South, which in the end required the application of laws, old and new, the use of federal troops to ensure order and stability, and significant amounts of money. One controversial extension of federal power serves nicely as an example of the application of the government's willingness to use its expanded political and military power to carry out domestic policy—namely, the division of the South into military districts and the stationing of U.S. troops in Southern states to carry out federal law and to prevent reactionary and violent responses to reconstruction. The government played an important role in altering the South's social and political institutions, though in some cases only temporarily.

THE ECONOMIC AND POLITICAL FOUNDATIONS OF RECONSTRUCTION POLICIES

It can be argued that Reconstruction began even before the Civil War ended. When President Lincoln issued the Emancipation Proclamation, in 1863, he redefined the nature of the struggle by giving the Union cause a broader meaning. A significant development in U.S. race relations did come about with the end of the war and the abolition of slavery. But though laws can be changed, people's attitudes are often considerably more difficult to alter. As we will see, many whites in the South, and even numerous whites in the North, were not about to give freed blacks access to the major institutions, rights, and privileges of American citizenship. Tragically, many blacks were free in name only. In fact, many white Northerners favored a policy of containing blacks in the South for two key reasons:

■ **Racism** Although Lincoln made abolition a cause of the Union war effort, many Northerners preferred that blacks stay in the South.
■ **Economic competition** Northern whites worried that blacks might migrate to the North, where there were more economic opportunities than could be found in the war-torn South. This in turn would drive down workers' wages. Consequently, while the wage-earning classes felt threatened by black migration North, the capitalist class desired an expanded labor pool, which would drive down wages.

There were political objectives as well. The Civil War indeed ended slavery and reestablished the Union, but it had two other desired consequences from the perspective of the North's political and economic leaders. The South's defeat had ended the reign of the planter aristocracy and decimated the Democrats (sneeringly referred to by Republicans as the "party of secession"). To ensure that neither the planters nor the Democrats would reemerge in the postwar South, Northern political and economic interests maintained that both of these objectives could be met if the Republican party was firmly entrenched in the South. This would make the Republicans a national party and make the Democrats a nuisance at worst, but certainly not a threat to Republican hegemony. The Republicans attempted to realize their goals by implementing the following measures:

■ They denied to the former Confederate leaders, many of them from the planter-slaveholding class, their political rights, which in turn would remove them as an obstacle to the Republicans' economic and political agenda.
■ They provided blacks in the South with just enough political and economic rights and opportunities so that they would choose to stay in the South, thereby establishing a base for the Republican party as well as obviating the racial and economic tensions that would occur if blacks began moving north.

PLANNING RECONSTRUCTION: CONFLICTING METHODS

Had Lincoln not been assassinated at the end of the war, Reconstruction and, in fact, the subsequent history of the nation might have been fundamentally different. Lincoln's plan for reconstructing the South was moderate in every sense of the word, especially in comparison with a wing of his party that became known as the radical Republicans. Lincoln's successor, Andrew Johnson, applied a plan that was quite similar but one that would bring him into direct confrontation with the radical Republicans. The stage would soon be set for a clash between the executive and legislative branches over how best to reconstruct the South and address the status of black Americans.

Lincoln wanted to quickly—and for the most part, painlessly—reincorporate the South back into the Union. His ideological rationale for this was his view that the people of the South did not secede; their economic and political leaders initiated secession and war. Lincoln argued that because the government was indivisible, secession was politically impossible. Instead, the Civil War represented a rebellion by a small minority who had brazenly violated the authority and laws of the national government. (Shortly after the war's end, in *Texas v. White*, the Supreme Court affirmed the contract theory of government.) This explains why he was opposed to the radical Republicans' plan (see below). Lincoln's design included the following features:

- Before a state could be readmitted into the Union, (only) 10 percent of voters needed to take a loyalty oath to the United States.
- The South had to repudiate the compact theory of government and accept the contract theory.
- Until the above requirements were met, military governors would oversee the conquered Southern states.

Initially, Johnson was accepted by many Republicans, for his contempt of the planter aristocracy in his home state of Tennessee was well known. But he quickly became an obstacle to those seeking a more radical and punitive solution to reconstructing the South. Johnson's plan was very similar to Lincoln's, though with a few additions, such as the disenfranchisement of very wealthy and politically powerful former Confederates. But one loophole that Johnson used frequently was the right to grant pardons to the same individuals that he claimed he sought to exclude from power. Given this approach, it was not long before most of the South's elites were back in power and every Southern state had been readmitted to the Union. In fact, the 1872 Amnesty Act lifted the last political restriction on former ex-Confederate leaders. Imagine the irritation of Northern senators at seeing the former vice president of the Confederacy, Alexander Stephens, reclaim his seat in the United States Senate. Although the readmitted states drew up constitutions that repudiated secession and abolished slavery, accepting the Thirteenth Amendment, nothing was done to enfranchise the South's black population. Enter the radical Republicans.

Not satisfied with disenfranchising blacks, the newly formed Southern state governments went even further by establishing what became known as Black Codes. The codes were designed to limit severely the movement of millions of dislocated blacks as well as to deny them the right to own property, including much-needed farms. Further, they were returned to a form of perpetual servitude by being compelled to sign work contracts that were little more than a thinly disguised attempt to make them dependent once again on their former owners. Legally, their rights were abridged as well; they still could not testify in a court of law against a white person (even if they had the courage to do so). For Southern reactionaries, the Thirteenth Amendment was irrelevant; they would, in the postwar years and following the end of Reconstruction, find other methods to subordinate and repress the newly freed slaves. Although steps were taken to address these abuses, in the decades following Reconstruction blacks were in fact returned to a state of subordination and degradation. Infuriated at how suddenly reactionaries reclaimed control of the South, Northern politicians openly challenged Southern elections that had returned the former Southern elite to power. The radical Republicans seemed to have anticipated these developments. Even before the war was over, they offered up their most decidedly punitive Reconstruction plan in 1864, referred to as the Wade-Davis Bill:

- Slavery was banned in the United States.
- All former high-ranking military, political, and economic (planter class) leaders of the former Confederacy, like Robert E. Lee and Jefferson Davis, were disenfranchised.
- Unlike Lincoln's modest 10 percent requirement for readmission, the radical Republicans required a more substantial commitment: 50 percent of a state's citizens must swear loyalty and allegiance to the United States.

A little over a year after becoming president, Johnson was in direct confrontation with the radical Republicans, led by Senator Charles Sumner (who before the war had been beaten to within an inch of his life by a South Carolina congressman, Preston Brooks, *in the Senate chamber*), and Representative Thaddeus Stevens. The conflict centered on a piece of legislation called the Civil Rights Act of 1866, which included the following features:

- Blacks were to be considered citizens of the United States, entitled to all the rights and privileges expressed in the U.S. Constitution.
- Attempts to restrict basic rights, such as owning property and testifying in a court of law, were illegal.
- The federal government, not the states, would enforce the act.

Johnson's veto of the bill was overridden by Congress; however, supporters of the legislation feared that the Supreme Court would rule the bill unconstitutional. Something more permanent was necessary.

THE FOURTEENTH AMENDMENT

Whereas the Thirteenth Amendment ended slavery, the Fourteenth defined citizenship rights, not only for freed slaves, but for all Americans. At least that was the implication. Women and minority groups would have to continue their battle for equal rights as citizens under the Constitution. Pointedly attacking the Black Codes, Congress's passage of the amendment established the following constitutional limitations on a state's power to modify or eliminate the rights of its citizens under the federal government. (Keep in mind that not until the 1950s would the federal government expand protection of Fourteenth Amendment rights to other civil rights groups, such as women, children, and those accused of a crime.) The most important provisions of the Fourteenth Amendment include the following:

- All persons who are born in or who are naturalized in the United States are citizens.
- A citizen of the United States cannot be denied *equal protection under the law* and must be provided *due process rights* under the law regardless of race, gender, class, religion, political views, or ethnicity.
- Any state that refuses a segment of its population protection and rights accorded them by this amendment would suffer a reduction in its congressional representation.

Knowing they had an ally in the White House, Southern states refused to ratify the Fourteenth Amendment, especially since one clause prohibited former Confederate leaders from holding state or federal offices. Again, battle lines were drawn. The radical Republicans mobilized their forces and sought to outmaneuver their opponents, whether they were in Southern state assemblies, the U.S. Congress, or even in the Oval Office.

THE RADICAL REPUBLICANS ASCENDANT

In the summer of 1866 the radical Republicans acted after a joint committee of Congress recommended that those Southern politicians elected to Congress under Johnson's lenient requirements for readmission and representation be barred from taking their seats. Moreover, the committee placed the responsibility and authority for Reconstruction under the direction of the legislative branch, thus devaluing the chief executive's role. Consequently, from 1867 to 1870 the radical Republicans were at the height of their power. In that brief time they instituted sweeping policies, with the Fourteenth Amendment as their guide. First and foremost they replaced Johnson's Reconstruction plan with their own.

The former Confederate states would be divided into five military zones, each governed by a U.S. army general entrusted with considerable powers.

In order for a state to be readmitted into the Union it had to ratify the Fourteenth Amendment and establish state constitutions that would guarantee black suffrage and disenfranchise ex-Confederate leaders. (In 1870, Hiram Revels of Mississippi became the nation's first black congressman when he was elected to the Senate seat previously occupied by the former president of the Confederacy, Jefferson Davis. Ironically, Davis, who had been captured at the end of the war, had recently been released from a federal prison.) These state constitutions had first to be ratified by Congress before readmission was possible.

The right of blacks to vote would be guaranteed by the federal government, which would oversee voting in the Southern states.

By the end of Reconstruction in the late 1870s, only three states had not been readmitted into the Union and were therefore still under the control of the military.

THE IMPEACHMENT OF PRESIDENT JOHNSON

Fully aware that their nemesis in the White House would continually attempt to thwart their plans, the radical Republicans passed the Tenure of Office Act over the president's veto. In retrospect, the act appears as a trap waiting to ensnare President Johnson, for it prohibited the president from removing civilian or military officials without the consent of the Senate. In essence, it profoundly reduced his authority as commander in chief. As expected, Johnson believed that the law encroached on the authority granted to the executive branch by the Constitution, and he set about to challenge the Tenure of Office Act. The obvious target was Secretary of State Edwin Stanton, who not only was allied with the radical Republicans, but also supervised the South's military districts. When Johnson fired Stanton, the radical Republicans impeached him. Charged with numerous counts of "high crimes and misdemeanors," Johnson avoided removal from office by merely one Senate vote. Retrospectively, the impeachment and trial seem purely politically motivated. Had Johnson been removed from office, a dangerous precedent would have been established. Not only would it have seriously damaged the system of checks and balances—not to mention the independence of the executive branch—it would encourage any subsequent majority political party in Congress to remove a sitting president for political reasons. Although he survived removal, Johnson was greatly weakened and posed no further serious threat to the radical Republican agenda.

REACTIONARIES AND RACISTS RESPOND TO RECONSTRUCTION

Most Southerners disdained the Republicans' reconstruction of the south. Over time they took the following steps to regain control:

- Many in the South's upper class believed it best to accept the Republicans' measures, gain the trust of the new black voters, and proceed to use this newfound relationship to entice them to become Democrats.
- They worked to gradually regain control of the state legislatures from, among others, "scalawags" (Southerners allied with radical Reconstruction). While some white politicians hoped to appeal to black voters, poor whites rejected this since the war had exacerbated their condition. The last thing they wanted was political and economic competition from poor blacks.
- Violence and intimidation were used against blacks to maintain their subordination. To this end, various antiblack, anti-Republican reactionary groups, such as the Ku Klux Klan (KKK) and the

Knights of the White Camellia, were created. Utilizing violence and intimidation as their methods of control, such as burning homes, whippings, and lynching, the Klan and the Knights were determined to keep blacks and sympathetic whites from voting. Garbed in white hoods and gowns, carrying torches, and firing weapons, the KKK would sweep down on unsuspecting victims, whether in their homes or at political meetings, and terrorize them. Although moderate whites condemned such actions, many terrified blacks and white Republicans stayed away from the polls. Not to be deterred, Congress passed the Force Act and the Ku Klux Klan Act, which made it illegal to use force or intimidation with the intention of disenfranchising citizens and denying them their Fourteenth and Fifteenth Amendment rights. The president was authorized to use military force to carry out these acts. Although membership in the Klan diminished, their use of fear and terror had panicked enough voters that by 1876 only three Southern states (South Carolina, Florida, and Louisiana) still had radical Republican state governments.

By the time the Force Act and the Ku Klux Klan Act were passed, the radical Republicans had already reached the zenith of their power and influence. Soon they would experience a precipitous decline, to be replaced by more conservative-minded political leaders. Yet they had at least one more significant bill left to pass: the Civil Rights Act of 1875. This far-reaching piece of legislation called for full equality in all public facilities—in other words, access to public accommodations and institutions could not be denied based on race. Unfortunately, the Supreme Court ruled the act unconstitutional in 1883. The nation would not see the likes of such legislation for over eighty years.

THE END OF RECONSTRUCTION: THE ELECTION OF 1876 AND THE COMPROMISE OF 1877

Reconstruction's life span did not exceed two decades, leaving students of history to ponder the circumstances of its short existence and sudden demise. Just as paleontologists often reflect on why the dinosaurs died off after flourishing for millions of years, historians are compelled to ask the same of Reconstruction's very brief life. Of course, there are any number of plausible explanations, one of which has to do with the state of the nation in the mid-1870s, when the motivation for continuing Reconstruction was waning.

- Starting in 1873, the nation experienced a depression. Funding to sustain Reconstruction was drying up. At the same time, sympathetic whites in the North were more concerned with their own economic situation than with those in the South.
- The hegemonic upper classes in both the North and South were concerned that the masses would somehow unite and threaten their interests. And, at the end of Reconstruction, the railroad strike of 1877 did little to assuage their fears.
- Because they were no longer enemies, the ruling elites in the North and South were increasingly interdependent as a result of their mutual economic interests.

- Given its power in the North and ever-expanding West, the Republican party no longer believed it had to dominate in all regions of the United States.
- Corruption and scandal were rampant.
    - The Grant administration was riddled with corrupt officials ("spoilsmen") and illegal deals—for example, the Crédit Mobilier scandal and the Whiskey Ring.
    - In some municipal governments, such as New York City's Tweed Ring, there were glaring abuses. Through the efforts of political cartoonist Thomas Nast, the extent of the Tweed Ring's corruption was conveyed to the public in persuasive images that influenced citizens to demand investigations into the abuses. As a result, some began to hold the view that Reconstruction programs were another way for corrupt and opportunistic politicians and businessmen to get rich at the public's expense.
    - Some Northerners were appalled by reports of corruption in Reconstruction governments.
    - There were abuses on Wall Street—for example, the attempt by financiers Gould and Fisk to corner the gold market in 1869,

Given these factors, many were tiring of the Grant administration and the Republican party. Conditions were rife for a change. However, the election of 1876 showed just how politically divided the nation had become. The Republicans ran a Civil War veteran and governor of Ohio, Rutherford B. Hayes. His Democratic opponent was New York's reform governor, Samuel J. Tilden. Tilden initially won both the electoral and popular vote, but Republicans charged that several Southern states had denied many blacks their right to vote; they contended that these were votes lost to the Republican candidate. For a time, there seemed to be no clear winner. On the one hand, the Democrats were certain their candidate had won; on the other hand, the Republicans claimed the election results in the states where the alleged abuses occurred should be nullified. A special electoral committee was established to decide which candidate was entitled to the disputed votes. Given the makeup of the commission (eight Republicans, seven Democrats), a partisan decision was made to give all of the contested votes to the Republican Hayes. Outraged Democrats threatened to filibuster the decision in the House of Representatives. The nation was in political limbo. And then, a deal was struck. The Southern Democrats relinquished the contested votes and therefore the election to Hayes and the Republicans in return for

- the removal of the remaining federal troops from the South
- federally funded development of a Southern railroad network
- the appointment of a Democrat to Hayes's cabinet

With this agreement, Reconstruction came to a sudden and, some would argue, premature end.

THE LEGACY OF RECONSTRUCTION

In the short term, blacks in the South found themselves languishing in a form of agrarian servitude once more. They were relegated to sharecropping whereby, under contract, they often labored in the same fields they had worked as slaves. Even as tenant farmers (a slight improvement over sharecropping) who received tools and seed in return for usually half their crop, freedmen toiled their lives away once again in abject poverty and misery.

Decades later, at the turn of the twentieth century, blacks were still living a marginal existence. Following the Supreme Court's *Plessy v. Ferguson* ("separate but equal") decision in 1896, whatever hope they may have had about equal protection under the law and social acceptance had turned to dust. "What happens to a dream deferred?" asked the black poet Langston Hughes. "It dries up like a raisin in the sun." For many blacks who had lived through slavery, the Black Codes, and the terror of "night riders" such as the KKK, the end of Reconstruction bequeathed to them a new form of misery known by the name Jim Crow laws, which further subordinated blacks in the South in the following ways:

- Political restrictions were imposed to circumvent the Fifteenth Amendment:
  - Poll taxes, a fee for voting, disenfranchized the poor, blacks and whites alike.
  - Literacy tests worked because there were very few schools for blacks in the South.
  - The grandfather clause (if your grandfather had the right to vote, you did as well) excluded most blacks because their grandfathers had been slaves.
  - Gerrymandering, the redrawing of voting districts to alter a racial, ethnic, or political majority, was used to neutralize votes.
- Blacks were denied access to many public and municipal facilities such as parks, theaters, housing, and mass transit. When Jim Crow laws failed to intimidate recalcitrant blacks, they were often threatened, beaten, and lynched.
- Various economic sanctions were placed on blacks in order to maintain their subjugated status and keep them dependent on their fellow white Southerners.

Still, Reconstruction did set a precedent that would stand the test of time. Government can and often does intervene to redress grievances and address the social, economic, and political needs of those who have been exploited. Reconstruction was quite possibly a failure, especially for those who lived through its promise of hope and equality. Yet, as with all reform movements, it did at the very least attempt to raise the consciousness of Americans about their own definitions of democracy, and at times it succeeded. For blacks, some educational opportunities were now available, and as a race they had finally experienced the cherished right to vote and elect fellow blacks to important positions during Reconstruction.

Unfortunately, over one hundred years after the last federal troops were withdrawn from the South, black Americans were still fighting for their rights and hoping that, unlike their ancestors, their dream would not be deferred.

Multiple-Choice Questions

1. The original purpose of the Freedmen's Bureau was to
   (A) generate support among Southern whites to attempt to end federal military occupation
   (B) organize blacks as sharecroppers
   (C) provide freed blacks with food, clothing, and educational opportunities
   (D) register blacks to vote
   (E) enroll poor whites and blacks in trade unions

ANSWER: **C**. The Freedmen's Bureau, which helped poor blacks and whites, is considered an important success of Reconstruction, despite various claims that some Bureau employees were corrupt (*The American Pageant*, 12th ed., p. 476/11th ed., p. 485).

2. Lincoln's plan for Reconstruction, developed in 1863, allowed for a state to be readmitted once
   (A) fifty percent of its voters took an oath of allegiance to the Union
   (B) the state legislature ratified the Fourteenth and Fifteenth Amendments
   (C) ten percent of its voters repudiated the contract theory
   (D) it paid for war damages caused by the Confederate army
   (E) it abolished slavery

ANSWER: E. Option A describes the radical Republicans' Reconstruction plan. Option B is incorrect since both amendments were passed after the war. Southern citizens were never asked to repudiate the contract theory--option C. If anything, they would be asked to repudiate the compact theory, which the Supreme Court nevertheless did in the *Texas v. White* decision. The South was never called on to pay war reparations—option D (*The American Pageant*, 12th ed., p. 483/11th ed., p.493).

3. The Fourteenth Amendment to the Constitution
   (A) abolished slavery
   (B) gave to the federal government supreme authority over the states
   (C) gave black males the right to vote
   (D) defined citizenship rights
   (E) gave to women the right to vote

ANSWER: **D**. The Thirteenth, Fourteenth, and Fifteenth Amendments were all passed between 1865 and 1870. The Fourteenth Amendment entitled blacks to the same citizenship rights as other Americans (*The American Pageant,* 12th ed., p. 476/11th ed., p. 485).

4. Carpetbaggers were
   (A) Southerners who supported radical Republican governments in the South
   (B) Northerners such as teachers and ministers who traveled South after the war to aid the freedmen
   (C) former Confederate political leaders who regained their political seats in Congress when Reconstruction ended
   (D) freed blacks who fled the South after being emancipated
   (E) Southern governments that refused to accept the Thirteenth Amendment

ANSWER: **B**. Though unwelcome by some Southerners as opportunists seeking to get rich off the South's misfortune, many sacrificed the comforts of home to help the freed slaves and poor whites of the South (*The American Pageant,* 12th ed., p. 492/11th ed., p. 502).

5. Andrew Johnson was impeached because
   (A) Southerners were opposed to his radical Reconstruction policies
   (B) he failed to enforce federal law in combating the KKK
   (C) he was involved in the assassination of President Lincoln
   (D) his administration was involved in a number of corrupt activities
   (E) he was an obstacle to the radical Republicans' Reconstruction plan

ANSWER: **E**. President Johnson's policies conflicted with the radical Republican agenda. When he challenged the Tenure of Office Act he was impeached (*The American Pageant,* 12th ed., pp. 486-487/11th ed., p. 496).

6. In the election of 1876
   (A) the Republicans swept the South
   (B) the contested election was decided by the Supreme Court
   (C) Tilden received more electoral votes but far fewer popular votes than Hayes
   (D) most white Southerners refused to vote
   (E) Republicans claimed that blacks had been denied the right to vote in several Southern states

ANSWER: **E.** Due to this claim, the election was thrown into turmoil. Whites in the South generally voted Democrat—options A & D; a special electoral commission, not the Supreme Court, decided in Hayes's favor (*The American Pageant*, 12th ed., pp. 508-509/11th ed., p. 519).

7. Which of the following did NOT attempt to disenfranchise black voters?
   (A) Force Act
   (B) gerrymandering
   (C) literacy test
   (D) grandfather clause
   (E) poll tax

ANSWER: **A.** The Force Act was passed to address the abuses of groups such as the KKK (*The American Pageant*, 12th ed., p. 493/11th ed., p. 503).

8. Jim Crow laws
   (A) were ruled unconstitutional by the U.S. Supreme Court immediately following the end of the war
   (B) were designed to subordinate blacks
   (C) allowed for the integration of all public facilities
   (D) were passed by the radical Republicans
   (E) were designed to address the abuses of racist organizations such as the KKK and the Knights of the White Camellia.

ANSWER: **B.** Years after the end of Reconstruction, Jim Crow laws were passed to segregate and subordinate blacks in the South (*The American Pageant*, 12th ed., pp. 510–511/11th ed., pp. 521-522).

9. Hiram Revels
   (A) was the leader of the radical Republicans in the House of Representatives
   (B) was head of the Freedmen's Bureau
   (C) was involved in a scandal which seriously damaged the Grant administration
   (D) was the first black American elected to Congress
   (E) was instrumental in organizing the KKK

ANSWER: **D.** Elected to the Senate in 1870, Revels was the first of his race to serve in Congress (*The American Pageant*, 12th ed., p. 491/11th ed., p. 501).

10. In the compromise that was reached by Republicans and Democrats over the impasse in the presidential election between Hayes and Tilden,
    (A) Tilden was given the presidency in return for selecting Republicans for every cabinet position in his administration
    (B) The radical Republicans agreed to disband if Hayes was given the presidency
    (C) Southerners generally voted for a third-party candidate
    (D) Hayes was given the presidency if the South agreed to ratify the Fifteenth Amendment
    (E) Hayes was given the presidency in return for the removal of federal troops from the South

ANSWER: E. This agreement effectively ended Reconstruction (*The American Pageant*, 12th ed., p. 509/11th ed., p. 520).

Free-Response Questions

1. Analyze the differences and similarities of the three major Reconstruction plans: Lincoln's, Johnson's, and the radical Republicans'.

RESPONSE You should point out the similarities between Lincoln's and Johnson's plans. Both sought a quick readmission process. Lincoln maintained that the political leadership of the South, not the Southern people, had seceded. The radical Republicans believed in a punitive Reconstruction plan that would also guarantee the rights of blacks. Generally speaking, the Republicans in Congress sought to enfranchise blacks and provide economic aid in the South for two reasons: to keep blacks in the South so that they would not compete with Northern laborers for jobs, and to create the nucleus of a Southern Republican party. Thus it is important to discuss Reconstruction as a struggle between the executive and legislative branches.

2. To what extent can Reconstruction be considered both a success and a failure?

RESPONSE As with all questions that begin with "To what extent," there can be a wide range of responses. Organize your information based on a list of the successes and failures—categorized as economic, political, or social—of Reconstruction. Remember that the question does not ask whether Reconstruction was a success *or* a failure but to what extent it was a success *and* a failure. Thus pointing out, say, the economic accomplishments of Reconstruction may include the work of the Freedmen's Bureau and the development of black educational institutions, as well as a negative economic effect: sharecropping and the crop-lien system.

10

THE INDUSTRIAL ERA: 1876–1900

When Reconstruction ended in 1877, the United States was still a mostly agricultural nation that contained some large commercial urban areas, such as New York and Philadelphia, yet also small towns, villages, and hamlets. In many places the economic landscape had been scarcely changed by the Civil War. After all, economic development never occurs evenly in a nation. Yet by the end of the century, new major metropolitan areas such as Chicago and Pittsburgh had sprung up where a few decades earlier there had been an "urban frontier." By 1885 Chicago boasted a ten-story skyscraper. By 1900 America's urban population was three times larger than it had been just thirty years earlier. By 1920 more Americans would live in cities than on farms or in small rural towns. Think of a person who was born around 1830. When he is in his seventies he leaves, say, rural Vermont for a visit to New York City. Amazed, he sees electric trolleys and buildings that dwarf anything in the towns nearest his home. He notices that many buildings have indoor plumbing, electricity, and even telephones. Large commercial areas dot the urban landscape. Department stores are many times larger than the stores in which he has ever shopped. Urban dwellers converse with one another in languages he has never heard before, for many are foreign-born. Looking across the East River toward Brooklyn, he sees the engineering marvel of his day, a massive steel structure, the Brooklyn Bridge. Yet behind the technology, the architectural wonders, and the excitement of city life, our traveler soon notices the darker side of modernization, industry, and urbanization: poverty, congestion, pollution, corruption, and crime.

KEY CONCEPTS

- The state and federal governments played significant roles in promoting business interests.
- This period witnessed the rise of the corporation.
- Proponents and opponents of the government in assisting laissez-faire capitalism offered numerous justifications for their positions.
- The U.S. economy expanded enormously during the late nineteenth century, easily surpassing European industrial nations.
- Representing different objectives and memberships, labor unions formed, and major strikes occurred in the period.
- The Supreme Court handed down decisions that for the most part favored business by controlling unions and undoing legislation that would interfere with capital accumulation.

Industrialization and the period of rapid capital accumulation are discussed in depth in *The American Pageant,* 12th ed., Chapters 23-25/11th ed., Chapters 24-26

THE RISE AND DEVELOPMENT OF INDUSTRIALISM IN AMERICA

At the end of the Civil War the United States ranked fourth in industrial output, behind Britain, France, and Germany. By the close of the century, in many industries, the United States produced more than the other three *combined.* So extensive was U.S. industrial growth in the late nineteenth and early twentieth centuries that one historian referred to this era as "the Second American Revolution." Consider some statistics:

- Between 1869 and 1913 the GNP rose by 56 percent.
- Between 1860 and 1900 wheat and corn production, spurred by the new technology in agricultural machinery, grew by 200 percent.
- Bituminous coal production increased 2,000 percent.
- Petroleum production increased over 9,000 percent.
- Steel production increased over 10,000 percent.
- Over 150,000 miles of new railroad track was laid between 1865 and 1895.
- By the first decade of the twentieth century, the United States accounted for one-third of the world's manufacturing capacity.

By 1900 the transition of the U.S. economy to an advanced, centralized, and government-supported industrial-capitalist system was complete in every region of the nation. (This is not to imply, however, that every region experienced industrialization and the impact of technology simultaneously.) As the United States entered the twentieth century it was well on its way to becoming a nation of industry, large urban areas, interconnected economies, and large-scale business enterprises. While much of this transformation was occurring in the nation's industrial hub, the Northeast, the West and the South were experiencing profound changes as well. The South, which had been devastated by the Civil War, experienced dramatic economic growth and diversification. Before the century was out, major southern cities such as Birmingham, Alabama, and Memphis, Tennessee, were producing enormous amounts of steel and lumber. In large part the availability of cheap labor (southern workers faced even more significant obstacles in organizing unions than their counterparts in the North), well-developed transportation and communication systems, and the acceptance of capitalist principles played central roles in the development of the New South. Out West, as the frontiers of the nation expanded, so too did industry and commerce. Stimulated by demand in the East and aided by the continuing construction of an integrated national railway system, western cattle and mining industries flourished. What accounts for this incredible transformation? Remember that every effect has numerous causes.

AP Tip

A College Board essay dealing with this period will most certainly require you to understand the causes and effects of the enormous expansion of the U.S. economy in the post-Civil War period.

Although less active than today, the federal government in the late nineteenth century played a decisive role in promoting business interests.

- The federal government imposed protective tariffs.
- The government encouraged a boom in railroad construction through, for instance, land grants (over 200 million acres were offered to railroad companies by states and the federal government). The Pacific Railroad Act not only provided enormous tracts of land to railroad companies but also granted them substantial loans as well. Unfortunately, the price of western land rose higher than what the government intended when railroad companies sold their surplus land at ever-higher prices.
- By aiding in the settlement of the West, a national market was created. When the Republican Congress passed the Homestead Act, in 1862, it freed up many acres of excellent land for settlers moving to the West.
- Mineral-rich land was sold by the Public Land Office for as little as $2.50 an acre.
- The federal government adopted a loose immigration policy that, by providing more laborers, increased production and demand in the domestic market. While the problem of labor shortages was effectively addressed by this policy, it also had the undesired effect of driving down wages for laborers.
- The government also encouraged capital investment by leaving large-scale businesses virtually untaxed.
- Foreign capital investments helped stimulate the creation of new industries and businesses in the United States.

The ascendancy of the corporation was the result of the capitalist class's success in controlling the free market system, thereby ensuring profitability and economic growth. This was accomplished by

- regulating production
- creating stable markets
- setting prices and wages

The following were factors that brought about the enormous production of industrial commodities, which in turn concentrated considerable wealth in the hands of the nation's most successful capitalists:

- new technological developments, such as the steam engine, conveyer belt, and better construction materials (steel)
- a huge labor force of men, women, and even children
- large-scale factories and production centers
- an enormous amount of capital

With abundant resources—technological, economic, and human— and little government restraint, some larger-than-life personalities emerged from the capitalist class.

- **Andrew Carnegie** A poor Scottish immigrant, he eventually came to dominate the steel industry. Using new technological innovations such as the Bessemer process, he was able to produce better steel at a lower price than his competitors. With considerable surplus capital at his disposal, he purchased everything necessary for the production of steel, such as land rich in iron-ore deposits (the Mesabi Range in Minnesota), and railroads and ships to transport the ore. This is called vertical integration—the control of all the steps necessary to turn raw materials into finished commodities. He retired in 1900 after selling his corporation to J. P. Morgan, but not before playing a major role in the development of the modern corporation. In his retirement he became a philanthropist and a living example to the defenders of the capitalist system that anyone could get rich in America.
- **John D. Rockefeller** Even at a young age he had his eyes set on accumulating great wealth. He paid a substitute to serve for him in the Civil War and set about amassing his fortune. His name was synonymous with the oil industry, which he came to control. He further concentrated his wealth through a variety of often extralegal methods such as the creation of trusts, horizontal and vertical integrations, and the holding company. Although oil prices decreased significantly (in early 1861 from $10 a barrel to merely 10 cents later that year), Rockefeller's Standard Oil controlled approximately 90 percent of the nation's oil market. Prices again rose, but to an acceptable level.
- **William H. Vanderbilt** Like his father, Cornelius (who once ranted at a competitor, "I won't sue you...I'll ruin you!"), William was a railroad magnate. For decades the family dominated the railroad industry.
- **J. P. Morgan** An investment banker, he was instrumental in funding corporations. By eliminating cutthroat competition in the railroad industry, whereby competing companies drove down prices and thus their own profits, he was able to consolidate rival railroad lines. He later went on to create U.S. Steel, the nation's first billion-dollar corporation. Due to a skin ailment, he had an enormously bulbous nose. His piercing eyes added to his persona.

Morgan was also lucky. At the last minute he canceled a cruise on a luxury liner, the *Titanic*.

THE ERA OF RAPID CAPITAL ACCUMULATION

For every Rockefeller or Carnegie success story, there were millions of citizens who lived in squalor and despair in America's industrial urban areas. Trade unions and social settlement houses as well as a few municipal aid societies tried to help the destitute worker and his family, but for most, life in industrial America was severe. Industrialists and their adherents continued to press for limited regulation of business and limited social spending to address poverty. After all, they argued, America was a land of opportunity for those willing to work hard, maintain self-discipline, and overcome whatever obstacles stood in the way of advancement and financial success. Few really believed that given these attributes you could become a Carnegie or a Morgan, but defenders of the status quo maintained that social mobility was available to all who sought it. Further, they contended, business functioned best when government limited its intervention. In 1776, the same year the American colonies declared their independence from Britain, economist Adam Smith had published *The Wealth of Nations,* a book that would become the economic bible for those later generations that favored limited government intervention (laissez-faire) in the affairs of business. Smith's thesis was that prices and wages and supply and demand were already regulated, not by government, but by the "invisible hand" (a self-seeking equilibrium) of the marketplace. A capitalist, Smith maintained, will not sell a commodity that is too costly for the consumer, nor will he offer wages that are unattractive to workers. Taking into account his costs to produce a commodity, the capitalist will naturally seek out a balance between costs and profit. The result is that supply will ultimately equal demand and the capitalist will realize a profit, all without government's "artificial" interference.

Yet most capitalists were not necessarily opposed to all government intervention—they were happy to see tariffs imposed—but they rejected any regulations that could reduce profits. Following the Civil War the U.S. government assisted industrial capitalism by protecting it from challenges by those who sought its regulation.

The relationship between government and big business took on two forms:

- State and federal court systems were used to prevent regulation of business by state legislatures. One critic has claimed that the Supreme Court became the "handmaiden" of private enterprise.
- Trade unions were suppressed. Again, the federal court system was enlisted to achieve this goal. The Supreme Court fortified its protection of private enterprise under the "due process" clause in a series of landmark cases. Police, state militias, and the U.S. Army were also used to suppress labor activities.

The outcome of this view was, in many industries, not fair and equal competition, but the rise of monopoly capitalism. Ironically, the same competition that would drive capitalism was marginalized by monopolies, which sought to reduce competition.

With this view in mind, justifications that reinforced this idea of laissez-faire capitalism were developed to complement Smith's thesis. While certainly not a homogeneous group, advocates of the views presented below all saw capitalism, especially laissez-faire capitalism, as a highly developed step in social evolution.

- **Social Darwinism** Possibly the most influential justification of laissez-faire capitalism, this philosophy was developed by British social philosopher Herbert Spencer and popularized in the United States by Yale University's William Graham Sumner. It applied Charles Darwin's theory of evolution and natural selection to government, the marketplace, and society. Social Darwinists argued that government should not provide assistance to those who were unable to make it on their own, businesses and private citizens alike. Rather, society's "fittest," the wealthy, should be protected because it was this class through its development of businesses and as financial contributors to educational and cultural institutions that was improving the species.

- **Horatio Alger** His rags-to-riches stories popularized the notion that self-sacrifice, determination, and hard work could overcome poverty and result in financial success and social status. His fictional characters, such as Mark the Matchstick Boy, became an inspiration to young men pursuing the American Dream.

- **Russell Conwell** For those who were poor and could see no way out of their predicament, Conwell's "Acres of Diamonds" sermon was deflating to say the least: "It is your duty to get rich. It is wrong to be poor." Now the poor were not only destitute, they were "wrong" as well. Yet this view mirrored nicely the Social Darwinist notion that, as Shakespeare put it, "The fault...is not in our stars, But in ourselves, that we are underlings."

- **Carnegie's "Gospel of Wealth"** Why Carnegie ultimately became a philanthropist was explained in his article "(Gospel of) Wealth": It is the duty of the wealthy to contribute to society the wealth they have accrued through philanthropic programs. In other words, the wealthy, not government, was society's benefactor.

People who were most directly affected by the social consequences of industrialization advocated for reforms that would alleviate much of the suffering they were enduring socially, economically, and politically. Unfortunately, their political influence paled in comparison with the entrenched capitalist class. Reformers were not without their allies, however, for citizens who were important politically, religiously, and economically viewed reform as a way to prevent the radicalization and potentially revolutionary tendencies of the working class. For them, capitalism could be democratized, and qualitative changes could be made to living and working conditions without jettisoning the free market system. Still others interpreted Darwinism noticeably differently from the way Social Darwinists did. These Reform Darwinists maintained that through planning and cooperation, human evolution could and should overcome many of the challenges and obstacles that confronted previous generations. The following groups raised concerns about the impact of unregulated capitalism on the economy and society:

- **Journalists** such as Edward Bellamy, Henry George, and Henry D. Lloyd wrote articles critical of big business's "unethical" practices and monopolistic tendencies. One of their goals was to compel the government to impose regulations that would maintain the competitive nature of capitalism. Bellamy's *Looking Backward,* for instance, envisions a future world in which government applies socialist principles to society and the economy, such as the nationalization of industry.
- **Small producers** such as farmers complained of artificially inflated shipping rates that drove up their costs and increased commodity prices. Small businessmen complained that their powerful competitors engaged in unfair labor practices, which drove them out of business.
- **Consumers** demanded probing investigations into the ways that corporations used their control of the market to charge exorbitant prices. Many opposed trade barriers, removal of which would permit the law of supply and demand to operate effectively.
- **Social reformers** such as those associated with the social gospel movement, a Christian liberal following, established social settlement houses.
- **Radicals and revolutionaries** such as anarchists, socialists (led by Eugene Debs), and marxists maintained that capitalism was inherently exploitative and must be replaced by a more humane economic system.

LABOR UNIONS AND LABOR STRIKES

Disgusted by the poverty wages they were receiving while the owners of the means of production were reaping enormous profits, workers organized into trade unions that agitated for change. It is important to note that the methods and goals of trade unions were often quite disparate. The four major national trade unions in the late nineteenth century were

- **National Labor Union (NLU)** Formed right after the end of the Civil War, in many ways this union was years ahead of its time. It was the first trade union to organize workers regardless of their race and gender, whether they were skilled or unskilled. It was open to workers in both the agrarian and industrial sectors of the economy. Some of its goals were more modest (higher wages, the eight-hour workday) than others (gender and racial equality). At a time when the ten-hour workday was the norm and many workers toiled even longer hours, it was able to win the eight-hour workday for federal employees.
- **Knights of Labor** Organized in 1869 and led by Terence Powderly, its objectives were often radical though its methods were more modest. Like the NLU, which sought racial and gender equality, Powderly preferred arbitration to the strike. Its membership peaked at nearly three-quarters of a million members before its star faded in the wake of the Haymarket riots in 1886.

- **American Federation of Labor (AFL)** Very much a "bread and butter" union that was not out to change the world but to achieve what it considered were realistic and attainable goals, the AFL under its president, Samuel Gompers, was open exclusively to skilled workers. Far from being reform-minded, Gompers used the power of his membership (1 million by the turn of the century) to win concessions from management. By the standards of its time, it was more successful than the other major unions. Even so, it was not nearly as potent as it would become in the twentieth century.

- **Industrial Workers of the World (IWW)** If you were a radical imbued with a revolutionary spirit and willing to challenge the owners for control of the factories and businesses, the IWW was your ticket. The Wobblies, as they were called, were not content with merely increasing wages; ownership of the means of production by the working class was the only solution to the exploitative nature of the wage labor system, they believed. Sometimes violent, sometimes victimized by the government, the IWW presented a perspective of labor and social agitation that few unions could match. Naturally, they were led by a colorful figure, "Big Bill" Haywood.

You should also know the causes and effects of the major labor strikes of the period.

- **Railroad Strike of 1877** This was the first major post-Civil War strike and was indicative of labor unrest following the war. Employees of the Baltimore and Ohio struck when the company lowered their wages. The strike soon turned violent, and ultimately President Hayes called out the U.S. Army to suppress the strike.

- **Haymarket Square (Chicago) Riot of 1886** A labor demonstration organized to protest the treatment of workers at the nearby McCormick Harvester factory as well as methods used by police in dealing with the protestors abruptly ended when an unknown assailant threw a bomb that killed a number of police officers who had been ordered to break up the demonstration. Although there was no proof that they had been involved, eight anarchists were arrested, four of whom were executed. The public blamed trade unions for the violence.

- **The Homestead (Pennsylvania) Strike of 1892** Despite higher profits, the Carnegie Steel Company cut workers' wages. Accordingly, the workers went on strike. This in turn provided the company an opportunity to crush the union by hiring a private security company, the Pinkerton Detective Agency, to engage the strikers. When the strikers opened fire on the Pinkertons, killing several, the state militia was called in. Out of funds and out of hope, the union itself ended the strike.

- **The Pullman Strike of 1894** To be sure, no one likes to have his or her wages cut. Having it done during a major depression, however, so that the company can maintain stockholders' dividends, is demoralizing, to say the least. But that's what happened to employees of the Pullman Palace Car Company. A number of workers were even laid off. Led by the American Railway Union and its president, the soon-to-be head of the Socialist party Eugene Debs, a boycott was established that greatly affected the railroad industry in the Midwest. Members of the Railway Managers Association responded by calling on the federal government to intervene; they argued that the strikers were in restraint of trade. An injunction by a federal court, citing the Sherman Antitrust Act, did little to stop the strikers. The boycott was ended when President Cleveland sent in troops to make certain that the strikers did not interfere with the train delivery of the U.S. mail and when Debs and other union leaders were jailed for violating the federal injunction.

THE SUPREME COURT, CONGRESS, AND STATE LEGISLATURES WEIGH IN

The executive branch was not the only ally of big business. The judicial and legislative branches were also fundamental to the expansion of monopoly capitalism. However, on the state level actions were taken to address the needs of the exploited and impoverished lower classes. Essential to this concern was the Fourteenth Amendment, which defines citizenship rights. Specifically, the due process clause of this amendment, which gave state governments an indispensable responsibility to protect the life, liberty, and property of its citizens, was taken to mean by more reform-minded state governments that they had the authority to enact legislation that would address issues such as work and living conditions. A short list of problems addressed by such legislation would include

- housing laws
- regulating safety and health conditions in the workplace
- regulating corporations when their behavior and actions contradicted the well being of citizens and of the capitalist system
- sanitation laws
- minimum wage and maximum hour laws
- child labor laws

Reform governments were motivated to take such bold action for a variety of reasons:

- Many feared that the lower classes might demonstrate and riot if conditions deteriorated even further. In order to defuse this agitation, reforms to quell any potential revolutionary or radical spirit that might emanate from the masses were needed.
- Some individuals in positions of power were motivated by altruistic tendencies. For whatever personal and philosophical reasons, they could no longer maintain their neutrality given the abuses that swirled around them.
- The lower classes pressed the government to act on their behalf.

Paradoxically, many of these reforms were ruled unconstitutional by state and federal governments and the Supreme Court on the grounds that they violated corporations' due process rights! In other words, the Court ruled that corporations had the same Fourteenth Amendment rights as citizens; they were entitled to due process rights. One major piece of legislation and one federal court case sum up the sentiments of the nation's political and legal vanguard in the late nineteenth century:

- **The Sherman Anti-trust Act** The key clause of this law declares that "any combination or condition which is *in restraint of trade* is illegal." Many historians and political scientists have traditionally interpreted this to mean that the legislative branch was acting on behalf of the nation's economic system and its citizens by attacking monopolies (which, after all, seek to limit competition). Other historians claim the opposite is true. The act was passed in order to defuse public criticism of corporations, to restore the legitimacy of the government as the supporter of the public interest and not a mere appendage of business, and to attack trade unions. In the end, they argue, due to government undertakings such as the Sherman Anti-trust Act, monopoly capitalism was preserved, and unions that went out on strike were promptly served with a court injunction for being in restraint of trade.
- *United States v. E. C. Knight Company* After purchasing a competitor, the American Sugar Refining Company, the E. C. Knight Company controlled approximately ninety-eight percent of the sugar refining industry. Because of its economic power, E. C. Knight could prevent further challenges to its domination and determine market prices for its product. In retrospect, this appears to be a textbook example of a monopoly. But not so to the pro-business Supreme Court in the late nineteenth century. The Court ruling involved a rather creative rationale: because E. C. Knight was engaged in *manufacturing* sugar and not in interstate *commerce* (at least within the meaning of the law), it was regulated by state and not federal law. Therefore, it could not be dismantled by the federal government.

MAXIMIZING PROFITS: THE RATIONALE AND TACTICS OF THE CAPITALIST CLASS

To increase profits, a capitalist has to find a way to neutralize the competition. If you consider that capitalists are playing a game, albeit a very serious one, then understanding why they seek to concentrate as much capital as possible will help you comprehend the turn American businesses and the economy in general took in this period. The concentration of capital was accomplished in a number of ways, including

- using pools, gentlemen's agreements, mergers (horizontal and vertical), holding companies, and conglomerates
- cutting prices in the hope that the competition would not be able to sustain a loss of profits
- introducing labor-saving technology when the outlay of capital for new production technology is not so prohibitive as to be harmful
- expanding commodities into a competitor's marketplace
- engaging in industrial spying (for instance, the theft of research and development information)
- employing innovations in industrial and managerial organization and techniques

Because a major cost in the production process is labor, reducing this expense can not only lead to greater profits; it can allow the capitalist to use surplus funds to reinvest in the business, making it even more efficient and therefore more competitive. Naturally, trade unions, which seek higher wages and shorter hours, not to mention medical insurance, drive up the cost of production. Not surprisingly, unions were the bane of the capitalists' existence. Various tactics and methods were used by the capitalists to counteract trade union activities:

- The open shop gave workers a choice as to whether they must join a union if they work in a certain industry. Obviously, unions opposed the open shop because it undermined collective bargaining, the source of unions' effectiveness and strength; the potency of labor demands in a particular industry relates to the number of workers who are unionized.
- Replacement workers (derisively called "scabs" by union members) who are willing to take the jobs of those out on strike and often work for less pay were hired.
- Government was used to suppress trade union activities, such as strikes.
- Blacklists prevented union organizers and activists from employment opportunities.
- Workers were compelled to sign yellow-dog contracts in which they agreed not to join a union.
- Subsistence wages were offered while the workday was often lengthened.
- Labor was intensified—informally referred to as "speed up."
- Low-wage immigrants, women, and children were employed.
- Divisions were created within the working class by paying differentiated wages, often based on race.

Workers, however, had their own tactics in attempting to convince their employers to recognize their unions as the legitimate collective bargaining agent:

- Closed shop meant that union membership was required. The rationale behind this seemingly undemocratic policy is to counteract the tactics of the employees.
- Unions picketed noncompliant businesses in the hope that the public would ally itself with the workers on strike.
- They slowed down the production process, which naturally reduces profits.
- They used sabotage to destroy company property.
- Workers physically occupied the factory or workplace ("sit-down strike"), though this was more popular in the 1930s than in the late nineteenth century.

Despite these tactics, membership in U.S. trade unions never exceeded more than three percent by the turn of the century.

As the nineteenth century came to a close, the United States had reached new heights in its economic development. To be sure, it had taken its place among the other economic giants of the Western world. Its growth was testimony to the enormous productive capabilities of the capitalist system. What is more, enormous fortunes had been made and important companies were created, many of which continue to shape our lives. But a substantial price had been paid in terms of misery, poverty, and the despair of America's wage laborers. True,

America's workers did experience an improvement in their standard of living, but the industrial process reduced them to mere cogs in the machine. Although the federal government had failed to address the plight of the nation's workers, it recognized their contribution in at least one way. In 1894 the U.S. Congress made Labor Day a national holiday.

Multiple-Choice Questions

1. Andrew Carnegie's use of the vertical integration was significant in that it
   (A) synthesized the various immigrant labor groups into one cohesive productive force
   (B) led to substantial cooperation between industry and banking
   (C) stimulated competition in the steel industry
   (D) allowed a capitalist to control all aspects of the production process
   (E) ultimately led to the construction of massive steel factories in Pittsburgh

ANSWER: **D**. Vertical integration allowed Carnegie, for example, to cut out the "middleman" by owning businesses necessary for the production of a commodity (*The American Pageant*, 12th ed., pp. 537-538/11th ed., pp. 545-546).

2. Which of the following statements accurately reflects the impact that industrialization had on the American worker?
   (A) The standard of living for most workers had declined by the late nineteenth century.
   (B) The standard of living for most workers improved by the late nineteenth century, but workers had become mere mechanisms in the production process.
   (C) Many wage laborers ultimately saved enough of their salaries to start their own small businesses.
   (D) Most workers came to develop a lasting economic and social bond with their employers.
   (E) Most workers experienced ever higher wages and even greater control over what they produced.

ANSWER: **B**. While there was an increase in worker salaries, the laboring class had little control over the production process. In other words, they were dispensable (*The American Pageant*, 12th ed., p. 548/11th ed., p. 555).

3. In his "Gospel of Wealth," Andrew Carnegie articulated the view that
    (A) the wealthy were entitled to their riches and had no responsibility to share it with others
    (B) only those born into wealth were the real economic leaders of the nation
    (C) religious leaders had a responsibility to convince their parishioners that success was attainable to those who worked hard
    (D) capitalism and Christianity were intimately related in the progress of individuals and nations
    (E) the wealthy were morally obligated to use some of their wealth for the improvement of society

ANSWER: **E**. This helps to explain why Carnegie became a philanthropist after he retired from business. His contributions made Carnegie Hall and the Carnegie Endowment for Peace possible (*The American Pageant*, 12th ed., p. 542/11th ed., p. 550).

4. By the late nineteenth century
    (A) the U.S. economy ranked fourth in the industrialized world
    (B) the United States had bypassed France and Germany industrial output, but still lagged behind Great Britain
    (C) the U.S. economy had fallen to fourth in industrial output behind Britain, France, and Germany
    (D) the U.S. economy was producing as much as Britain, France, and Germany combined in many sectors
    (E) the U.S. economy had not grown significantly since the 1860s

ANSWER: **D**. Incredibly, the United States ranked fourth after the Civil War and more than bypassed the other three major industrial nations by the turn of the century.

5. The Industrial Workers of the World differed from the other major trade unions in that
    (A) it sought to negotiate and mediate its differences with management
    (B) unlike the other unions, it disdained using boycotts and strikes against capital
    (C) its objective was to eliminate the private ownership of the means of production
    (D) it was recognized by capitalists as the legitimate bargaining agent of its members
    (E) it was outlawed by the U.S. government

ANSWER: **C**. Composed of radicals, the IWW wanted to eliminate private ownership of factories and major businesses.

6. Which of the following would NOT be used by a supporter of the capitalist system as it existed in the Gilded Age?
    (A) Reform Darwinism
    (B) Social Darwinism
    (C) Russell Conwell's, "Acres of Diamonds" sermon
    (D) the novels of Horatio Alger
    (E) the perspective held by Herbert Spencer

ANSWER: **A**. Options B-E justify, condone, or support the capitalist class's control of society, government, and business.

7. In order to promote the interests of labor, trade unions would support
    (A) the open shop
    (B) collective bargaining
    (C) subsistence wages
    (D) yellow-dog contracts
    (E) the closed shop

ANSWER: **E**. Options A-D would harm the interests of workers, whereas the closed shop would increase union membership (*The American Pageant*, 12th ed., p. 554/11th ed., p. 559).

8. The railroad strike of 1877
    (A) was the first time a president ordered U.S. troops to stop a strike
    (B) led to significant wage increases for railroad workers
    (C) was the first time that management recognized the legitimacy of a trade union
    (D) was the only time in the nineteenth century that government sided with the strikers
    (E) led to significant improvements in worker safety laws but not wage increases

ANSWER: **A**. President Hayes became the first U.S. president to use troops to quell a strike (*The American Pageant*, 12th ed., p. 511/11th ed., p. 522).

9. This capitalist created U.S. Steel, the nation's first billion-dollar corporation
    (A) Andrew Carnegie
    (B) J. P. Morgan
    (C) "Big Bill" Haywood
    (D) Cornelius Vanderbilt
    (E) John D. Rockefeller

ANSWER: **B** (*The American Pageant*, 12th ed., pp. 539-540/11th ed., pp. 547-548).

10. In *United States v. E. C. Knight Company,* the Supreme Court ruled that
    (A) trade unions that were on strike were in restraint of trade
    (B) monopolies such as the E.C. Knight Company were illegal combinations
    (C) since the company was involved in production and not commerce, it fell under state jurisdiction
    (D) monopolies were in restraint of trade
    (E) vertical integration was not in restraint of trade

ANSWER: **C**. Ruling in the company's favor the Court interpreted the meanings of commerce and production in a literal and narrow sense.

Free-Response Questions

1. To what extent did government assist in the rise of corporate capitalism following the Civil War?

RESPONSE You may want to begin your essay with a brief discussion of the expansion of the role of government during the Civil War and its continued expansion in the postwar era. Policies that the government used to assist corporations include a protective tariff and land grants to railroad companies. Keep in mind that the question is asking "to what extent" the government assisted. Also, discuss the role played in suppressing labor as well as the pro-business decisions handed down by state and federal courts.

2. How successful was the trade union movement in the post-Civil War era? In your answer cite the following:
   organizing workers
   achieving economic goals

RESPONSE You should indicate that the growth of industry and corporate capitalism during and after the Civil War led to tensions between the capitalists and their employees. Keeping in mind that the government and business were allied, you many want to briefly discuss the various strikes and the responses of the government and capitalists to them as well as the divisions within labor itself—some unions were more radical than others; some were exclusionary based on race or skill level. Thus a response may indicate that trade unions were generally successful in organizing workers but not particularly successful in achieving their goals.

11

POSTWAR POLITICS AND THE POPULISTS: 1870s–1896

Republican administrations, which dominated the federal government in the late nineteenth century, did much to support the rise of big business. The populists represented a wide coalition of groups that had a broad political platform. With the demise of the movement, many would find a home in the Democratic party.

KEY CONCEPTS

- Republican presidents dominated the postwar era and tended to support big business.
- The Grange, Farmers' Alliances, and Populists emerged to contest big business's control over the marketplace.
- The Populists were a diverse coalition that sought to confront a wide variety of urban and rural problems.
- The Populists and Democratic party fused in the late nineteenth century.

This period is discussed in depth in *The American Pageant*, 12th ed., Chapters 23-26/11th ed., Chapters 24-27.

POLITICS IN THE GILDED AGE

Despite his success as a military leader, Ulysses S. Grant's two terms in the White House (1869-1877) were anything but stellar. In fact, historians consistently rank Grant among the two or three worst presidents in the nation's history. Skilled on the battlefield, Grant obviously lost his edge upon becoming president. Although honest himself, he was surrounded by corrupt officials, friends, and appointees who did not know or care to know the meanings of honesty and responsibility. But with a diminished Democratic party, at least in the North and West (it was very strong in the South), Americans ultimately were faced with a dubious task of selecting from different varieties of Republicans. This they did with great regularity. In fact, with the exception of Grover Cleveland's two nonconsecutive terms (1885-1889 and 1893-1897), the United States did not elect a Democrat to serve in the White House until Woodrow Wilson's victory in the 1912 election. Unfortunately for the American people, the vast majority of presidents who served the nation after the Civil War and until the turn of the century were mediocre political leaders. The administrations of Hayes, Garfield, Arthur, and Harrison reflected the political stalemate and patronage problems that shaped the Gilded Age as well as a desire by many Americans for a "do-little" government following the abuses that occurred in Grant's terms.

- **Hayes** Although his election (or, critics would say, selection) ended Reconstruction, he did try to restore honesty to government after the corruption that plagued the Grant administration. A temperance supporter, he also unfortunately sought to limit Chinese immigration.

- **Garfield** Because of an assassin's bullet, he served only four months, but his election reflected the bitter division that existed within the Republican party between the conservative "Stalwarts" (led by Senator Roscoe Conkling) and the more reform-minded "Halfbreeds" (led by James Blaine). The commonality between the two wings of the Republican party was that they both vied for power in order to have access to treasured patronage positions. A third wing of the Republican party, the Mugwumps, refused to join the patronage game. Eventually, the patronage problem was addressed in 1883 by the Pendleton Act, which established the Civil Service Commission.

- **Arthur** No reformer, he nonetheless distanced himself from the Stalwarts and supported civil service reform to address the problems of patronage and nepotism in government hiring practices. A supporter of a strong navy, his opposition to a high protective tariff cost him his party's renomination as president in 1884.

- **Harrison** In a long line of second-rate presidents, Harrison may very well be considered the most mediocre. More Americans voted for his opponent, Cleveland, but Harrison received more electoral votes, and therefore the presidency. In his one term in office, he played second fiddle to Congress—the legislative branch in this era was generally more influential. The emergence of the executive branch as the more dominant force coincided with the growing crises, both domestic and in foreign affairs, faced by the United States at the turn of the century.

THE TARIFF (AGAIN) AND THE "BILLION DOLLAR CONGRESS"

The tariff issue, always lurking below the surface, yet again played a role in the politics of the nineteenth century. The combatants this time were western farmers and eastern capitalists. During the war, the United States had been able to adopt a high protective tariff (the Morrill Tariff of 1861) because the southern obstacle to such a bill was no longer present in Congress. Not long after the war's end, southern Democrats and some of their northern Democratic allies objected to a high protective tariff on the grounds that it would increase the price of consumer goods as well as perhaps provoke a retaliatory tariff by foreign producers affected by the tax. As the agrarian sector began producing more and more food, foreign markets were increasingly playing a larger role in their sales. In the election campaign of 1888, an important question shaped the debate: Was a (high) protective tariff necessary? It was a question that for the first time in many years truly differentiated the two major political parties. Republican candidate Harrison and his party were able to convince many voters that lowering the tariff would wreck business prosperity and lead to mass unemployment, an issue that resonated with the nation's laboring classes. Not only was a Republican returned to the White House, where Harrison safeguarded the tariff but the party also had majorities in both houses of Congress. The new Republican Congress was active over the next decade politically and fiscally. (It became known as the first "billion-dollar Congress" due to its enormous expenditures.) Key pieces of legislation passed by this Congress include

- the McKinley Tariff of 1890
- the Sherman Silver Purchase Act of 1890
- the Sherman Anti-Trust Act of 1890
- a Negro voting rights bill, which was defeated
- the Wilson-Gorman Act of 1894, which increased the tariff
- increased monthly pensions to Civil War veterans and their families (a transparent attempt, opponents claimed, for the Republican party to retain the support of northern Civil War veterans and their families)

Although the tariff was a significant issue in the election, for many Americans it was not the only political issue. Possibly even more controversial was the debate over currency.

DEBATE OVER EXPANDING THE MONEY SUPPLY

Following the end of Reconstruction the nation engaged in an intense debate over whether to expand the amount of money in the economy. (Recall how this issue developed into a politically explosive controversy during the second Jackson term.) Too little money could have serious consequences for the financial system, not to mention those who would benefit or be hurt by one policy or the other.

Supporters of an expanded money supply included expectant capitalists, debtors, and farmers because this would enable them to

- borrow money at lower interest rates
- pay off their loans faster and easier with inflated dollars
- increase prices for the commodities they produced

After an economic depression called the Panic of 1873, many Americans suspected that the cause of the slump was the government's policy of backing its currency with gold, which restricted and therefore contracted the amount of money in the system. They favored a "soft" (or inflationary) currency (greenbacks) as well as unlimited minting of silver coins, which is also more inflationary than gold.

Opponents of an expanded money supply included bankers, entrenched capitalists (established businesses), creditors, and investors. They favored a "hard" (or deflationary) policy in which currency was backed by gold in U.S. government vaults. The benefits of this policy would be

- to allow currency to hold its value, since gold-backed money is less susceptible to inflationary instabilities
- to increase the value of gold as the population expanded (which it ultimately did, by as much as 300 percent in the thirty-year period following the end of the war)

In the short term the supporters of a hard money supply won out when Congress passed the Specie Resumption Act, in 1875, and thus withdrew the last of the greenbacks from circulation. Advocates of a soft money policy responded by creating the Greenback party to counteract the deflationary effects of the Specie Resumption Act. In the 1878 congressional elections, Greenback candidates received over 1 million votes, and fourteen of their candidates were elected. The most noteworthy of these was James B. Weaver, of Iowa, who would soon go on to form a broader party, the Populists. As for the Greenback party, it died out when the economic hard times of the 1870s ended, though the goal of expanding the supply of money was still very much alive. In the 1870s when Congress halted the coining of silver (referred to by critics as the "Crime of '73"), the debate intensified. When silver deposits were discovered in the West, demand for the use of silver to expand the money supply grew. Eventually a compromise was worked out in 1878, the Bland-Allison Act (which was passed over Hayes's veto). It allowed only a limited coining of silver ($2-4 million in silver each month at the standard silver to gold ratio, which was set at 16:1). Not satisfied with this deal, farmers, debtors, and western miners continued to press for unlimited coinage of silver.

Though certainly not limited to any two or three issues, farmers and their allies began to consider organizing to protest the government's adoption of what they viewed as injurious policies in regards to the railroads, the tariff, and hard money. At that very time, they were feeling most vulnerable because of changes in their sector of the economy.

THE GROWTH OF DISCONTENT: FARMERS ORGANIZE

Between the end of the Civil War and the turn of the century, the nation experienced enormous growth in terms of population, production, and demand for foodstuffs and commodities. In this thirty-five-year period the nation's population more than doubled and the number of farms tripled. As the nation urbanized, the demand for food increased significantly. Americans grew and consumed enormous amounts of food, leaving little for export. A number of factors (mostly having to do with technology and mechanization) led to this enormous burst of productivity in the agrarian sector of the economy:

- improvements in the cotton gin
- the introduction of harvesters, combines, and reapers
- improved plows made of stronger materials such as steel
- greater specialization in agricultural production—for example, wheat was grown mostly in the West

Consequently, the number of hours necessary to grow and harvest crops was more than halved in this period. But greater production doesn't always mean greater profits. Many forces and factors came together to harm farmers engaged in the free market economy of the late nineteenth century, among them the following:

- Grain elevator operators stored grain when it was not in transit, and often charged excessive rates.
- Manufacturers kept raising prices on their commodities, even as farmers found they had less disposable income.
- Banks increased interest on credit. Farmers in particular are reliant on credit and are therefore hurt by interest rate increases. Also, wealthy planters provided credit so that farmers could purchase seed and equipment. Known as the crop-lien system, it created a level of indebtedness that was difficult to pay off.
- Industries that farmers relied on for machinery kept raising the cost of harvesters and combines.
- The railroad industry became the symbol and focus of farmer discontent. It affected the profit levels farmers could earn from their labor because of shipping price increases. Furthermore, in many states the railroad industry was immune to regulations, especially the amounts they charged for long and short hauls, and set shipping rates arbitrarily. In addition, the industry was not beyond using nefarious measures to maximize profits.
- In some states regulations were nonexistent.

Within a twenty-year period, from about the end of Reconstruction to the mid-1890s, the market price of important crops such as wheat, corn, and cotton dwindled. Mary Elizabeth Lease, an attorney active in Farmers' Alliance affairs, provided farmers with a solution to their overproduction problems: "What you farmers have to do," she told them, "is to raise less corn and more hell!" This they indeed would do. In the last decade of the century, they would organize the Populist party.

As the United States continued its drive to industrial supremacy and as the capitalist class raked in enormous profits, the nation's growers experienced a downturn in their fortunes. There were a number of factors that help to explain the serious economic crisis that confronted the nation's farmers after the war, such as

- **The cost to introduce new time- and labor-saving technology** While this would undoubtedly increase production, it required significant expenditures, which often had to be borrowed with interest charged by the banks.
- **A great increase in the value of land** The availability of land was limited because so much land had been granted to railroad companies or sold to land speculators.
- **High taxes** Because states often rewarded railroad and grain storage companies with reduced taxes, the remainder was paid by private citizens.
- **The cost to store and ship grains and crops** These costs were very high.

Most farmers were not prepared for a transformation of the American economy following the Civil War, one that made them even more susceptible to the fluctuations that often occur in a market economy and frequently dry up profits, as happened to many farmers. By the 1880s numerous farms had been foreclosed on by banks; others were no longer owned but rented. Farmers were not willing to stand idle, however, while their livelihood was undermined by the frequent instability in market prices and ruinous interest, freight, and storage costs. Rather than sink into powerlessness, they organized. Not long after the end of the war, the National Grange of the Patrons of Husbandry was formed both to educate its members about new developments in agriculture and to create a social and cultural bond among farmers. It was not long, however, before the Grange became actively involved in politics. As membership in the organization quickly rose to 1.5 million members by mid-1870, it became a force to be reckoned with, especially in the Midwest and the South.

Utilizing their political clout, the Grangers were able to enact a number of laws that sought to address the abuses that were so damaging to their businesses. To this end, several "Granger laws" were passed to regulate the railroads and the grain elevator operators. However, though they were a potent force in the rural areas of the nation, farmers were met with strong opposition. Confronted by the railroad industry and the operators of the grain elevator and storage facilities, the farmers and their opponents faced off in federal court. In a series of landmark Supreme Court decisions, the farmers generally experienced success.

- *Munn v. Illinois* (1877) In the same year that President Hayes called out federal troops to crush a strike by workers in the railroad industry, the court handed down a pivotal decision. As in other states, the Grangers in Illinois had already obtained regulations for maximum rates that could be charged by grain elevator and storage facilities. These laws were often challenged by the owners of these businesses (who said the Granger cases were in violation of Fourteenth Amendment rights), and sometimes they ended up in federal court, such as the *Munn* case. So long as property was "devoted to public use," the court ruled, the states could place regulations on the railroads for the good of the public. The decision was not a complete victory for the farmers, for the Court decided that states could not regulate rates for long hauls. To compensate for their loss in short-haul rates, the railroad companies responded by inflating the long-haul rates.

- ***Peik v. the Chicago and Northwestern Railway* (1876)** The Supreme Court's decision in this case held that the Granger laws were not in violation of the federal government's power to regulate interstate trade and commerce and that states could establish their own interstate regulations when federal law was not present.
- ***Illinois v. Wabash* (1886)** The court reversed its earlier decision in the *Peik* case and ruled that commerce and trade that crossed state lines was directly under the authority of the federal government, not the states. Even Congress got into the act, passing the Interstate Commerce Act (which in turn created the Interstate Commerce Commission). Under the ICA's guidelines certain rules had to be obeyed, such as reasonable shipping rates and the elimination of abuses by the railway companies. It was given the authority to use the courts to compel recalcitrant railway companies to obey its policies.

In the early twentieth century, under the influence of the progressives (those who sought political and economic reforms), further legislation would regulate the railroad industry. Until then, the various Farmers' Alliances—such as the Southern Farmers' Alliance, the Northern Farmers' Alliance (successor to the Grange), the Louisiana Farmers' Union, the Texas Alliance, the Northwestern Farmers' Alliance, and the Colored Farmers' Alliance—represented agrarian interests. By the turn of the century the various alliances had merged into the National Farmers' Alliance and Industrial Union. In 1890 the Farmer's Alliance formulated a platform in Ocala, Florida, that enumerated their demands, which in 1892 would become the foundation of the Populist party's goals as expressed in the Omaha Platform:

- Government should own the major utilities such as the railroads.
- There should be free and unlimited coinage of silver.
- The fixed income tax should be replaced with a graduated income tax.
- All excess lands granted to the railroads should be returned to public ownership.
- Laborers should have an eight-hour day as well as the right to collective bargaining.
- A plan to establish federal offices near grain storage facilities into which farmers could deposit their nonperishable crops should be adopted. This would allow farmers to market their crops when their value was highest and store it when they were low.
- Immigration should be limited to control the expansion of the labor pool.
- Private detective and security agencies such as the Pinkerton and Baldwin-Felts agents should not be used to break up strikes.
- The U.S. political system should be democratized through the following measures:
  - direct election of U.S. senators (prior to the ratification of the Seventeenth Amendment in 1913, senators were commonly elected by state legislatures)

- ▥ use of the secret ballot to end the intimidation associated with publicly announcing one's choice for office
- ▥ a single term for presidents
- ▥ use of the initiative, by which a proposed law can be voted on if the advocates of the bill submit a petition beforehand and with the required number of signatures—in this way, legislative bodies would not have a monopoly on initiating legislation
- ▥ use of the referendum to allow voters to vote on governmental legislation and programs

To be sure, the Alliance was effective in electing its members to offices in the state and federal governments. For example, in 1890, over fifty candidates allied with or sympathetic to the Farmers' Alliances were elected to Congress. But discontent was not limited to the nation's farmers. By the late 1880s many throughout the nation had become disconcerted by government corruption, the ever-expanding concentration of economic power, as well as the tariff, money supply issues, and the railroad industry's abuses. True, government had taken steps to address some of their concerns; however, it would take a third party and a major depression in 1893 to shake the Democrats and Republicans from their lethargy.

The depression of 1893 represented the worst collapse of the American economy up to that time. Twenty percent of the work force was without jobs, and many Americans were living at or below the poverty level. Employers continued to cut wages, and unions went out on strike. In the spring of that year, Jacob S. Coxey, an Ohio businessman, led hundreds of unemployed and desperate men—Coxey's Army—on a march to Washington, D.C., to appeal to the government for assistance in the form of work-relief. They received none, but a few of Coxey's lieutenants were arrested, not for disturbing the peace or for starting a riot, but for walking on the grass! Police dispersed the rest of Coxey's Army.

THE POPULIST PARTY

Many economic, social, political, and cultural factors led to the dramatic rise and ultimate decline of the Populists. At the time the Populist movement seemed revolutionary, not only because of its attack on laissez-faire and monopoly capitalism, but also because of its attempt to form a political alliance between poor whites and blacks. The Populists were in every sense of the word a coalition of seemingly disparate groups, unions, and political parties: Grangers, Farmers' Alliances, former Greenback party members, Knights of Labor, socialists, Free Silver party members, prohibitionists, women's rights groups, anarchists. If the Populist movement suffered from internal divisiveness, its members were still deeply passionate about their organization's effort to address the problems that undermined their livelihood.

In the election of 1892, Populist candidate James Weaver received 1 million votes. He even won electoral votes, rare for a third-party candidate. Although he lost the presidential race, the Populist party experienced some remarkable victories: almost 1,500 Populist candidates were elected to state legislatures, three won gubernatorial elections, five were elected U.S. senators, and ten were elected to the House of Representatives. Unfortunately for Weaver and his party, they fared poorly in the South primarily because conservative southern Democrats were fearful of the Populists uniting poor blacks and whites. Remember that at this point, blacks in the South were politically neutralized by Jim Crow laws, and many white southerners were in favor of maintaining this racial status quo. Surprisingly, the party failed to attract many northern urban workers, despite the fact that the Populists fought for labor's rights in the halls of Congress, in state legislatures, and in public forums. Additionally, they provided financial support to workers out on strike.

In the 1896 presidential election the Democrats were split between "Gold Bugs," who were loyal to Cleveland and his advocacy of the gold standard, and pro-silver advocates, who did not yet have their own candidate—that is, until William Jennings Bryan (only thirty-six at the time) gave a speech on the silver issue to the delegates at the Democratic Convention. His speech not only electrified the audience but remains one of the most memorable speeches in U.S. history: "You shall not press down upon the brow of labor this thorn of crowns," he exclaimed, "you shall not crucify mankind upon a cross of gold." The Democrats had their candidate for the presidency, except of course for the Gold Bugs, who ran their own contender. Because the Democrats had already incorporated into their platform much of the Populists' platform, such as outlawing injunctions in labor disputes, the free coining of silver, and a lower tariff, the Populist party also nominated Bryan as their candidate, though not without some difficulty. Many Populist delegates opposed a "fusion" ticket for fear that their goals would be neutralized by allying themselves with a Democratic candidate. In fact, Bryan's support was sectional. Southern and western delegates had earlier fused with the Democrats on the state and local levels; southern delegates opposed such an alliance. In order to satisfy the southerners, Tom Watson, a Populist, was selected as the vice-presidential candidate instead of a Democratic candidate. Consensus had been reached. For their part, the Republicans had effective and potent campaign leadership. Under the campaign direction of Mark Hanna, the Republicans effectively cast blame on the Democrats for the depression in 1893. Further helped by the defection of the Democratic Gold Bugs, by increasing crop prices, especially for wheat, and by employers who frightened their workers into voting Republican by claiming that a low protective tariff would lead to business closings, the Republican, William McKinley, decisively defeated the "fusion" Democrat-Populist candidate Bryan.

After the 1896 election, the Populists ceased to exist as a national political party. The power of the monopolies, combined with the shortcomings of its own membership—who, according to some historians, could not leap the hurdle of racism despite their common economic interests—led to the party's demise. But there was one consolation for its leaders and rank-and-file members: much of its platform was ultimately absorbed into those of the Democrats and the Republicans. In the early twentieth century, during the progressive era, issues that the Populists had fought so hard for, such as the direct election of U.S. senators and a graduated income tax, would become a reality.

The Populist party was indeed unique in the history of the nation's political evolution. While some historians claim its downfall came in part from its inability to resolve the racial divides that existed within the party, other historians take the opposite view. At a time when black Americans were, at best, second-class citizens, these historians argue that the party fought for black economic and political rights because exploitation had to be confronted, regardless of the victim's skin color. To this end Populists viewed government not as a force to be overthrown, but to be redefined, because government could, in the right hands, be a tool to bring about opportunities for all citizens, not just the politically and economically entrenched. Hand in hand with this outlook was a total rejection of Social Darwinism, which Populists maintained was an obstacle to humanity's efforts to triumph over its own shortcomings. But this is not the only legacy of the Populist party. At a time when the American family farm is rapidly being replaced by enormous agribusinesses, one can more easily sympathize with the plight of the nation's food producers as the country moves into the twenty-first century.

Multiple-Choice Questions

1. All of the following were political objectives of the Populists EXCEPT
   (A) government ownership of major industries such as the railroads and telegraphs
   (B) replacing the fixed income tax with a graduated income tax
   (C) the free and unlimited coining of silver
   (D) direct election of U.S. senators
   (E) creating a national system of unemployment insurance

   ANSWER: E. Unemployment insurance would have to wait until the New Deal in the 1930s. Options A-D were important features of the Populists' platforms (*The American Pageant*, 12th ed., p. 521/11th ed., pp. 625-626).

2. William Jennings Bryan became the presidential candidate of both the Democrats and Populists in 1896 because of his support for
   (A) high protective tariffs to protect domestic industries
   (B) unlimited and free coinage of silver
   (C) nationalizing the railroad industry
   (D) policies that would unite poor black and white farmers
   (E) a single six-year term for presidents.

ANSWER: **B**. The silver issue and the condemnation of the gold standard were at the heart of Bryan's appeal. His "Cross of Gold" speech catapulted him into the national spotlight (*The American Pageant,* 12th ed., p.617/ 11th ed., p. 634).

3. A major reason why McKinley was able to defeat Bryan in 1896 was
   (A) the Populists ultimately withdrew their support for Bryan
   (B) the Republicans were split between gold and silver advocates
   (C) American farmers experienced an increase in farm prices during the campaign
   (D) Bryan's repudiation of the silver cause during the campaign
   (E) most Democrats favored Cleveland over Bryan

ANSWER: **C**. An increase in farm prices was one of the key factors that helped McKinley win support from farmers. B is incorrect because the Democrats and not the Republicans were split over the silver/gold issue. Bryan would never repudiate his primary campaign issue— option D. True, Gold Bugs (who had more in common with Cleveland than Bryan) did desert the party in the 1896 election, but most Democrats supported Bryan's candidacy.

4. Coxey's Army
   (A) reflected discontent with the government's response to the depression in 1893
   (B) was the military wing of the Populist party
   (C) was the name given to supporters of Jacob Coxey's candidacy for president in 1896
   (D) were strong advocates of the gold standard
   (E) were Democrats who switched their political allegiance to the Republicans in the 1896 election

ANSWER: **A**. Coxey and his supporters marched to Washington, D.C., in 1894 to appeal for aid for those unemployed as a result of the economic collapse in 1893 (*The American Pageant,* 12th ed., p. 614/ 11th ed., p. 630).

5. Which of the following did the nation's farmers advocate in the
   late nineteenth century?
   (A) government should reduce farmers' costs by providing farmers
       with seed and farm implements
   (B) the government should privatize the railroads
   (C) a sub-Treasury system should be established that would allow
       farmers to sell their crops on the market when prices rose
   (D) the use of federal troops to ensure farmers' safety against
       private security agents hired by the railroads
   (E) a high protective tariff

ANSWER: **C**. The sub-Treasury system would provide farmers some
control over the prices they could receive for their crops (*The
American Pageant,* 12th ed., p. 612/ 11th ed., p. 618).

6. Which of the following did NOT lead to greater productivity by
   farmers in the late nineteenth century?
   (A) iron and steel plows
   (B) the use of new farm machinery, such as harvesters
   (C) improved cotton gins
   (D) greater specialization of agricultural production
   (E) the rates charged by grain elevator owners

ANSWER: **E**. Farmers maintained that the grain elevator operators
charged exorbitant fees (*The American Pageant,* 12th ed., p. 611/ 11th
ed., p. 617).

7. In which Supreme Court case did the Court rule that as long
   property was "devoted to public use," states could place
   regulations on the railroads for the good of the public?
   (A) *Peik v. the Chicago and Northern Railway*
   (B) *Munn v. Illinois*
   (C) *Illinois v. Wabash*
   (D) *Pollock v. Farmers Loan and Trust*
   (E) *Dred Scott v. Sandford*

ANSWER: **B**. *Munn v. Illinois.*

8. Which industry, *more than any other,* became the symbol and
   source of agrarian discontent in the post-Civil War period?
   (A) the insurance industry
   (B) companies that developed harvesters and combines
   (C) railway companies
   (D) telephone and telegraph companies
   (E) banks

ANSWER: **C**. While farmers were often susceptible to rate changes in
other businesses, it was the railroad industry that most noticeably cut
into farmer's costs to get their crops to market and thus became a
symbol for their exploitation (*The American Pageant,* 12th ed., p. 611/
11th ed., p. 617).

9. Which of the following groups was NOT identified with the
    Populist party?
    (A) supporters of the gold standard
    (B) anarchists
    (C) Knights of Labor
    (D) Grangers
    (E) Greenback party

ANSWER: **A**. Populists were strong supporters of the free and unlimited
coining of silver. They sought to devalue the currency, which is what
silver, not gold, would achieve (*The American Pageant,* 12th ed., p. 617/
11th ed., pp. 608, 625).

10. The Specie Resumption Act of 1875
    (A) led to a dramatic increase in the amount of silver in the
        economy
    (B) was a compromise bill that allowed for an equal amount of
        gold and silver to be introduced into the economy each month
    (C) established the ratio of gold to greenbacks at 16:1
    (D) removed all of the greenbacks from circulation
    (E) dramatically inflated currency, which led to a depression

ANSWER: **D**. Passed by the Republican Congress, it called for redeeming
all greenbacks and replacing them with gold certificates (*The
American Pageant,* 12th ed., p. 507/11th ed., pp. 517-518).

Free-Response Questions

1. To what extent did the Populists and Farmers' Alliances effectively
    challenge the established Democratic and Republican parties in the
    late nineteenth century? In your answer discuss TWO of the
    following:
    a. the economic agenda of the Populists and Farmers' Alliances
    b. the degree of political success experienced by the Populists and
        Farmers' Alliances
    c. the ability of the Populists and Farmers' Alliances to organize
        farmers and others into a cohesive political force

RESPONSE You should begin by explaining why the Populist movement
and Farmers' Alliances were created in the first place. To this end,
provide some of the economic and political factors that negatively
affected those who joined these organizations. An explanation of their
goals (such as public ownership of the railroads and inflated paper or
silver currency) is also necessary. The second aspect, b, is similar to a
question that begins with "To what extent." Responding to this
question, you should identify which of the important objectives set
forth by the Populists and Farmers' Alliances were actually achieved.

2. Evaluate the response of government to the plight of America's
    farmers and laborers in the late nineteenth century.

RESPONSE For this essay you should address the relationship between
government and business and how this relationship affected laborers

and farmers. Identify the response of government to strikes; are there any patterns you can see? Did government address the needs of farmers by alleviating the problem of overproduction and declining farm prices? Discuss the decisions of the Supreme Court—for example, *Munn v. Illinois*—in this period as they relate to the plight of workers and farmers.

12

U.S. FOREIGN AFFAIRS FROM 1860 TO 1914

Prior to the American Civil War, the United States embarked on a systematic policy of territorial expansion across the continental United States. In the process, through wars, treaties, and conquests, it acquired land from Native Americans and Mexicans and settled territorial disputes with Britain and Spain. In the decades after the Civil War, the United States continued to expand across the continent, but by the late nineteenth century it turned its attention to noncontiguous territories—land beyond the continental United States. If the United States did not emerge from the Civil War with its sense of nationalism intact, it was nevertheless most certainly a rising power. By the end of the nineteenth century, the United States would be an economic giant and a military power with international colonial possessions. Less than two decades into the twentieth century, it would emerge from World War I an even stronger economic and military power. One of the driving forces behind this development was the same both before and after the Civil War: territorial expansion. Industry, immigration, the enormous expansion of the economy, all played a role in making the United States a major participant on the international scene. First it had to control the continental United States, and that meant removing Native Americans as an obstacle to expansion.

KEY CONCEPTS

- The clash between the U.S. government and Native Americans resulted in atrocities and attempts by the government to create policies to deal with the remaining tribes.
- The United States created an international empire as a result of its one-sided victory in the Spanish-American War.

- Those who supported or opposed U.S. imperialism provided theories and justifications for their views.
- The United States penetrated Asia, establishing the Open Door policy in China.
- Throughout this period, the United States intervened in Central and South American internal affairs.

U.S. foreign policy during this period is discussed in depth in *The American Pageant,* 12th ed., Chapters 26–28 and 30–31/11th ed., Chapters 27–30 and 32–33.

U.S. Policy Towards Native Americans Following the Civil War

In the years following the Civil War, thousands of settlers poured into areas that were home to Native American tribes such as the Cheyenne, Nez Perce, and Lakota Sioux. Both sides committed various atrocities as white Americans and Native Americans clashed over western lands. Treaties concentrated many tribes on small reservations, where in some cases they became dependent on federal agencies. Other tribes fought on, most famously the Comanche and the Sioux. The latter, in fact, wiped out General George Armstrong Custer's entire command at the Battle of Little Big Horn in 1876. Revenge was taken at the expense of Sioux women and children who were slaughtered alongside the male warriors by U.S. troops at the Battle of Wounded Knee in 1890. Before the Native Americans were completely destroyed or placed on reservations, reformers sought other options:

- **Assimilation** Native American children were given a Christian education (for example, the Carlisle School in Pennsylvania) that eventually would allow them to be assimilated into white American society.
- **The Dawes-Severalty Act** Congress persuaded Native Americans to relinquish their tribal ways by granting them plots of land and citizenship if they stayed on the land for twenty-five years and made a concerted effort to become "civilized." Unfortunately, the best land had been sold to speculators, railroad companies, and mining companies, so the policy failed. Not until the 1920s did the U.S. government grant citizenship rights to Native Americans.

The Purchase of Alaska

In 1867 Secretary of State William Seward brokered a deal in which Russia agreed to sell Alaska to the United States for approximately $7.5 million. In acquiring Alaska, Seward, an expansionist, eliminated Russian influence in the Western Hemisphere. The American public and many in Congress thought the purchase was a waste of funds and dubbed the deal "Seward's Folly" and Alaska itself "Seward's Icebox." Seward was later vindicated when gold and coal were discovered.

THE NEW IMPERIALISM: THEORIES

To be sure, the United States was not alone in building an international empire. In fact, it came late to the race. The New Imperialism of the late nineteenth century differed from earlier imperialist rivalries in the number of competitors vying for empire. Great Britain, France, Germany, Japan, and Russia, among others, had created empires by the late nineteenth century. The impetus for this enormous burst of expansionist activity was the growing opinion that the opportunities for creating an empire were fading as more and more land was coming under the influence and control of rivals. Yet there are other theories to explain why nations adopted an imperialist foreign policy. Social scientists have for decades attempted to create an explanation as to why nations embark on a policy of imperialism. Many have been critical of the imperialist activity for different reasons. Below is a sampling of some of the more notable theorists:

- **John Hobson (1858-1940)** A liberal economist, Hobson contended that underconsumption (or overproduction) convinces governments to adopt an imperialist policy: the colony becomes a source of demand for commodities that go unsold in the imperialist nation. Hobson, who was critical of imperialism, maintained that increasing wages would allow workers to purchase the goods they produced, thereby resolving the problem of underconsumption and eliminating the need to adopt an imperialist policy.
- **V. I. Lenin (1870-1924)** The leader of the Bolshevik Revolution in 1917, Lenin argued that when the rates of profits fall the capitalist class seeks new markets to dominate and invest surplus capital. Because all capitalist nations take the same approach, dangerous interimperialist rivalries result.
- **Rosa Luxemburg (1870-1919)** A German Marxist revolutionary, Luxemburg claimed that when supply exceeds demand, capitalist nations must find new markets in noncapitalist areas. Eventually, however, capitalism would have nowhere left to expand and, she hoped, would collapse.
- **Joseph Schumpeter (1883-1950)** A German economist, Schumpeter held that underconsumption led to imperialism as the center, the mother country, sought a larger market. He maintained that imperialism represented atavistic behavior—that it was a reflection of a more primitive state—and that capitalism represented a sophisticated system of supply and demand.

METHODS ADOPTED BY THE UNITED STATES TO ACHIEVE ITS IMPERIALIST GOALS

- **Formal imperialism** One of the most pervasive methods used by the United States and other imperial powers, formal, or direct, imperialism involves the physical presence of the center—the mother country—politically and often militarily. Examples of formal imperialism by the United States include the acquisition of
  - Hawaii
  - Guam

■   Puerto Rico
■ **Informal imperialism** In this form of imperialism, formal control is not necessary. Instead, the imperial power can dominate a colony, nation, or region in several different ways. The imperial power can support those in power in the dominated area whose policies are beneficial to the center. It can draft treaties that subordinate the economic, social, and political interests of the dominated nation to the interests of the center. The Open Door policy, adopted by the United States at the turn of the century, would allow any area to be penetrated by the imperial nations. John Hay, President McKinley's secretary of state, was a strong advocate of the policy, which was initially applied to China, but eventually extended to other continents as well.

Despite the enormous productive capabilities of U.S. capitalism, the nation in the late nineteenth century was experiencing a period of economic stagnation and social and political instability, not unlike what was occurring in other capitalist nations. In order to combat these problems, the United States, like other capitalist nations, adopted a dual plan. Domestically, the government attempted to reform capitalism by addressing the problems that led to discontent. The Progressive Era was a period of intense interest in reform. Internationally, the government adopted an expansionist—imperialist—foreign policy.

Whether their expectations regarding the benefits of imperialism were realistic is still debated today. Nevertheless, the decision to adopt this foreign policy option was based on policy-makers' perceptions of what an imperialist policy could achieve in the short and long term. Specifically, U.S. and other world leaders believed an imperialist policy would have the following effects:

■ An imperialist policy would bring the economy out of immediate financial crisis—a severe depression struck the United States in 1893.
■ An imperialist policy would help create conditions that would allow for future investments.
■ An imperialist policy would reduce domestic conflict—for example, between the working class and the capitalist class. (Remember, industrialization and rapid capital accumulation brought on serious confrontations between labor and capital following the Civil War.) This could be achieved by
   ■ reducing the extent of unemployment because of the favorable conditions imperialism would bring, such as increased demand from overseas colonies
   ■ passing on some of the economic benefits derived from imperialism to the working class
   ■ appealing to the patriotism of the working class to mute class tensions

A primary reason why the United States embarked on a policy of creating an international empire was the closing of the frontier, as officially reported in the 1890 census. The significance of this report was that all of the areas within the continental United States had been settled by the late nineteenth century. There was only one direction left to expand—overseas.

AP Tip

According to the renowned historian Frederick Jackson Turner, the frontier helped shape the democratic attributes of the American character and culture. In his famous 1893 essay, "The Significance of the Frontier in American History," Turner put forth the thesis that as Americans moved to the West, they had consistently regenerated the societies and cultures they had previously created in the East. In the process, they had cultivated a unique American system based on democratic values and individualism. Turner's thesis has prompted considerable discussion between historians who support his view and those who challenge it. Keep this in mind should you be presented with a College Board free-response question that deals with topics such as Jacksonian Democracy, Manifest Destiny, and the New Imperialism of the late nineteenth century.

IDEOLOGICAL JUSTIFICATIONS FOR AN AMERICAN IMPERIALIST POLICY

Because imperialism tends to be a highly controversial course of action, various justifications are utilized to explain the need for such a foreign policy and to mollify those who question its necessity. In the late nineteenth century, the following were important justifications for U.S. imperialism:

- **Alfred T. Mahan's** *The Influence of Sea Power upon History* **(1890)** In one of the most influential books of the era, Mahan proposed that for the United States to become a world power it must develop a first-class navy. This would give the United States a global reach and considerably increase its military power. However, in order to have a great navy, coaling stations and naval bases were necessary—in other words, the acquisition of colonies. A staunch advocate of imperialism, Mahan's book had a profound influence on President Theodore Roosevelt, himself a supporter of a global U.S. empire.
- **Frederick Jackson Turner's "The Significance of the Frontier in American History" (1920)** This essay sums up Turner's belief that territorial expansion promotes social, economic, and political stability. His essays, published in professional journals in the late nineteenth and early twentieth centuries, influenced President Woodrow Wilson, himself a historian.
- **Religious justifications** The notion that imperialism allowed "civilized" Christian cultures an opportunity to spread their way of life to "lesser" cultures was advocated by the nativist Reverend Josiah Strong among others. Often, in an attempt to mute criticism of the economic motives behind the adoption of an imperialist policy, noneconomic justifications such as the missionary rationale were used.

■ **Social Darwinism** Advocates of imperialism maintained that the United States was simply biologically and morally superior to those cultures and peoples that were being dominated. Imperialism was merely a reflection of that superiority.

AP Tip

Some social scientists maintain that U.S. foreign policy should not be shaped by theoretical and ethical justifications, but by *Realpolitik*—the "politics of reality"— the practical and realistic needs and concerns of the nation. They hold that U.S. economic imperatives and political/military objectives helped shape the foreign policy adopted by the United States beginning in the late nineteenth century. The realization of a global empire was a realistic and necessary objective of U.S. policy makers, they contend. Others argue that morality should be a primary factor in adopting a particular or general course of action when adopting a foreign policy, for the implementation of a policy based on realpolitik has its limitations and unintended deleterious consequences. A brief discussion of realpolitik as it applies to U.S. foreign policy (in any period) may add a compelling dimension to a free-response question that asks you to address foreign affairs.

OPPONENTS OF AMERICAN IMPERIALISM

Not all Americans supported their government's foreign policy. Even President Cleveland opposed the annexation of Hawaii in 1894. In fact imperialism was so controversial that it became the key issue in the 1900 presidential campaign between William McKinley and William Jennings Bryan. By then, an influential association opposed to expansionism had been organized, the Anti-Imperialist League. Its members included politicians (for example, Bryan), literary figures (for example, Mark Twain), economic leaders (for example, Andrew Carnegie), and scholars (for example, Charles Francis Adams and William Sumner). Their opposition to imperialism ran the gamut from distress over the costs necessary to maintain an empire to the immorality of denying others self-determination to the racial notion that incorporating "lesser" cultures into a U.S. empire would weaken American "purity."

U.S. FOREIGN RELATIONS IN EAST ASIA AND THE PACIFIC

To U.S. political and economic leaders in the late nineteenth century, China was a region that offered infinite economic possibilities. The United States was not alone in this analysis. All imperial powers knew that gaining a foothold in China, and eventually in the rest of Asia, would enhance their power in relation to one another. While the United States looked to China for opportunities, a new force in East Asia was demonstrating its power—Japan. In the late nineteenth century, it became clear that the United States and Japan were emerging as the leading contestants for hegemony in Asia. Beginning with Japan's victory over China in the Sino-Japanese War in 1895 and over Russia in the Russo-Japanese War in 1905, U.S.-Japanese enmity grew as each sought to influence East Asia. This antagonism would ultimately take them down the path to war in 1941. Several examples show how the United States and Japan tried to address their strained diplomatic relations throughout the first half of the twentieth century:

■ President Theodore Roosevelt organized the Treaty of Portsmouth ending the Russo-Japanese War in 1905. Japan was clearly the victor and thus received concessions from Russia; however, many in Japan blamed Roosevelt's treaty, and therefore the United States, for what many Japanese claimed were only modest gains.

■ The Taft-Katsura Agreement (1905): Japan recognized U.S. control over the Philippines and the United States recognized Japan's control over Korea.

■ In order to show the extent of the U.S. global reach, President Roosevelt sent the U.S. Navy on an international cruise in 1907, making certain it stopped in Japan. The fleet of warships duly impressed the Japanese. They welcomed the American Navy, but they may have seen this Great White Fleet (so called because of the ships' distinctive coloring) as a possible threat to its plans to dominate East Asia.

■ The Root-Takahira Agreement (1908): At the time, the Japanese and Americans desired to improve relations; by this agreement, they promised to preserve China's independence, support the Open Door policy, and recognize each other's possessions in the Pacific.

Although they were allies in World War I, from this point on, and despite efforts to forestall conflict, relations between the United States and Japan were never entirely amicable.

As for the other imperial powers in Asia, their grab for wealth and power in China in many ways resembled their scramble in Africa during the same period. This spurred the United States to formulate the Open Door policy. The goal of the policy was to prevent the total dissection of China, which would further weaken the country and allow the competing imperial powers to create spheres of influence in China, and to ensure that the United States had the same opportunities to trade in China as did the other powers.

In 1900 a Chinese group called the Boxers attempted to drive out the foreign powers. The United States was in the vanguard in organizing an international military response that eventually put down this nationalist uprising. Later the United States worked out an agreement that attempted to preserve China's independence. However, the other nations involved—Britain, France, Russia, Italy, Germany, and Japan—compelled China to pay enormous indemnities, which weakened it considerably; the United States returned a majority of its share of the indemnities to an appreciative Chinese government.

Around the same time, the United States was acquiring territorial possessions east of China, in the Pacific:

■ **Samoa** A trade relationship had developed between American merchants and Samoans even before the Civil War. In the decade following the Civil War the United States was permitted to establish a naval base on one of the Samoan islands. Soon Germany and Britain wanted what the Americans had in Samoa. When the American and Germany navies almost fought each other over the islands, a treaty was worked out. It gave Germany two of Samoa's islands; the other islands were given to the United States; Britain received other concessions.

- **Hawaii** As was the case in Samoa, American merchants had opened trade with the Hawaiians in the decades before the Civil War. The key commodity was sugar. The export of sugar benefited both American merchants and Hawaiian traders. Standing in the way of an even more lucrative trade relationship was the monarch of Hawaii, Queen Liliuokalani, who opposed foreign economic and political intervention in her country. In short order the queen was overthrown by Hawaii's white population under the leadership of Hawaiian Supreme Court justice Sanford Dole and assisted by U.S. Marines. The U.S. government quickly recognized the new government, one amenable to increased trade. On July 4, 1894, the Republic of Hawaii was proclaimed. Ostensibly Hawaii was an independent nation. However, many Hawaiians opposed a key provision in their new constitution that would allow the United States to annex the Hawaiian Islands.

While Samoa and Hawaii were indeed important acquisitions, it was not until the United States went to war against the Spanish Empire that it fully established itself as a major global power. Nevertheless, the U.S. interest in Cuba did not begin in the late nineteenth century. In the antebellum era, Southern economic and political leaders wanted to annex Cuba, a Caribbean island that was certainly suitable for a Southern-styled slave plantation system. President Polk attempted to purchase the island from Spain but was refused. Even independent proslavery military expeditions failed to wrest Cuba from Spain. Later President Pierce sent several proslavery U.S. representatives to Ostend, Belgium, to negotiate for the sale of Cuba; they implied that if Spain refused to give up Cuba, the United States would take it by force. When the negotiations were leaked to the press, angry antislavery forces in Congress saw to it that the Ostend Manifesto, as it was called, was repudiated.

THE SPANISH-AMERICAN WAR (1898)

The war that made the United States a global power in possession of an overseas empire came about because of a variety of causes:

- Spain's treatment of the Cubans was brutal.
- The United States supported the Cuban independence movement.
- Cuba's strategic location in the Caribbean was enticing to the United States.
- Financial interests in the United States were being hurt by the ongoing war between the Cuban rebels and the Spanish military.
- The influence of the "Yellow Press": William Randolph Hearst's and Joseph Pulitzer's newspapers unscrupulously sensationalized Spanish atrocities in Cuba in order to increase sales, correctly speculating that a war in Cuba would stimulate newspaper readership. Although some of their stories were outright

fabrications, the reading public devoured the graphic and sometimes salacious stories.

Relations between Spain, whose glory days as Europe's first major empire in the Western Hemisphere were well behind it, and the United States, which was a newcomer to global empire-building, deteriorated even further as a result of two events:

- **The DeLôme letter** In 1898 a U.S. newspaper published private correspondence stolen from the Spanish minister in Washington, Dupuy DeLôme. In the letter the minister made derogatory comments about President McKinley, which, when made public, outraged the American people. Although DeLôme resigned, the damage had been done.
- **The sinking of the *Maine*** The U.S.S. *Maine* was sent to Havana Harbor to protect U.S. citizens and property. Just one week after the DeLôme incident, a massive explosion blew up the ship, killing over 250 American sailors. Given the mood of the American people at this point, they believed the obvious culprit was Spain. After the Hearst and Pulitzer papers sensationalized the story, the public was, for the most part, decidedly sympathetic to a war with Spain. To this day the cause of the sinking is a mystery, though many experts believe the explosion was a tragic accident.

Following the sinking of the *Maine*, President McKinley demanded a cease-fire in Cuba. Spain agreed. But in the minds of the American people and the U.S. Congress, a line had already been crossed. Under pressure, McKinley asked Congress for a declaration of war. Congress's affirmation came in the form of a congressional resolution, the Teller Amendment. In it the United States assured the Cuban people that they would be granted autonomy and self-determination once Spain was defeated. The United States prepared to engage Spain's forces in the Caribbean and in the Pacific.

The Spanish-American War lasted several months, cost more American lives from disease and spoiled food than from Spanish bullets, and in the end provided the United States with a global empire. Secretary of State John Hay knew it had been "a splendid little war." The following were major military events of the war:

- One Spanish fleet was destroyed by U.S. warships under the command of Commodore George Dewey in Manila Bay on June 1, 1898.
- Manila, capital of the Philippines, was captured two months later.
- In Cuba the U.S. military force was unprepared for tropical conditions. Despite the loss of thousands of soldiers to malaria and other diseases, Cuban rebels and American soldiers were able to wear down the Spanish forces. One of the most famous land battles occurred in the American attack on San Juan Hill, an event made popular by the rousing charge of the Rough Riders, led by Theodore Roosevelt, on Spanish forces.
- The destruction of the other Spanish fleet at Santiago Bay on July 3 convinced the Spanish to open negotiations to end the fighting. That month, the United States annexed Hawaii. It would soon add other territories as well.

These are the principal terms of the peace treaty signed in Paris in December 1898:

- Cuba received its independence from Spain. The United States would have liked to annex Cuba, but it could not because it had gone to war to win Cuban freedom.
- Spain relinquished control of Puerto Rico, in the Caribbean, and Guam, in the Pacific.
- In return for $20 million, the United States acquired the Philippines. Opponents claimed this violated America's basic principles as expressed in the U.S. Declaration of Independence, but the pro-imperialist forces in Congress won the day. Unfortunately for the United States, the Filipinos had other thoughts. Led by Emilio Aguinaldo, a former U.S. ally, Filipino rebels fought for three years against the U.S. military before the uprising was put down.

By then the United States had compelled the Cubans to agree to the Platt Amendment, which denied Cuban self-determination by allowing the United States to intervene in Cuban affairs when it believed its own interests were threatened and by allowing the United States to lease naval bases such as the one at Guantanamo, on the eastern tip of the island. In reality, while the United States claimed it had fought for Cuban freedom, the Platt Amendment effectively made Cuba an American protectorate.

Puerto Rico, on the other hand, had an unusual relationship with the United States. It was neither a U.S. territory nor an independent nation. Under the Foraker Act (1900), Congress provided the Puerto Ricans with substantial political autonomy, although the United States continued to exert heavy political and economic influence on the island's government. The Puerto Ricans had a civil government and an American governor. But were they entitled to the same constitutional rights as American citizens? In the early twentieth century the Supreme Court ruled on this question about constitutional rights in a series of cases called the *Insular Cases*: in a controversial decision, the Court ruled that the Constitution does not follow the flag—all the rights, privileges, and provisions accorded U.S. citizens under the Constitution do not apply to those living under the U.S. flag in overseas territories and possessions.

The war was a windfall for McKinley and the Republican party. Late in the century, the United States experienced domestic prosperity and prestige overseas. To many Americans the rise in economic prosperity was well worth the financial and military burdens of empire. The depression of 1893, the worst in the nation's history to that time, seemed like a memory. Not surprisingly, the 1900 presidential race was a particularly difficult one for the Democrats, who tended to oppose overseas imperialism. The Republican President McKinley rode a wave of popular support for the war and the public's general acceptance of U.S. imperialism. He received nearly twice the number of electoral votes as the Democratic candidate, William Jennings Bryan.

U.S. Foreign Relations in Latin America and the Caribbean

Since the 1890s, U.S. intervention in the domestic affairs of many Latin American nations has been extensive. In 1904 President Roosevelt extended the authority of the United States in the Western Hemisphere as articulated in the Monroe Doctrine. Responding in part to the bellicose actions of several European nations in 1902 regarding money owed to them by Venezuela, Roosevelt believed the Monroe Doctrine had to be strengthened. In the Roosevelt Corollary, the president recognized the principle of self-determination, but only for nations that acted "with reasonable efficiency and decency in social and political matters," adding that "chronic wrongdoing" would result in the United States acting as an "international police power." In other words, the United States would intervene when it thought it was necessary to do so. This firm approach became known as the "Big Stick" policy, in reference to an African proverb: "Speak softly and carry a big stick, [and] you will go far." Citing the Corollary, the United States opposed nationalist and reform governments and those movements that sought greater autonomy as a threat to U.S. political, military, and economic interests. Roosevelt's successor, William Howard Taft, added a new ripple to the Roosevelt Corollary in the form of "Dollar Diplomacy." Taft believed that economic and political instabilities in Latin America required U.S. intervention to protect American financial interests. (Following World War I, the most intense U.S. responses have been reserved for leftist and communist movements.) Not surprisingly, many Latin Americans resented the policy. Below is a sampling of U.S. interventions in Latin America:

- **Cuba** The United States occupied Cuba from 1898 to 1902 and intervened again militarily in 1906, 1909, 1917, and 1961.
- **Dominican Republic** The United States militarily occupied the island nation from 1916 to 1924. It was a U.S. protectorate from 1905 to 1940. The United States last sent troops to the Dominican Republic in 1965.
- **Haiti** A U.S. protectorate from 1915 to 1941, it was militarily occupied by the United States between 1915 and 1934. U.S. troops were sent to Haiti in the late twentieth and early twenty-first centuries.
- **Nicaragua** The United States militarily and politically intervened in 1909, 1912–1925, 1927–1933, and again in the 1970s and 1980s.
- **Mexico** The United States militarily intervened in 1916 during the Mexican Civil War.
- **Colombia** In 1903 the United States helped establish a secessionist movement in northwestern Colombia (Panama), which soon came under U.S. control. It would later be the site of the Panama Canal.

The next American president, Woodrow Wilson, claimed he was an opponent of imperialism and repudiated the policies of his predecessors, Roosevelt and Taft. During his administration the United States took the following actions:

- **Panama Canal Tolls Act of 1912** The act allowed U.S. ships to use the Panama Canal toll-free. Wilson convinced Congress to repeal the act, which angered strong nationalists like Roosevelt but was appreciated by the British, who had earlier challenged the exemption.

■ **Jones Act of 1916** The act provided for eventual Filipino independence, made the Philippines a full-fledged U.S. territory, and granted universal male suffrage.

■ **Jones Act of 1917** The act conferred citizenship rights on all Puerto Ricans and made democratic improvements to their legislative system.

In just over fifty years, from the end of the American Civil War to the eve of World War I, the United States had taken its place as an economic leviathan and international world power. Coincidentally, the first phase of U.S. territorial expansion, the period of Manifest Destiny, coincided with the advent of a major reform movement, Jacksonian Democracy. Likewise, the U.S. role in the New Imperialism coincided with two domestic reform movements: the Populists in the late nineteenth century and the progressives in the early twentieth century. As the United States looked outward beyond its borders, many began to take stock of the domestic conditions shaping the nation. Again, the government and grassroots movements would take steps to democratize the institutions of American life.

Multiple-Choice Questions

1. The Dawes-Severalty Act
    (A) made Puerto Rico a protectorate of the United States
    (B) placed limitations on the political rights of the citizens of Guam
    (C) punished Spain for its abuses of the Cuban people
    (D) was an attempt by the U.S. government to assimilate Native Americans
    (E) denied Native Americans their rights as citizens of the United States

ANSWER: **D**. The act attempted to assimilate the Native Americans by breaking their connection to tribal customs (*The American Pageant*, 12th ed., p. 597/11th ed., p. 534).

2. This theorist claimed that underconsumption in the center, or mother country, is the primary reason why nations adopt an imperialist policy.
    (A) Joseph Schumpeter
    (B) V. I. Lenin
    (C) Rosa Luxemburg
    (D) Sanford Dole
    (E) John Hobson

ANSWER: **A**. Schumpeter, a German economist, later taught at Harvard.

3. The Open Door policy was initially applied to
(A) Korea
(B) Japan
(C) China
(D) Africa
(E) Latin America

ANSWER: **C**. Secretary of State John Hay designed the Open Door policy to make certain the United States had continued access to the China market (*The American Pageant,* 12th ed., pp. 648-649/11th ed., pp. 666-667).

4. Alfred T. Mahan was influential during the era of New Imperialism because of his
(A) support for self-determination for conquered peoples
(B) advocacy for a large U.S. Navy in order to extend the nation's power internationally
(C) opposition to the U.S. adoption of an imperialist policy
(D) candidacy for the U.S. presidency as an advocate of imperialism
(E) defeat of the Spanish fleet in Havana Harbor

ANSWER: **B**. Mahan's *The Influence of Sea Power upon History* convinced the government to expand its naval fleet as a prerequisite to expanding its global power (*The American Pageant,* 12th ed., p. 624/11th ed., p. 642).

5. Which of the following was NOT an opponent of U.S. imperialism?
(A) Theodore Roosevelt
(B) Mark Twain
(C) William Jennings Bryan
(D) Charles Francis Adams
(E) Andrew Carnegie

ANSWER: **A**. Roosevelt vigorously supported U.S. imperialism (*The American Pageant,* 12th ed., p. 662/11th ed., pp. 680-681).

6. In the Taft-Katsura Agreement, Japan recognized the U.S. control over the Philippines and the United States recognized Japan's control of
(A) China
(B) Korea
(C) Guam
(D) Hawaii
(E) Cuba

ANSWER: **B**.

7. Which of the following held that those living in U.S. territories are not accorded the same constitutional rights as U.S. citizens?
   (A) Foraker Act
   (B) Jones Act of 1916
   (C) Root-Takahira Agreement
   (D) Insular Cases
   (E) Platt Amendment

ANSWER: **D**. This was the conclusion of a badly split Supreme Court. The decision concerned constitutional questions raised by the Foraker Act (*The American Pageant,* 12th ed. p. 639/11th ed., pp. 656-657).

8. The Teller Amendment
   (A) granted independence to the Philippines
   (B) convinced the Filipino rebels to lay down their arms in return for financial concessions
   (C) recognized Japan's influence in East Asia
   (D) was a U.S. guarantee of self-determination to the Cubans once Spain was defeated
   (E) was Congress's formal declaration of war against Spain

ANSWER: **D**. Unfortunately for the Cubans, the lure of economic incentives convinced the United States to rethink its promise (*The American Pageant,* 12th ed., p. 631/11th ed., pp. 648-649).

9. Which U.S. president repudiated the imperialist policies of his predecessors?
   (A) Roosevelt
   (B) McKinley
   (C) Polk
   (D) Wilson
   (E) Taft

ANSWER: **D**. Wilson loathed imperialism (*The American Pageant,* 12th ed., pp. 693-694/11th ed., p. 710).

10. Which one of the following was NOT a cause of the Spanish-American War?
    (A) the yellow press
    (B) the U.S. desire to prevent European nations from controlling the Caribbean
    (C) the U.S. desire to control Cuba for its strategic location in the Caribbean
    (D) the sinking of the *Maine*
    (E) the DeLôme letter

ANSWER: **B**. A European nation, Spain, already controlled Cuba (*The American Pageant,* 12th ed., p. 628/11th ed., p. 646).

Free-Response Questions

1. To what extent is this statement correct?
   The primary factor in the United States adopting a policy of imperialism was economic.

RESPONSE You can discuss the limitations of this view while addressing the importance of economic factors. To this end, discuss the economic imperative to expand and find new markets for investments, surplus commodities, and raw materials. Point out that there were socio-political and cultural objectives and imperatives as well: Social Darwinism as a justification for expansion, the desire to develop a hegemonic relationship with, for example, South America, and the desire to create a world empire.

2. Was the United States justified in going to war against Spain in 1898? In your response, take into account political, economic, moral, and diplomatic factors.

RESPONSE To support this view, you should discuss the terrible treatment of the Cubans under Spanish rule, U.S. support for Cuban independence, the sinking of the *Maine,* and the DeLôme letter. To refute this view, you should address the influence of the Yellow Press; the desire on the part of the U.S. to create a global empire at the expense of Spain, a waning European power; and the demand for war on the part of U.S. business interests because the war between Spain and the Cuban rebels was hurting U.S. economic interests.

13

THE PROGRESSIVE ERA: 1900-1920

By 1900 the United States was a world power; its aggressive foreign policy and dynamic domestic growth were powered by enormous industrial production and the federal government's more assertive domestic and international policies. At the turn of the century, the United States had unprecedented prestige and power. Its seemingly ever-expanding economic opportunities and basic democratic rights were a magnet for millions around the world who had few of these things. For America's large businesses, corporations, and the upper class, life was good. For the most part, they operated with little government interference other than measures that facilitated the concentration of capital. Approximately half of the nation's wealth was in the hands of 1 percent of the population.

Yet under the surface were serious problems. In some cases, not much had changed since the Gilded Age in the 1870s and 1880s when a small percentage of the nation's population was enormously wealthy while millions suffered in abject poverty, scratching out an existence in America's bustling, overcrowded, and filthy cities. Industrialization had made the American worker simply a cog in the production process. Some laborers were mere children, compelled to work so that their families did not sink deeper into poverty. Throughout most of the late nineteenth century, America's farmers also experienced hardship, as farm prices fluctuated and farmers in increasing numbers lost their property and their livelihood. As for black Americans, decades earlier they had been relegated to a second-class status. Women were still disenfranchised; they could not vote or run for political office. What is more, they continued to languish as subordinates to men economically and socially.

While industrialization had brought despair to millions of urban workers, it was the impetus for the emergence of a middle class of professionals, office workers, social workers, educators, and government employees. As in the antebellum period, the middle class was willing and had the time to take up the challenge of addressing America's social ills. Their motives were sometimes altruistic but often simply personal, as these problems affected their class as well. Because of reform-minded public officials and private citizens and organizations, a concerted effort was made to address the maladies that undermined American democracy. This period in U.S. history, 1900-1920, is referred to as the progressive era, and it was the first manifestation of liberalism in the twentieth century.

KEY CONCEPTS

■ The progressive movement was one major phase of liberalism in the twentieth century.
■ Grassroots and government reformers attempted to address the abuses and deficiencies in American life at the local, state, and federal levels.
■ Important reforms were enacted by Congress to address abuses in business, the economy, and the environment.
■ Women and African-Americans organized to improve their condition and status, but despite major economic and political reforms, they continued to experience hard times.

The progressive era is discussed in depth in *The American Pageant,* 12th ed., Chapters 28-30/11th ed., Chapters 30-32.

LIBERALISM IN THE TWENTIETH CENTURY: HISTORIANS' PERSPECTIVE

To place the progressive era in perspective, it is important to view it as one phase in the ongoing struggle to reform American society, the economy, and government. In the twentieth century alone, there have been five major reform periods:

1900–1920 Progressive Era	1933–1945 New Deal	1945–1953 Fair Deal	1961–1963 New Frontier	1963–69 Great Society
Roosevelt, Taft, and Wilson	Franklin D. Roosevelt	Harry S Truman	John F. Kennedy	Lyndon B. Johnson

Before exploring the details and dimensions of the progressive movement, you will need a working knowledge of the term "liberalism"—it is often considered synonymous with reform and progressivism, but it is not. On this topic there is little consensus among social and political scientists. Some historians, for example, view liberalism this way:

■ Liberalism is the true expression of American democracy and represents the traditions established by Jefferson and Jackson and further developed by twentieth-century presidents (see above).

■ Liberalism represents an alliance between the public and the government to guard against and correct the abuses of capital. In the process, equilibrium is established between the interests of the public and the interests of corporations.

■ Reforms and reform movements have two fundamental objectives:

  ■ to alleviate immediate short-term economic, political, and social problems

  ■ to bring about significant fundamental change within existing economic, political, and social relationships and institutions

Reforms

Economic	Political	Social
reforms that seek to control corporate behavior and check the abuses practiced by large corporations	reforms that 1) extend or protect the political rights of previously disenfranchised groups, 2) are intended to make public officials more accountable to the public, 3) attack corruption and abuses of power by political officials	reforms that seek to protect and promote the human and social rights of deprived groups in society

Other historians do not agree that liberalism is an expression of American democracy. They hold that liberalism represents an alliance between the government and corporations designed to preserve and enhance the following conditions and relationships:

■ maintaining power in the hands of a small elite class

■ maintaining this class's hegemony over other classes in American society

■ preserving the status quo, a goal of both the liberal elite and the conservative elite, who differ only in their methods

THE EARLY TWENTIETH-CENTURY PROGRESSIVES

The progressives were a composite of a variety of groups, individuals, and movements. Like reformers before and since, they held to the view that humanity and the institutions created by humans could be improved. To this end, progress and advancement of U.S. society and culture were the foundations of progressive thought and actions. In the vanguard were professionals, both men and women, who represented the middle class. Rather than rely exclusively on traditional sources of reform—the church, private benefactors, and municipal government—they approached societal problems systematically and pragmatically. Progressives rejected both laissez-faire capitalism and a radical approach to the crises—recessions and depressions, for example—inherent in the capitalist system:

- They viewed government as a potentially positive force for change and reform, one that could be used to combat monopolies and corruption in government.
- They maintained that government could neutralize special-interest groups that had long been a drain on the nation's governmental resources.
- A long-term objective of the progressives was to instill order and stability to the institutions and relations of American life.
- Some progressives combined the Protestant religion and humanitarian work, a synthesis that became known as the social gospel movement. Operating predominantly in urban areas, those belonging to this movement believed it was their Christian duty to be concerned about the plight of the poor and the immigrant and to take steps to improve their lives.
  - The Salvation Army is an excellent example of the social gospel movement at work. It provided material and spiritual assistance to the urban poor.
  - One of the leaders of the movement, Walter Rauschenbusch, distinctively combined socialist thought with religious principles to bring salvation through Christianity and reform ideals.
  - Settlement houses served as centers for the urban poor and immigrants; they provided the needy with educational services, child care, technical skills, and recreational activities. The most famous American social settlement house was Jane Addams's Hull House, situated in one of Chicago's most distressed wards.
- The muckrakers were investigative reporters and journalists who wrote about the abuses that were prevalent in American society. (They received this unflattering label from President Theodore Roosevelt, who believed they were sensationalizing their stories to attract readership.) The graphic and hard-biting exposés inspired a public uproar against those causing the abuses. Examples include
  - Jacob Riis's *How the Other Half Lives* (1890) is one of the earliest examples of muckraking. Riis's photos of urban poverty evoked an emotional response from the public, especially his photographs of forlorn young street orphans.
  - Upton Sinclair's *The Jungle* (1906) exposed gruesome working conditions and the tainted meat that emerged from Chicago's meatpacking plants. Although it did not generate support for socialism, which was Sinclair's intention, it did lead to legislation to correct the abuses: the Pure Food and Drug Act and the Meat Inspection Act.
  - Ida Tarbell's *History of the Standard Oil Company* (1904) targeted the company's abuses so effectively that it was successfully prosecuted in 1911.
  - Frank Norris's novel *The Octopus* (1901) exposed corrupt politicians conspiring with the powerful Southern Pacific Railroad to exploit California farmers.

■ Lincoln Steffens's *The Shame of the Cities* (1904) exposed municipal corruption.

REFORMING LOCAL AND STATE POLITICAL SYSTEMS

Political machines are organizations that manage, sometimes illegally, the administration of local and state governments. Favoritism, sordid dealings, and nepotism are features of the political machines. They often work in conjunction with municipal governments but have often come to dominate the city in which they operate. Most machines have been corrupt, financially and politically. After the Civil War and well into the twentieth century, in return for performing favors for residents, especially new immigrants, the recipient was expected to be politically loyal to the machine. The most famous machine was "Boss" Tweed's "Ring," which dominated New York City's government during and after the Civil War. As boss of Tammany Hall, the nickname of New York's political machine, the Tweed Ring essentially ran the city, in the process bilking it of millions of dollars. The famous cartoonist Thomas Nast (who introduced the elephant and donkey as symbols for the Republicans and Democrats) exposed the corruption and abuses of the Tweed machine in a series of startling political cartoons. Tweed went to prison, but other cities had their machines as well. Years later, in Kansas City, Tom Pendergast ran a powerful Democratic party machine. One if his protégés—Harry S Truman—eventually became president.

To many progressives, political corruption, disenfranchisement, and unequal political influence prevented substantial changes in all realms of American society. To this end, a number of initiatives were taken at all levels of government. Reforms at the local and city levels of government include the following:

■ Home-rule charters gave cities greater flexibility and autonomy by taking away many powers from the state governments and allowing local governments to draw up their own plan of government. In the process, local areas were freed from corruption on the state level that affected their communities.

■ The National Municipal League was formed to carry out fact-finding investigations related to government's role in urban problems and to make recommendations in the hope of producing a model government.

■ The city-manager system and the commission system placed executive and legislative powers in the hands of a small elected commission that would manage a city much like a business enterprise—with great emphasis on efficiency. Thus, the management of local municipalities would be taken out of politics and operated on a nonpartisan basis.

■ In some urban areas reformers pressed for public ownership of utilities. Referred to as "gas and water socialism," it was an idea that came to fruition. Today, most municipalities own their utilities.

■ Minimum wage and maximum working hours were established for city employees in various municipalities.

■ Some municipalities funded recreational and day-care facilities.

In order to correct urban problems, it was first necessary to correct the abuses at the state level. Various reform-minded governors focused on the abuses that weakened their state. For example, in New Jersey, Governor Woodrow Wilson brought about reforms to regulate public utilities and address corrupt business practices. California's Hiram Johnson sought railroad regulations, and New York's Theodore Roosevelt addressed urban living conditions. Other major state reforms adopted in some states in the period include the following:

- Attempts were made to ban child labor.
- Minimum wage and maximum hour laws to protect women laborers were established.
- Workers' compensation was set up to protect workers against on-the-job accidents.
- Pensions were provided for widows and children when the husband/father was killed on the job.
- Building codes and state inspections acts were passed. Designed to protect workers against hazardous working conditions, the catalyst for this reform was the Triangle Shirtwaist Company Fire in New York (1911), which killed almost 150 young women textile workers.
- Businesses such as railroads and insurance companies and the food industry were regulated. A graduated income tax was imposed on businesses, replacing the inequitable fixed income tax.

The most far-reaching state reforms, however, occurred under the tutelage of Wisconsin's Senator Robert La Follette. In what became known as the "Wisconsin Idea," La Follette brought about a series of reforms geared to address a variety of problems and abuses. So extensive was his program in bringing about social and political reforms that Wisconsin became the model of a progressive state. They included the following:

- A direct primary system was adopted to nominate presidential candidates, in the process removing this power from the hands of political machines, which were a phenomenon of city politics.
- La Follette was instrumental in the passage of the Corrupt Practices Act, which made political figures liable to prosecution for wrongdoing.
- The state of Wisconsin passed laws limiting campaign expenditures (a precursor to today's campaign finance reforms) and lobbying activities.
- Utilizing professionals, intellectuals, and experts, La Follette created special commissions and agencies to investigate problems in conservation, taxes, education, highway construction, and politics.

REFORM UNDER REPUBLICAN PRESIDENTS

Piecemeal state and city reforms, while important, did not solve the problems of society and the increasing complexity of the economy. Federal policies and legislation were needed to address the problems associated with industrialization and urbanization. Three presidents are associated with the progressive era: Theodore Roosevelt (1901–1908), William Howard Taft (1909–1912), and Woodrow Wilson (1913–1920). All three supported progressive reform.

Theodore Roosevelt, a Republican, had campaigned on the promise of a square, or fair, deal for citizens while reconciling this with the needs of business. This promise resonated with many Americans. As president, he was amenable to legislation that monitored and regulated big business. Unlike his predecessors, he believed a president should take an active role as an arbiter between the demands of laborers and profit-driven businesses.

In 1902 the United Mine Workers (UMW), led by John Mitchell, went out on strike. They demanded 20 percent higher wages, a reduction from a ten- to nine-hour workday, and recognition for their union by the coal companies. The mine operators had raised wages a few years earlier but now refused to budge on any of the union's demands. Since most homes and businesses were heated by coal, Roosevelt was so concerned that the strike would last into the winter that he invited the coal operators and UMW representatives to the White House to negotiate an end to the strike. When the mine company heads stubbornly refused to negotiate with the UMW, a frustrated Roosevelt threatened to send the U.S. Army to occupy and run the mines. Frightened that he might actually seize their property, the operators agreed to have an arbitration committee settle the dispute. The strike ended in the fall; the workers received a 10 percent wage increase, their workday was shortened to nine hours, but the operators refused to recognize the union as a legitimate bargaining agent of the workers. Some historians are quick to point out that Roosevelt's actions were driven less by his support for labor than by his concerns about the effect of the strike on the economy and, indeed, capitalism itself. He challenged individual corporate giants when their actions endangered the interests and viability of capitalism as a whole. To them, Roosevelt was adamantly opposed to recognizing unions as a collective bargaining agent for labor, and his antipathy prevailed in this conflict.

Often viewed as an opponent of monopolies and other unfair business practices, Roosevelt was considered a "trust buster." However, his successor, William Howard Taft, actually dismantled more trusts than he did. During Roosevelt's time in office, Congress passed key legislation integral to regulating business. Many of these reforms had Roosevelt's support.

- In 1903 the Department of Commerce and Labor was created.
- Passage of the Elkins Act (1903) strengthened the Interstate Commerce Act of 1887 by requiring railroad companies to charge only the published rate and made illegal secret rebates. The railroad companies generally favored the act because it minimized the effects of a rate war between railroad companies that was driving down profits.
- Also in 1903 the Bureau of Corporations was created to investigate antitrust violations. By this time, 1 percent of corporations produced nearly 40 percent of the nation's manufactured goods. A key example in attacking monopolies that were clearly in restraint of trade was the Northern Securities Company, a railroad holding company that controlled nearly all long-distance railroads west of Chicago. In *Northern Securities v. United States* (1904), the court ordered the company to be dissolved.

- The Hepburn Act (1906) further empowered the Interstate Commerce Commission (ICC) to set maximum railroad rates and established other standards and regulations. The large railroad companies did not welcome government intervention, but they did welcome the establishment of fair rules of competition.

- In 1906 the Pure Food and Drug Act and the Meat Inspection Act barred the sale of adulterated foods involved in interstate commerce. All meatpacking facilities engaged in interstate commerce were to be federally inspected.

- An avid sportsman, Roosevelt took an active role in conservation policies. In so doing, he confronted the business sector, which wanted unfettered opportunities to harvest natural resources wherever they could be found. Over time, many corporate leaders did come to recognize the need for a rational policy for the nation's resources. By no means was Roosevelt antibusiness, but his administration sought a balance between the needs of the America's environment and the needs of America's businesses. To preserve the environment, Roosevelt's administration was active in the following:

  - enactment of the Newlands Reclamation Act Bill, by which a further 150 million acres were added to the national forest reserve

  - establishment of the Conservation Congress to address national conservation efforts

  - appointment of Gifford Pinchot, a strong conservationist, to head the Department of Agriculture's Division of Forestry

When Roosevelt's second term ended, he designated his confidant William Howard Taft as his successor. In Taft's four years in the White House, the following initiatives were taken:

- Passage of the Mann-Elkins Act (1910) strengthened the Interstate Commerce Commission (as had the Elkins Act and the Hepburn Act) by giving to it the power to regulate the new communications industry. In addition, the ICC was given more authority to regulate railroad companies' short- and long-haul rates. (Often railroad companies charged more for transportation of passengers and commodities between two points on a railway line than for a longer journey on the same line.)

- Taft "busted" twice as many trusts in four years as Roosevelt did in eight, including one, U.S. Steel, that had been approved by Roosevelt. This was one factor in a split between Roosevelt and Taft that eventually divided the Republican party. During Taft's one term, the Supreme Court dissolved two major corporations: American Tobacco Company and the Standard Oil Company.

THE REPUBLICAN PARTY SPLITS

As Roosevelt's handpicked successor, Taft proved to be a disappointment, both to Roosevelt and to progressives in general. During his presidency, Taft moved closer to the conservative wing of his party, alienating his political base in the process. Four major issues eventually divided the Republican party:

- **The Payne-Aldrich Tariff** (1909) was a high protective tariff (up to 40 percent tax on imports) that was supported by conservatives but opposed by progressives. Taft decided to support the conservative wing on this issue.
- **The Ballinger-Pinchot controversy** (1910) grew out of western opposition to conservation measures because they inhibited the development of the West. Ballinger, secretary of the interior, was identified with those westerners and conservatives who opposed conservation measures. Pinchot represented the progressive (and eastern) wing that favored conservation measures. Once again, Taft threw his weight behind the conservatives and sided with Ballinger, who proceeded to open over 1 million acres of land that Roosevelt had reserved. (Taft did, however, set aside some of that reserved land for public use.)
- **The Speaker of the House controversy** erupted over Joseph Cannon. Few Speakers of the House of Representatives have been as powerful as Cannon, nor as conservative. Cannon opposed nearly all social-welfare programs. As chairman of the Rules Committee, he decided which bills would be discussed in the House. The progressives wished to curtail the Speaker's power by, for instance, making membership on the Rules Committee an elected rather than appointed position. The conservatives opposed any erosion of the Speaker's power. Taft further alienated the progressive wing by supporting the conservatives.
- **Taft's antitrust suit against U.S. Steel** (1911) dated back to 1908, when U.S. Steel purchased the bankrupt Tennessee Coal and Iron Company. The combination seemed to be in violation of the Sherman Anti-Trust Act. Roosevelt's position had been that U.S. Steel had provided a public service to the nation by acquiring a company that, if it defaulted on its loans, could have dire consequences for the economy. Roosevelt assured U.S. Steel that the Justice Department would not prosecute the company, but under Taft that is exactly what happened. Roosevelt felt as if Taft had undermined his integrity. The enmity that had developed between the two former friends split the party.

At the Republican party convention in 1912, the progressive wing, led by "Battling Bob" La Follette, attempted to replace Taft as the party's candidate. Roosevelt refused to support either Taft's renomination or La Follette's attempt to unseat Taft. Instead, he chose to run as a candidate on a third-party ticket, the Progressive party (more commonly referred to as the "Bull Moose party," named for an animal that Roosevelt had admired for its strength and vigor). Roosevelt's campaign program (the "New Nationalism") advocated use of the federal government as a positive interventionist tool to advance democracy. The Democratic candidate, Woodrow Wilson, argued in his campaign program (the "New Freedom") that government should intervene only when democracy was threatened by social, economic, and political privilege and unfair business practices.

There was yet another candidate in the race, Eugene Debs, of the Socialist party. Debs promoted public ownership of the nation's natural resources and those industries vital to the nation's economic health. Amazingly, he received nearly 1 million votes. As for the Republicans, the party's division was a major factor in the election of

Woodrow Wilson, only the second Democrat to win the presidency in over fifty years.

REFORM UNDER WOODROW WILSON

Before becoming president, Wilson had been a popular reform governor of New Jersey. He took this reform spirit with him to the White House, where he was bent on tackling the "triple wall of privilege": the tariff, the trusts, and banking. Whereas Roosevelt regulated monopolies, Wilson regulated competition. His support for certain policies and his rejection of others were shaped by his general support for big business. In his two terms in office, he took an active role in seeing that the following domestic measures were taken:

- **The Underwood Tariff** (1913) was the first significant reduction in the tariff in fifty years. Wilson sided with consumers, who he believed were paying inflated prices because of the protection accorded businesses. Yet he believed that lowering tariffs and thereby increasing foreign competition would compel U.S. businesses to become more efficient, lower their prices, and make better products. The nation's corporate leaders agreed, though the idea of lowering tariffs is often a hard pill for business to swallow.
- **The Clayton Anti-Trust Act** (1914) was the response to Wilson's call for steps to be taken to break up monopolies. The new law modified the Sherman Anti-Trust Act (1890) by now exempting unions from restraint of trade provisions, but only when pursuing legitimate aims. This provided the government an opportunity to limit labor's power. For example, the Supreme Court, in *Duplex Printing Press Company v. Deering* (1921) upheld an injunction against a secondary boycott. The Clayton Act supplemented the Sherman Act by including new provisions prohibiting unfair and illegal business practices such as price fixing.
- **The Federal Trade Commission** was created in 1914 to regulate business by controlling trusts and monopolies, investigate misconduct, and issue cease and desist orders to intractable businesses.
- **The Federal Reserve Act** (1913) addressed glaring currency problems: the inability of the federal government to regulate the amount of money in the economy and to regulate banking practices. All national banks were required to join the Federal Reserve System.
  - The nation was divided into twelve regional Federal Reserve Banks.
  - The Federal Reserve System served banks, not private citizens.
  - The district banks extended credit and accepted deposits from member banks based on the needs of the specific district. The Federal Reserve regulated credit by either raising or lowering interest rates.
  - The district banks issued national currency in the form of Federal Reserve notes. This currency could be expanded (more money in the system) or contracted (less money in the system) depending on the status of the economy.

■ A board of directors composed of financial experts was to oversee the Federal Reserve System.

■ **The Adamson Eight-Hour Act** (1916), growing out of concern that a railroad strike would severely damage the economy, had Wilson's support. The act also provided compensation for overtime work.

■ **The Keating-Owen Child Labor Act** (1916) prohibited interstate trade involving commodities produced by children under the age of fourteen. It was subsequently ruled unconstitutional in the 1918 Supreme Court case *Hammer v. Dagenhart*. In 1924 a constitutional amendment to abolish child labor failed to receive the approval of the required three-fourths of the states for ratification.

Progressives had mixed success with the Supreme Court. Some of the court's key cases in the Progressive era are the following:

■ *Lochner v. New York* (1905) invalidated a New York State law that had limited night work hours in bakeries. The court contended that the law was a violation of the work contract between employer and employee.

■ *Muller v. Oregon* (1908) upheld a law that limited work hours for women laundry workers only. It did not apply to other workers (see the *Adkins* case below) and did not overturn the *Lochner* decision. In the *Muller* case, the Court decided that the inherent "weakness" of females required their protection by the government.

■ *Adkins v. Children's Hospital* (1923) held that a maximum ten-hour workday for women workers in Washington, D.C., was unconstitutional.

AP Tip

During the progressive era four constitutional amendments were adopted. Keep them in mind for AP free-response essays.

■ The Sixteenth Amendment (1913) provided for an income tax. As you recall, the Supreme Court had ruled in *Pollock v. Farmers Loan and Trust Company* (1895) that the Income Tax Act of 1893 was unconstitutional.

■ The Seventeenth Amendment (1913) replaced the method of selecting U.S. senators as prescribed in the Constitution—by state legislatures—with direct election of senators by popular vote.

■ The Eighteenth Amendment (1919) repealed in 1933 by the Twenty-first Amendment) prohibited the "manufacture, sale, or transportation of intoxicating liquors" within the United States. Some reformers blamed alcohol for many of society's problems.

■ The Nineteenth Amendment (1920) granted women the right to vote. No state could deny or abridge this right.

THE WOMEN'S RIGHTS MOVEMENT

While a milestone in the women's rights effort had been reached with ratification of the Nineteenth Amendment, women continued to be relegated to a second-class status, both economically—in the workplace—and socially. More and more women entered clerical and factory work, and some entered the professions, but their pay was considerably lower than men's pay, and they were denied access to certain professions and jobs. Roosevelt and Wilson, while progressive-minded in other ways, were certainly not strong advocates of the federal government's involvement in the women's rights cause. Some progressive women sought alternatives. For example, Charlotte Perkins Gilman's *Women and Economics* advocated for female financial independence. Another reformer, Margaret Sanger, observed the ill effects that unwanted pregnancies had on women, especially the poor, and thus advocated for the legalization of birth control. Even though she was arrested for disseminating contraceptive literature through the U.S. Mail, the indomitable Sanger set up the nation's first birth-control clinic in 1916. Alice Paul, a militant suffragist, engaged in acts of civil disobedience to draw attention to the need for a constitutional amendment guaranteeing women the right to vote. In addition, Jeannette Rankin became the first woman elected to Congress (1917). She promptly involved herself in the peace movement and would vote against U.S. intervention in World War I and World War II.

THE SOCIALIST CHALLENGE

Formed in 1901 by Eugene Debs and V. L. Berger as a radical alternative to the two dominant political parties, the Socialist party of the United States was dedicated to the welfare of the laboring class. Socialists called for policies and programs that went beyond the aspirations of the progressives, such as public ownership of utilities, railroads, and major industries such as oil and steel. On issues such as workers' compensation and minimum-wage laws, however, progressives and socialists cooperated. Over time, state, local, and federal governments embraced some Socialist ideas: public ownership of utilities, the eight-hour workday, and pensions for employees. During World War I, the party's supporters were persecuted, and following the war, the party was decimated in the first Red Scare. Yet the Socialist party offered Americans a viable alternative to the platforms of the Democrats and Republicans.

Debs was the party's presidential candidate five times. He embraced socialism while imprisoned for participating in the Pullman Strike in 1894. Debs did best in 1920 while in prison for violating the Espionage Act by opposing America's entry into World War I; in that election he garnered 6 percent of the popular vote.

The Wobblies

While most unions, such as the American Federation of Labor (AFL), sought to compromise and coexist with big business, the Industrial Workers of the World (IWW, founded in 1905 by revolutionary socialists and nicknamed the Wobblies) took a radically different approach. To them, capitalism was a tool of oppression that extended beyond the workplace into every aspect of one's social, economic, cultural, and political life. Led by "Big Bill" Haywood, the Wobblies dreamed of "one big union" of skilled and unskilled workers as the only way to challenge the enormous clout of America's corporations. When the United States entered World War I, the Wilson administration began to prosecute the Wobblies for treasonous acts; they had engaged in strikes and supported others to do so, which the administration claimed was undermining the war effort. At its height, it had enrolled 100,000 members, but its power waned after World War I.

BLACK AMERICANS AND THE PROGRESSIVE MOVEMENT

While Roosevelt and Wilson were catalysts for numerous reforms in the early twentieth century, the status and rights of black Americans were not priorities for them. Wilson, born in Virginia during the Civil War, did not appear to have much sympathy for the plight of black Americans. (Some historians maintain Wilson was a blatant racist.) Roosevelt concurred. He saw no political solution to the problem despite his outcries against the lawless acts perpetrated against blacks. Most progressives were frankly indifferent to the discrimination that was so very much a part of the black experience in the United States at this time. The most reform-minded politician could also be a racist. In most cases, black Americans had to look to their own leaders to develop a response to the political, economic, and social barriers that confronted them daily. Three gifted leaders emerged in this period:

- **Booker T. Washington** gained national attention in 1895 when he spoke at the Cotton States and International Exposition in Atlanta. Washington advised blacks to "put down your bucket where you are" and work for individual self-improvement. Once blacks were economically independent, he maintained, social change would follow. To this end, he started the Tuskegee Institute, a vocational school for blacks. For many white Americans, Washington's advice to his fellow blacks was sound. Washington (who was born a slave) was not advocating a radical or militant solution to the condition of blacks in America, but one that was moderate and therefore generally acceptable to white America. When President Roosevelt invited Washington to dine at the White House, it caused a national furor.
- **W. E. B. Du Bois**, like many other blacks, had serious reservations about Washington's approach. Born after the Civil War, he had been educated at Harvard University. His views were more expansive than Washington's in that he looked to white Americans to eliminate racism and segregation. In 1903 he published *The Souls of Black Folk*, in which he attacked Washington's patient approach to racial acceptance and equality. Instead, talented blacks should go

beyond developing a trade or skill and seek a university education. This "talented tenth" would be the vanguard in the effort to have black rights restored without delay and would became the nucleus of an organization called the Niagara Movement, forerunner to the National Association for the Advancement of Colored People (NAACP). Started in 1909, the NAACP soon went to work challenging Jim Crow laws. In *Buchanan v. Worley* (1915) the court struck down a Louisville, Kentucky, law that required segregated communities. In *Guinn v. United States* (1919), the Supreme Court ruled unconstitutional Oklahoma's use of the grandfather clause. To this day, the NAACP is active in promoting the rights of black Americans.

■ **Marcus Garvey** embraced nationalism as the solution to the black struggle. Believing that blacks would never gain acceptance and equality in the United States, he created the Universal Negro Improvement Association (UNIA), which had as its goal the creation of an independent nation in Africa. Although other civil rights leaders such as Du Bois repudiated him, thousands of blacks, mostly in poor urban areas, purchased stock in the Black Star Line, whose fleet would ostensibly transport them to Africa. Garvey's scheme failed, and many lost what little money they had in their investment. Ironically, Garvey's desire for a segregated black nation was exactly what reactionary and racist organizations like the Ku Klux Klan supported.

THE END OF THE PROGRESSIVE ERA

By the early 1920s the progressive movement had run its course. However, many progressive organizations' supporters were imbued with a spirit of reform that would continue to thrive. As war loomed, the foreign threat siphoned off the attention that domestic conditions had received. The devastation of World War I dampened the enthusiasm of many who believed that through government a more democratic society could be realized. Others embraced the notion that the material growth the nation was experiencing following the war was an indication that life in America had indeed improved. Still others believed that, given the tribulations of war and the social, economic, and political struggles of the previous twenty years, a "return to normalcy" was needed.

Multiple-Choice Questions

1. Which of the following took the lead in reforming the United States in the early twentieth century?
   (A) corporate leaders
   (B) the lower classes
   (C) the middle class
   (D) the House of Representatives
   (E) the conservative wing of the Republican party

ANSWER: **C.** The middle class was interested in reform because it felt pressure from big business and from labor and the poor (*The American Pageant,* 12th ed., p. 667/11th ed., p. 686).

2. Which one of the following presidents is NOT associated with a major reform movement in the twentieth century?
   (A) Warren Harding
   (B) Woodrow Wilson
   (C) Franklin D. Roosevelt
   (D) Lyndon Johnson
   (E) Theodore Roosevelt

ANSWER: **A.** Harding was a conservative who wanted to return the nation to "normalcy" after the changes that occurred because of the progressive movement and the impact of World War I (*The American Pageant,* 12th ed., p. 754/11th ed., pp. 771-772).

3. This muckraking novel addressed the abuses that occurred in Chicago's meatpacking industry.
   (A) *The Octopus*
   (B) *How the Other Half Lives*
   (C) *Shame of the Cities*
   (D) *The Jungle*
   (E) *The History of the Standard Oil Company*

ANSWER: **D.** Upton Sinclair's novel caused a national uproar over working conditions and the unsafe foods that emerged from meatpacking plants (*The American Pageant,* 12th ed., p. 675/11th ed., p. 691).

4. Which one of the following did NOT divide the Republican party on the eve of the 1912 election?
   (A) the Ballinger-Pinchot controversy
   (B) Taft's antitrust suit against U.S. Steel
   (C) the progressive wing's advocacy for black rights
   (D) the Speaker of the House controversy
   (E) the Payne-Aldrich Tariff

ANSWER: **C.** Most progressives were indifferent to the plight of black Americans (*The American Pageant,* 12th ed., p. 685/11th ed., pp. 699-700).

5. Which Supreme Court case decision made the Keating-Owen Child Labor Act unconstitutional?
   (A) *Lochner v. New York*
   (B) *Hammer v. Dagenhart*
   (C) *Muller v. Oregon*
   (D) *Northern Securities v. U.S.*
   (E) *Adkins v. Children's Hospital*

ANSWER: **B**.

6. This constitutional amendment provided for a federal income tax.
   (A) Fourteenth
   (B) Fifteenth
   (C) Sixteenth
   (D) Seventeenth
   (E) Eighteenth

ANSWER: **C**. The Sixteenth Amendment provided for a graduated income tax (*The American Pageant,* 12th ed., p. 691/11th ed., p. 707).

7. Marcus Garvey
   (A) was head of the Federal Reserve System in the early twentieth century
   (B) was a powerful Speaker of the House in the early twentieth century
   (C) advocated for equal rights for women, including the right to vote
   (D) was a reform-minded senator from Wisconsin who made his state a model of reform
   (E) was a black leader whose nationalist movement advocated a return to Africa for the nation's exploited black population

ANSWER: **E**. Garvey's Universal Negro Improvement Association maintained that blacks would never gain acceptance in a white-dominated United States and should instead develop their own nation in Africa (*The American Pageant,* 12th ed., p. 748/11th ed., pp. 764-765).

8. Which one of the following did NOT occur during Woodrow Wilson's presidency?
   (A) Federal Trade Commission
   (B) Federal Reserve Act
   (C) Clayton Anti-Trust Act
   (D) Department of Commerce and Labor
   (E) Underwood Tariff

ANSWER: **D**. The Department of Commerce and Labor was created in 1903, nine years before Wilson became president (*The American Pageant,* 12th ed., p. 673/11th ed., pp. 789-790).

9. The Socialist party of America
    (A) opposed civil rights legislation
    (B) supported government ownership of utility companies
    (C) was led by Booker T. Washington
    (D) was eventually absorbed into the conservative wing of the
        Republican party
    (E) advocated for the creation of the Federal Reserve System

ANSWER: **B.** The Socialist party, led by Eugene Debs, maintained that industries vital to the health of the nation's economy should not be owned by individuals whose only objective is to make a profit (*The American Pageant,* 12th ed., pp. 614-615/11th ed., pp. 631, 696).

10. The Salvation Army is identified with
    (A) the women's rights crusade
    (B) the black civil rights movement
    (C) the social gospel movement
    (D) trade unions
    (E) the conservation movement

ANSWER: **C.** The social gospel movement combined Christian ethics and social responsibility (*The American Pageant,* 12th ed., p. 571/11th ed., p. 578).

Free-Response Questions

1. Discuss the role government played in reforming American social, economic, and political life in the early twentieth century. In your response include TWO of the following:
   a. reforms at the federal level
   b. reforms at the state level
   c. reforms at the local/city level

RESPONSE You want to keep in mind that reforms emanate from both the government and from grassroots movements. However, the question asks you to address only government-related reforms. This is a straightforward question in which you identify those reforms that you deem significant and discuss what abuses they were intended to correct.

2. Evaluate the administrations of Roosevelt, Taft, and Wilson in relation to their records as progressive presidents.

RESPONSE Again, this is a straightforward question. It nonetheless requires a high-level thinking skill: the ability to evaluate a president's record on reform. Identify the reform measures taken by each, evaluate the success of the reforms, and discuss whether there is a pattern of social, economic, and political reforms initiated by these presidents.

14

WORLD WAR I: 1914–1918

By the early twentieth century the United States had established an international empire that stretched from the Caribbean to the Pacific. Ironically, while acquiring the land of others, the government and various grassroots movements were engaged in democratizing the nation's social, economic, and political systems, in a reforming spirit known as the progressive movement. As the United States entered the second decade of the century, storm clouds were appearing on the horizon in faraway Europe. Before long, a considerable part of the globe was engaged in what would become the most destructive war in history up to that time. When World War I broke out in 1914, Americans looked warily from across the Atlantic Ocean at the political machinations of Europe's powers, and they were determined to follow the advice given by President Washington over a century earlier: maintain the nation's neutrality in foreign disputes. Despite this sentiment, in 1917 American troops were fighting in France and Belgium in a war that would ultimately elevate the United States to world-power status.

KEY CONCEPTS

- German violations of American neutrality, strong economic and political ties to Britain, and effective British propaganda helped shape American public opinion about the combatants.
- Despite a strong desire on the part of the American public to remain neutral, the United States entered the conflict in 1917.
- World War I affected American civil liberties as the government suppressed dissent.
- The punitive nature of the Treaty of Versailles laid the foundation for resentment in Germany.

■ Woodrow Wilson's idealism, as articulated in the Fourteen Points, including the establishment of a League of Nations, was challenged at home.

World War I is discussed in depth in *The American Pageant,* 12th ed., Chapters 30 and 31/11th ed., Chapters 32-33.

CAUSES OF WORLD WAR I

While the United States entered the war fully three years after it began, it is important for the student to identify the major factors that brought the European powers into conflict. All historical events involve a multiplicity of short- and long-term causes, but four primary factors led to the onset of World War I in 1914.

■ **The rise of nationalism** Those ethnic groups that had earlier been absorbed into large European empires sought self-determination and desired freely elected governments that would best represent their interests. The Austro-Hungarian Empire is a prime example of a patchwork nation comprising a variety of ethnic and religious groups held together by an autocratic monarchy.

■ **The growth of imperialism** In the late nineteenth and early twentieth centuries, European powers raced to acquire colonies—in some cases simply to prevent their rivals from obtaining land that often had dubious benefits, as expressed in the term, the "scramble for Africa." This in turn led to increased tensions and threatened military conflicts among the European imperial powers. For example, the French and Germans nearly came to blows over control of Morocco, and German-British competition for markets in Africa and the Middle East increased tensions between the two. To make matters worse, there was no permanent international organization to settle disputes between nations.

■ **The formation of sometimes-secret military alliances** Distrust among rival imperialist European nations led to the creation of antagonistic alliances. The two most important were the Triple Alliance (later known as the Central Powers and comprising Germany, Austria-Hungary, and the Ottoman Empire) and the Triple Entente (later known as the Allies and comprising Great Britain, France, and Russia). The United States, Italy, and Japan would later side with the Allies.

■ **Increased militarism** The major European powers had been stockpiling military arms and expanding the size of their armies and navies. For example, the naval arms race between Britain and Germany exacerbated relations between the two. Further, in France a strong sense of revenge against the Germans for the French defeat in the Franco-Prussian War over thirty years earlier was still strong. In that conflict, the French had suffered a humiliating defeat and the loss of two of its key provinces, Alsace and Lorraine.

The stage was set for war. The spark that started it was the assassination of the heir to the Austro-Hungarian throne, Francis Ferdinand, by a Serb nationalist in June 1914. Tensions rose to a fever pitch when the Austrian government blamed Serbian authorities for the assassination. Reeling from the murder, Austrians nonetheless saw it as an opportunity to crush Serb nationalism once and for all and quell Serb dissent within the Austro-Hungarian Empire. A harsh ultimatum was given to the Serbs, who failed to meet the Austrian demands. On July 28 Austria-Hungary declared war on Serbia. Two days later Serbia's ally, Russia, entered the war, followed in short order by the other European powers—and ultimately non-European nations as well.

AMERICAN NEUTRALITY

When war broke out, President Woodrow Wilson was determined to keep the United States out of the conflict. He was deeply concerned that the war would seriously interrupt international trade and, worse, that the United States might be drawn into the maelstrom. Somewhat unrealistically Wilson believed that a neutral United States could somehow mediate an end to the dispute. But as we will see, if Wilson's hope of mediating an end to the war in 1914 or 1915 was near impossible, working out the peace terms proved equally challenging.

For both the Allies and Central Powers the demands of war required that they interrupt each other's expansive trade relationships, which included, of course, the United States. To this end, the British blockaded Germany in hopes of cutting off supplies to the Central Powers. In violation of international maritime law, the British deemed a wide range of goods contraband that could be seized by the Royal Navy. When the United States complained that the British were in fact in violation of international law, the British government claimed it was seizing contraband obviously intended for Germany and that it was not interfering with trade destined for neutral ports.

To the delight of the British, German violations of neutrality soon overshadowed their own transgressions. Early in 1915 the Germans declared that British waters would be deemed a war zone and that all shipping in that area could be attacked by German U-boats (submarines). From Germany's perspective, the loss of civilian lives could be avoided if neutrals stayed outside this zone and refrained from sailing on Allied ships. The very nature of submarine warfare—namely, stealth—often required U-boat captains to attack ships without first stopping and searching them for contraband. Not surprisingly, this led to the sinking of neutral ships and the loss of civilian lives. For the United States, the policies of both warring sides seriously interfered with freedom of the seas and placed American citizens in harm's way. The same year the British instituted their blockade, the inevitable happened. A British passenger liner, the *Lusitania,* was sunk by a German U-boat, resulting in the loss of over a thousand passengers, including 128 Americans.

In 1916 Wilson threatened to cut off diplomatic relations with Germany if unrestricted submarine warfare continued to cost the lives of Americans and jeopardize American shipping. Secretary of State William Jennings Bryan resigned in protest, believing that Wilson's rhetoric would bring the United States into the war. But when two Americans were injured after a French ship, the *Sussex,* was torpedoed, Wilson threatened to break off diplomatic relations with Germany. The Germans were at the time fighting the war on two fronts, against the British and French in the west and the Russians in the east. Keeping the United States out of the war was a German priority, and so the Germany promised not to sink passenger ships carrying noncombatants without warning and without care for the lives of the passengers (the "*Sussex* pledge"). For the better part of 1916, the Germans held true to their word.

U.S. RELATIONS WITH BRITAIN AND FRANCE, PUBLIC OPINION, AND WAR PROPAGANDA

Prior to the war the United States had experienced a recession, but French and British military contracts helped stimulate a recovery. By 1915 the economy had rebounded in terms of production and business profits. Of course, U.S. manufacturers wanted to ship supplies to the Germans as well as to the Allies, but the British blockade of Germany prevented this. Whereas between 1914 and 1917 U.S. trade with the Allies quadrupled, trade with Germany all but dried up. U.S. economic interests and the Allied war effort became even closer when U.S. financiers such as J. P. Morgan were given permission by the U.S. government to extend $3 billion in credit to Britain and France. To be sure, had the Allies lost the war, that money would be lost to U.S. bankers, a factor that probably played a role in the eventual decision by the U.S. government to intervene in the war.

Most Americans supported the Allied war effort for noneconomic reasons, a perspective that was shaped in part by the effectiveness of British propaganda, which depicted the Germans as modern-day Huns brutalizing Belgians and anyone else who stood in their way. Yet support for one side or the other depended in large part on one's ethnicity. For example, German-Americans supported the Central Powers, whereas Italian-Americans supported the Allies after Italy entered the war in 1915. Many Irish-Americans supported the Central Powers because of their hatred for the British government. Some Americans identified with the French because of their perceptions of a shared revolutionary past and French help during the American Revolution. Still, even by early 1917, most Americans, especially in the Midwest and West, were opposed to U.S. involvement in what they perceived as an entirely European affair. National leaders such as former Secretary of State Bryan, social activist Jane Addams, and Jeanette Rankin, the first woman elected to Congress, gave voice to sentiment for American neutrality, though once the United States entered the war most opposition dwindled. However, American socialists, unlike European socialists, maintained their opposition to the war from beginning to end and were often imprisoned for expressing their views or refusing to serve in the military.

U.S. INTERVENTION

In early 1917 the Germans decided to resume unrestricted submarine warfare. While probably a necessary military measure, it was one of the primary reasons the United States entered the war in November of that year. The immediate response of the United States was "armed neutrality"—that is, U.S. merchant ships would be armed in order to protect themselves from the stealthy U-boats. The Germans fully realized that their resumption of unrestricted U-boat warfare would probably draw the United States into the war, but they gambled that American intervention would come too late to effect a change in the course of the war. In February 1917 the British intercepted a diplomatic telegram written by Germany's foreign minister to Mexico, Alfred Zimmerman. When the telegram, referred to as the Zimmerman note, was published, Americans were shocked by the offer made by Zimmerman to Mexico: in return for Mexico's military assistance in the event the United States entered the war, Mexico would receive most of the land it had lost in the Mexican-American War if the Central Powers were victorious.

In March 1917 the Romanov Tsar Nicholas II of Russia was overthrown by revolutionary democratic forces. The provisional government kept Russia in the war until Lenin's Bolsheviks took power and signed a peace treaty with Germany, the Treaty of Brest-Litovsk, in 1917. But the overthrow of the tsar convinced Wilson that repressive regimes like Tsar Nicholas's and Kaiser Wilhelm II's represented a threat to democracy and economic liberalism. Wilson inched ever closer to the idea that the war, and specifically U.S. involvement in it, was a struggle "to make the world safe for democracy." On April 2, 1917, President Wilson called for a special session of Congress at which he asked for a declaration of war in order to stop Germany's "warfare against mankind." On April 4 Congress concurred; the United States was at war with Germany and its allies.

AP Tip

In explaining any historical effect, you should distinguish between short- and long-term causes. U.S. intervention in World War I did not suddenly occur. For example, German violations of American neutrality had long been a source of tension between the two nations. However, there were important short-term causes of President Wilson's decision to declare war on the Central Powers:

- Germany's decision to renew U-boat attacks on neutral shipping
- the Zimmerman note, which had a profound impact on American public opinion
- the Russian Revolution, which overthrew the Romanov dynasty—and satisfied Wilson's concerns regarding a U.S. alliance with an autocratic Russia's and allowed him to claim the war was being fought to make the world safe for democracy

WORLD WAR I AND SUPPRESSION OF CIVIL LIBERTIES AND DISSENT

Given the nearly unanimous support in Congress for the war, one would think that the entire nation embraced U.S. intervention. But the actions of the government in 1917 and 1918 indicate that it was deeply concerned with domestic dissent. For example, the following legislation was passed to address this "problem":

■ **Espionage Act of 1917** This called for fines and imprisonment for anyone "aiding the enemy" by obstructing the war effort. The postmaster-general was authorized to ban the dissemination of "treasonable literature." Socialist leader and 1912 presidential candidate Eugene Debs was convicted and imprisoned for violating the act. In 1919 the Supreme Court upheld the constitutionality of the Espionage Act in its decision in *Schenck v. United States,* a case involving an individual who used the U.S. mail to attempt to dissuade draftees from reporting for induction in the military. Justice Oliver Wendell Holmes argued that such actions presented a "clear and present danger" to national interests and therefore First Amendment free-speech rights could be limited by the government.

■ **Sedition Act of 1918** This law made it a criminal act punishable by fine or imprisonment to attempt to persuade or discourage the sale of war bonds or to in any way disparage the military, the Constitution, or the government.

To complement its attack on dissenters, the government created the Committee of Public Information (run by George Creel, who, interestingly enough, was a progressive). In the process of equating the government's case for war and patriotism, the committee's work set off a groundswell of distrust. Immigrants and those with foreign-sounding names were considered "un-American."

THE ECONOMICS OF WAR

The federal government's intervention in the economy increased profoundly during the war as more and more agencies and resources were centralized under the government's control. This would serve as a foundation and precedent for later governmental interventions (the New Deal, for instance) and as a way to resolve economic problems and organize the expansive nature of American capitalism. The following are representative of this centralization:

■ **War Industries Board (1917)** Led by Bernard Baruch, the board was created to coordinate all aspects of industrial production and distribution.

■ **Lever Act (1917)** Led by Herbert Hoover as food administrator, this act aimed to mobilize agriculture and establish prices to encourage production.

■ **War Labor Board (1918)** This board arbitrated management-labor disputes, prevented labor strikes, and regulated wages and work hours.

To be sure, U.S. economic and military intervention (over 1 million troops) in the war helped break the stalemate that had shaped warfare on the Western Front, where the Allies and Central Powers battered each other month after month, with neither side able to gain a decisive advantage. For Germany, the war was sapping its resources and public support for continuing the fight. After the Allies launched a major offensive in the fall of 1918, it became abundantly clear to the Germans that their nation would ultimately be invaded. The kaiser abdicated and was replaced by a representative government, which agreed to an armistice in November 1918. The "war to end all wars" had ended, but not before claiming millions of lives, of which over fifty thousand were American. The war had cost over $300 billion. Four great empires—Russian, German, Ottoman, and Austro-Hungarian—collapsed in the process.

TREATY OF VERSAILLES AND THE LEAGUE OF NATIONS

The "Big Four" (Wilson, France's Clemenceau, Britain's Lloyd George, and Italy's Orlando), representing the victorious Allied Powers, met in Paris and Versailles, France, in 1919 to work out the details of the peace treaty that would be imposed on the defeated Central Powers. Having suffered enormous losses, the European Allies sought a punitive peace treaty. Despite Wilson's misgivings about the harsh punishment meted out to Germany in the Treaty of Versailles, the followings provisions were adopted:

- The provinces of Alsace and Lorraine (lost by the French in the Franco-Prussian War) were returned to France.
- Germany was prevented from placing troops on the western side of the Rhine River.
- The German military was dramatically reduced in size and strength.
- Germany was to ship coal from the occupied Saar region to France for a period of fifteen years.
- Germany lost all of its colonies.
- New nations were created: Estonia, Latvia, Yugoslavia, Czechoslovakia, and Poland.
- Austria-Hungary lost three-fifths of its land and three-fifths of its population.
- The Central Powers were to pay crushing war reparations.
- Germany was branded with "war guilt" as the primary perpetrator of the war.

For his part, Wilson was greatly disturbed by the harshness of the treaty, even threatening at one point to negotiate a separate treaty with Germany. Instead, he outlined his vision for the postwar world in a list of political and economic objectives referred to as The Fourteen Points. They included

- the elimination of secret treaties, the stimulus for which was the Bolshevik revelation that Britain and France had engaged in this diplomatic practice prior to the war
- open access to the seas in times of war and peace, which was important for economic expansion and trade
- reduction of military stockpiles
- adjustment of colonial claims
- self-determination for Europeans, but not for those under colonial control
- the creation of an international assembly (the fourteenth point) that would "afford mutual guarantees of political independence and territorial integrity"

Wilson believed that the fourteenth point—his call for the creation of what ultimately became the League of Nations— could be the basis for resolving the problems associated with the first thirteen points. Open to all nations, this international body would be the forum for resolving international disputes and making military confrontations obsolete.

Wilson worked tirelessly to convince the American people and Congress to support the Versailles Treaty. Unfortunately, the commissioners he selected to represent the United States at the peace conference were all Democrats, which angered and antagonized the Republican party and key Republican political leaders, especially the most influential member of the Senate, Henry Cabot Lodge. Wilson's second political blunder was to travel to France for the peace talks rather than mobilize support for the treaty at home. Wilson's emphasis on the treaty made it the most important issue of the 1918 Senate elections. He took his appeal for its ratification directly to the American people in an exhausting national speaking tour, which ultimately broke his health. A stroke, in September 1919, paralyzed not only his body, but his personal crusade to see the treaty ratified. Senator Lodge, for his part, offered certain important reservations to the treaty that would have diminished the role and commitment of the United States to the League of Nations. With Senator Lodge and the "irreconcilables" (ultraconservatives opposed to the treaty) in the vanguard, the opponents of ratification won the day. Although the issue of admission to the League was taken up after Wilson left the White House, the United States never became a member of that body.

THE INTERWAR YEARS

Shocked by the enormous loss of life in the war, world leaders grasped at ways to prevent such a thing from happening again. The League of Nations was seen as one method, but without U.S. and Soviet involvement, its potential for solving international disputes was limited. Nevertheless, various international agreements were made in the interwar years to limit the size of militaries and resolve potential political disputes. Some were practical, others, rested on naïve optimism.

- **The Five-Power Naval Treaty** At the Washington "Disarmament" Conference (1921-1922), convened by President Harding, the United States, Britain, Japan, France, and Italy agreed to limit their capital ships to the following ratio respectively: 5:5:3:1.7:1.7. The participants also agreed to ban the use of certain insidious weaponry such as poison gas and restricted submarine warfare.
- **The Four-Power Treaty** At the same conference, the United States, Britain, Japan, and France agreed to respect one another's Pacific territorial possessions by, in part, not creating forward military bases in the Pacific.
- **The Nine-Power Treaty** Yet another product of the same conference, this treaty reaffirmed the Open Door policy in China.
- **Kellogg-Briand Pact (1928)** This international agreement outlawed war. However, it made no provision for enforcement, nor did it provide for defensive wars.

ECONOMIC IMPERATIVES: INTERVENTION, WORLD WAR I DEBTS, AND REPARATIONS

The interwar years were dominated by Republican presidents whose domestic and foreign policies were designed to advance American business interests. To this end the Coolidge administration saw to it that a new constitution passed by Mexico in 1917, which called for nationalizing Mexico's important industries, would not jeopardize American investments in those businesses. Throughout the 1920s U.S. troops were sent to South America and the Caribbean to reinforce U.S.-backed regimes and to protect U.S. financial interests. Of equal concern to U.S. policymakers and financial institutions were the billions of dollars in loans extended to the Allies during the war. President Coolidge wanted the debts repaid, but the Europeans balked, claiming that they were unable to collect the billions in war reparations owed to them by a bankrupt Germany and adding that U.S. losses paled in comparison to their losses. Equally troubling was the U.S. passage of the Fordney-McCumber Tariff. The tariff made it exceedingly difficult for Europeans to sell their products in the United States and make the money that could be used to pay back the war loans. In response to this problem, the United States offered the following solutions:

■ **The Dawes Plan** This plan significantly reduced Germany's reparations and provided loans to Germany in a roundabout way: the United States loaned money to Germany, Germany used this to pay its reparations to the Allies, who in turn used these funds to pay off the interest on its war debts to the United States.
■ **The Young Plan** This plan further reduced Germany's payments and established the Bank for International Settlements to assist in the process of reparations payments.

Nevertheless, the collapse of national economies brought on by the Great Depression caused most nations to default on their debt payments to the United States.

Throughout the 1920s and well into the 1930s, the United States continued to influence the affairs of its own hemisphere as well. Time after time it intervened in Central and Latin America in order to protect U.S. economic and political interests while simultaneously it attempted to draw those nations closer to the United States, especially in light of the rise of antagonistic governments in Japan, Germany, and Italy. At the Pan-American Conferences of 1923 and 1928, the United States agreed to treat all nations on an "equal footing." The Clark Memorandum of 1928 took this rapprochement one step further by repudiating the Roosevelt Corollary to the Monroe Doctrine. Later, in the 1930s, President Roosevelt would replace Dollar Diplomacy with the Good Neighbor policy, which stated that no nation would interfere in another's internal affairs. For the time being, this new, less hegemonic policy satisfied most South Americans. Even in the far reaches of the American empire, the Philippines, the United States, partially recognizing the costs of maintaining an international empire, promised Filipino independence by 1946 (Tydings-McDuffie Act). Post-World War II international affairs, however, would convince U.S.

administrations to pull back from these prewar agreements and statements.

In the two decades following the war, as the horrors of World War I battlefields faded from public consciousness, the United States experienced an economic boom, highlighted by the "Roaring Twenties." But the harshness of the Versailles Treaty, the onset of the Great Depression, and the rise of militarism and imperialism in Europe and Asia would guarantee that the peace would not be maintained for long. By 1939 the world was again at war. Two years later, the United States, which had emerged from World War I as a major economic and military power, would for the second time in less than twenty-five years send its young men to fight and die on foreign battlefields. But this time, the stakes seemed so much higher.

MULTIPLE-CHOICE QUESTIONS

1. Which of the following was NOT a cause of World War I?
    (A) imperialism
    (B) militarism
    (C) secret military alliances
    (D) the Russian Revolution
    (E) nationalism

ANSWER: **D.** The Russian Revolution took place during the war (*The American Pageant*, 12th ed., p. 706/11th ed., p. 724).

2. Which of the following was a member of the Central Powers?
    (A) Germany
    (B) France
    (C) Britain
    (D) Italy
    (E) United States

ANSWER: **A.** The others were members of the Allied Powers (*The American Pageant*, 12th ed., p. 706/11th ed., p. 714).

3. The spark that ignited World War I was
    (A) the Zimmerman note
    (B) the assassination of the Austrian heir to the throne by a Serb nationalist
    (C) Germany's ultimatum to Serbia
    (D) the sinking of the *Lusitania*
    (E) the sinking of the *Sussex*

ANSWER: **B.** Austria-Hungary declared war on Serbia, and the other nations quickly followed by declaring war on each other (*The American Pageant*, 12th ed., pp. 696-697/11th ed., pp. 713-714).

4. In the Zimmerman note
   (A) Germany offered to compensate the United States for the American lives lost in the *Lusitania* sinking
   (B) the United States agreed not to intervene in the war if Germany halted its sinking of neutral shipping
   (C) the Germans agreed to help the Russian Bolsheviks overthrow the tsar of Russia
   (D) the United States secretly agreed to supply the Allies with war supplies in return for concessions following the war
   (E) the Germans promised to restore to Mexico the land it lost in the Mexican-American War in return for a military alliance with Germany

ANSWER: **E.** The Zimmerman note played a significant role in aggravating U.S.-German relations (*The American Pageant*, 12th ed., p. 706/11th ed., p. 723).

5. In the *Sussex* pledge
   (A) Germany promised to cease sinking passenger ships without warning or care for the passengers
   (B) Germany promised to resume U-boat attacks on neutral shipping if the United States continued to supply the Allies
   (C) President Wilson promised the Allies that the United States would halt all U.S. trade with Germany
   (D) the Germans promised to stop using U-boats to attack Allied warships and merchant ships
   (E) the United States agreed not to arm its merchant fleet

ANSWER: **A.** The *Sussex* pledge did not hold throughout the war (*The American Pageant*, 12th ed., pp. 700, 705/11th ed., pp. 716, 722).

6. In the U.S. Supreme Court case *Schenck v. United States,* the Court ruled that
   (A) the government could prohibit U.S. citizens from traveling on ships of nations at war
   (B) conscientious objectors could not be forced to serve in the U.S. military
   (C) the government was not obligated to protect the lives or property of those American citizens who opposed the war
   (D) the Espionage Act of 1917 was constitutional
   (E) the American Socialist party represented a clear and present danger to the United States

ANSWER: **D.** The *Schenck* decision was a serious attack on civil liberties (*The American Pageant*, 12th ed., pp. 708-709/11th ed., pp. 726-727).

7. Which of the following was NOT a feature of the Treaty of Versailles?
    (A) Germany would be occupied by France and Britain for twenty years.
    (B) Germany would provide France with coal for fifteen years.
    (C) Germany would pay reparations to the Allies.
    (D) Alsace and Lorraine were returned to France.
    (E) Germany would be demilitarized.

ANSWER: **A.** Parts of Germany were indeed occupied, but not the entire nation. The other features were indicative of the punitive nature of the treaty (*The American Pageant*, 12th ed. p., 721/11th ed., pp. 737-738).

8. Which of the following was an international agreement designed to outlaw war?
    (A) the Five-Power Naval Treaty
    (B) the Treaty of Versailles
    (C) the Kellogg-Briand Pact
    (D) the Four-Power Treaty
    (E) the *Sussex* pledge

ANSWER: **C.** The Kellogg-Briand Pact failed because it did not include provisions for enforcement (*The American Pageant*, 12th ed., p. 758/11th ed., p. 776).

9. The same year (1917) that the United States entered World War I on the Allied side, this Allied power dropped out of the war:
    (A) Britain
    (B) France
    (C) Italy
    (D) Belgium
    (E) Russia

ANSWER: **E.** The Bolsheviks, under the leadership of V. I. Lenin, signed a peace agreement, the Treaty of Brest-Litovsk, with the Central Powers (*The American Pageant*, 12th ed., p. 715/11th ed., p. 732).

10. The Dawes Plan and the Young Plan
    (A) increased U.S. financial aid to South America
    (B) repudiated the Roosevelt Corollary to the Monroe Doctrine
    (C) assisted Germany with its reparations payments
    (D) provided for Filipino independence
    (E) placed significant limitations on the role the United States would play in the League of Nations

ANSWER: **C.** The plans were designed to help Germany pay back its loans to the U.S., from which it had borrowed to pay war reparations to the European Allies (*The American Pageant*, 12th ed., p. 764/11th ed., pp. 782-783).

FREE-RESPONSE QUESTIONS

1. Agree or disagree with the following statement:

    President Wilson had no choice but to enter World War I on the side of the Allies.

RESPONSE To agree with the statement, you can begin with a discussion of American neutrality, the Zimmerman note, and Germany's use of unrestricted U-boat warfare. To refute it, you should discuss Britain's violations of U.S. neutrality, the effectiveness of British propaganda, the economic investment U.S. capitalists made to the Allied war effort, and the suppression of domestic dissent.

2. Agree or disagree with the following statement:

    Woodrow Wilson's vision for the postwar world and the methods he used to achieve these goals was riddled with naïve thinking and political miscalculations.

RESPONSE To agree with the statement, you should discuss the resistance of the European Allies to a peaceful settlement with Germany, favoring instead a punitive peace treaty, much to Wilson's chagrin. Further, you can address the shortsighted approach the president took in not making his mission to the peace talks a bipartisan one—he took only Democrats to Paris with him. Wilson may have also miscalculated the strong neutral and isolationist sentiments among Americans after the war. To refute the statement, point out that Wilson's idealism was expressed in the expectation that an international body, the League of Nations, would resolve future problems and therefore prevent military conflicts. His Fourteen Points were an attempt to address some of the abuses and problems that led to World War I.

15

CONSERVATISM AND CULTURAL DIVERSITY IN THE 1920S

The period between the end of World War I and the collapse of the nation's economy in 1929 is often referred to as the "Roaring Twenties." Indeed, in many ways that characterization is appropriate, for the 1920s witnessed an explosive cultural transformation that affected the lives of the nation's youth, its African-American population, and women. In some ways, the decade has a counterpart in the civil rights and women's rights movements and with youth rebellion associated with American life in the 1960s. Yet in the 1920s there were contradictions: women and black Americans were still subordinated, and despite the burst of cultural development that took place, the nation was led by conservative presidents who represented the social, cultural, economic, and political status quo. Political radicalism and trade unionism would challenge the economic and political relations that prevailed, bringing radicals and trade unions into direct confrontation with a government that would not tolerate deviations from the accepted political ideology.

What then made the Twenties "roar?" Following the war, the nation experienced an economic boom. Many Americans, especially in the nation's urban areas, helped the expansion of the economy by increasingly participating in America's growing consumer culture, from the automobile to the phonograph. New cultural forms such as jazz and modern art revolutionized American civilization, and the Harlem Renaissance offered black poets, artists, and authors an opportunity to make valuable contributions to American cultural life. Still, under the surface there were pressures, contradictions, and the same racial and ethnic maladies that had always plagued the nation. Increasingly, the nation was divided demographically, as rapidly changing, dynamic urban life stood in stark contrast with the more static, traditional, and—to a certain sense—more Protestant rural areas. Also, while the economy boomed, not all benefited. Many who were poor after the war remained that way through the 1920s and beyond. Millions of immigrants entered the nation during this period, alarming indigenous Americans that the United States would soon be overwhelmed by foreign cultures, especially from southern and eastern Europe. An investigation of the features, tensions, and passions of the 1920s offers an opportunity to view the nation at a pivotal point in its history, when many sought to leave the past behind and others yearned for a "return to normalcy."

KEY CONCEPTS

- The 1920s were dominated by conservative Republican presidents.
- Americans experienced an unprecedented burst of consumer activity as new mass-produced commodities were made available.
- Tensions prevailed between rural and urban America.
- The decade witnessed a rise in nativism and racism.
- The period was culturally vibrant as new forms of music and art became popular.
- The U.S. government persecuted radicals in the red scare.

The decade of the 1920s is discussed in depth in *The American Pageant,* 12th ed., Chapters 32 and 33/11th ed., Chapters 34-35.

POLITICAL DEVELOPMENTS

The presidential election of 1920 focused on whether to accept President Wilson's idealism (for example, to enter the League of Nations) or to, as the Republican candidate Warren G. Harding stated, "Return to normalcy"—in other words, return to an earlier time when Republicans occupied the Oval Office and the nation was not embroiled in foreign problems. The Democratic ticket was composed of presidential candidate James M. Cox and his running mate, Franklin D. Roosevelt. The election, the first in which women nationally had the right to vote, was a landslide for Harding and his running mate, Calvin Coolidge. It appeared the Republicans were given a mandate from the American people, who rejected the policies and philosophy of Wilson's administration by returning a Republican to the White House in such a convincing way. In the meantime a reconversion of the nation's economy had taken place as wartime government regulations on business were relaxed. Two pieces of legislation serve as significant examples of this reconversion:

- **The Jones Merchant Marine Act (1920)** The act authorized the sale of ships built by the government to private bidders.
- **The Esch-Cummins Act (1920)** Control of the railroad industry was returned to private companies. Unions had offered the Plumb Plan (named after a railway union's legal counsel), which would have allowed the government to purchase the railroads; management of the industry would comprise government officials,

railway employees, and railway operators. Congress rejected the plan, however.

The Harding administration sought to cut taxes, especially for the wealthy—as could be seen in the Mellon Tax Plan—reduce government spending, and to protect American industries from the demands of labor and from foreign competition. In the case of the latter, Congress passed the Fordney-McCumber Tariff, which placed high taxes on imports, a policy that the nation's trade partners would adopt in retaliation.

Harding had never really wanted to be president. Content as an Ohio newspaper owner and U.S. senator, he found the role of chief executive more stressful than his mind and body could endure. Three years into his term, in 1923, he died suddenly, catapulting Calvin Coolidge into the Oval Office. Had Harding lived, he would have endured the humiliation of congressional investigations that revealed widespread corruption on the part of Harding's associates and advisers. The most infamous case involved the sale of U.S. naval oil reserves at Teapot Dome, Wyoming, to private businesses. Harding's secretary of the interior, Albert Fall, was convicted of bribery and sent to prison, the first cabinet member in U.S. history to suffer such a disgraceful fate. Other political associates, such as Attorney General Henry Daugherty and Secretary of the Navy Edwin Denby, barely escaped conviction. However, one of Harding's closest friends, Jesse Smith, who had arranged the payoffs, committed suicide.

"SILENT CAL" COOLIDGE AND THE "DO-NOTHING" HERBERT HOOVER

The new president, Calvin Coolidge, the former governor of Massachusetts, rose to national prominence by putting down a police strike in Boston. A man of very few words, Coolidge believed the best thing a president could do for the nation was to do very little, especially when it came to government control or regulation of the economy. Under his conservative stewardship the business sector flourished, though his critics claimed he maintained the status quo by failing to address important social and economic concerns. Farmers, for one, could find little support from the administration, especially after farm prices slumped in the postwar years. Even though Congress passed the McNary-Haugen Bill (in 1927 and 1928), which provided for the government to purchase crops in order to maintain price levels comparable to what they were before the war, both times Coolidge vetoed the legislation as being an economic burden on the government.

Because he had not been tainted by the scandals of the previous few years, Coolidge ran for election in his own right in 1924. He easily defeated his Democratic opponent, John W. Davis, and a third-party candidate, the progressive senator from Wisconsin, Robert La Follette, who nevertheless received 5 million votes. Throughout the nation, women were elected to serve in local, state, and federal positions. The nation's first two women governors, for example, were elected in 1924. When it came time for Coolidge to seek reelection in 1928, the taciturn president told reporters, "I choose not to run for president in 1928," and kept to his word. In the '28 election another Republican, Herbert Hoover, was elected over New York's Governor Al Smith. Smith's religion (he was a Catholic) probably cost him significant support among Protestants. (It would be another thirty-two years before the nation would elect its first Catholic president, John F. Kennedy.) Sadly for Hoover, the Great Depression struck less than two years into his one and only term. Unfortunately for the American people, Hoover, who had done so much as an administrator for Belgian war relief in 1917, did so little to provide aid to Americans suffering from the effects of the economic collapse. His detractors called him a "do-nothing" president. His successor, Democrat Franklin D. Roosevelt, would oversee the nation as it made its way through the perilous waters of the worst economic collapse in the nation's history.

MASS CONSUMERISM

After a brief recession in the first two years of the decade, the economy quickly rebounded. It would soon reach unprecedented heights as the nation engaged in a torrent of consumer spending stimulated in part by the stock-market "bubble" and available surplus capital that often comes with periods of economic recovery. Purchasing on credit (installment buying) allowed Americans to "buy now and pay later." Consequently, those items that had earlier been considered out of reach for millions of Americans, such as home appliances, could now be purchased and paid off over time. Unfortunately, this spending spree led many to fall into debt. The advent of department-store catalogs, such as those offered by Sears Roebuck and Montgomery Ward, made it easier to purchase commodities, especially for people who did not have access to large urban department stores. And mass advertising convinced the consumer of the need to purchase new and improved commodities. The advent of the radio provided Americans a new form of entertainment and faster access to national and international news, as well as a venue for the nation's advertisers.

The period's most notable consumer item was the automobile. Although there were very few cars in the United States prior to World War I, by the end of the 1920s over 25 million autos would be registered; 20 percent of Americans owned cars by 1930. Of course not everyone could afford to purchase such an expensive commodity, but Henry Ford's revolutionary use of the assembly line made the Model T accessible to many, including his own workers, who were paid an unprecedented $5 per eight-hour day! The expansion of the auto industry spurred associated developments, such as highway construction, increased suburbanization, and the growth of the rubber, oil, insurance, and advertising industries. By the mid-1920s, many in the middle class came to associate their status with automobile ownership. Yet the expansion of one form of transportation spelled the decline of another—namely the railroad industry.

Entertainment: The Motion Picture Industry and Professional Sports

Like the birth of radio and the recording industry in the 1920s, of television in the post- World War II years, or of the Internet today, the motion picture industry provided Americans with a revolutionary new source of entertainment and information. The first one-reel movie (*The Great Train Robbery*) had been produced in 1913, followed by the first feature-length film, *Birth of a Nation* (1915). Utilizing editing techniques, *Birth of a Nation* captivated the American public despite its politically charged representation of racist stereotypes and glorification of the KKK. The 1920s movie industry built on the successes of the previous decade as silent motion pictures became enormously popular. The first movie documentary, *Nanook of the North,* was released in 1922. Animated films also became very popular in the 1920s as the American public was drawn to such cartoon characters as "Krazy Kat" and Walt Disney's "Steamboat Willie" (later known as Mickey Mouse). It was not until 1927 that Americans had the opportunity to hear their first "talkie," *The Jazz Singer.*

Although baseball had suffered a serious black eye as a result of the Black Sox scandal of 1919 when members of the Chicago White Sox threw the World Series, the sport rebounded in the 1920s as athletes such as Babe Ruth became national icons. Boxing and football also grew as popular diversions in the 1920s.

While the economy boomed, there were social and cultural undercurrents that indicated that all was indeed not well domestically. By 1930 many Americans who had spent enormous sums on consumer items in the 1920s would find it difficult to purchase even the most basic needs of life.

DIVISIONS ON THE DOMESTIC SCENE

Many social scientists see the 1920s as a time when the ideals of modernism clashed with the stability of tradition, secular and religious. These tensions manifested themselves in a variety of political, social, and cultural ways:

- **Urban versus rural** To those living in rural America, the nation's cities represented vice and sin. Ironically, as the nation was prepared to enter into the decade known as the Roaring Twenties, the sale, distribution, and consumption of alcoholic beverages was outlawed in the United States by the Eighteenth Amendment and enforced by the Volstead Act. The campaign to outlaw alcohol, launched by Protestant fundamentalists—the "drys"—was based on the assumptions that liquor caused crime, poverty, poor health, and broken families. With prohibition, speakeasies popped up in cities large and small. There, "wets" would dance—for example, the frenetic Charleston played by jazz musicians like Louis Armstrong—and drink illegal alcohol. Rural Americans viewed it as an exceedingly provocative lifestyle. (Prohibition ultimately led to the rise of urban gangs, such as the one led by Chicago's Al Capone. It also cost millions to enforce, and it failed to resonate on a moral level with the American people. Having outlived its welcome, the Eighteenth Amendment was repealed in 1933 by the Twenty-first Amendment.) The attitude of urban women as represented in their clothing and behavior (in part shaped by advertising) seemed equally disturbing to small-town Americans. Each year, it seemed, women's hemlines inched ever higher, and some women were wearing cosmetics and smoking cigarettes. Known as "flappers," these women flaunted their disdain for traditional women's roles in a manner that angered those who favored a more Victorian comportment for women.

■ **Moderate versus radical unionism** Major moderate unions such as the American Federation of Labor (AFL) experienced a decline in their membership due to their limited successes in achieving real gains for workers when the nation's economy was booming. Radical unions such as the Industrial Workers of the World (the "Wobblies") had been effectively neutralized by the government during the war. The 1920s witnessed the growth of industrial unions whose members identified with radical political and economic solutions to their plight.

■ **Science versus religion: the Scopes Monkey Trial** In 1925 a Tennessee teacher was arrested for teaching Darwin's theory of evolution in defiance of state law. The case provided fundamentalist Christians an opportunity to silence those who questioned the theory of creation as described in the Book of Genesis. Moreover, the case pitted the ideals and ideas of urban modernism against the religious fundamentalism of rural Protestant America. Three-time presidential candidate William Jennings Bryan was the prosecutor in the case; the famous attorney Clarence Darrow represented John Scopes. The jury ruled against the teacher, but the verdict was eventually overturned. To this day, the role of religion in education is debated in the halls of Congress and across the nation.

■ **Modern versus traditional art forms** The emergence of abstract art forms such as impressionism and cubism provoked controversy. At the infamous Armory Show, held in New York City in 1913, the highly controversial works of Pablo Picasso and other modern artists were exhibited. Picasso's use of geometric abstract shapes in his paintings outraged traditionalists, as did Marcel Duchamp's "Nude Descending a Staircase," which seemed suggestive and provocative to those with more modest sensibilities. Ultimately the modernists won out. In 1929 the Museum of Modern Art opened in New York City. By that time many had come to accept and even appreciate the new art form, whose case was prejudiced by the nativist sentiment that consumed the nation in this decade. Following World War I, New York's Harlem became the center of black American cultural and intellectual life. Black artists, poets, authors, musicians, and painters flocked to this cultural mecca, where they produced some of the finest literary, musical, and artistic works in the 1920s—or in any decade, for that matter. James Weldon Johnson, Jean Toomer, Countee Cullen, Langston Hughes, and other authors and poets touched a chord in white and black Americans alike. The musical arrangements that emerged from this movement tended to be a synthesis of gospel music, jazz, and African rhythms. Known as the Harlem Renaissance, the movement also provided an opportunity to protest racial attitudes and promote black pride.

AP Tip

What was it about the 1920s that seems so important and unique that it deserves a separate chapter? As with all historical questions, the answer is very much interpretive. Some historians see the period as essentially one in which Americans became increasingly identified with consumerism and materialism, repudiating the reforms associated with the pre-World War I era and embracing conservatism and even racist and reactionary politics, in part as a response to the Progressive era. Other historians see the reaction by more traditional and conservative citizens as a legitimate attempt to preserve the values they associated with being an American, which was expressed, for example, in nativism and antimodernism. What is more, many Americans were responding to what they viewed as an unhealthy expansion of federal power that they attributed, in part, to the progressive era and World War I. Other historians view this expansion of federal power as a not unexpected consequence of the development and expansion of the American economy. To be sure, this is a sampling of interpretations, but you should be conscious of divergent perspectives, as well as how many of the issues that shaped an earlier historical period are contemporary concerns as well.

NATIVIST ANXIETY

The success of the Bolshevik Revolution in Russia in 1917 gave rise to the first red scare (1919-1920). Americans and their government believed that communism was on the rise and could someday spread to the United States. When bombs exploded outside the home of Attorney General A. Mitchell Palmer in 1919 and on Wall Street the following year, killing thirty-eight people, the attacks were blamed on communists. Paranoia swept the nation in what became known at the "red scare," a period when the government reacted against domestic radicals, many of whom, though opponents of capitalism, were law-abiding citizens who should have been protected by the First Amendment. Under Palmer, deportations soon followed, as did attacks on trade union members, socialists, and immigrants.

After the red scare died down, the 1920s were characterized by a conservative reaction to immigration and political radicalism. Foreigners were perceived as somehow posing a radical challenge to the American way of life. Nativist sentiment consumed the nation in this decade. It can be seen on a number of fronts:

■ **The reemergence of the Ku Klux Klan** The KKK had fallen on hard times in the late nineteenth and early twentieth centuries as membership declined. By 1915, however, it had returned with a vengeance. Its targets were now Jews, eastern Europeans, Catholics, radicals, and unions, as well as black Americans. By 1924 the organization's membership peaked at 5 million, and it had expanded into northern states. The Klan was even successful in electing its members to important political positions in the 1920s.

- **The Sacco and Vanzetti Trial** In some ways this legal case was a microcosm of the political and ethnic problems and tensions that existed in the 1920s. Accused of murder, the two Italian anarchists were convicted and executed in 1927, despite claims that there was insufficient evidence to convict them. Many of their contemporaries argued that the men's ethnicity and political views, not their complicity in the crime, convicted them. Historians are still divided over the nature of the case.
- **The "Hundred Percenters"** Considering themselves 100 percent American, not foreign-born, this group attempted to limit foreign cultural and political influences on the United States and sought a foreign policy that would isolate the United States from foreign entanglements and relations.

Anxiety about foreigners inevitably gave rise to immigration restrictions. Despite the growing need for cheap labor, intense anti-immigration sentiment for cultural and racial reasons again took hold, as expressed in the following legislation:

- **Literacy Test Act (1917)** Passed over Wilson's veto, it required immigrants to pass a literacy test in English or their own native tongue.
- **Emergency Quota Act (1921)** This act reduced southern and eastern European immigration.
- **Immigration Act (1924)** Based on the belief that immigrants from eastern and southern Europe were more difficult to assimilate, this legislation provided a national origins plan that dramatically restricted immigration to 2 percent for each nationality represented in the 1890 census.
- **Chinese Exclusion Act (1882)** This act limited Asian immigration, which was not significantly changed until 1965.

In 1929 the Roaring Twenties came to an abrupt and unexpected end when the stock market crashed, bringing down with it the nation's economy. To be sure, the lives of millions of Americans, black and white, rural and urban, had been untouched by either the prosperity or cultural achievements that defined the 1920s. As the nation entered one of its darkest hours, the Great Depression, the lives of those already marginalized would deteriorate even further. For those who had flourished in the 1920s, their lives in the next decade would be in stark contrast to the excitement and sense of newness of the 1920s.

MULTIPLE-CHOICE QUESTIONS

1. Politically the decade of the 1920s
   (A) was dominated by conservative presidents
   (B) experienced one of the major reform periods in the nation's history
   (C) was dominated by Democratic presidents
   (D) was favorable to unions as government passed collective bargaining laws
   (E) was dominated by women who had recently been given the vote

ANSWER: **A.** Harding, Coolidge, and Hoover were all Republican conservatives (*The American Pageant,* 12th ed., p. 753/11th ed., p. 771).

2. The Eighteenth Amendment
   (A) gave women the right to vote
   (B) ended Prohibition
   (C) made it illegal to belong to a radical organization
   (D) made it illegal to purchase, distribute, or consume liquor
   (E) made it legal to teach evolution in public schools

ANSWER: **D.** For the text, see *The American Pageant,* 12th ed., pp. A47-A48/11th ed., pp. A17-A18.

3. The Volstead Act
   (A) allowed the government to purchase railroad companies from private companies
   (B) provided a tax cut to wealthy Americans
   (C) placed railroad companies under combined government and private management
   (D) restricted immigration
   (E) provided for the enforcement of the Eighteenth Amendment

ANSWER: **E.** (*The American Pageant,* 12th ed., p. 732/11th ed., pp. 580-81.)

4. Which of the following is NOT associated with the Harlem Renaissance?
   (A) Countee Cullen
   (B) Langston Hughes
   (C) James Weldon Johnson
   (D) Jean Toomer
   (E) Booker T. Washington

ANSWER: **E.** Booker T. Washington was an educator, not an artist (*The American Pageant,* 12th ed., pp. 573-574/11th ed., p. 765).

5. A. Mitchell Palmer is associated with
   (A) the Harlem Renaissance
   (B) prohibition
   (C) the motion picture industry
   (D) baseball
   (E) the red scare

ANSWER: **E.** Palmer led the mass arrests of suspected "subversives" in the red scare (*The American Pageant*, 12th ed., p. 729/11th ed., p. 747).

6. Sacco and Vanzetti were
   (A) leaders of the prohibition movement
   (B) arrested and convicted for placing bombs on Wall Street
   (C) trade union leaders arrested by the government for organizing illegal strikes
   (D) anarchists who were controversially convicted and executed for murder
   (E) Major League baseball players

ANSWER: **D.** Italian immigrants Sacco and Vanzetti were convicted of the murder of a paymaster and his guard. Many believed they were victims of nativist fear (*The American Pageant*, 12th ed., pp. 729-730/11th ed., pp. 747-748).

7. The Teapot Dome scandal occurred during which president's administration?
   (A) Coolidge
   (B) Hoover
   (C) F. D. Roosevelt
   (D) Harding
   (E) Wilson

ANSWER: **D.** The Teapot Dome scandal was the most infamous of the scandals for which the Harding administration was famous (*The American Pageant*, 12th ed., pp. 758-759/11th ed., pp. 776-777).

8. A major reason why Al Smith was defeated in the 1928 presidential race was because
   (A) of his vocal support for radical movements
   (B) he had been president of a militant trade union
   (C) he had been involved in the Teapot Dome scandal
   (D) he was associated with Wilson's idealism
   (E) he was a Catholic

ANSWER: **E.** Many historians believe Smith's Catholicism was a factor in his defeat (*The American Pageant*, 12th ed., p. 766/11th ed., p. 784).

9. Which of the following was considered to be the symbol of post-World War I consumerism?
   (A) television
   (B) automobile
   (C) refrigerator
   (D) phonograph
   (E) radio

ANSWER: B. The automobile defined American consumerism and had a profound impact on other industries as well (*The American Pageant*, 12th ed., pp. 739-740/11th ed., pp. 757-758).

10. The "Hundred Percenters"
    (A) advocated for the repeal of the Volstead Act
    (B) favored a loose immigration policy
    (C) were rural Americans who condemned urban life
    (D) favored an isolationist policy
    (E) opposed the teaching of Darwin's theory of evolution in public schools

ANSWER: D. The Hundred Percenters sought to reduce foreign influence on American culture and favored an isolationist foreign policy.

FREE-RESPONSE QUESTIONS

1. Discuss how the 1920s represented social, economic, and cultural discord among Americans. In your essay discuss THREE of the following:
   a. urban versus rural attitudes
   b. nativism versus immigration
   c. science versus religion
   d. the red scare

RESPONSE While in some ways a lively decade that witnessed important cultural innovations, the 1920s also represented an era of conformity, repression, and bigotry. Significant tensions developed during this period that you should discuss. As the nation's cosmopolitan urban areas reflected modernism and consumerism, rural America continued to represent tradition and stability. Urban areas were ethnically and culturally heterogeneous, whereas rural America was homogeneous culturally and religiously as well; this is an appropriate opportunity for you to discuss the tensions that prevailed between "Bible Belt" areas and those areas that were exposed to scientific literature and ideas. This is indicated in the tensions that existed between U.S.-born Americans and the millions of immigrants who were arriving in the United States in this decade. Even events outside of the United States had an impact on the discord and intolerance that prevailed in the 1920s. For example, the red scare was in large part caused by the success of the Bolshevik Revolution in Russia.

2. Discuss the extent to which the United States underwent a cultural transformation in the 1920s.

RESPONSE In responding to this question, you should take into account the profound effect consumerism had on American culture. New consumer items shaped the way Americans lived in many unprecedented ways. Radio, motion pictures, the automobile, and modern art were both causes and effects of a cultural transformation that helped to shape the Roaring Twenties. Further, you can incorporate into your essay a discussion of the causes of prohibition and its effects, such as the cultural phenomenon known as the speakeasy. You might discuss changing gender roles as well. Keep in mind that the question asks you to "discuss the extent" of this cultural transformation; therefore, you should also identify its limitations. For instance, much of the Roaring Twenties was an urban experience; the rural areas of the nation did not experience the 1920s in the same way as those living in major cities did.

16

THE GREAT DEPRESSION AND THE NEW DEAL: 1929–1941

In 1929, a little over a decade after the most devastating war in modern times up to that point, the United States and the rest of the world endured the worst economic crisis in history in terms of intensity and duration. The economic, political, and social crises that resulted from the Great Depression required massive intervention by the government on an unprecedented scale in order to preserve the capitalist system and recover from the ruinous effects of the depression. During the 1920s there were many weaknesses in the economy that were ignored by both politicians and economists and that were symptomatic of deep-seated problems that became more apparent over the next ten years. The election of Franklin Delano Roosevelt in 1932 marked the end of twelve years of Republican rule and the emergence of Roosevelt's New Deal, which represented the second manifestation of liberalism in the twentieth century. (The first was the progressive movement in the early twentieth century.) Ultimately the New Deal preserved capitalism by balancing the needs of the capitalist class with the demands of the working classes. Equally important was that the New Deal represented the federal government's expansion and implementation of its authority to tax, borrow, and spend in order to help find solutions for both short- and long-term problems in the economy. In short, Roosevelt and the New Deal took great strides in ending the depression, but it was not until World War II that the United States recovered from the despair of the Great Depression.

KEY CONCEPTS

■ A number of major factors caused the Great Depression, among them underconsumption and high protective tariffs.

■ The extent of the economic collapse for the U.S. and the world was unprecedented.

■ President Hoover failed to stem the decline of the economy.

■ Upon becoming president, FDR instituted a vast array of relief, recovery, and reform policies and agencies to address the collapse of the economy.

■ Several New Deal programs were ruled unconstitutional by the conservative Supreme Court.

The Great Depression and the New Deal are discussed in depth in *The American Pageant,* 12 ed., Chapters 32-34/11th ed., Chapters 34-36.

CAUSES OF THE GREAT DEPRESSION

Politically conservative Republican administrations dominated the 1920s: Warren G. Harding (1921-1923), Calvin Coolidge (1923-1929), and Herbert Hoover (1929-1933). Each of these administrations was in some way accountable for creating and/or intensifying the maladies that led to the collapse of U.S. capitalism in 1929. Collectively, the following economic factors played a role in the worst depression in U.S. history:

■ **Unequal distribution of wealth** Differences in income and wealth are inherent in the capitalist system; however, the extent of the concentration of wealth in the United States prior to the Great Depression was enormous. In 1929 the top 5 percent of income earners averaged $13,960 and controlled 30 percent of the nation's total wealth; the bottom 40 percent of income earners controlled 12.5 percent of the income. What is more, the median income in the nation at the time was $2,335, yet nearly 16 percent of the income-earning population received under $1,000 per year. Repressive labor policies used by the government and business in the previous decades had prevented the working class from making substantial financial gains. This in turn affected the purchasing power of millions of Americans. The tax polices of the Republican administrations—most famously the Mellon tax plan—aggravated the problem by concentrating even more wealth in the hands of a small percentage of the population, thus lowering aggregate demand and consumption.

■ **Underconsumption** As the per capita income of the working class declined, so too did its ability to consume the products it was producing. The absence of adequate credit also reduced demand. There simply was not enough stimulation of the economy by the federal government to address effectively the problem of underconsumption. (A study by the prestigious Brookings Institution in 1929 revealed that 42 percent of all consumers lived at or below the subsistence/poverty level, while another 36 percent were at the minimum-comfort level.) The short-term effect of underconsumption was overproduction, leading to surpluses. Capitalists then cut back on production, which affected

The Mellon Tax Plan: An Early Version of Supply-Side Economics

Andrew Mellon, Harding's secretary of the Treasury, dominated his administration despite the presence of other capable and strong-minded cabinet secretaries, such as Herbert Hoover (secretary of commerce) and Charles Evans Hughes (secretary of state). Mellon was an experienced financier and a highly seasoned presidential adviser, having served three administrations. Extremely probusiness like his former superiors, Presidents Harding and Coolidge, Mellon believed U.S. industry must be protected from overseas competition, and so advocated a high protective tariff. He also maintained that taxes on the wealthy were too high, thus limiting the expansion of the economy. His position on tax cuts for the wealthy rested on the assumption that if the wealthy had more money, they would invest it in new business enterprises or expand already established businesses. Consequently more workers would be employed, they would spend more money, and demand would again increase, necessitating more investments and even more employment. In other words, he believed that tax breaks for the wealthy would invariably "trickle down" to the rest of society so long as the wealthy invested their money in new enterprises. In the 1920s Congress passed Mellon's tax plan and other new tax laws. Critics maintain that Mellon's tax policies provided the wealthy even more surplus capital, much of which was invested in the stock market, thus dramatically inflating the price of stocks.

employment levels, and the downward spiral continued. Added to this were the problems of deflation and falling prices, which in turn led to more layoffs as profits dwindled in many sectors of the economy.

- **The rise of protectionism** On Mellon's recommendation, the Fordney-McCumber Tariff was introduced in 1922. This tariff raised taxes on agricultural, chemical, and metal imports to an unprecedented level. While ostensibly protecting domestic production, this tax had serious ramifications on Europe and the United States. Before the war, overseas capital had played a significant role in expanding the U.S. economy through foreign investments. World War I had transformed the United States from a debtor to a creditor nation because of U.S. financial aid given to the Allies during the war. In the 1920s the U.S. demanded repayment. The trade barrier established by the Fordney-McCumber Tariff prevented the former Allies from selling their commodities in the United States, which would have allowed them to pay off their debts. Yet, throughout the 1920s, U.S. loans and investments continued. Once the depression hit, Congress made another ill-fated attempt to protect American industry and manufacturing from foreign competition. In 1930 it passed the highest protective tariff in the nation's history, the Hawley-Smoot Tariff, which only aggravated the problems created by the Fordney-McCumber Tariff.

- **Inadequate capital investment** Profitability is the major reason why a capitalist invests in a business. However, there was little incentive to invest given the decline in the overall rate of profit that occurred with increasing frequency in the late 1920s and continuing into the 1930s.

■ **The fragility of the banking system** Banks overextended themselves to individuals and corporations whose financial situation was precarious. In other words, they made numerous bad loans. The fragility of the banking industry in the United States was revealed by the collapse of the European banking system. Because economic systems had become increasingly interdependent in regards to trade, finance, and production, a problem in one part of the world affected other markets.

■ **Borrowing on margin: the speculation bubble bursts!** A substantial amount of the money invested in stocks prior to the collapse of the market in 1929 was borrowed on margin—the amount a buyer uses as a down payment to purchase stock. In the 1920s, the down payment was often substantially lower than the actual price of the stock. Technically, the stockbroker who handled the transaction loaned the balance of the investment to the buyer. In reality, the banks often provided the difference between the margin and the actual cost because the interest rates on such loans were uniformly high. Consequently stock prices became highly inflated. For example, the price per share of AT&T stock on the New York Stock Exchange in March 1928 was $179.50. Within six months, the price had nearly doubled. RCA's stock price went from $94.50 to $505.00 in the same period. There was obviously a substantial risk in all of this, for as long as the original price of the stock remained stable or increased, the buyer was safe. If the price fell, however, the stockbroker could legally demand immediate payment of part or all of the money loaned. This is exactly what happened in the autumn of 1929 as many loans were called in. On Thursday, October 24, panic swept the stock market. Nearly 13 million shares were traded. Five days later, a record 16.5 million shares were dumped on the stock exchange, shattering the market. Banks went under, and hundreds of thousands of investors, many of whom had invested whatever surplus funds they had on hand, were ruined. The collapse of the stock market in specific and the state of the economy in general had a profound effect on the nation's most vulnerable citizens: the elderly, the poor, blacks, women, and the working class, despite the efforts of reformers on the local and state levels to alleviate their condition.

■ **Technology** In order for capitalists to remain competitive, they often utilize laborsaving methods. The consequences for the worker are obvious: machines turn out more commodities using fewer workers, resulting in higher unemployment, overproduction (because machinery increases production), and underconsumption.

THE EXTENT OF THE COLLAPSE (1929-1933)

The entire capitalist world experienced the collapse. The crisis was most devastating in the most highly industrialized countries—the United States, Germany, and Great Britain. In the United States alone eighty-five thousand businesses closed. Listed below are the other major effects and symptoms of the economic crisis:

- The gross national product (the total net value of goods and services produced nationally within a given time, usually one year) fell from $104 billion in 1929 to $56 billion in 1933.
- Per capita disposable income (the money available after taxes, inflation, and other necessary expenses are taken out) fell from $678 in 1929 to $369 in 1933.
- Farmers' income declined from $5.7 billion in 1929 to $1.7 billion in 1933. Four hundred thousand farmers lost their land through foreclosures; many became tenant farmers. By 1932 farmers began destroying their own crops to drive up prices.
- Unemployment increased from 1.5 million in 1929 to 12.8 million (or 25 percent of the working population) in 1933. In 1931 three-quarters of the nation's cities banned married women from holding jobs as teachers while at the same time children were forced to look for work.
- New investments declined from $10 billion in 1929 to $1 billion in 1933.
- Exports fell from $5.2 billion in 1929 to $1.7 billion in 1933.
- Building construction decreased from $300 billion in 1929 to $500 million in 1933.
- In 1928 and 1929, bank failures averaged 550 per year. Between 1930 and 1933, there were 1,700 bank failures per year.
- Hunger, homelessness, and mental depression and other social maladies increased dramatically.
- Capacity utilization (the percentage of functional factories and mines in use) fell from a high of 91 percent in 1925 to 42 percent in 1932.

HOOVER AND THE COLLAPSE OF THE ECONOMY

When the depression intensified, Hoover argued that direct federal assistance to the victims of the crisis should not occur. Believing that the marketplace was resilient and would soon recover from the effects of the depression, he reasoned that government intervention would establish an unhealthy precedent that would undermine the very character of hardworking, independent Americans with a state-supported welfare system. Instead, Hoover preached about the virtues of:

- **Localism** Addressing the needs of the unemployed and impoverished was the responsibility of local and state governments, not the federal government.
- **Voluntarism** Charitable organizations would see people through the difficult times, providing them with basic needs.
- **Rugged individualism** Only through hard work, sacrifice, and determination have Americans found success. These attributes would allow them to weather the depression; they should not rely on government, but themselves, to recover.

Given Hoover's laissez-faire philosophy and policies, his critics—both historians and his contemporaries alike—have labeled him as a "do-nothing" president who was a prisoner of ideologies (laissez-faire capitalism and social Darwinism) that were destined to fail. To suggest that he did absolutely nothing, however, is incorrect.

- On June 20, 1931, Hoover proposed an international moratorium on war reparations and debts.

- The following year he established the Reconstruction Finance Corporation (RFC). This agency had more than $2 billion at its disposal to loan to failing banks, farm mortgage associations, building and loan societies, railroads, and insurance companies. Regrettably, Hoover did not go far enough. As with his successor, Calvin Coolidge, the idea of an unbalanced budget so worried him that he declined to pump enough money into the system. Hoover believed that the depression was an overseas phenomenon and that a strong U.S. economy would convince foreigners to invest in the U.S. economy. To this end, he attempted simultaneously to balance the budget and raise taxes. A bill passed the same year allowed the RFC to loan millions of dollars to state and local governments.

- At Hoover's request, Congress passed the Federal Home Loan Bank Act. This legislation was designed to increase funds to banks, which would then be able to finance loans for home mortgages.

Despite these and many other efforts, the depression deepened. Throughout the nation, homeless families lived in makeshift shacks and tents on the outskirts of America's towns and cities. These "communities" were derisively called "Hoovervilles." As the depression intensified, citizens began to take action into their own hands. Often their conduct stemmed from frustration and despair. Two dramatic developments during the Hoover years demonstrate the growing anger and disenchantment of large parts of the population:

- **The Bonus Army** Over fifteen thousand World War I veterans camped in the nation's capital, hoping to persuade Congress to allow them to cash in the bonus certificates given them in 1924 as recognition of their military service. On orders from Hoover, the U.S. Army, under the command of General Douglas MacArthur, destroyed the primary encampment at Anacostia Flats.

- **The Farmers' Holiday Association** Congress had taken some steps in the 1920s that were favorable to farmers. For example, the McNary-Haugen Farm Relief Bill proposed that the government become a purchaser of surplus farm crops. The government, in turn, would sell the surplus overseas. Nevertheless, declining farm prices and foreclosures after 1929 led farmers to organize the Farmers' Holiday Association. This group clamored for an end to bank foreclosures and in favor of government-regulated price controls for farm commodities.

It seemed to some, even the owners of the means of production, that capitalism was collapsing, and the government, under Hoover, had no idea how to save it. The nation's laborers, at the very least, were becoming disenchanted with the free-market system, and they were now mobilizing. To be sure, thoughts of riotous workers destroying private property, overthrowing the government, and even initiating a reign of terror must have crossed the minds of even the most resolute patricians. By this time, the majority of Americans were more than ready for a political change. It came in the form of the Democratic governor of New York, Franklin Delano Roosevelt (FDR).

FDR

Upon assuming office, FDR recruited intellectuals and university professors—many from Columbia University—to play major roles in his administration. The press dubbed them the "Brain Trust." Some were unofficial advisers; others held cabinet-level positions. New Dealers came from a variety of backgrounds and political shades, including progressive Republicans, agrarian and urban interest groups, Democrats who had earlier supported Wilson's reforms, and labor leaders. With the assistance of his Brain Trust and others advisers, Roosevelt adopted a reform program he called the New Deal. It had two primary objectives:

- **Maintain Americans' loyalty to the government and to the capitalist system as a whole** Given the staggering unemployment rate, rural discontent, and the growing attraction of communist and fascist alternatives, discontent with capitalism and the government was a real concern.
- **Create conditions favorable to capital accumulation** Roosevelt had to jump-start the sluggish economy and convince capitalists and investors to reopen closed businesses and invest in new businesses.

To achieve these goals, the president and his advisers established a wide range of federal programs and agencies to attack the various trouble areas of the economy. FDR's approach tended to be pragmatic and methodical. His handling of the Great Depression can be divided into three major phases:

- spring of 1933 to summer 1935: the "Hundred Days"
- summer of 1935 to 1939: the First New Deal
- 1939 to 1945: the Second New Deal

The New Deal articulated three major efforts to address short- and long-term goals:

- relief, to provide immediate assistance to businesses and individuals
- recovery, to make recovery of the economy permanent
- reform, to address those abuses that had helped cause the depression

FDR'S FIRST HUNDRED DAYS TO THE FIRST NEW DEAL

On March 4, 1933, Democrat Franklin Roosevelt took over the reins of government from a tired, demoralized, and exceedingly unpopular Herbert Hoover. In his inaugural address the new president declared how he would attack the economic collapse and disillusionment of the American people: "I shall ask Congress for the one remaining instrument to meet the crisis—broad executive power to wage a war against the emergency as great as the power that would be given me if we were in fact invaded by a foreign foe." Over the next three months (the first hundred days) the new chief executive initiated in rapid succession a series of measures designed to alleviate the effects of the Great Depression. In this so-called honeymoon period, enhanced by his party's congressional majority, Roosevelt initiated the following measures to promote economic recovery and relief for the millions of unemployed:

- **National Bank Holiday (Emergency Banking Relief Act)** More banks closed in 1933 than in the previous four years combined. Confidence had to be restored in America's banking system, so FDR closed all banks for four days. Only those banks that were solvent were allowed to reopen. The nation was also taken off the gold standard. This was intended to give the government more flexibility in determining the amount of money in the system and to inflate prices and stocks. Paper currency was no longer redeemable in gold.

- **Glass-Steagall Act** Also known as the Banking Act of 1933, this forbade commercial banks from engaging in excessive speculation, added $1 billion in gold to the economy, and established the Federal Deposit Insurance Corporation (FDIC), which guaranteed bank deposits up to $5,000.

- **Agricultural Adjustment Act (AAA)** To control the wild fluctuations in farm prices the government paid farmers to reduce their crop yield, thereby—it was hoped—increasing prices. After the Supreme Court ruled the 1933 AAA unconstitutional, a second AAA, designed to circumvent the Supreme Court's wording in outlawing the first act, was passed in 1938.

- **Federal Emergency Relief Act (FERA)** This provided funds to states to aid in unemployment relief and to subsidize public works projects.

- **Home Owners' Refinancing Act** This created the Home Owners' Loan Corporation (HOLC), which made funds available to refinance mortgages.

- **Tennessee Valley Authority (TVA)** The brainchild of Nebraska Senator Frank Norris, the TVA constructed hydroelectric dams in the Tennessee River Valley to control flooding and bring electricity to rural communities.

- **Civilian Conservation Corps (CCC)** The federal government's first public works project, the CCC employed thousands of young men in conservation work. It provided employment and as a result injected much-needed money into the economy.

- **National Industrial Recovery Act (NIRA)** This created the National Recovery Administration (NRA), which allowed industry to establish voluntarily its own regulations such as price and production guidelines and fair competition codes. The NRA supervised business policies and agreements and had the authority to approve or reject these agreements. It recognized the right of workers to establish unions and engage in collective bargaining. The act also established the Public Works Administration (PWA), which employed hundreds of thousands of men to build roads, bridges, and public buildings. Like other work relief programs, the PWA is an example of "pump priming"—stimulating both capital investment and consumer demand. The latter would grow as a result of increased employment.

There were other programs in the First New Deal:

- **The Civil Works Administration (CWA)** Through this agency, the federal government employed workers for construction jobs.
- **The Securities and Exchange Commission (SEC)** This commission was established to regulate the stock market and reduce wild speculation.
- **The Federal Housing Administration (FHA)** This agency was created to stimulate the construction of new homes.

Many of the reforms of the First New Deal focused on relief, recovery, and reform, a focus that was carried over into the next phase. To understand better why this second phase of the New Deal was launched, keep the following factors in mind:

- Throughout the 1930s, there was growing disillusionment among segments of the population, not only with the capitalist system, but also with New Deal programs that were considered ineffective or did not address specific needs. Farmers and laborers, for example, were quite vocal in their discontent, and this resonated with the government.
- Conservative business leaders were becoming increasingly antagonistic to the New Deal. The economy still seemed to be stagnant, and some were opposed to FDR's attack on laissez-faire capitalism.
- Vocal critics such as Francis Townsend, the Reverend Charles Coughlin, and Huey Long offered what to many seemed viable alternatives to the New Deal, which threatened to siphon off support for FDR's reelection bid in 1936.
  - **Francis Townsend** Townsend's Old Age Revolving Pension Plan called for a monthly stipend of $200 to citizens over the age of sixty; the recipients, however, would be required to spend the money, which would stimulate the economy.
  - **Charles Coughlin** A Catholic priest, Coughlin established the National Union for Social Justice. Appealing to the public in his weekly radio addresses, he garnered millions of supporters. A harsh critic of the New Deal, his increasingly anti-Semitic remarks convinced the Catholic Church to take him off the radio.
  - **Huey Long** The governor of Louisiana, Long organized the "Share Our Wealth" program, which called for the federal government to provide each American family a home and an annual $2,000 income. Nationally, Long's popularity might have posed a serious challenge to Roosevelt's reelection bid, but in 1935 Long was assassinated.

THE SECOND NEW DEAL

With a Democratic victory in the 1934 congressional midterm elections, FDR believed his New Deal had been given a mandate from the public. Though his three goals—relief, recovery, and reform—overlapped throughout his administrations, the Second New Deal concentrated on relief and reform:

Labor Strikes

Workers—especially factory employees—who had earlier been exempt from joining craft, or skilled, unions now had their own collective bargaining agent, the Congress of Industrial Organizations (CIO). One consequence of labor's right to collective bargaining as protected by the federal government was the frequency of strikes. Many of the major strikes, however, predated the creation of the National Labor Relations Act. Some historians contend that even after its creation, the NLRA was often lax in carrying out its mandate and that it was the workers themselves who played a decisive role in ushering in a period of industrial democracy. Major industries such as steel, textiles, and automobiles experienced strikes in the 1930s. The response of businesses to unions was mixed; some accepted them while others opposed them violently. By 1938 the rights of workers and unions were bolstered by the passage of the Fair Labor Standards Act, which set the maximum workweek at forty hours, established a minimum wage, and limited child labor. Several measures were adopted to limit the power and right to strike. In several southern states, right-to-work legislation that banned the closed shop and outlawed picketing was passed.

- **Works Progress Administration (WPA)** A massive work relief program, the WPA employed millions who had been receiving assistance from state and local governments. The WPA built roads, airports, public buildings, and other major construction projects. It also employed actors, musicians, artists, and writers. Wages were higher than state relief rates, but so as not to compete with the free-market system, they were lower than what businesses offered.
- **Resettlement Administration (RA)** This provided assistance to the agrarian sector of the economy, especially small farmers, those renting farmland, and sharecroppers.
- **Rural Electrification Administration (REA)** This brought electricity to rural areas not served by private utility companies.
- **National Labor Relations Act (NLRA)** Also known as the Wagner-Connery Act, this superseded the NIRA, which the Supreme Court ruled unconstitutional in 1935. The act created the National Labor Relations Board to address unfair labor practices and confirmed workers' rights to collective bargaining and to form and join unions.
- **Tax restructuring** A higher income tax was placed on the wealthy as well as on capital gains (income generated from investments such as stocks).
- **Social Security Act** One of the longest lasting New Deal programs, it established a trust fund to which workers and employers contributed. At age sixty-five, individuals could retire and collect monthly payments. The act also applied to those who suffered from a disability, were unemployed, or were dependent mothers and children. Social Security remains an important government program.

> **AP Tip**
>
> When studying this period, students are frequently overwhelmed or confused by the vast assortment of New Deal alphabet programs. You will find that organizing the agencies according to the three phases (for example, work relief programs or farm assistance programs), by dates, or by category (relief, recovery, or reform) is helpful.

Obviously, these programs had large budgets requiring the federal government to engage in an enormous outlay of capital intended to stimulate capital accumulation in hopes of expanding the economy through new investments. Despite their concerns about an unbalanced budget, the president and his advisers maintained that through deficit spending, the economy would recover. They were echoing the ideas of the influential economist John Maynard Keynes.

KEYNESIAN ECONOMICS

Roosevelt had always been apprehensive about pouring too much money into the system. He was never comfortable with the principle and practice of deficit spending, despite the fact that two of the leading advocates of Keynesian economic policy, Harry Hopkins and Harold Ickes (head of the Public Works Administration), were two of his most valuable advisers.

According to Keynes, the private sector was unable to prevent severe cyclical downturns in the economy. Consequently Keynes asserted that it was imperative for the government to play a major role in the economy.

- Government should create additional demand by becoming a major purchaser/consumer of goods and services.
- Government should encourage investments by the private sector through tax policies that lower the corporate tax rate.
- Government should facilitate the growth of exports.
- Government should make use of deficit spending. If the primary emphasis of government spending policy during an economic downturn is on balancing the budget, the economic crisis will continue. Therefore, the government must spend more than it takes in during periods of economic stagnation.

When the economy did pick up in the 1930s, FDR made the ill-fated decision to balance the federal budget in 1937. A recession ensued: capacity utilization fell from 83 percent to 60 percent; unemployment rose from 14.3 percent to 19 percent. The attempt to balance the budget in the midst of an economic recovery was quickly abandoned. On the advice of his advisers, FDR returned to the idea of deficit spending as articulated by Keynes. However, because of Roosevelt's inhibitions and reservations on Keynesian policy, the federal government never spent enough money to lift the United States out of the Great Depression. In fact, not until the United States became involved in World War II did FDR adopt the kind of spending programs prescribed by Keynes.

By 1939 the economy began to recover, but those who had lost their jobs—again, in some cases—saw their faith in the New Deal begin to erode.

THE COURT-PACKING SCHEME

In the first two phases of the New Deal, the Supreme Court revealed its aversion to some of FDR's most important programs such as the NIRA and the AAA:

- *Schechter Poultry Corporation v. United States* **(1935)** In this case, called the Sick Chicken Case, the court invalidated the NIRA on several grounds—for example, that the federal government could not constitutionally regulate wholly intrastate commerce.
- *Butler v. United States* **(1936)** The court invalidated the AAA on the grounds that Congress did not have the power to create a tax that would benefit one sector of society and that agriculture was a responsibility of the states, not the federal government.

FDR called the Court's decisions "horse and buggy thinking" and looked for a way around the intransigent justices.

Support for FDR declined because of his attempt to "pack" the Supreme Court. A majority of the justices had been appointed by FDR's conservative predecessors. Discouraged by the Court's rulings against a number of key New Deal programs such as the AAA and the NIRA, FDR aimed to solve the problem by reorganizing the Court: he proposed a bill to increase the number of Supreme Court justices from nine to fifteen (giving FDR an opportunity to appoint six justices of his choosing). Even his supporters had misgivings about this scheme because it posed a threat to the principle of checks and balances. Fortunately, the bill never saw the light of day, but from that point on the Supreme Court upheld the constitutionality of a number of key New Deal programs. Before he died in office (in his fourth term!), FDR would go on to appoint seven new justices, among them three of the Supreme Court's greatest judges—Felix Frankfurter, William O. Douglas, and Hugo Black.

Despite efforts to address ongoing problems in the agricultural and industrial sectors and to supplement the relief programs of the earlier phases of the New Deal, by the end of the decade no new policy goals or measures were offered by the president. Although FDR and the New Deal were still very popular, opposition continued to grow. Southern Democrats were increasingly nervous about the New Deal's social agenda, conservatives were organizing to oppose FDR's bid for a fourth term, and the Republicans increased their membership in both houses of Congress in the 1938 congressional elections.

BLACK AMERICANS, WOMEN, FDR, AND THE NEW DEAL

Ironically, many black Americans came to revere FDR. In fact his election in 1932 signaled the end of black support for the Republican party that had begun during Reconstruction. Unfortunately FDR's

Historians and the New Deal

Many historians consider FDR one of the few great presidents in the nation's history. They praise him for the substantial transformation that occurred under the New Deal, such as minimum wage/maximum hour laws, extensive energy programs like the TVA, expanded rights for workers and unions, and assistance programs such as Social Security. Addressing the problems that caused the Great Depression, they argue, is also part of FDR's legacy. But critics are not so enamored with FDR. Some claim the New Deal was in fact conservative in nature, that it did not fundamentally change social conditions and left the same class of people in power. While filled with great expectations, the New Deal did not go far enough in addressing the inequality that prevailed in American life. For their part, conservative critics contend that the New Deal established a precedent for enormous government spending and the creation of the welfare state.

record does not necessarily reflect a great concern for the condition and future of the nation's black population. As bad as the national unemployment rate got, it was worse for blacks, who tended to be the last hired and the first fired. Few Americans suffered more than black farmers, who were already at the bottom of the socioeconomic scale when the depression struck. Some New Deal agencies segregated blacks, some excluded them entirely, and some were clearly discriminatory. Black tenants and sharecroppers lost their property when they were forced from their land by the AAA in order to reduce crop yields and drive up prices. Nevertheless, some gains were made, as blacks were able to find employment opportunities in the PWA and the WPA. FDR himself took some steps to address the abuses. He appointed the first black federal judge in the nation's history and created a Civil Rights Division in the Department of Justice. In addition, black Americans sat for the first time as delegates to the Democratic National Convention in1936.

If the president was often indifferent to the plight of the nation's black population, his wife, Eleanor, was not. Blacks had no greater ally in the White House than the First Lady, who advocated for increased rights for blacks and raised funds for the NAACP. Although black Americans made limited gains in the 1930s, those gains were enough for most blacks to switch from the party of Lincoln to the Democrats.

The New Deal's record regarding women is equally mixed. More and more women entered the workplace in order to keep their families from sinking into or below poverty levels, but they received lower wages than did men, they were laid off first, and they rarely received promotions. In some cases they were denied access to certain jobs so that they would not compete with men. Yet women did benefit from employment in various New Deal agencies, as well as from the employment protection accorded them by NRA. Some women found opportunities in government. In fact, the first woman to hold a cabinet position, Frances Perkins, was appointed secretary of labor by FDR.

THE LEGACY OF THE NEW DEAL

Unquestionably, FDR's expansionist fiscal and monetary policies stimulated the nation's moribund economy, as witnessed in the 1930s by increases in prices, production, and investment. By the end of the decade, wages had returned to predepression 1929 levels in many industries, and real wages had increased as well. Confidence in the economy and the government had also improved. Yet on the eve of America's entry into World War II, the effects of the depression continued to plague the nation. In 1940 unemployment continued to hover at approximately 10 percent. World War II helped remedy the vestiges of despair and economic malaise that continued to linger. By 1942 approximately one-third of the economy was devoted to the war effort. Consequently industrial and agricultural demand grew and unemployment shrank, especially because millions of young men and women were by then employed by the military. Corporate profits and real wages reached high levels. Even the earning power of the bottom one-fifth of the nation's population increased dramatically. Finally, the gross national product doubled during the war.

World War II and the New Deal changed the size and scope of the government as well as how Americans viewed the role of the federal government. Many came to accept its expanded role as indispensable in confronting economic problems and, in general, the problems of industrial society. Prior to the Great Depression, the federal government did not play a large role in people's lives, but the New Deal changed that. Government programs, from education to infrastructural development to relief, in one way or another affected every aspect of life. To this day, some view the New Deal and subsequent reform programs as undermining states' rights, the free-market system, and social and cultural traditions. Others contend that this is not the case, and furthermore, they argue, the alternative to government intervention is far worse, as witnessed by the collapse of the nation's economy and the resulting despair that traumatized the nation in the 1930s.

Multiple-Choice Questions

1. Which of the following was NOT an underlying cause of the Great Depression?
    (A) underconsumption
    (B) the effects of World War I
    (C) the fragility of the banking system
    (D) the vastly unequal distribution of wealth
    (E) inadequate capital investment

ANSWER: B. Many Americans experienced economic prosperity following the war (*The American Pageant,* 12th ed., p. 728/11th ed., p. 746).

2. The Mellon tax plan
    (A) helped lift the nation out of the Great Depression
    (B) was adopted by FDR as a remedy for underconsumption
    (C) distributed wealth evenly between the nation's social classes
    (D) led to underconsumption and wild speculation in the stock market
    (E) was instituted to pay for the enormous cost of the New Deal agencies

ANSWER: D. The Mellon tax plan concentrated even more capital in the hands of the relatively small wealthy class. This in turn gave them an opportunity to invest in the stock market, in some cases inflating stock value, and left less money in the hands of the rest of the population, which exacerbated the problem of underconsumption (*The American Pageant,* 12th ed., pp. 751-752/11th ed., p. 768).

3. The Hawley-Smoot Tariff
    (A) facilitated improved trade relations between the United States and its trade partners
    (B) reduced the tax on imported industrial goods, thus hurting American industry
    (C) was the highest tariff in the nation's history, and an underlying cause of the Great Depression
    (D) was ruled unconstitutional by the Supreme Court
    (E) was vetoed by Roosevelt, but passed by Congress over his veto

ANSWER: C. The Hawley-Smoot Tariff set import tax rates so high in order to protect American industries that it led to other nations enacting their own trade barriers (*The American Pageant,* 12th ed., pp. 767, 769/11th ed., pp. 785, 787).

4. Which of the following is NOT associated with Hoover's ideology in regards to addressing the problems created by the collapse of the economy in 1929?
   (A) deficit spending
   (B) localism
   (C) voluntarism
   (D) laissez-faire
   (E) rugged individualism

ANSWER: **A.** Deficit spending is associated with FDR, not Hoover (*The American Pageant,* 12th ed., p. 771/11th ed., pp. 788-789).

5. Which opponent of FDR introduced an alternative to the New Deal in the form of an Old Age Revolving Pension Plan?
   (A) Herbert Hoover
   (B) Huey Long
   (C) Calvin Coolidge
   (D) Father Coughlin
   (E) Francis Townsend

ANSWER: **E.** A retired physician who had lost his savings, Townsend proposed the pension plan (*The American Pageant,* 12th ed., p. 786/11th ed., p. 804).

6. Which of the following programs was instituted by President Hoover?
   (A) Federal Deposit Insurance Corporation
   (B) Home Owners' Loan Corporation
   (C) going off the gold standard
   (D) Reconstruction Finance Corporation
   (E) Tennessee Valley Authority

ANSWER: **D.** The RFC was a source of government lending (*The American Pageant,* 12th ed., p. 772/11th ed., p. 790).

7. The U.S. Supreme Court ruled this New Deal agency unconstitutional in the 1930s.
   (A) Home Owners' Loan Corporation
   (B) Tennessee Valley Authority
   (C) Federal Deposit Insurance Corporation
   (D) National Industrial Recovery Act
   (E) Federal Housing Administration

ANSWER: **D.** The court invalidated the NIRA in the *Schechter Poultry Corporation v. United States* case (*The American Pageant,* 12th ed., pp. 787-788/11th ed., p. 805).

8. In order to address the problem of rampant speculation in the stock market, FDR
   (A) closed the stock exchange for four days
   (B) placed a limit on how much money an individual or company could invest in the stock market
   (C) established the Securities and Exchange Commission
   (D) set a ceiling on how high the price of a stock could go
   (E) established the Reconstruction Finance Corporation

ANSWER: **C.** The SEC is still the "watchdog" of the stock exchange (*The American Pageant,* 12th ed., p. 791/11th ed., p. 810).

9. FDR's goal to reorganize the federal judiciary
   (A) provided him the opportunity to replace conservative judges who had been appointed by the previous administration
   (B) was achieved, but it was ruled unconstitutional by the Supreme Court
   (C) allowed him to bypass the judiciary when considering new programs and agencies
   (D) was described by angry critic as "court packing"
   (E) was intended to give more power to the states

ANSWER: **D.** Many Americans met FDR's "court-packing scheme" with considerable derision, and he therefore dropped the plan (*The American Pageant,* 12th ed., pp. 798-799/11th ed., pp. 816-817).

10. The Social Security Act
    (A) was designed to provide assistance to the agrarian sector of the economy
    (B) employed musicians, artists, actors, and writers
    (C) provided assistance to the elderly and handicapped and to dependent women and children
    (D) established codes of conduct for corporations and unions
    (E) allowed workers to form unions and engage in collective bargaining

ANSWER: **C.** The Social Security Act addressed the needs of the unemployed and the elderly (*The American Pageant,* 12th ed., p. 794/11th ed., p. 812).

Free-Response Questions

1. Support or refute this statement:
   A key feature of the New Deal was that it gave too much authority to the federal government and specifically the executive branch.

RESPONSE For many conservatives and proponents of laissez-faire capitalism, the New Deal is seen as an overexpansion of the federal government in regulating the economy and business. You can support this claim by discussing legislation promoted by FDR that overstepped his authority—for example, by establishing New Deal programs that were in competition with private businesses or adopted various aspects of a socialist economy such as the Tennessee Valley Authority. To support the idea that FDR used his authority properly, you can point out that he took extraordinary steps because the economic collapse was so extensive. As a contrast, discuss the policies of the conservative Hoover—laissez-faire economics, volunteerism, and localism—that were insufficient to lift the nation out of its economic woes.

2. To what extent is it correct that the New Deal was a conservative effort to maintain the social, economic, and political status quo?

RESPONSE Few would initially associate the New Deal with conservatism, instead viewing it as a major manifestation of liberalism. However, critics on the left believe the New Deal was not particularly liberal. You can support this position by pointing out that the New Deal did not go far in addressing the socio-economic problems confronting women and minorities and that the goal of the New Deal was to preserve capitalism. To this end, the New Deal did not fundamentally change class, gender, and racial relations in the U.S. To support the view that the New Deal was profoundly liberal, discuss the legislation displayed an unprecedented expansion of government power and authority in establishing social programs for the aged, the unemployed, and those ordinarily marginalized such as black Americans. Furthermore, you can write on ways the New Deal leveled the playing field for labor and business, not to mention engaging in deficit spending to fund New Deal programs and agencies.

17

WORLD WAR II: 1939– 1945

As nations struggled to survive the ordeal of the Great Depression, they would soon be confronted with malevolence greater than the horrors of World War I or the desperation associated with the collapse of the world's economy. For in Europe and Asia imperialism, militarism, and fascism were taking hold and would soon envelope the world In a catastrophe that made other modern wars pale in comparison.

Germany's capitulation in World War I combined with devastating war reparations and the collapse of its economy in the 1930s provided fertile ground for various extremist organizations to flourish, most infamously the Nationalist Socialist party, the Nazis. But Germany's defeat in the war did not have only economic ramifications. Saddled with "war guilt" by the victors, its national psyche was damaged by the extremely punitive nature of the Treaty of Versailles. One member of the Nazis, Adolf Hitler, would rise to head that group, and in the process exploit Germany's shame and humiliation to elevate himself and the Nazi party to the nation's political leadership. Using powerful and passionate oratory, Hitler convinced the German people that their defeat in the war, the humiliating peace terms, and the collapse of the German economy had been the result of poor political leadership, defeatism on the home front, and the economic machinations of Germany's Jewish population. Hitler's Nazi party synthesized nationalism with populist rhetoric, while simultaneously rejecting liberal values, communism, and republicanism. Utilizing coercion and violence, his regime promoted the "cult of personality," in which the leader—Hitler in this case—was portrayed as being larger than the nation itself. Tapping into the average German's nationalistic sentiments, in little more than a decade Hitler rose from being an obscure World War I veteran and third-rate artist to become chancellor of Germany in 1933. Without pause, he began to rebuild Germany's military in order to restore its commanding presence in Europe.

The story was not profoundly different in Italy. There, another would-be demagogue named Benito Mussolini took advantage of his nation's postwar crises—labor strikes, the breakdown of law and order, and ongoing battles between right- and left-wing groups—to catapult himself and his Fascist party to the leadership of Italy. Like his fascist comrade in Germany, Mussolini would assume dictatorial powers. Likewise in Japan, there were those who believed that only through extreme nationalism and militarism could Japan take its place in the sun.

Although these events increasingly concerned American political leaders, the developments in Europe and Asia could not shift the American public away from the belief that these were uniquely European and Asian problems, and that the United States should most certainly avoid involvement in yet another war that, like World War I, had dubious benefits for the United States. Thus, throughout the interwar years, the United States maintained an increasingly fragile policy of neutrality.

KEY CONCEPTS

- The rise of fascism, militarism, and imperialism were significant developments that ultimately led to World War II when Germany, Italy, and Japan embarked on policies of territorial expansion and conquest.
- The 1930s Neutrality Acts limited but did not entirely prevent FDR from providing assistance to Great Britain.
- Deteriorating relations between Japan and the United States ended in war.
- The United States adopted a discriminatory policy towards Japanese-Americans.
- The Holocaust brought unprecedented suffering to millions of European Jews and others the Nazis found objectionable.
- The dropping of the atomic bombs on Japan ended the war, but some later questioned whether the attacks were necessary.
- The roots of the Cold War lay in the tensions that developed between the Soviet Union and the Western Allies.

World War II is discussed in depth in *The American Pageant*, 12th ed., Chapters 35 and 36/11th ed., Chapters 37 and 38.

GERMAN AND ITALIAN MILITARISM AND TERRITORIAL EXPANSION

After assuming control of their respective nations, Hitler and Mussolini embarked on a massive rearmament program that was a prerequisite for them to carry out their foreign- policy objective: territorial expansion through conquest. For Hitler the buildup of Germany's military was in direct violation of the Treaty of Versailles. No matter, Hitler simply withdrew Germany from the League of Nations when that body forbade his request to rearm his nation. Hitler

Neutrality or Isolationism?

Some textbooks refer to American foreign policy in the interwar years as one based on isolationism. True, following World War I many Americans believed that the United States should curtail or, in extreme cases, end its involvement in international affairs, especially in Europe. This sentiment was given added weight in 1934 when a Senate investigation headed by Senator Gerald P. Nye concluded that political pressure exerted on American policymakers by U.S. bankers, financiers, and munitions corporations had been a determining factor in the U.S. government's decision to enter World War I. In order to maintain a neutral stance, a bill authored by Senator Hiram Johnson and passed into law in 1934 (the Johnson Act) forbade foreign nations that had defaulted on their debt payments to the United States from receiving further loans. In 1935, 1936, and 1937 the U.S. Congress passed neutrality acts designed to keep the United States out of foreign conflicts. The acts ran the gamut from preventing exports to nations at war, to warning Americans that they traveled on ships of warring nations at their own risk, to preventing loans to belligerents. The president was even authorized to deny the ships of belligerent nations access to American ports. After the outbreak of World War II in 1939, the American isolationist movement found its voice in the America First Committee, which maintained that isolationism was in the nation's best interest. However, given the U.S. intervention in Latin America in the postwar decades, the presence of its military in Asia, the strong economic relationship between the United States and many European and Asian nations, and the military assistance given to Britain once war broke out, some historians question whether the United States was even neutral by 1940, let alone isolationist. A close investigation of U.S. policies and objectives in the interwar years is therefore necessary in order for you to develop your own interpretation of the nature of American foreign affairs in this period.

continued to defy the League by occupying the demilitarized Rhine Valley in 1936. He next set his sights on repatriating the over 1.5 million German-speaking citizens who were then living outside of Germany and Austria because of the collapse of Austria-Hungary and the creation of new states following World War I. To this end, his forces occupied the Rhineland and annexed Austria. In the Munich Conference of 1938, Hitler secured an agreement from the French and British that gave him the German-speaking area of Czechoslovakia known as the Rhineland. Hitler promised that his thirst for territorial expansion had been quenched. British Prime Minister Neville Chamberlain, and his French counterpart, Edouard Daladier, believed him, mistakenly thinking they had prevented another European war. "Peace in our time," Chamberlain naively declared upon his return to Britain.

But this was wishful thinking, given what we now know of Hitler's ambitions. Not long after the Munich Agreement, Germany occupied all of Czechoslovakia. Paralyzed by the thought of another world war, Britain and France assumed that a policy of appeasement would satisfy the German dictator. The occupation of Czechoslovakia convinced them of the folly of such a policy. On September 1, 1939, Germany invaded Poland. Negotiations, appeasement, and agreements having run their course, France and Britain declared war on Germany. A few years before the German expansion into Czechoslovakia, their ally Italy invaded Ethiopia. The League of Nations imposed an embargo on war-related items but did little else to assist the overmatched Ethiopians, despite a personal appeal to the delegates by Emperor Haile Selassie. The Soviet Union would not engage German troops until 1940, for, to the shock and surprise of the world, the two ideological antagonists—one communist, the other fascist—had signed a nonaggression pact in 1939.

AP Tip

In order to comprehend the conflict in ideologies that shaped the economic and political structures of the combatants, the following definitions may be helpful:

- **Fascism** An authoritarian, antidemocratic economic and political system that subordinates the individual to the needs of the state and party. For example, trade unions are outlawed because they promote the interests of laborers, not of the nation. Obedience to the nation's leader is required. Italy and Germany in the 1930s are examples of fascist countries.
- **Totalitarianism** Similar in several respects to a fascist society, a totalitarian system requires obedience to the leader and the needs of the state. Consequently, the government controls most aspects of society, such as education and the legal system. Germany and the Soviet Union in the 1930s were totalitarian.
- **Democratic-Republicanism** A political system in which certain basic rights and privileges are guaranteed to all citizens, who in turn have the right to elect representatives to serve their interests and those of the nation at various levels of government. Great Britain and the United States are examples of democratic-republics.
- **Communism** A social, political, and economic system in which private ownership of the means of production is controlled by the state. A key objective of communism is to rid society of class-based interests and the exploitation of the working class by those who own the means of production. The Soviet Union from 1917 to 1989 was a communist nation.

THE SPANISH CIVIL WAR

The Spanish Civil War is considered a prelude to World War II in that it pitted forces representing divergent ideologies—fascism and republicanism—against each other in a war to determine Spain's political future. Both sides in the conflict were assisted by outside forces. Supplementing the Republican government (the Loyalists) were 52,000 volunteers from around the world, including the most famous American unit, the Abraham Lincoln Brigade. Soviet dictator Stalin sent war matériel and military personnel to assist the government's forces as well. Hitler and Mussolini, on the other hand, sent air and ground units to assist fascist general Francisco Franco overthrow the Spanish government. Although President Roosevelt supported the Loyalists, his hands were tied by the Neutrality Act of 1937, which forbade arms shipments to the belligerents in the Spanish Civil War.

He recommended that the United States join with the other powers to "quarantine" aggressor nations. But by 1939, the same year World War II broke out, Franco's fascist forces prevailed.

JAPANESE IMPERIALISM

Once Japan entered the modern age in the late nineteenth century, it had embarked on an intensive program of industrialization, westernization, militarism, and territorial expansion. In the late nineteenth century Japan had defeated China, and to the surprise and chagrin of westerners, it had decisively defeated Russia in 1905. Its success continued. In World War I it had fortuitously joined the Allied side. Although its troops saw limited combat in the war, Japan received China's Shandong Peninsula and Germany's colonies in the Pacific. Yet Japan still believed that it was not given the respect it deserved as a major world power by the other victorious nations. It would therefore create its own Asian empire (the Co-Prosperity Sphere), a decision that would culminate in a war with the United States over which nation would be the hegemonic power in the Pacific.

The first step in its imperialist objective was to occupy the Chinese province of Manchuria in 1931, in complete defiance of the League of Nations, establishing a puppet government called Manchukuo. Despite refusing to take steps to join other nations in economically punishing Japan, the United States did take umbrage with its invasion of China, seeing it as a violation of the Open Door, and a host of other interwar agreements. But the Hoover administration's response was tepid and sanctimonious at best: Secretary of War Henry Stimson declared in the Stimson Doctrine that the United States would not recognize the pseudogovernment established in China by the Japanese and would adhere to the Nine-Power Treaty by condemning the acquisition of territory taken by force. The League of Nations endorsed the doctrine but did little else. In 1937 a full-scale war erupted between the Japanese and Chinese. In the course of events a U.S. gunboat, the *Panay,* was sunk by Japanese planes. Not wanting the incident to escalate any further, a Japanese apology was quickly accepted by the U.S. government. Four years later, however, Japan would intentionally attack U.S. warships at Pearl Harbor, Hawaii, a decision that could only be met by a declaration of war by the United States.

ROOSEVELT AND THE ALLIES

By the late 1930s, despite the continued public support for the Neutrality Acts, the militarist actions of Japan, Germany, and Italy (who eventually formed the Rome-Berlin-Tokyo alliance and were known thereafter as the Axis Powers) made Congress more amenable to President Roosevelt's request for increased military expenditures. After the German conquest of Denmark and Norway, and the fall of France in 1940, Great Britain stood alone against Nazi domination of Europe. Still, the American public was wary of U.S. military involvement despite growing concerns that the Nazis might soon conquer all of Europe.

From Roosevelt's perspective the defeat of Great Britain would pose dire consequences for U.S. national security. Thus FDR worked around the Neutrality Acts, finding ways to aid Britain and, in the process, U.S. self-interest. In a series of policies designed to aid Britain the president methodically eroded the Neutrality Acts:

- **"Cash and Carry"** A belligerent could purchase arms from the United States if it paid in cash and transported the supplies in its own vessels. FDR reasoned that this policy was in line with the Neutrality Acts because it allowed access to U.S. matériel for any nation at war. But inasmuch as the British Royal Navy dominated the seas, it obviously benefited the British.

- **Lend-lease** In order to help a financially strapped Britain, Roosevelt ended cash and carry and instead provided credit to the British so that they could continue to purchase much-needed military supplies. Roosevelt justified this action by telling the American people that "we must be an arsenal of democracy" and that the policy was designed to defend the "four freedoms" that Americans valued: freedom of religion, freedom of speech, freedom from want, freedom from fear. Despite the strong opposition to assisting Britain in this manner from isolationists and those advocating a policy of neutrality, the Lend-Lease Act became law in early 1941 and was further expanded when Roosevelt ordered that U.S. warships escort British ships carrying lend-lease items for part of their journey. When a German submarine attacked one of the warships, Roosevelt ordered that all German ships should be attacked on sight. For all intents and purposes, the United States was fighting an undeclared war with Germany. Little did the American public know that before the year was out the U.S. would formally be at war with the Axis Powers.

- **Destroyers for bases** Even though Britain's surface ships "ruled the seas," German submarines were wreaking havoc on British shipping. Although resolute in their defiance of Hitler's attempt to pummel them into submission, by late 1940 Britain's ability to sustain itself was in dire straits. Roosevelt desperately wanted to provide direct military assistance to Britain, but he could not openly violate the Neutrality Acts. Instead, he came up with a creative way to circumvent the acts and in the process augment the British Royal Navy. In return for fifty dated U.S. Navy destroyers, the British allowed the United States to construct military bases on Britain's Caribbean islands.

- **The draft** In order to prepare the nation in the event it was drawn into the war, Roosevelt took the momentous step of convincing Congress to institute a peacetime draft, the Selective Training and Service Act of 1940. Predictably, those who wanted to keep the United States out of the war at all costs interpreted the act as a prerequisite to U.S. military involvement. The legal bulwark that kept the United States from participating in the war—the Neutrality Acts—by now seemed like a guiding principle in name only. In the summer of 1941 Roosevelt met with British Prime Minister Churchill in a secret meeting held on a warship off the coast of Newfoundland and declared in the Atlantic Charter that both nations stood for the four basic freedoms, self-determination for all nations, opposition to territorial expansion, freedom of the seas, a repudiation of any territorial gains made as a result of the war, and arms control. In other words, their declaration avowed all the beliefs that were inconsistent with the behavior of the militarist Axis Powers: Germany, Italy, and Japan.

DETERIORATING RELATIONS WITH JAPAN

The antecedents of the war between Japan and the United States can be found in the escalating tensions between the two nations in the 1930s, which culminated in the Japanese attack on Pearl Harbor in 1941. As the Japanese sought to extend their hegemony in Asia, the United States became increasingly concerned with Japan's aggressive foreign policy. The invasion of China confirmed American fears that the Japanese would not be satisfied until they dominated Eastern Asia and the Pacific. The creation of the Rome-Berlin-Tokyo military alliance only confirmed Japan's bellicose intentions, which were realized when the Japanese military occupied French Indochina in the summer of 1941. The British and Americans responded by imposing a trade embargo on Japan, cutting off resources it needed to sustain its industries and military, such as rubber and oil. It was made clear to the Japanese government that further expansionist acts would provoke a military response. In the months leading up to Japan's attack on the United States, both nations engaged in what were fruitless attempts to forestall war, as neither country was prepared to do battle with the other. From the Japanese perspective, however, war with the United States seemed inevitable if Japan was to successfully carry out its foreign-policy objectives.

In order to neutralize the most potent U.S. obstacle to Japanese control of the Pacific—the U.S. Seventh Fleet stationed at Pearl Harbor, Hawaii—a surprise attack was launched on December 7, 1941. Although the attack killed thousands of U.S. servicemen and destroyed approximately twenty U.S. ships and hundreds of airplanes, the United States was fortunate that its aircraft carriers were out to sea at the time of the attack. Simultaneously, Japanese forces conquered the Philippines, Guam, and Hong Kong. December 7, "a day which will live in infamy," according to Roosevelt, propelled the United States into a war against Japan as well as Germany and Italy. Though some Americans still hoped for a peaceful solution, whatever doubts most had about their nation's involvement in the war were now put to rest as the U.S. government and the American people mobilized their resources for the war effort.

Unfortunately the U.S. government and the military remained segregated. Although black Americans served the nation at home and in the armed forces, they continued to suffer discrimination in the workplace even after the nation's economy expanded as a result of the demands of the war. To be sure, some gains were made, such as the creation of the Fair Employment Practices Committee, a federal agency that attempted to address discrimination in the economy. Due to the federal government's less discriminatory hiring practices, the number of blacks employed by the government increased profoundly. But it was not until 1948 (as a result of an executive order by President Truman) that the military was desegregated.

Japanese-American Internment

One tragic consequence of the Pearl Harbor attack was a virulent anti-Japanese sentiment that culminated in the persecution of Japanese-Americans. President Roosevelt exacerbated this racism by issuing Executive Order 9066, which resulted in the resettlement of over 125,000 Japanese-Americans to miserable internment camps in the western United States for fear that they would undermine the American war effort against Japan. While this travesty of justice was taking place, Japanese-American servicemen were serving honorably in the U.S. military. What is more, the U.S. government did not expand this program to include Italian-Americans or German-Americans. The message was clear: Asians could not be trusted. Though the U.S. war against Germany, Italy, and Japan was noble, the legacy of the unjust treatment of U.S. citizens of Japanese descent is an unfortunate legacy of a war that was fought to stop racism and fascism.

The Holocaust

One nefarious aspect of the Nazi regime was its treatment of political opponents, dissidents, homosexuals, and most especially Jews. Hitler had a long-standing hatred of Europe's Jews, whom he blamed for a variety of German and European problems. Tragically, they became scapegoats for all that the dictator claimed was wrong in the world. During his twelve-year reign his government systematically destroyed approximately 6 million German Jews and those who lived in nations overrun by the German army. Initially Jews were terrorized, as in the infamous 1938 "Night of Broken Glass"—*Kristallnacht*—in which synagogues and Jewish homes and businesses were destroyed. Next, Jews were rounded up and sent to concentration camps or restricted to ghettos, where they starved to death or fell victims to diseases. Finally, in what the Nazis referred to as the Final Solution, millions of Jews, as well as millions of Russians, homosexuals, and political opponents, were killed in death camps designed to eliminate the victims in large numbers.

It was not until the middle of the war that the Allies became aware of the extent of the atrocities. Some critics argue the United States should have taken steps to stop the attempted genocide, whereas others claim that the best way the Allies could have ended the Holocaust was to defeat the German military. Only when the death camps were liberated by U.S. soldiers was the full extent of the horror made known. Entire families had been destroyed, millions had been gassed, and others worked and starved to death. Horrifically, the Germans had conducted "scientific experiments" on live subjects. It was later revealed that the Japanese had also committed atrocities. After the war, at the Nuremberg War Crimes Trial and similar legal proceedings against Japanese military and political leaders, the defendants were charged with crimes against humanity. Important German and Japanese leaders were executed and others given prison sentences as punishment for their actions.

WARTIME CONFERENCES AND THE COLD WAR

In the last two years of the war the Allied leaders met with one another in a series of conferences designed to discuss strategies and objectives, as well as to discuss the post-war world. Often the Allied leaders seemed unified in their thinking; at other times there appeared to be tensions and suspicions between the Americans and British on one hand and the Soviet dictator Josef Stalin on the other.

- **Casablanca Conference (January 1943)** President Roosevelt and Prime Minister Churchill agreed that Allied forces would invade Sicily and end Italy's participation in the war. A strategy was discussed to defeat the Japanese as well. Most important, the two leaders announced that they would accept nothing less than the unconditional surrender of Japan and Germany.

- **Teheran Conference (November-December 1943)** This was the first conference of the "Big Three" (Stalin, Roosevelt, and Churchill), and though it ended amicably, it was not without its tense moments. The leaders discussed strategies for ending the war, including an invasion of Nazi-held France. Stalin agreed to enter the war against Japan upon the defeat of Germany. Roosevelt and Stalin supported the idea of a postwar international body that would settle disputes between nations, though Churchill had some misgivings about the effectiveness of such an organization. For the time being, the leaders decided that Germany would be severely punished for its role in causing the war.

- **Yalta Conference (February 1945)** By the time the Big Three met at Yalta, it was obvious that the defeat of Germany was imminent. Once again Stalin agreed to enter the war against Japan in return for the restoration of its pre-1905 status in East Asia. The leaders also began working out the details of the organization that would soon become the United Nations. The most controversial issue, the status of postwar East European countries, especially Poland, was vaguely defined. Some historians believe the origins of the Cold War can be found in this meeting, when a gravely ill Roosevelt was outmaneuvered by a wily and deceitful Stalin, who promised free elections in Soviet-controlled Eastern Europe. To these historians, Yalta laid the groundwork for Soviet domination of Eastern Europe in the postwar period. Others argue that Russia, which had been invaded twice in less than twenty-five years, required a buffer zone between it and its potential future enemies to the west.

- **Potsdam Conference (July-August 1945)** By the time this conference was convened, Roosevelt had died and Churchill had been succeeded by Clement Attlee as Britain's prime minister. The fissures that appeared in the Allied relationship at Yalta had widened by the time the leaders met at Potsdam (Berlin). All agreed that Germany must be demilitarized and the Nazi influence purged from German culture. But reparations and the occupation of Germany were left unresolved, thereby intensifying the uneasiness that now seemed to define the relationship between the Western Allies and the Soviet Union.

THE WAR

In the early stages of the war the Axis Powers experienced considerable success. The Japanese overran much of East Asia and islands in the Pacific. Germany conquered its neighbors, until Britain stood alone. The Battle of Berlin, in which the Royal Air Force defeated the German Luftwaffe (air force), put an end to Hitler's aim of invading Britain. Stymied, he turned east and invaded the Soviet Union, his troops reaching Stalingrad in 1941; they then laid siege to the city. By 1942, however, the Germans were cut off, exhausted, and demoralized. Over 300,000 of Germany's best troops surrendered. The Russians then launched a massive counteroffensive, which ultimately took them to the outskirts of Berlin.

In the meantime the United States had entered the war and, with their British allies, was successful in establishing a foothold in Europe as a result of the successful, though costly, D-Day landing (June 6, 1944). Over the next ten months the Germans were driven from France and Italy. Mussolini was killed and Italy sued for peace. Finally Berlin itself was under siege. By early 1945 the Americans and British were also on the outskirts of Berlin, where Hitler had taken refuge in his underground bunker. Rather than be captured alive, he chose to commit suicide. On May 8, 1945, the Germans surrendered (V-E Day).

The war against Japan continued on for three more months. In a series of bloody battles Japanese military units holding strategically important islands such as Iwo Jima and Okinawa were eventually defeated, until the Japanese mainland itself was open to attack. Before an invasion could take place, President Truman, who had ascended to the presidency upon FDR's death in April, ordered that atomic bombs be dropped on Hiroshima and Nagasaki. U.S. scientists had for several years been working on an atomic weapon in a secret program known as the Manhattan Project. Five days after the second bomb was dropped on Nagasaki, the Japanese unconditionally surrendered.

When the atomic bombs were first dropped on Japan, few questioned the military necessity of such a decision. After all, the Truman administration's convincing argument that the bombs, though devastating, would save the lives of 1 million Allied servicemen if Japan itself was invaded was proof enough that the dropping of the atomic weapons was necessary. The bloody battles on Iwo Jima and Okinawa, in which the Japanese fought almost to the last man, convinced many that an invasion of the Japanese mainland would be even more bitterly contested. Thus President Truman was forced to sacrifice the lives of thousands of Japanese civilians in order to convince the emperor and the Imperial War Cabinet that capitulation was Japan's only option.

In the past few decades historians have questioned whether Truman's decision was intended to end the war with Japan or to send a clear message to the Soviet Union that the United States had the military capability to challenge the Soviets if necessary in the postwar period. Furthermore, the United States may have been concerned that the Soviet Union's imminent entry into the war against Japan would provide it an opportunity to, along with the United States, occupy that nation after the war, possibly leading to the type of territorial division that had occurred in Korea. In fact, it seems that by 1945 the once-formidable Japanese military was but a shell of its past power. For example, the Japanese Navy had essentially been neutralized, Japan's merchant fleet was nearly destroyed, millions of Japanese soldiers were isolated in China and elsewhere and could not be returned to Japan to defend the homeland, and the Japanese Air Force was reduced to using kamikaze pilots. Moreover, every major military target in Japan had already been bombed at least once. Even the projected estimate of 1 million casualties is also questioned. To this day, the decision whether the United States should have used atomic weapons on Japan triggers passions on both sides of the issue. It is important for you to understand that every controversial issue or decision has its supporters and detractors.

World War II cost approximately 50 million lives, hundreds of billions of dollars, and untold suffering and despair for millions of others. Although the international price was massive, the defeat of Germany, Japan, and Italy ended the horrors perpetrated by those nations against humanity. Importantly, the year the war ended, the United Nations was established in the hopes of preventing such barbarity from ever happening again. As for the United States, it had endured over 1 million casualties, killed and wounded, but had emerged from the war a superpower. For the time being it had a nuclear-weapons monopoly that gave it an advantage over the Soviets in the first few years of the Cold War. Yet, as the nation entered into a postwar period of consumerism and economic reconversion, foreign and domestic concerns would profoundly shape the quality of life for the American people.

Multiple-Choice Questions

1. Which of the following is NOT associated with the Axis Powers?
   (A) Hitler
   (B) Mussolini
   (C) Japan
   (D) Franco
   (E) Italy

ANSWER: **D**. While Germany and Italy assisted Franco's fascists, Spain remained neutral in the war (*The American Pageant*, 12th ed., p. 855/11th ed., p. 876).

2. In the Munich Conference
   (A) Hitler agreed to form an alliance with Italy and Japan
   (B) the Big Three agreed to demand unconditional surrender from the Germans and Japanese
   (C) Britain and France gave in to Hitler's territorial demands
   (D) the United States promised Germany that it would remain neutral in the war
   (E) the Nazis worked out the details of the Final Solution

ANSWER: **C**. Hitler promised an end to his territorial ambitions if Czechoslovakia was compelled to relinquish control of the Sudetenland to Germany (*The American Pageant*, 12th ed., p. 813/11th ed., pp. 831-832).

3. Which future Allied nation provided support to the Loyalists in the Spanish Civil War?
   (A) United States
   (B) Britain
   (C) France
   (D) China
   (E) Soviet Union

ANSWER: **E.** The Soviet Union provided aid, though not as much as Germany and Italy provided (*The American Pageant,* 12th ed., p. 811/11th ed., p. 830).

4. The America First Committee
   (A) was strongly in favor of providing economic assistance to Britain, but opposed military aid
   (B) believed the United States should enter the war only if its ships were attacked by German submarines
   (C) was strongly in favor of the assistance President Roosevelt gave to the British
   (D) believed "cash and carry" would not jeopardize American neutrality
   (E) strongly opposed U.S. intervention in the war

ANSWER: **E.** The America First Committee favored isolationism (*The American Pageant,* 12th ed., p. 818/11th ed., p. 837).

5. At which conference did the Big Three first meet?
   (A) Casablanca
   (B) Munich
   (C) Potsdam
   (D) Yalta
   (E) Teheran

ANSWER: **E.** An earlier conference, the Casablanca Conference, was between Roosevelt and Churchill (*The American Pageant,* 12th ed., pp. 843-844/11th ed., pp. 864-865).

6. In the *Panay* incident
   (A) the Japanese inadvertently sank a U.S. gunboat on patrol in China
   (B) the Japanese launched a surprise attack on the Seventh Fleet at Pearl Harbor, Hawaii
   (C) Japan invaded China
   (D) the Japanese government agreed not to invade China in return for territorial concessions in Southeast Asia
   (E) Chinese troops attacked the Japanese embassy in China

ANSWER: **A.** Japan apologized for the sinking of the U.S. gunboat rather than risk escalating tensions between the two nations (*The American Pageant,* 12th ed., p. 812/11th ed., p. 831).

7. The Stimson Doctrine
   (A) was widely condemned by the America First Committee
   (B) stated that the United States would not recognize Japan's puppet government in China
   (C) implied that the United States would not challenge Soviet influence in Eastern Europe
   (D) declared that the United States would sink German submarines on sight
   (E) stated that the United States would seek unconditional surrender terms from Japan and Germany

ANSWER: **B**. The Stimson Doctrine is widely viewed as a tepid response to Japan's aggression in China (*The American Pageant,* 12th ed., pp. 774-775/11th ed., pp. 791-792).

8. When President Roosevelt stated that this event was "a date which will live in infamy," he was referring to:
   (A) the D-Day landing
   (B) the dropping of the atomic bombs on Japan
   (C) the beginning of the Holocaust
   (D) the surprise attack on Pearl Harbor
   (E) Germany's invasion of Poland

ANSWER: **D**. This attack was the basis of the U.S. entry into World War II (*The American Pageant,* 12th ed., p. 824/11th ed., p. 843).

9. In order to establish a new Italian empire, Mussolini ordered his military to invade
   (A) Poland
   (B) France
   (C) Belgium
   (D) Ethiopia
   (E) Egypt

ANSWER: **D**. The defeat of the Ethiopians and Italian occupation of portions of the Adriatic and Balkans was the extent of Mussolini's empire (*The American Pageant,* 12th ed., p. 810/11th ed., p. 829).

10. The Manhattan Project was a top-secret plan
    (A) to prevent Japan from acquiring raw materials necessary for the expansion of its military
    (B) devised by the Nazis to eliminate Europe's Jews
    (C) by the United States to develop the atom bomb
    (D) that led to the formation of the Rome-Berlin-Tokyo Axis
    (E) that culminated in the Allies' D-Day landing

ANSWER: **C**. Albert Einstein convinced Roosevelt to start the project (*The American Pageant,* 12th ed., p. 814/11th ed., p. 834).

Free-Response Questions

1. Analyze President Roosevelt's foreign policy in light of the considerable opposition and obstacles he faced in helping Great Britain. Discuss the following in your response:
    Neutrality Acts
    America First Committee
    assistance provided to the British

RESPONSE In this essay you should indicate that President Roosevelt wanted to assist Britain in its war against Germany but was prohibited from directly providing aid by the Neutrality Acts. You should discuss the specific restraints placed on the president by the acts as well as the efforts of those individuals and groups who sought to keep the United States neutral in what they viewed as a European war, such as the America First Committee and Charles Lindbergh. Over time, however, Roosevelt was able to assist Britain. You should therefore discuss "Cash and Carry," lend-lease, and the "bases for destroyers" agreement.

2. Support or refute the following statement:
    The United States was justified in using the atomic bombs against Japan in 1945.

RESPONSE If defending the use of the atomic bombs on Japan in 1945, you should address the enormous cost of the battles that led up to Truman's decision, such as the Battles of Iwo Jima and Okinawa. Include in your essay the reasoning that if the Japanese military had fought almost to the last man in those battles, and in the process inflicted staggering casualties on the Americans, the cost in lives for conquering Japan itself would make the other battles pale in comparison. To refute the statement you should discuss the condition of the Japanese military and Japan itself in 1945: its air force and navy had been decimated, its merchant fleet had been reduced to insignificance, and every major military target in Japan had already been bombed at least once. Added to this is the willingness of the Japanese to surrender weeks before the bombs were dropped. Another major argument that supports this perspective is the view that the United States attacked Japan with atomic weapons in order to defeat that nation before the Soviets could enter the Pacific War.

18

U.S. DOMESTIC AFFAIRS FROM 1945 TO THE 1980S

In 1945 much of Europe lay in ruins, economics and political systems had been shattered, and millions were displaced. Asia too had been a battleground. The United States occupied Japan, China was poised to revert to civil war, and Southeast Asia and the Korean peninsula would soon be divided between communist and anticommunist groups and governments. The war had taken approximately 50 million lives, and had cost hundreds of billions of dollars. It had taken its toll on the United States as well, which suffered over 1 million casualties, of which 300,000 were killed in action. In monetary terms, it had cost well over $300 billion. In many ways, however, the United States emerged from the war more powerful in political and economic terms than the other combatants. To be sure, the number of Americans killed was staggering, but it pales in comparison with the Soviet Union's losses—approximately 8 million civilians and 14 million soldiers. Many nations in Europe and Asia had experienced invasion as well; the continental United States was untouched by such an experience during the war. The United States had furthermore entered the war as an international power and emerged a superpower, the only nation in the world at that time with a nuclear arsenal.

Numerous problems lay ahead for the United States despite its success in the war and its healthy condition relative to other nations. President Roosevelt had died in April 1945, just weeks before the surrender of Germany's Third Reich. The vice president was the untested and seemingly inexperienced Harry Truman. His task was daunting. The United States and its allies would first have to defeat Japan and then decide how to integrate millions of service members back into the economy. Demobilization was not the only economic concern; reconversion from a war to a consumer economy would also present a considerable challenge. As Americans adjusted their lives to the new realities of the postwar years, they would soon find that relations with their former ally, the Soviet Union, would rapidly deteriorate, leading to decades of tension, conflict, and enormous military expenditures. The Cold War—the adversarial relationship between the United States and its allies and the Soviet Union and its allies—defined in many ways the quality of life in the postwar era, made worse by the knowledge that there were more than enough nuclear weapons to destroy the planet.

KEY CONCEPTS

- In the postwar period, the U.S. economy reconverted from one geared to the production of military supplies to one that was consumer-oriented.
- The postwar years witnessed an enormous expansion of the economy, highlighted by the baby boom, suburbanization, and massive consumer spending.
- The civil rights movements helped black Americans, but they were still relegated to a second-class status economically, politically, and socially.
- The presidential administrations in the postwar decades expanded the size and scope of government.
- Some administrations addressed the demands of labor, whereas others had an adversarial relationship.
- Liberalism reshaped social, economic, gender, racial, and political relations.
- A conservative backlash evolved in response to the liberal policies of the 1960s.
- The Watergate scandal undermined the American people's trust in their political system.

This period is discussed in depth in *The American Pageant,* 12th ed., Chapters 37-41/11th ed., Chapters 39-43.

THE ECONOMIC "BOOM"

Of course it is easy to see the United States after World War II as a nation overwhelmed by the Cold War and the arms race that developed between the two powerful adversaries, the United States and the Soviet Union. Yet conditions were still dreadful for millions of Americans at the end of the war, and they would stay that way. Poor whites, blacks, Latinos, and others lived desperate lives, struggling to stay above the poverty line, as postwar prosperity did not touch their lives. For example:

- Twenty percent of the population lived in poverty.
- Parts of rural America had been untouched by modern developments in sanitation, housing, education, and health care.

Yet for many Americans the postwar years represented a new level of national and personal prosperity few had ever known. The generations that had fought the war had not only experienced the unparalleled devastation of World War II but also endured the Great Depression. The decade following the war, when the nation achieved unprecedented and sustained economic growth, must have seemed like an illusion to some. Citizens and the government embarked on a massive spending spree, stimulated by the carefree spending habits of many Americans, who had saved millions of dollars during the war, and government spending. The government had stimulated the economy out of necessity during the war, but it continued to do so when the conflict ended. Billions of dollars were budgeted for public education and welfare programs. The Interstate Highway Act of 1956 allotted over $30 billion to highway development. The primary beneficiaries of this infrastructural development were the trucking and automobile industries (the auto became the symbol of postwar prosperity), and the integrated highway network, a major conduit between urban central business districts and the "bedroom communities" of suburbia, altered the national landscape forever. Government spending for former service members covered a variety of areas: the Veterans Administration and the Federal Housing Administration provided low-interest loans for purchasing homes and for low-cost public housing. The Servicemen's Readjustment Act, commonly known as the GI Bill, provided veterans low-interest loans to start businesses and enroll in technical schools and universities.

The vitality of the economy was remarkable:

- Production of goods and services doubled as Americans engaged in unprecedented consumerism.
- Unemployment and inflation stayed below 5 percent.
- The gross national product had increased fivefold during the war.

DEMOBILIZATION AND ECONOMIC RECONVERSION

Shortly after becoming president, Harry Truman changed the paperweight on his desk; one modeled after a gun was replaced by one modeled after a plow. The message was clear: reconvert the economy from a war footing to a consumer one. As more and more service people returned home—approximately 7 million servicemen and -women had returned to civilian status just one year after V-J Day—economic reconversion was a high priority for the administration.

Another concern soon surfaced: postwar inflation. Some feared inflation could spark a recession and widespread unemployment. The Office of Price Administration (OPA), created during the war, had imposed price controls—and therefore controlled inflation. But what would happen after the war, when it was anticipated that consumer demand would drive up prices and the general cost of living? Fortunately, the OPA, rapid reconversion to producing consumer goods, and considerable demand offset a temporary increase in inflation. By late 1947 most concerns had dissipated. The growth of the economy was further sustained by the military demands of the Cold War; the government continued to be a major purchaser of goods and services. With so much money in the system, combined with ever-growing consumer demand, businesses introduced a new phenomenon in consumer spending, an early form of the credit card, in order to further stimulate consumer demand.

THE BABY BOOM AND SUBURBANIZATION

Between 1945 and 1960 the total U.S. population increased by 40 million. In the 1950s alone the population increased by 28 million. This expansion represented an almost 20 percent population increase, the largest since the height of immigration earlier in the century. Americans who were born in the decade and a half after the war and came of age in the midst of the Cold War are known as "baby boomers."

The population explosion created a demand for affordable family housing in the late 1940s and 1950s, which precipitated dramatic demographic changes:

- The need for housing immediately following the war spurred the remarkable growth of the suburbs. However, almost the entire population increase in this period was an urban experience, as millions settled in the nation's bustling cities.

- Much of the demographic shift that took place led to substantial growth in what became is as the "sunbelt" states, an arc that stretches from the Carolinas to Florida, Texas, and California. Millions of Americans relocated, lured by lower taxes, a more temperate climate (aided by the introduction of air conditioning in businesses and homes), and economic opportunities in defense-related industries. The industrial areas of the Northeast, which became known as the "rustbelt," experienced economic hard times and a reduction in representation in the House.

- The Northeast, however, remained the most densely populated section of the nation. Twenty years after the end of the war, one in five Americans lived in the narrow corridor that stretched from Massachusetts to Virginia.

- By the early 1960s population growth was mostly a suburban phenomenon, so that by the 1970s many more Americans were living in suburban neighborhoods than in cities.

- With military spending increasing employment opportunities in the North from 1941 to 1945, black Americans had migrated to the North in significant numbers; this trend would continue well after the end of the war.

- The growth of suburbia was the consequence of numerous factors: the automobile, the highway system, consumer demand to live outside congested urban areas, and the efforts of development contractors such as William Levitt. Levitt mass-produced low-priced family homes (the prototype was Long Island, New York's Levittown). This massive construction project, offering low-interest rates on mortgages that were government insured and tax deductible, paved the way for millions to own their own suburban homes. Unfortunately, Levitt homes were not made available to black Americans. The effect of this demographic shift and racial discrimination was "white flight" from urban to suburban areas. Consequently, inner cities became increasingly poorer and racially segregated.

  - Advocates of suburbanization claim that it represents the American dream of home ownership, a cleaner environment, and less crime.

■ Critics contend that it despoils the environment, leads to conformity, promotes racial segregation, and weakens the economic and cultural qualities of urban areas.

DOMESTIC DEVELOPMENTS DURING THE TRUMAN ADMINISTRATION (1945–1953)

Harry Truman had been vice president of the United States only three months when President Roosevelt died in April 1945. Many skeptics were convinced that he lacked the experience and leadership skills necessary to run the nation at such a pivotal moment. It did not take him long, however, to form his own identity independent of the long shadow cast by his predecessor. As president Truman wanted to adopt many of the features of the New Deal into his reform program, called the Fair Deal. One critic implied that he came up with so many programs and policies that resembled the New Deal that not even the Brain Trust had thought of them. Political consequences would doom many of his programs to failure. The short postwar recession convinced enough Americans to vote for Republicans, who proceeded to take over both houses of Congress in 1946. Consequently, Republican conservatives in Congress blocked most of Truman's domestic programs, such as a comprehensive civil rights program, a national health insurance program, agricultural reforms, and aid to education. Actually, the last had bipartisan support, but the issue floundered on whether to fund religious parochial schools as well.

Labor's relationship with Truman was rocky at times. Postwar wages had not kept up with inflation, and by 1946 nearly 2 million workers went out on strike. When railroad workers struck, Truman threatened to seize and operate the railroads, thus ending the work stoppage. When the United Mine Workers union went out on strike and refused to heed the same warning, the government took over the mines until a compromise contract was worked out.

Labor's fortunes took a turn for the worse when Congress changed hands. Dismayed at the frequency of strikes and intensity of labor unrest, the probusiness Republican party acted quickly to stop the strikes, passing the controversial Taft-Hartley Act in 1947 over Truman's veto. The bill defined "unfair labor practices" as boycotts, sympathy strikes, and the closed shop, and required unions to adhere to a sixty-day cooling-off period before workers could strike. Union leaders were required to swear that they were not communists.

Undaunted, Truman pushed ahead with his own domestic agenda. In his two terms, the following measures were taken:

■ **Housing Act of 1949** This act budgeted $3 billion for slum clearance and new low-rent housing.
■ **Minimum Wage Act of 1949** The Fair Labor Standards Act of 1938 was amended to increase the minimum wage.
■ **Social Security Act of 1950** Coverage to individuals who were self-employed was added, and retirees were given increased benefits.
■ **Civil rights** Truman's policies alienated the southern wing of the Democratic party, or Dixiecrats, who in turn created their own States' Rights party and ran South Carolina Governor Strom

Thurmond against Truman in the 1948 election. Truman took the following steps despite the anticipated opposition from southern Democrats and Republican conservatives:

- created the Committee on Civil Rights, which proposed, for instance, that public institutions engaging in racial discrimination be denied federal funds, segregation in interstate transportation be prohibited, and lynching made a federal offense—all matters for which Congress refused to enact legislation
- desegregated the federal government and the armed forces
- appointed black federal judges

Despite strong opposition from the progressive wing of his own party (which ran Henry A. Wallace) and the Dixiecrats, not to mention his popular Republican opponent, Thomas E. Dewey, Truman surprised pollsters and political pundits by receiving over one hundred more electoral votes than did Dewey in the 1948 election. Prevented from seeking a third term when the Twenty-second Amendment was ratified in 1951, and with his popularity waning, Truman retired from public office.

DOMESTIC DEVELOPMENTS DURING THE EISENHOWER ADMINISTRATION (1953–1961)

Dwight Eisenhower emerged from World War II a national hero. As supreme allied commander, he was enormously popular. In 1952 he ran as a Republican and easily defeated Illinois's Adlai Stevenson. His campaign slogan, "Time for a Change," resonated with the public after two decades of Democratic leadership. He would repeat his victory over Stevenson again in 1956. The cabinet he selected comprised wealthy advocates of business. Despite this, labor did better in the 1950s compared with other sectors of the economy. In 1955 the AFL and the CIO merged, forming a powerful union. That year the government raised the minimum wage from seventy-five cents to one dollar an hour. In Eisenhower's two terms in office, the following steps were taken:

- The Department of Health, Education, and Welfare (initially recommended by Truman) was organized as a cabinet-level position in 1953. Its first secretary was Oveta Culp Hobby.
- Social Security was amended in 1954 to include new groups: state and local government employees and farmers. Retirees received cost-of-living increases. Two years later it was amended again to cover physicians. The eligibility requirement was lowered to age sixty-two for women and to age fifty for the disabled.
- The National Defense Education Act (1958) appropriated $1 billion for education, in large part because of concerns about Soviet advances in aeronautics. The act provided financial aid to college students, and provided matching federal funds for state education to improve courses in science, math, and language arts.

Civil rights claimed much of the country's attention. Blacks had experienced some important gains under Truman and some assistance from the Eisenhower administration when they took bold steps to challenge segregation and discrimination in the 1950s. With the *Brown v. Board of Education of Topeka, Kansas* decision (1954), the Warren Court shattered the eighty-year history of Jim Crow laws in the South and forever transformed black rights in relation to the Fourteenth Amendment. In overturning the 1896 *Plessy v. Ferguson* decision, the court ruled that separate but equal is unconstitutional because facilities for the races were inherently unequal.

Some southern communities refused to abide by the new law. When Arkansas's Governor Orval Faubus sent the National Guard to turn away black students from Little Rock's Central High School, Eisenhower sent the U.S. Army to the school to guarantee the safety of its newly registered black students. When the Little Rock School Board challenged the president's authority to integrate Little Rock's schools, the court decision in *Cooper v. Aaron* (1958) reiterated its rationale in the *Brown* case as a fundamental right of citizens under the Fourteenth Amendment. Legalized segregation was dead, though the struggle for integration continues to this day.

As segregation lingered on in the South, blacks took it upon themselves to challenge municipal and state laws that sustained inequality and segregation. In late 1955 Rosa Parks, a black resident of Montgomery, Alabama, refused to relinquish her seat to a white person in accordance with the city's segregation statute. Parks's arrest galvanized Montgomery's black community. Led by a twenty-six-year-old Baptist minister, the Reverend Dr. Martin Luther King, Jr., a successful, nonviolent boycott of Montgomery's buses was organized. The following year the Supreme Court ruled that segregated seating in municipal buses was unconstitutional. The boycott, Dr. King, and his philosophy of nonviolent resistance received international attention.

One year after the Montgomery bus boycott, Congress passed the Civil Rights Act of 1957, the first civil rights legislation since Reconstruction. It was designed to enforce voting rights that had been systematically denied to blacks throughout the South. A bipartisan Civil Rights Commission was established to oversee and prosecute (through the Justice Department) those interfering with a citizen's Fifteenth Amendment rights. In 1960 the act was strengthened to make such abuses a federal crime. Further, in response to a wave of bomb attacks on mostly southern black churches and homes in the 1950s, the act made transporting explosives across state lines a federal crime.

DOMESTIC DEVELOPMENTS DURING THE KENNEDY ADMINISTRATION: "THE NEW FRONTIER" (1961–1963)

John F. Kennedy (JFK) narrowly defeated the Republican candidate, Richard M. Nixon, in a campaign notable for the first presidential television debates. An assassin's bullet ended his life less than three years into his term in office, but in that brief time, JFK sought to expand on FDR's New Deal and Truman's Fair Deal programs. Like FDR he sought out the advice of intellectuals and university professors. As in Truman's presidency, Congress rejected most of Kennedy's most progressive programs. The following are representative of the programs and measures enacted during his short term in office:

- The Housing Act of 1961 budgeted $5 billion for slum clearance.
- The Minimum Wage Act of 1961 increased minimum hourly wages to $1.25.
- Amendments to Social Security extended coverage to children of unemployed workers and increased payments to retirees; however, a penalty was imposed on retirement before age sixty-five.
- Congress approved a Federal Water Pollution Control Act.

Civil rights still dominated the domestic scene. Kennedy was at first hesitant to use all of the federal government's power to tackle civil rights problems, but events compelled him to act. He eventually took important steps to guarantee black Americans their constitutional rights. Under the direction of his brother, Attorney General Robert F. Kennedy, the Justice Department sued in federal court to protect voting rights for black Americans. In 1961 he dispatched federal marshals to protect the Freedom Riders, who had been brutally attacked when they attempted to integrate interstate bus facilities. After announcing his support for the Voter Education Project, which was designed to register southern blacks to vote, JFK told Dr. King, "I may lose the next election, but I don't care." When a black Korean War veteran named James Meredith attempted to enroll in the all-white University of Mississippi in 1962, the governor of the state ordered that Meredith be rejected despite having met the academic requirements for admission. President Kennedy ordered federal marshals to Mississippi to compel the school to enroll Meredith. Violence erupted and two people were killed. It eventually took over five thousand federal marshals to register Meredith at the university. The following year Medgar Evers, the head of Mississippi's NAACP, was assassinated by a white racist in front of his home. Ironically, that very evening Kennedy had appeared on television to persuade the nation that stronger civil rights legislation was needed.

In 1963 another southern governor, George Wallace, attempted to accomplish what his fellow governors in Arkansas and Mississippi had failed to do: stop the enrollment of qualified black students in a state university. Again, the result was the same. Wallace symbolically and ceremoniously stood in the doorway of the registrar's office at the University of Alabama, preventing the black students from registering. Careful not to send the U.S. military into the state for fear it would result in rioting, Kennedy outmaneuvered Wallace: he nationalized the Alabama National Guard and commanded its senior general to order Wallace away. His act of bravado complete, Wallace left the university and it was soon integrated. That same year, under the leadership of Dr. King and his organization, the Southern Christian Leadership Conference (SCLC), the "cradle of the Confederacy," Birmingham, Alabama, was integrated.

Inspired by these gains, but not satisfied that almost ten years had passed since segregation was outlawed in the *Brown* decision, over 200,000 black and white demonstrators participated in the March on Washington, demanding an end to segregation and racial discrimination. Three months later Kennedy was dead, and it was left to a progressive southerner, Vice President Lyndon B. Johnson, to continue the series of reforms started by his predecessors.

DOMESTIC DEVELOPMENTS DURING THE JOHNSON ADMINISTRATION: "THE GREAT SOCIETY" (1963–1969)

A great admirer of Franklin Roosevelt, Lyndon Johnson sought to emulate him as a political leader. Like FDR, Johnson came to the White House during a traumatic moment in U.S. history, but fortunately he had had considerable experience in government. Domestically Johnson sought to combat poverty, disease, inadequate education, racial injustices, and generally improve the quality of life for millions who knew little more than hardship and discrimination. His approach appealed to the voting public. When he ran for election in 1964 he received over 61 percent of the popular vote, even more than FDR had received in his four successful bids for the presidency. Johnson's Great Society reform program brought about or inspired the following:

- **The Economic Opportunity Act of 1964** The act authorized $1 billion for the War on Poverty. In addition, it created the Job Corps to provide vocational training and educational opportunities for underprivileged youth.
- **Appalachian Regional Development Act of 1965** The act set aside $1 billion for aid to the poverty-stricken Appalachian mountain regions.
- **Elementary and Secondary Education Act of 1965** The act provided extensive financial aid to public and parochial schools.
- **Medicare Act of 1965** The act provided nursing and hospital care, funded by the Social Security system, to the elderly.

Johnson also oversaw the creation of two cabinet-level agencies: the Department of Housing and Urban Development (HUD) 1965, which was led by Robert Weaver, the nation's first black cabinet secretary; and the Department of Transportation in 1966, which oversees and coordinates national transportation policies. In addition two constitutional amendments were ratified: the Twenty-fourth Amendment (1964) prohibited the use of a poll tax as a prerequisite for voting; and the Twenty-fifth Amendment (1967) provided for the vice president to assume the duties of the president if the chief executive is incapacitated.

Two crucial civil rights acts were passed in the mid-1960s:

- **Civil Rights Act of 1964** This act strengthened antisegregation policies by withholding federal funding to states that did not comply with federal laws regarding voting rights, education, and public facilities.
- **Voting Rights Act of 1965** The act forbade literacy tests under certain circumstances and authorized the president to enforce the Fifteenth Amendment.

To Martin Luther King, these two civil rights acts gave crucial federal protection for blacks seeking to exercise their constitutional rights. More radical and militant black leaders and groups such as Malcolm X and the Black Panthers challenged this view. Malcolm X, who had converted to Islam while in prison in the 1950s, advocated racial separation and black nationalism, but eventually modified his position somewhat before he was assassinated in 1964. The Black Panthers, led by Bobby Seale, Huey Newton, and Eldridge Cleaver, advocated a militant response to police harassment, inequality, and systematic racial subordination. The police regularly arrested Black Panther members until the early 1970s, when the organization decided to redirect its energies from armed defense of black rights to community development programs. In fact, in 1973, Bobby Seale was a mayoral candidate in Oakland, California. Other groups that had experienced discrimination and were mired in poverty, such as Puerto Ricans and Mexican-Americans, also organized. Labor leader César Chávez, for instance, organized Mexican-American farm workers in a bid for higher wages. He appealed to the public to boycott certain crops such as grapes in order to force employers to raise wages.

Even though he had been elected in a landslide in 1964, the war in Vietnam eroded much of Lyndon Johnson's initial support. In 1968, weary and overwhelmed by the quagmire in Vietnam, he surprised the nation by deciding not to run for reelection.

AP Tip

The postwar decades were filled with turmoil, especially the 1960s. In order to understand this decade better, you need a working understanding of the countercultural movements that shaped American domestic life. The decade was characterized by the rebelliousness of America's youth in response to what many perceived as the socially stifling mores and lifestyles of the previous decades.

- Many of the nation's "baby boomers" sought to combat the social ills they saw as fundamentally undemocratic: racism, poverty, inequality, and American foreign policy, especially in Vietnam. In the early 1960s, for example, Students for a Democratic Society (SDS) was formed with the intention of democratizing the institutions that shaped American life, such as universities and government.
- A new generation of feminists re-energized the women's movement, which worked to raise the consciousness of women themselves and society as a whole and pressed for profound changes in both social and economic life.
- Sexual mores were under attack as earlier changes in sexual attitudes inspired even more criticisms of traditional sexual values. The advent of birth control ("the pill") as well as increasingly risqué advertising and sexuality in movies and television loosened certain stereotypes about sexuality. The 1980s would witness a backlash to the revolution in sexuality that took place in the previous decades.
- The music of the 1960s, as well as the dress of many young people ("hippies"), was seen as an expression of a frustrated, sometimes angry, but politically conscious American youth.

The Presidency of Richard M. Nixon (1969–1974)

Richard Nixon's unfortunate legacy is that he is the only chief executive to resign the office of president. Nixon ran for election as the Republican candidate on the promise that he could end the war in Vietnam honorably. Although foreign affairs often dominated his presidency, a number of key domestic events and policies shaped his administration as well. Nixon appealed to the "silent majority," middle-class Americans, some of whom were Democrats, who had not participated in one or another sort of demonstration, were opposed to "big government," and rejected the nation's cultural and social direction. His cabinet secretaries, reflecting Nixon's probusiness, conservative constituency, were initially white Christian males, hardly a reflection of the social crusades sweeping the nation at the time.

Nixon entered the White House in January 1969 and immediately faced significant economic problems. The cost of Johnson's Great Society programs and the war in Vietnam had led to inflation, increasing unemployment, and a moribund gross national product. Nixon tried to cut government spending while reducing personal income taxes to encourage consumer spending, but the economy worsened. Even a ninety-day wage and price freeze did not have the desired effect. Surprisingly, the fiscally conservative Nixon turned to a Keynesian solution: deficit spending. In order to address the nation's huge trade deficit, Nixon devalued U.S. currency by taking the dollar off the gold standard, thereby making products manufactured in the United States more affordable to foreign consumers. By 1972 the economy was showing signs of recovery.

At that same time, Nixon was exploring his reelection bid. Having received only 43.3 percent of the popular vote in the 1968 election, Nixon and his advisers formulated a strategy to appeal to the disaffected "silent majority" and southern voters discontented with the Democrats' domestic and foreign affairs policies. When he attempted to slow integration and nominated two conservative southerners to the Supreme Court, Congress rejected both maneuvers. He even took steps to "reform" welfare, but was again thwarted by Congress. Yet Nixon, with his abrasive Vice President Spiro Agnew in the vanguard attacking liberals and antiwar protestors, won over many southerners. In the 1972 election he defeated his Democratic opponent, George McGovern, in a landslide.

Nixon's administration coincided with two important developments, one constitutional, the other scientific. In response to the cry "Old enough to fight, too young to vote," the Twenty-sixth Amendment, lowering the voting age to eighteen, was ratified in 1971. In 1969 Apollo 11 landed on the moon, profoundly boosting American morale in the midst of domestic turmoil and the quandary in Vietnam. By 1973, however, the economy worsened again, in large part because of the Organization of Petroleum Exporting Countries' (OPEC) oil embargo against the United States for its support of Israel in the Six-Day War.

It was Watergate, however, that unraveled the Nixon presidency. The unfortunate acronym for Nixon's reelection organization was CREEP (Committee to Re-Elect the President). Having won the popular vote by a slim majority in 1968, Nixon's advisers were prepared to do everything possible to guarantee victory, even if that meant breaking the law and engaging in a vast array of "dirty tricks." When burglars (called "plumbers" by the White House because they plugged political leaks) were caught breaking into the Democratic party headquarters in Washington, D.C.'s Watergate complex, suspicions were raised that the plot had been formulated in the White House. CREEP officials and Nixon's administration, led by White House Chief of Staff H. R. Haldeman and domestic adviser John Ehrlichman, vehemently denied a connection to the "plumbers." Two determined reporters for the *Washington Post*, Carl Bernstein and Bob Woodward, dug deeper into the affair, ultimately exposing criminal acts and cover-ups at the highest levels of government. What is more, the administration had even used independent government agencies to do some of its dirty work and had created an "enemies list," which included politicians, actors, newspaper and television reporters, and opponents of the administration who could be harassed by the White House in a variety of ways (for example, with income tax audits).

Nixon and his aides attempted to cover up their activities, but unfortunately for the president, it was revealed that he habitually tape-recorded all of his Oval Office conversations. The Justice Department and the Senate demanded that Nixon release the tapes to them. Nixon's response was to appoint a special prosecutor, Archibald Cox, to investigate. Cox then demanded Nixon to turn over the tapes. On October 20, 1973, Nixon ordered Attorney General Elliot Richardson to fire Cox, but Richardson and his assistant both resigned in protest. Solicitor General Robert Bork (a future unsuccessful candidate to the Supreme Court) finally agreed to fire Cox in what became known as the "Saturday Night Massacre." Nixon's popularity plummeted. The House Judiciary Committee began to consider impeachment proceedings. At last, Nixon turned over what were obviously extensively edited tapes that conclusively proved that Nixon had been lying and had attempted to cover up a crime. The tapes also revealed that Vice President Spiro Agnew had engaged in criminal activities when he was governor of Maryland. Agnew resigned and was replaced by Congressman Gerald Ford. By this point even members of his own party considered Nixon a liability. When the House Judiciary Committee reported that it was prepared to impeach the president, and with his own advisers admitting that he lacked the support to survive such a proceeding, Nixon resigned the office of the president on August 9, 1974.

FORD AND CARTER (1974–1981)

Gerald R. Ford is the only vice president to become chief executive under the Twenty-fifth Amendment. In order to maintain continuity as the nation experienced a transfer of power because of Nixon's resignation, Ford kept most of Nixon's policies and even his cabinet secretaries. His first controversial act came one month into his presidency when he pardoned Nixon. Ford's domestic policy involved limiting government expenditures on social programs, such as welfare and education; high taxes on imported oil; and tax cuts to stimulate consumer demand. Ford spent much of his term unsuccessfully fighting the effects of inflation and the Democratic-controlled

Social Concerns in the 1970s and 1980s

Politics played a significant role in American life in the two decades following Nixon's resignation, but no more than social changes.

- By the early 1980s, Asian-Americans became the nation's fastest growing ethnic minority.
- Illegal immigration reached record proportions, possibly as high as 12 million in the late 1970s.
- Latino-Americans began entering politics and winning elected offices throughout the nation.
- Native Americans began organizing to preserve the vestiges of their culture from the effects of assimilation and to call attention to the terrible standard of living they were experiencing. The American Indian Movement (AIM), a militant organization, seized government property to generate awareness for the plight of the nation's original inhabitants.
- Inspired by the publication of Rachel Carson's *Silent Spring* (1962), a dire warning about the use of insecticides on plant and animal life, the American environmental movement came into its own in the 1960s and 1970s. The nation grew increasingly conscious of and concerned about the frequency and extent of industrial disasters: oil spills, a near-catastrophic accident at the Three Mile Island nuclear power plant in Pennsylvania, and the spoliation of the nation's land by companies that irresponsibly dumped toxic waste material. In New York an entire community, Love Canal, was built on a toxic waste dumpsite; over time, residents began experiencing serious health problems. Concerned citizens across the nation demanded that the federal government take action. In 1970 the government created the Environmental Protection Agency (EPA), and two years later, the Clean Water Act passed Congress.
- Many women sought a constitutional amendment (an equal rights amendment) to address gender abuses and discrimination in the workplace.
- Reproductive rights became a hotly contested issue, especially when the Supreme Court ruled in *Roe v. Wade* (1973) that states could not prohibit abortion in the first trimester of a woman's pregnancy.

Congress. In an act of futility, he endeavored to get the American people and U.S. businesses behind his economic policies by distributing WIN (Whip Inflation Now) buttons. Nevertheless, inflation was not whipped, and as it worsened, unemployment began to creep ever higher. As was the case during the Nixon years, the federal budget increased appreciably in Ford's term.

In 1976 the nation celebrated its bicentennial and the election of a new president, Georgia Governor Jimmy Carter, who defeated Ford in a close race. Carter's popularity rested largely on his claim to be a populist and an outsider—meaning that his political career had not been shaped by the machinations of Washington politics. His one term in office was marred by runaway inflation and a foreign policy that seemed at times amateurish. Domestically, President Carter pardoned thousands of Vietnam War draft evaders to illustrate to the American people that it was time to move on and not dwell on the turmoil and divisiveness of the late 1960s and early 1970s. During his presidency the following policies and legislation were enacted:

- The minimum wage was increased.
- The Social Security payroll tax was increased.

- Two cabinet-level departments were created: the Department of Energy (1977) and the Department of Education (1979).

Carter's budget, like the rest of the economy, was highly inflationary. The inability to harness runaway inflation ravaged the economy while unemployment, the deficit, and interest rates rose. But the nation's confidence in Carter declined. In his bid for re-election, Republican Ronald Reagan defeated Carter in a landslide.

THE REAGAN "REVOLUTION" (1981–1989)

Not since Hoover had an unambiguously conservative president like Ronald Reagan been elected to lead the nation. On the campaign trail and in the Oval Office he openly criticized the New Deal and the Great Society.

He fulfilled his campaign pledge to redefine the Supreme Court by nominating conservative justices. Three of his appointees, Antonin Scalia, Anthony Kennedy, and Sandra Day O'Connor (the first female Supreme Court justice), were confirmed by the Senate. However, the Senate rejected the outspoken conservative judge Robert Bork. Reagan's appointments shifted the balance away from a more progressive to a decidedly conservative Supreme Court, as evidenced by the limitations it placed on abortion rights and affirmative action.

His economic record is an indication of the direction he took the nation in his eight years as president. President Reagan's administration is associated with deep cuts in government spending and considerable business deregulation. For example:

- A freeze was placed on the number of workers on the federal government's payroll.
- Tax cuts for citizens and corporations were passed.
- Government funding for a range of social programs, such as student education loans and mass transportation, was significantly reduced. Welfare-related programs such as food stamps also suffered budget cuts. Medicare was not touched, but the age for Social Security recipients was raised.
- An attempt was made to reorganize the federal government by eliminating the Departments of Energy and Education.
- Previous restrictions on certain types of mergers and takeovers were removed, as were certain environmental protection standards that businesses contended were driving up their costs. Restrictions on the savings-and-loan industry were reduced while the government simultaneously increased the federal government's depositors' insurance from $20,000 to $100,000. Bad loans, opportunists, and crooks precipitated a flood of bankruptcies, leaving the American taxpayer to pay for the $200 billion bailout of the savings-and-loan industry.

President Reagan is the only former union president (of the Screen Actors Guild) to serve as president of the United States, so it is ironic that his presidency is associated with a strongly probusiness outlook (as indicated by his view that federal regulations inhibited business growth) and an adversarial relationship with unions. Nineteen months into his first term he eviscerated the air traffic controllers union

(PATCO) by firing strikers who refused to return to work. As with his predecessors, Reagan had to confront looming economic problems. The federal budget deficit was growing in part because of his tax cuts, which reduced the government's revenue. Reagan's solution was supply-side economics: corporations and the wealthy would be given significant tax cuts (through the Tax Reform Act), which, it was believed, would in turn stimulate the economy by starting new businesses and expanding others. Admirers called his plan "Reaganomics," but critics, reminded of Treasury Secretary Mellon's justification for tax cuts in the 1920s, called it "trickle down." Certainly the wealthiest citizens benefited from supply-side economics, but so did some middle-class investors, who could now invest some of their money in tax-free Individual Retirement Accounts (IRAs). Unfortunately the middle class's real wages (surplus capital after all other cost-of-living expenses have been paid for) did not increase in the 1980s. Offsetting the enormous budget cuts was unprecedented spending on the military, in part to undermine the Soviet Union's ability to keep pace with the United States in military expenditures.

When President Reagan entered the White House, the United States was the world's number one creditor nation. Eight years later it had a $200 billion a year federal deficit and an almost equally large trade deficit. Congress's response to the bloated deficit was to pass the Gramm-Rudman-Hollings Balanced Budget Act in 1985, which succeeded in reducing the deficit by approximately $60 billion in just one year. Despite the economic problems facing the nation, many Americans admired Reagan for instilling a sense of patriotism and pride in the United States that had seemed to dissipate over the previous decade. Critics blame him for a host of domestic and foreign policy debacles, but undeniably, his stature is greater than of any American president since Franklin Roosevelt.

Multiple-Choice Questions

1. President Reagan's nominations of Justices Scalia, O'Connor, and Kennedy to the Supreme Court
   (A) was warmly supported by Democrats in Congress
   (B) failed to win the approval of the Senate
   (C) reveal his attempt to make the Supreme Court more conservative
   (D) indicated to many Americans his moderate stance on constitutional issues
   (E) ultimately backfired, as the three justices were far more liberal than was Reagan

ANSWER: C. The three justices reflected Reagan's conservative ideology (*The American Pageant*, 12th ed., pp. 988-989/11th ed., p. 1004).

2. A stimulus to postwar prosperity was
   (A) the spending habits of Americans as more consumer items became available
   (B) the significant cuts in the military budget made by Presidents Truman, Eisenhower, and Kennedy
   (C) the purchasing power of millions of women who entered the work force at war's end
   (D) the elimination of the income tax
   (E) the elimination of foreign competition in most industries

ANSWER: **A**. Many consumer items were unavailable during the war. As more goods became available and wages rose, consumers happily spent (*The American Pageant*, 12th ed., p. 860/11th ed., p. 860).

3. Which U.S. president is associated with the Fair Deal?
   (A) Franklin Roosevelt
   (B) Harry Truman
   (C) Dwight Eisenhower
   (D) John Kennedy
   (E) Lyndon Johnson

ANSWER: **B**. The Fair Deal was the name given to Truman's domestic reform program (*The American Pageant*, 12th ed., p. 883/11th ed., p. 903).

4. The Supreme Court case *Roe v. Wade* dealt with
   (A) voting rights
   (B) environmental protection laws
   (C) reproductive rights
   (D) Social Security benefits
   (E) federal funding for welfare programs

ANSWER: **C**. The court prohibited states from interfering with a woman's abortion rights during the first trimester of pregnancy (*The American Pageant*, 12th ed., p. 989/11th ed., p. 1004).

5. In the Supreme Court case *Brown v. Board of Education of Topeka, Kansas*
   (A) the Court reaffirmed the *Plessy v. Ferguson* decision in 1896
   (B) the Court affirmed voting rights of all citizens in accordance with the Fifteenth Amendment
   (C) black Americans were outraged by the Court's support for segregation
   (D) segregation was ruled unconstitutional
   (E) the Court ruled that the federal government was not responsible for integrating facilities and institutions

ANSWER: **D**. The Court overturned the *Plessy* decision, opening the way for integration in all public facilities and institutions (*The American Pageant*, 12th ed., p. 895/11th ed., p. 914).

6. The National Defense Education Act
   (A) was passed during the administration of Lyndon Johnson
   (B) was designed in response to Soviet advancements in aeronautics
   (C) significantly increased the federal aid to military research programs
   (D) gave the president the power to declare war without Congress's approval when the nation is being threatened with attack
   (E) appropriated billions of dollars for developing peaceful uses for nuclear energy

ANSWER: **B**. One billion dollars was appropriated for improving science, math, and language arts courses in order to keep pace with the Soviet Union's advances (*The American Pageant*, 12th ed., pp. 903-904/11th ed., pp. 922-923).

7. The Taft-Hartley Act
   (A) helped fund the construction of schools and hospitals in economically depressed areas
   (B) provided billions in federal aid to communities faced with serious environmental problems
   (C) helped to fund the Medicare program
   (D) was ruled unconstitutional by the Supreme Court on the grounds that the federal government could withhold funds from states that refused to integrate
   (E) placed serious restrictions on the rights and powers of labor unions

ANSWER: **E**. The act forbade the closed shop, restricted boycotts and sympathy strikes, and required a sixty-day cooling off period before workers could strike (*The American Pageant*, 12th ed., p. 859/11th ed., pp. 880-881).

8. In which of the following events did the Reverend Dr. Martin Luther King, Jr. play a significant role?
   (A) the integration of the University of Alabama
   (B) the integration of the University of Mississippi
   (C) the Montgomery, Alabama, bus boycott
   (D) ending segregation in the military
   (E) the formation of the Black Panthers

ANSWER: **C**. His work on the bus boycott brought King to national attention (*The American Pageant*, 12th ed., p. 894/11th ed., p. 913).

9. Which postwar president is most associated with business deregulation?
   (A) Harry Truman
   (B) Dwight Eisenhower
   (C) Gerald Ford
   (D) Jimmy Carter
   (E) Ronald Reagan

ANSWER: **E**. Reagan's pursuit of deregulation freed businesses from costly and restrictive federal requirements but led to mergers, takeovers, and the savings-and-loan fiasco (*The American Pageant*, 12th ed., p. 990/11th ed., p. 1005).

10. Which of the following challenged President Truman in his bid for election in 1948?
    (A) northern Democrats who believed his integration of the military had been premature
    (B) corporate interests who wanted believed Truman was pro-union and anti-business
    (C) northern liberals who opposed his Fair Deal
    (D) southerners who were opposed to his civil rights policies
    (E) black Americans who had grown tired of the Democrats' social programs

ANSWER: D. Southern Democratic states' rights Dixiecrats nominated their own candidate, Strom Thurmond, to challenge Truman (*The American Pageant*, 12th ed., p. 881/11th ed., 901-902).

11. Which of the following is NOT associated with Lyndon Johnson's presidency?
    (A) the Medicare Act
    (B) Appalachian Regional Development Act
    (C) Voting Rights Act
    (D) the Twenty-fourth Amendment
    (E) supply-side economics

ANSWER: E. Johnson was inspired by the New Deal and engaged in deficit spending, not supply-side economics, to stimulate the economy. Supply-side economics is associated with Reagan's presidency (*The American Pageant*, 12th ed., p. 987/11th ed., p. 1003).

Free-Response Questions

1. To what extent did New Deal liberalism continue to shape the U.S. domestically in the decades after World War II? In your answer include relevant information from
       Truman's "Fair Deal"
       Johnson's "Great Society"
       Kennedy's "New Frontier"

RESPONSE You should discuss how the New Deal redefined the role of government by adopting a Keynesian approach to the economy and by budgeting millions of dollars to establish various social programs. Truman, Kennedy, and Johnson all in one way or another expanded on the ideology and policies of Roosevelt liberalism. You should identify those programs, like the War on Poverty, that have a correlation to similar programs of the New Deal.

2. Contrast the conservative ideology of President Reagan with the liberal views of Truman, Johnson, and Kennedy.

RESPONSE You should discuss how Reagan's election was in part a conservative response to the liberal programs under Roosevelt, Truman, Kennedy, and Johnson. Include a discussion as to why this occurred, such as the view that government bureaucracy and government spending had become too extensive. Point out that while Reagan's budget was enormous, much of his budget was used for military spending, whereas the liberal presidents—Truman, Kennedy, and Johnson—also sought to establish social programs as well as engage in enormous military spending. Another relevant contrast is the relationship Reagan had with labor as opposed to the lack of such relationship for Truman, Kennedy, and Johnson. Finally, a discussion of Reagan's supply-side ("trickle-down") economics versus the demand-side approach of the liberal presidents should be included in your response.

19

U.S. FOREIGN AFFAIRS
FROM 1945 TO THE 1980s

When Japan surrendered on September 2, 1945, ebullient Americans spontaneously broke into wild celebrations. Their sense of relief was universal. As people around the world took stock of the war's effects, they were appalled by the devastation in terms of lives, property, and money lost. In the major theaters of the war—Europe, Asia, and the Pacific—survivors had already begun to dig out of the wreckage caused by the war and rebuild their shattered lives; they could only imagine what the future held in store. They had lived through the worst economic disaster the world had ever seen; they had survived the worst military conflict, including attempted genocide, in modern times. They longed for a respite from suffering and despair.

Even before atomic bombs destroyed Hiroshima and Nagasaki, however, new storm clouds had appeared on the horizon in the form of a world divided into two armed camps, each ready to use whatever means were at its disposal to achieve its political objectives. As it turned out, there would be no reprieve from the anxiety and uncertainties millions had experienced since the Great Depression. Almost without pause, the world would shift from total war to what became known as "Cold War."

The two Cold War adversaries, the United States and the Soviet Union, had experienced World War II differently. The United States had suffered 1 million casualties; the Soviets, at least twenty times that number. For the second time in twenty-five years, Germany had invaded the Soviet Union. Millions of Soviet citizens had been killed, and its western agrarian and urban areas had been devastated by the Nazi invasion in 1941. The Soviet government, led by Josef Stalin, would make certain that no European nation ever invaded again. For Americans, the war had been fought from afar, and they were comforted by the protection accorded by the vast Atlantic and Pacific Oceans.

When the war ended, the United States and Soviet Union were the world's two most powerful nations—superpowers—and they were suspicious of each other's political and economic systems, not to mention foreign policy objectives. Despite tensions that had existed between the two nations ever since the communists overthrew Russia's czarist regime in the 1917 Bolshevik Revolution, the two had been wartime allies. One promising indicator that cooperation, rather than conflict, could guide postwar international affairs was the creation of the United Nations in 1945. The most powerful organ of the United Nations, the Security Council, comprised fifteen nations. The major allied powers in the war—the United States, the USSR, Britain, France, and China—each possessed veto power. Nevertheless, the Americans and Soviets remained wary of each other's intentions.

KEY CONCEPTS

■ Conflicting U.S. and Soviet postwar objectives played a significant role in creating the tensions between the two superpowers that led to the Cold War.

■ The United States sought to contain the spread of communism in Europe, Asia, South America, and Africa.

■ The second red scare (McCarthyism) affected the United States domestically as the public was led to believe that there were communists seeking to undermine American institutions.

■ The United States succeeded in containing communism in Europe.

■ The United States was unable to contain the spread of communism to China but did so in South Korea.

■ The Vietnam War seriously divided the American people and showed the limitations of the containment policy.

■ The collapse of the Soviet Union transformed international affairs.

U.S. foreign affairs after World War II are discussed in depth in *The American Pageant*, 12th ed., Chapters 37-41/11th ed., Chapters 39-43.

SOVIET AND AMERICAN POSTWAR OBJECTIVES AND PRIORITIES

The end of the war found the Soviets in possession of much of Eastern Europe. After the failure of Hitler's Operation Barbarossa—the invasion of the Soviet Union—the Soviets had counterattacked, driving the German invaders west and out of the East European nations that had been under their control. Germany itself was invaded and finally capitulated to the Allies in May 1945. It soon became abundantly clear that there were deep tensions between the wartime allies. The war ravaged the Soviet Union in human, military, and financial terms. The immediate Soviet priorities, then, were economic rehabilitation and military defense:

■ **Reconstruction of the economy** The Soviets demanded that Germany pay it $20 billion in war reparations. Initially, the United States promised large loans to the Soviets.

- **Military competition** The Soviets sought to remain on par with the United States militarily. This resulted in the nuclear arms race.
- **Self-defense** The Soviets wanted to make certain that they no longer would be surrounded by countries hostile to the USSR. They therefore created a buffer zone, referred to as the Soviet-bloc nations, in Eastern Europe.

The United States was deeply concerned that nations devastated by the war might be susceptible to Soviet-backed communism. Furthermore, if the United States itself were to grow its economy, it would need trading partners, which meant helping to rebuild Europe's destroyed infrastructure and manufacturing centers. Essential to the expansion of the U.S. economy was cheap energy sources. To this end the United States in 1953 helped overthrow Iran's government, which had promised to nationalize foreign- controlled oil companies, and replaced it with Shah Reza Pahlavi, who then proceeded to supply the West with inexpensive oil. In the immediate postwar period, the United States sought to achieve the following:

- **Reconstruction of Europe** This became a major goal of the United States. It set out to help rebuild the economies of West European nations such as France, Great Britain, Norway, the Netherlands, Denmark, Greece, and Germany for the following reasons:
  - These nations would be able to repay their war debts.
  - An economically stable Western Europe would eventually benefit the U.S. economy by importing U.S. goods.
  - For the United States to reap the economic benefits of a stable and reconstructed Western Europe, it was imperative that the Europeans eschew policies and political systems antithetical to U.S. postwar economic needs, including, but not limited to, socialist and communist systems. This policy was also applied to Asia, South America, and Africa during the Cold War.
- **Military superiority** This would be achieved through nuclear monopoly, later through nuclear superiority.
- **Containment of Soviet-backed communism** Ultimately containment became the focus of U.S. foreign policy in the decades after the war's end.

THE COLD WAR IN EUROPE

According to one school of thought, the Cold War began even before World War II ended. This view postulates that at the Yalta Conference—the final meeting in February 1945 between the Big Three: Churchill, Roosevelt, and Stalin—the Soviet premier deceived a gravely ill President Roosevelt. Stalin pledged to declare war on Japan in return for its pre-Russo-Japanese War status in the Far East. It was decided that the United States, the USSR, and Britain, with French participation, would divide and administer Germany and its capital, Berlin, following the German surrender. Several important issues dealing with Europe were left unresolved, with the expectation that post-war commissions and agreements would settle them. The most

AP Tip

Who Started the Cold War? The responsibility for starting the Cold War has been an enduring topic of discussion among historians for over half a century. Predictably, a simple answer is not the case here. For the most part historians are seriously divided in their analysis of the causes of the Cold War.

- One perspective claims that ideology was at the center of the conflict. That is, there existed an ideological incompatibility between the United States, which stood for freedom and democracy, and the tyrannical, imperialist Soviet Union. Thus the United States adopted a policy that at the very least would contain this "evil" or, possibly, even assist in its demise.
- Another viewpoint is that the Cold War was less an expression of ideology than an objective by which each power could enhance its national interests. As for the Soviet Union, it was behaving as it had always done, whether under the tsars or under the communists—namely, expansion and mistrust of the outside world. For example, the U.S.-sponsored Baruch Plan to regulate nuclear energy and nuclear disarmament was rejected by the Soviets, who may have mistrusted American intentions, believing the plan was an attempt to thwart their goal of nuclear parity with the United States.
- For other historians, the onus for starting the Cold War rests with both the United States and the USSR. The Cold War could have been prevented had it not been for misperceptions, misguided idealism, and unfounded suspicions.
- A fourth view places the responsibility for starting the Cold War with the United States. While not condoning the brutal aspects of the Soviet regime, tension between the two nations had its origins in the early twentieth century when the United States revealed its counterrevolutionary tendencies during the Russian Civil War. The Cold War was simply another expression of that predisposition. What is more, they argue, given the need for capitalism to expand, the United States itself had engaged in imperialism. The Cold War then is viewed as just another example of aggressive and exploitative U.S. foreign policy, which seeks to extend its hegemony worldwide. Whereas some historians view, say, the Soviet refusal to participate in the development of the International Bank for Reconstruction and Development (also known as the World Bank) as symptomatic of Soviet power politics, others acknowledge Soviet suspicions that the World Bank might become a tool of American capitalist hegemony.

troublesome issue involved the establishment of a Polish government, not to mention the other East European nations liberated by the Soviets. Military necessity may have convinced Roosevelt that Soviet support for the war against Japan required granting concessions to the Soviets in the Far East and an acceptance of Stalin's promise to hold elections in Eastern Europe. Nevertheless, the elections promised by Stalin exacerbated relations with the West when Soviet-supported communists took over the governments of what became known as the Soviet bloc: East Germany, Czechoslovakia, Hungary, Bulgaria, Poland, Albania, and Romania. Yugoslavia, a communist nation, remained independent of the USSR because of the efforts of its president, Tito. To the Americans the wartime conference had divided Europe into East European communist and totalitarian governments and Western capitalist democracies. The Soviets, from their perspective, had merely addressed a long-standing military necessity: protection of its vulnerable western border from invasions by creating a buffer zone between it and potentially hostile West European nations.

Later, Soviet refusal to remove its troops from oil-rich northern Iran further convinced Western leaders that the Soviets were bent on being the hegemonic power in more than Eastern Europe. A strident rebuke from Truman convinced Stalin to remove his troops from Iran, but suspicions remained. Former British Prime Minister Winston Churchill echoed the concern about Soviet expansionism when he warned that an "iron curtain" had "descended across the continent" as the Soviets attempted to extend "their power and doctrine." Churchill's recommendation was for the Western democracies to stop this expansion. President Truman concurred. "I'm tired of babying the Soviets," he fumed in response to what he perceived as Soviet intransigence in controlling Eastern Europe. For their part, the Soviets seemed equally resistant to thawing relations with the United States. When George Kennan, an American diplomat and specialist on Russian and Soviet affairs, warned that the Soviets would spread their ideology if given the opportunity but could be stopped if challenged, Truman took to heart his counsel. Just as A. T. Mahan's *The Influence of Sea Power upon History* had profoundly influenced U.S. policymakers at the turn of the twentieth century, Kennan's analysis became the foundation of an American foreign policy. In effect legitimizing the U.S. government's vigorous anti-Soviet position, Kennan's major observations included the following:

■ The United States can exploit the frailty of the Soviet economy, the lassitude of its people, and the brutal nature of the Soviet leadership if it adopts policies that would discourage Soviet expansion.
■ It is unrealistic to expect a thaw in U.S.-Soviet relations in the near future.
■ Soviet mistrust of the outside world borders on paranoia.

Kennan recommended that the United States adopt a policy of containment, although he later opposed the way in which his observations were interpreted and implemented, especially when NATO was created. What follows are important examples of the containment policy as applied by the United States to Europe. Keep in mind that for over forty years this policy was applied to other continents as well.

■ **Truman Doctrine (1947)** Just two years after the war's end, Truman came before Congress to request a $400 million aid package to Greece and Turkey in order to prevent communist rebels from overthrowing their governments. Soviet pressure on Turkey to relinquish control over the strategic Dardanelles was another incentive for Truman to act. Neither country became communist.

- **Marshall Plan (1947)** The United States was acutely concerned that Europe's depressed economic condition, common to those nations that had experienced the war firsthand, was susceptible to communist influences. In Italy, for instance, there was considerable popular support for leftist movements. In response, Secretary of State George Marshall recommended a program called the European Recovery Plan to rehabilitate over twenty nations, including the Soviet Union (which rejected the funds). Over $12 billion was distributed in four years, helping to restore the economies of important U.S. trade partners such as Britain, West Germany, and France and preventing the spread of communism to Western Europe.

- **Berlin Blockade and Airlift (1948–1949)** At war's end the former capital of Nazi Germany, Berlin, lay deep inside communist East Germany. As with the rest of Germany, Berlin had been divided into four zones, each administered by the United States, Britain, France, and the USSR. In an attempt to consolidate their control of East Germany, the Soviets ordered the access roads into West Berlin closed. Without needed supplies, the West Berliners would have nowhere to turn and would be absorbed into the rest of communist Berlin—or so the Soviets hoped. What they did not anticipate was a yearlong airlift that numbered one thousand planes per day and successfully provided 2 million West Berliners with basic necessities. Realizing the blockade was fruitless, the Soviets lifted it in May 1949. Although West Berlin did not become communist, tensions mounted between the two superpowers.

- **North Atlantic Treaty Organization (NATO)** Buoyed by the success of the Berlin airlift, but acutely concerned about the Soviet bloc's military power and suspicious of its intentions, the Western allies believed that a coordinated military alliance could thwart a potential communist invasion of Western Europe. In fact, a number of European nations, France and Britain among them, had already organized a mutual defense pact called the Brussels Treaty. The United States had never entered into a peacetime European alliance; however, the mounting friction with the Soviet Union convinced U.S. leaders to do just that. The U.S. rationale for the creation of NATO was deterrence—that is, an attack on one member nation would be considered an attack on all. By 1955 NATO had fifteen members, the largest permanent peacetime military coalition in history. That year the Soviets responded to NATO's expansion with its own military alliance of Soviet-bloc East European nations called the Warsaw Pact. Europe was now divided between two hostile and heavily armed camps, each possessing nuclear weapons—despite the U.S. government's contention that the Soviets were years away from developing and successfully testing an atomic weapon, its monopoly ended in the spring of 1949 when President Truman announced to the nation that the Soviets had in fact successfully tested such a weapon. The Cold War immediately entered into an even more potentially catastrophic phase, the nuclear arms race.

■ **The Division of Germany** In 1955 French, American, and British occupation of West Germany ended. Many hoped that this would be a prelude to German reunification. Although discussions with the Soviets about reunification went nowhere, four years later a summit was organized that brought together President Eisenhower and Premier Khrushchev of the Soviet Union. The two agreed to continue their discussion in Paris but the meeting was never held. In 1960 a U.S. spy plane piloted by Francis Gary Powers was shot down over the Soviet Union. The Eisenhower administration acknowledged responsibility for the surveillance mission, and an angry Khrushchev cancelled not only the Paris summit but also a personal invitation for Eisenhower to visit the USSR. In the meantime, Germany remained divided.

ROLLBACK, BRINKMANSHIP, AND RISING TENSIONS

Upon becoming president, Dwight Eisenhower selected John Foster Dulles, a Republican expert on foreign affairs, to be his secretary of state. Dulles saw serious limitations in the containment policy. He believed that communism was a moral evil that should be rolled back if possible, not merely contained. To achieve this aim, he based his diplomatic strategy on "brinkmanship" and "massive retaliation." Dulles maintained that the Soviets could be taken to the brink in disputes, at which point they would inevitably back down. Further, it would be in the best interest of the United States to build such a massive nuclear weapons stockpile that the Soviets would be deterred from ever challenging the United States. Given this approach, and the presence of hard-liners in the Kremlin (the center of Soviet administrative and political affairs), U.S.-Soviet relations continued to be tense.

Despite this mistrust, both nations still seemed determined to reduce the tensions that prevailed between the two nuclear superpowers. A summit meeting in 1956 between Khrushchev and Eisenhower failed to produce an "open skies" policy that would allow each nation to fly over the other's territory, thus preventing a "first strike" attack, but it did indicate that both sides were willing at least to negotiate. When the Soviet premier repudiated the actions and policies of his predecessor, Josef Stalin, a thaw in relations seemed possible. To some in the Soviet-bloc nations of Poland, East Germany, and Hungary, this was taken to mean that reforms could be instituted, giving them greater autonomy and expanded freedoms. In 1956 the Hungarians actually took the momentous step of overthrowing their Soviet-backed government, but the Soviets immediately crushed the rebellion; they would do the same in Czechoslovakia in 1968. The U.S. response, which was to do nothing for fear of sparking a nuclear confrontation, revealed the limitations of Dulles's policies. Essentially, Eastern Europe was in the Soviet sphere of influence, and the United States would not challenge that reality.

The Second Red Scare: McCarthyism

The Cold War was obviously at the center of U.S. foreign policy; however, it also influenced the nation domestically, sometimes in ways not foreseen. In 1947 Republicans pressured President Truman to establish a Loyalty Review Board to investigate current and prospective federal employees for possible affiliations with radical groups. Thousands consequently lost their jobs. Four years later the federal government prosecuted American Communist party leaders under the Smith Act (1940), which made it illegal to promote the overthrow of the U.S. government or belong to an organization that advocated this intention. In 1951 the Supreme Court upheld the constitutionality of the act in *Dennis v. United States.* Earlier, in 1938, the House Un-American Activities Committee (HUAC) had been formed to investigate political "subversives." It was resuscitated during the Cold War, in part because of the exposure of Soviet sympathizers such Ethel and Julius Rosenberg. The Rosenbergs were accused of providing atomic bomb information to the Soviets during World War II when the USSR was America's ally, thereby, according to federal prosecutors, accelerating the Soviet A-bomb program. Although it was peacetime, the nation was in the grips of the red scare, and the "loss" of China to Mao Zedong's communists and the Korean War all weighed heavily in the government's decision to electrocute the two convicted spies on June 19, 1953.

The most famous case to come before HUAC involved a former State Department official and adviser to President Roosevelt at the Yalta Conference named Alger Hiss. Hiss's accuser, Whittaker Chambers, claimed that Hiss had not only been a communist sympathizer in the 1930s; he had also transmitted secret information to the Soviets. Hiss was convicted of perjury in 1950, in large measure because of the efforts of a young California congressman named Richard M. Nixon. The case led some to question whether there were other Soviet "sympathizers" in public and private life.

HUAC ultimately became a postwar tool whereby anyone who had been even sympathetic to radical causes (and there were quite a few given the disenchantment with capitalism during the Great Depression) could be called to Washington to recant their suspected political allegiance and inform on neighbors, friends, and colleagues. Some refused and suffered dearly. Numerous politicians took advantage of the anticommunist hysteria that swept the nation after the war, but no one did it as effectively and reprehensibly as Wisconsin's junior Republican senator, Joseph R. McCarthy. Searching for a campaign issue on which to run for reelection, McCarthy found that making unsubstantiated claims and accusations about communist infiltration into every segment of American life generated for him considerable publicity. One week he would claim there were 250 communist sympathizers in the U.S. State Department; the following week the number would arbitrarily change. Before long McCarthy was one of the most powerful and popular political figures in the nation. Few in or out of government would challenge him, for to do so would invariably invite the charge that that person was "soft" on communism. McCarthy even accused George Marshall, the former U.S. Army chief of staff and Truman's secretary of state and defense, of taking part in a communist conspiracy. Not even President Eisenhower, Marshall's former comrade in the war, would defend him. Some Republicans personally rejected McCarthy's tactics, but as his victims tended to be Democrats, they said nothing—with the exception of Senators Margaret Chase Smith and Ralph Flanders, both of whom publicly repudiated their colleague.

Over the course of McCarthy's crusade, many lives and careers were ruined, among them entertainers, screenwriters, teachers, and government employees. Not until Senator McCarthy's "witch hunt" was televised (during the Senate's 1954 investigation into possible communist infiltration of the U.S. Army; there was none) did the American people see firsthand the abusive and arbitrary verbal tactics McCarthy used to assault his victims. Many did not like what they saw. The American public, at one time supportive of the showy senator, turned against him. Later that year the Senate censured McCarthy, finally ending the demagogue's crusade. McCarthy died three years later, leaving in his wake thousands of shattered lives and a legacy of unfounded hysteria.

The following year, 1957, the Soviets launched the world's first satellite, *Sputnik*. Similar U.S. efforts continually failed, raising suspicions that U.S. technological superiority may have been exaggerated. Emboldened by the successful orbiting of *Sputnik* and subsequent satellites, Khrushchev employed his own policy of brinkmanship when he demanded that the West vacate West Berlin. Eisenhower of course refused but invited the Soviet leader to a summit in Paris. The meeting was never held because of the downing of the American spy plane over the Soviet Union in 1960. Khrushchev persisted in his demand; the American response was to strengthen NATO. The following year the Soviets walled off East Berlin in an attempt to halt the flow of refugees to West Berlin.

To the West the Berlin Wall became a symbol of Soviet repression. Despite the increased tensions, the United States, Britain, and the Soviet Union (and eventually over one hundred other nations) signed the Limited Test Ban Treaty in 1963, which banned nuclear weapons tests in the oceans, atmosphere, and outer space. Over the years, other arms agreements followed:

- **Nuclear Nonproliferation Treaty (1968)** The treaty banned the transfer of nuclear weapons to nonnuclear nations.
- **Strategic Arms Limitation Talks (1969-1972)** Known as SALT I, this aimed to prevent the expansion of U.S. and Soviet nuclear arsenals. SALT II sought further reductions, but when the Soviets invaded Afghanistan, the Senate refused to ratify the treaty.
- **Anti-Ballistic Missile Treaty (1972)** ABM restricted the development of defense systems that could be used against strategic ballistic missiles.
- **Strategic Arms Reduction Talks (initiated in 1982)** START aimed to reduce long-range nuclear missiles. President Reagan's Strategic Defense Initiative (SDI), or "Star Wars," a satellite defensive system that would ostensibly destroy incoming missiles, was an impediment to START.
- **Intermediate-Range Nuclear Forces (INF) Agreement (1987)** The United States. and the Soviet Union agreed to eliminate all intermediate-range nuclear weapons from their arsenals.

THE CONTAINMENT POLICY AND LATIN AMERICA: FROM EISENHOWER TO REAGAN

Ever since the early nineteenth century, the United States had warned European nations not to intervene in the internal affairs of nations in the Western Hemisphere. Every U.S. president in the twentieth century had taken steps to prevent this, but after World War II, grassroots movements were often associated with Soviet infiltration into economically and politically vulnerable South American and Caribbean nations. Relations between the United States and South America had generally improved in the decades before World War II, but following the war resentment increased because of U.S. support for dictatorial governments that did little to address the poverty and despair many South Americans were experiencing. Years later the anger had still not subsided. When Vice President Nixon visited South

America in 1959, his car attacked by angry demonstrators—an act that symbolized the sentiment towards the United States held by many in Third World nations.

In 1949 the United States helped establish the Organization of American States (OAS) to address the continent's economic stagnation, but it did little to change the poor conditions under which so many lived. The ultimate priority of the United States was containing communism, and that often meant supporting dictators who were anti-communist. The following are examples of U.S. actions taken in South America and the Caribbean:

- In 1954 the people of Guatemala elected as their president Jacobo Arbenz, who promptly proceeded to alleviate his nation's economic problems by nationalizing land controlled by U.S. banana companies. The companies had considerable influence with important officials in the U.S. government and Central Intelligence Agency (CIA). With U.S. support, revolutionaries overthrew Arbenz's government and replaced it with a pro-U.S. military regime, adding to the frustration and anger South Americans felt towards the United States.

- In 1959 revolutionary leader Fidel Castro overthrew the corrupt military dictator of Cuba, Fulgencio Batista. A nationalist, Castro adopted radical solutions for Cuba's problems. This displeased the U.S. government. Castro then moved closer to the Soviet Union. When he began nationalizing foreign-owned businesses, the United States imposed a trade embargo. Near the end of Eisenhower's second term, in 1961, the United States cut all diplomatic ties with Cuba. President Kennedy extended the trade embargo to include all but essential medical supplies. To this day the embargo is still in effect.

- In 1961 newly elected President John F. Kennedy approved a plan, begun during the Eisenhower administration, to overthrow Castro. Although skeptical, Kennedy gave it his backing. The United States trained and equipped anti-Castro Cubans and landed them at Cuba's Bay of Pigs. Most of the soldiers were killed or captured. The fiasco was an international embarrassment to the United States and the new president.

- In 1962 U.S. spy planes photographed Soviet-built nuclear missile sites in Cuba. Although the United States had missiles in Turkey, which bordered the Soviet Union, President Kennedy warned that if the sites became operational, they would pose a dire threat to the United States. To prevent the Soviets from delivering the missiles, he ordered a "quarantine" of the Caribbean island. After a few tense days, Soviet premier Khrushchev agreed to dismantle the bases in return for a U.S. guarantee not to invade Cuba. The Cuban missile crisis was the closest the U.S. and the Soviet Union came during the Cold War to military—possibly nuclear—engagement.

- In 1965 President Johnson sent thousands of U.S. combat troops to the Dominican Republic to prevent the election of a leftist government.

- In 1973, under President Nixon and Secretary of State Henry Kissinger, the United States overthrew the democratically elected leader of Chile, Salvador Allende, who was killed in the coup; they replaced him with a military dictator, Augusto Pinochet. The Nixon administration saw Allende's Marxist programs and rhetoric as a threat to U.S. political and economic interests.

■ In 1979 a leftist revolutionary group called the Sandinistas overthrew the U.S.-backed corrupt dictator of Nicaragua, Anastasio Somosa. President Reagan, deeply opposed to their policies, instructed the CIA to destabilize the country in the hopes of eroding support for the Sandinista government. Millions of dollars were given to the Contras, a rebel group attempting to overthrow the Sandinistas, despite Congress's passage of the Boland Amendment prohibiting such aid. Nevertheless, advisers to Reagan developed a scheme to funnel weapons to the Contras, clearly circumventing federal law. Reagan claimed he knew nothing of the plan. Meanwhile, the Reagan administration was supporting the often-ruthless Salvadoran government's battle against leftist guerrillas.

■ In 1983 President Reagan sent U.S. combat forces to the tiny Caribbean island of Grenada. The American troops succeeded in overthrowing a Cuban-supported government, which itself had recently overthrown Grenada's government.

■ In 1989 President George H. W. Bush ordered the invasion of Panama to overthrow the government of Manuel Noriega and to stop what he claimed was Noriega's involvement in the drug trade.

U.S.-ASIAN AFFAIRS: THE LIMITATIONS OF CONTAINMENT

The United States was clearly successful in containing the spread of communism to Western Europe in the postwar years. The same could not be said of its involvement in Asia. Three major conflicts defined the U.S. containment policy in Asia: the Chinese Civil War, the Korean War, and the Vietnam War.

THE CHINESE CIVIL WAR

The Chinese Civil War began before World War II. Chinese communists under the guerrilla leader Mao Zedong had been fighting a civil war against Jiang Jieshi's anti-communist Nationalist government. When Japan invaded China in 1937, the two sides halted their civil war to fight the invaders, but in 1945 they resumed hostilities. The Truman administration sent over $2 billion in economic and military aid to supply Jiang's military. However, because of the growing popularity of the Chinese Communist Party (CCP) among China's mostly peasant population, and hurt by corrupt Nationalist government officials and generals, the communists won the civil war. In 1949 the Nationalists fled to Formosa (Taiwan).

It was a fateful year for U.S. policymakers. The Soviets had successfully detonated a nuclear weapon, and China, the nation with the world's largest population, had embraced communism. The question "Who lost China?" sparked criticisms that the Truman administration had not done enough to aid its ally, which was evidence to conservatives that it was soft on communism. The United States would not recognize the People's Republic of China until 1971, after President Nixon had made a surprise visit to that nation, considered a major thaw in the Cold War.

THE KOREAN WAR

Korea had been occupied during World War II by the Japanese. At the end of the war, Korea was divided along the 38th parallel, the Soviets occupying the area north of the dividing line, the United States south of it. Both nations left after North Korea and South Korea developed their military strength, though North Korea had a more formidable army. Elections were held; North Koreans voted for a communist government under Kim Il Sung, while South Koreans elected an anticommunist government led by Syngman Rhee. Both leaders were strong nationalists who wanted reunification. The Korean War broke out in June 1950, when North Korea invaded South Korea to unify the nation.

Just two months earlier, a U.S. National Security Council memorandum (NSC-68) had recommended to President Truman that the United States engage in a massive development of its conventional and nuclear capabilities in order to send a clear message to the Kremlin. Consequently the U.S. military budget skyrocketed from $13 to $50 billion. Some of that money would be used to supply U.S. troops in the ensuing Korean conflict. To counter North Korea's invasion, Truman, who mistakenly believed the attack had been planned in Moscow, ordered U.S. troops stationed in occupied Japan to Korea. In the meantime Truman asked the U.N. Security Council to pass a resolution condemning the invasion and to send troops immediately to assist South Korea. The resolution passed only because of the absence of the Soviets—they would have vetoed it, but they had been boycotting the U.N. over the U.S. veto of communist China's admission into the U.N. Troops were rushed to Korea from many nations, though the bulk of the force was American.

They were almost too late. The invasion was so sudden and overpowering that South Korean and U.S. forces had been driven into the southwestern corner of the Korean peninsula around the city of Pusan. General Douglas MacArthur, commander of U.N. troops in Korea, devised an audacious maneuver that outflanked the North Korean army at Inchon and drove it back across the 38th parallel. Not content with that, Truman sought to roll back communism by overthrowing Kim Il Sung; he therefore ordered MacArthur's forces to cross the 38th parallel into North Korea. China threatened to enter the conflict if MacArthur's troops continued their invasion of North Korea. MacArthur, an advocate of rollback as well, believed the Chinese would do no such thing, and he pressed on north to the Chinese-Korean border at the Yalu River. To his surprise, in November 1950 nearly a half million Chinese soldiers poured across the border and drove the U.N. forces back across the 38th parallel. MacArthur was insistent that China itself should be attacked, but Truman, now having second thoughts about invading North Korea, favored a political solution. Outraged, MacArthur publicly criticized the commander in chief's handling of the war and disobeyed his orders. Truman fired him. MacArthur returned to the United States a national hero, despite his insubordination.

By the summer of 1951, the war had settled into a stalemate. Negotiations for an armistice began that summer and dragged on for two more years. Finally, in 1953 at Panmunjom, on the 38th parallel, a cease-fire was agreed to. The United States had successfully contained communism in South Korea, but it had been compelled to use its military to do so. To this day, Korea is still divided, and thousands of U.S. troops continue to be stationed there.

THE VIETNAM WAR

The Vietnam War grew out of France's effort to reclaim its colonial possession, Indochina, which had been conquered by the Japanese during the war. Ho Chi Minh, the leader of the Vietnamese independence movement, appealed to the United States and the United Nations for assistance and recognition. Neither was forthcoming. Ho was more warmly received, however, by China and the USSR. When the French tried to crush the insurgents, the United States provided France with economic and military assistance. The French were nevertheless defeated by Ho's nationalist guerrilla force, the Viet Minh. Concern swept Washington that the rest of Southeast Asia would in turn fall like dominoes (the "domino theory").

At the 1954 Geneva conference, Cambodia, Laos, and Vietnam—the three had comprised the French colony of Indochina—received their independence. Vietnam, however, was temporarily divided along the 17th parallel. Ho became the leader of North Vietnam, and the U.S.-backed Ngo Dinh Diem took control in the South, with elections scheduled for 1956. Within South Vietnam, a guerrilla force comprising mostly communists known as the Vietcong were determined to reunite Vietnam under Ho's leadership. Almost immediately, civil war erupted between North Vietnam and South Vietnam. The United States sent more and more military advisers to help the South Vietnamese turn back the Vietcong. For his part Diem refused to participate in the election scheduled for 1956, and his brutal measures lost him whatever support he had from the citizens of South Vietnam. Diem's generals told American officials in Saigon of their plans for a coup and asked for assurances that the U.S. would not thwart the coup and that U.S. financial assistance would continue after it. The assurances were given. Diem was assassinated in the coup. Three weeks later, Kennedy was assassinated in Dallas, Texas.

In 1962 Soviet Premier Khrushchev prophetically remarked: "In South Vietnam, the U.S. has stumbled into a bog. It will be mired down there a long time." American presidents Kennedy, Johnson, and Nixon all sought one way or another to either win the war or, at the very least, to extricate the United States from the conflict. Johnson intensified U.S. involvement in 1964 after alleging that the North Vietnamese attacked two of its warships in the Gulf of Tonkin. In a near unanimous vote, Congress gave the president a "blank check" to wage war in Vietnam (Gulf of Tonkin Resolution). By 1965 the United States had nearly 200,000 troops in Vietnam. The war continued to escalate until by 1968 a half million U.S. troops were involved. They were bolstering what seemed to many to be an unpopular government under Nguyen van Thieu, whose forces, along with American troops, were battling the Army of North Vietnam and the Vietcong. Until this point, most Americans had supported the war, but by 1968, with no end to the conflict in sight and the American people now badly divided over Johnson's foreign policy, the president chose not to run for reelection. Richard Nixon, who claimed to have a secret plan to bring "peace with honor," was elected president. Nixon's plan was known as

Vietnamization: the United States would train and equip the South Vietnamese army while American forces were gradually withdrawn.

Throughout the United States demonstrations in favor of and opposed to the war broke out. Some turned deadly—for example, Ohio National Guard troops opened fire on antiwar demonstrators at Kent State University, killing four students, and police used machine guns and armor-piercing bullets to control demonstrators at Jackson State, killing two students. Now Americans were dying in the Vietnam War at home.

Television, which had considerably changed American culture in the postwar years, dramatically brought the Vietnam War into American living rooms. Search and destroy missions, the use of napalm and defoliants such as Agent Orange, and the massive bombing raids on North Vietnam such as Operation Rolling Thunder convinced many Americans that the war had become one of brutal attrition. Antiwar demonstrations increased and, ultimately, over one-half million American men resisted the military draft. Still, the government repeatedly attempted to convince the public that the end of the war was in sight.

However, doubts intensified when the North Vietnamese and Vietcong launched a major offensive on the Vietnamese New Year (Tet) in 1968 against every major city in South Vietnam, even breaching the grounds of the U.S. embassy in Saigon. Although the attackers suffered huge casualties, the Tet offensive was a political defeat for the U.S. government; it convinced even more Americans that the end of the war was not in sight and that it was time to withdraw from Vietnam. This position was given added weight when in 1971 the *New York Times* published the Pentagon Papers, a top-secret study of the war commissioned by the Johnson administration. It revealed that the government had misled the public and Congress about the reasons the United States entered the conflict and had escalated U.S. involvement.

From the end of Johnson's presidency through Nixon's, the United States sought a negotiated settlement to the war in peace talks that were convened in Paris in 1968. When talks broke down at one point, Nixon ordered a massive bombardment of Hanoi, the capital of North Vietnam. Finally, on January 23, 1973, an agreement was announced, followed shortly thereafter by the withdrawal of all U.S. troops. Two years later North Vietnamese troops overran Saigon, the capital of South Vietnam, and unified the nation, but not before an estimated 2 million Vietnamese and 56,000 Americans had been killed.

FOREIGN AFFAIRS IN THE POST-VIETNAM ERA

In the late 1970s President Carter initiated a shift in the U.S. approach to foreign policy. In an attempt to rebuild America's image, especially in the Third World, he infused morality and human rights into his policies. To Carter, U.S. support of anticommunist totalitarian governments had serious limitations. Conservatives were deeply opposed to this approach, as they believed it would ultimately weaken U.S. power and influence worldwide. However, Carter proved to be inconsistent in his application of human rights to foreign policy:

- He negotiated the Panama Canal Treaty, which returned the Canal Zone to the Panamanians in 2000, angering many conservatives.
- In Central America after the Marxist Sandinistas took over Nicaragua, Carter thought it best to provide aid to the government of El Salvador, which itself was engaged in a civil war. Despite the Salvadoran government's tolerance of right-wing death squads, turning a blind eye to those abuses, Carter obviously preferred this regime to another leftist government in the region.
- Carter's greatest success came in the Middle East, when he negotiated a peace treaty between Egypt and Israel. It did not bring peace to the region, however.
- Despite his rhetoric to end the Cold War, and the Strategic Arms Limitation Treaty (SALT) he signed with his Soviet counterpart in 1979, Carter's actions often proved that he was as much a cold warrior as his predecessors. When the Soviets invaded Afghanistan in 1979 to support a faltering Marxist government, Carter refused to send American athletes to participate in the 1980 Moscow Olympics and supplied the Afghan guerrillas with weapons and supplies. Both actions obviously infuriated the Soviets.
- The overthrow of the U.S.-backed shah of Iran in 1979 reverberated through the White House. Angered that the United States had maintained the corrupt and repressive shah's government in power for so long, as well as U.S. support for Israel, Islamic fundamentalists led a successful popular revolution against their leader. They proceeded to take U.S. embassy officials hostage after Carter allowed the shah to seek medical treatment in the United States. Carter's futile attempts at a negotiated settlement, an attempted military solution, and neutral intervention all failed. His contradictory foreign policy, the inability to resolve the Iranian crisis, and the slumping U.S. economy were factors in his failed bid for reelection.

If Carter intended to infuse foreign affairs with morality, President Reagan represented the alternative view. In Reagan's view, the Carter administration had failed to protect the nation's self-interests, its prestige, and the morale of its people. For Reagan the enemy of the United States was still the "evil empire," the Soviet Union. It was the Soviet Union, not political repression and poverty, that was behind the instability in the Third World. With this view in mind, Reagan did not hesitate to intervene in all parts of the world when he believed it was in the best interests of the United States to do so. The 1980s saw the United States involved in one way or another in Central America and the Caribbean, Lebanon, the Persian Gulf, Libya, Angola, Afghanistan, and Cambodia.

The events in Lebanon revealed a weakness in Reagan's objective of making the United States the world's policeman. When a civil war ripped that nation apart, the president sent Marines to restore order. In 1983, in a precursor of what would become an increasingly common tactic, a truck packed with explosives blew up the U.S. barracks, killing 241 Marines. The Reagan administration then ordered a "strategic deployment" of its forces out of the area.

The end of the Cold War was a watershed event in the 1980s. When Reagan denounced SALT II and proceeded to take a hard-line approach to the Soviet Union, the Soviets reacted by deploying more nuclear missiles. It seemed as if the Cold War would continue indefinitely. In the meantime a new Soviet government, led by Mikhail Gorbachev, came to power in 1985. Gorbachev took over a country whose economy could not maintain both an arms race and a consumer economy. He was tired of the economic burden of sustaining the Cold War, especially given the expansion of the U.S. arms buildup under Reagan. Moreover, he wanted to introduce greater democratic freedoms into the Soviet system. To achieve this goal he initiated two important reforms:

- **Perestroika** This restructured the Soviet economy by introducing features of a free-market system.
- **Glasnost** This expanded citizens' democratic and political freedoms.

Then, in an historic decision, Gorbachev redefined his nation's relationship with its East European allies by removing Soviet troops from those countries. Beginning with Poland, one after another Soviet-backed governments fell from power in Eastern Europe. Finally, in 1989, the Berlin Wall was torn down, and the two Germanys were reunited. It was not long before the USSR itself was dismantled, as nine of its republics broke away and formed the Commonwealth of Independent States.

The end of the Cold War did not make the United States and the world as safe as most had hoped. Now the Persian Gulf Wars; the terrorist attacks on the World Trade Center, the Pentagon, and other international targets; and the enduring Middle East crisis have come to define post-Cold War anxieties.

Multiple-Choice Questions

1. An objective of the Marshall Plan was to
   (A) provide military assistance to the Chinese Nationalists
   (B) limit the nuclear stockpiles of the United States and Soviet Union
   (C) rebuild West European nations that had been devastated during the war
   (D) roll back communism in Eastern Europe
   (E) divide Korea into two separate nations, one communist the other noncommunist

ANSWER: **C.** The Marshall Plan provided billions in aid to rebuild Europe's war-torn economies (*The American Pageant,* 12th ed., p. 875/11th ed., pp. 895-896).

2. Joseph McCarthy
   (A) was commander of U.N. forces in Korea
   (B) was successful in exposing thousands of communist sympathizers in the U.S. government
   (C) was a congressman who strongly opposed U.S. intervention in Vietnam
   (D) is associated with the second red scare in the 1940s and 1950s
   (E) was arrested and executed for revealing U.S. nuclear secrets to the Soviets

ANSWER: D. McCarthy was at the center of the red scare that profoundly affected American life in the 1940s and 1950s (*The American Pageant,* 12th ed., pp. 890-891/11th ed., pp. 911-912).

3. Which of the following is NOT a permanent member of the U.N. Security Council?
   (A) Germany
   (B) France
   (C) Britain
   (D) United States
   (E) China

ANSWER: A. (*The American Pageant,* 12th ed., p. 871/11th ed., p. 892.)

4. In order to prevent the Soviets from placing nuclear missiles in Cuba, President Kennedy
   (A) threatened to strike Moscow with U.S. intercontinental ballistic missiles
   (B) imposed a trade embargo on Cuba
   (C) appealed to the U.N. to send combat troops to Cuba
   (D) placed a naval quarantine around Cuba
   (E) agreed to remove U.S. missiles from Europe

ANSWER: D. In an act of brinkmanship, Kennedy blockaded Cuba (*The American Pageant,* 12th ed., pp. 922-923/11th ed., p. 942).

5. The Korean War
   (A) ended in a stalemate
   (B) resulted in the first successful attempt by the United States to contain communism in Asia
   (C) was a direct cause of the Chinese Civil War
   (D) ended when the U.N. sent peacekeeping forces to the Korean Peninsula
   (E) is the only example of U.S.-Soviet cooperation in the immediate post-World War II period

ANSWER: A. After three years of fighting, the war essentially ended where it began, with the two Koreas divided along the 38th parallel (*The American Pageant,* 12th ed., p. 889/11th ed., p. 889).

6. Which U.S. president advocated the development of a satellite-based defensive system known as Strategic Defense Initiative?
   (A) Truman
   (B) Eisenhower
   (C) Kennedy
   (D) Johnson
   (E) Reagan

ANSWER: **E.** It was popularly referred to as Star Wars (*The American Pageant,* 12th ed., p. 982/11th ed., p. 998).

7. The Tonkin Gulf Resolution
   (A) was passed by the U.N. authorizing the United States to send combat troops to Vietnam
   (B) was passed by Congress giving President Johnson unlimited powers to wage war in Vietnam
   (C) ended hostilities in Korea
   (D) stated that the United States would not intervene in the Chinese Civil War
   (E) recognized the Viet Minh as the legitimate government in Vietnam

ANSWER: **B.** Congress gave Johnson a blank check to wage war in Vietnam (*The American Pageant,* 12th ed., p. 929/11th ed., pp. 947-948).

8. President Nixon authorized a military coup that toppled the popularly elected government of Salvador Allende in
   (A) Guatemala
   (B) Hungary
   (C) El Salvador
   (D) Chile
   (E) Mexico

ANSWER: **D.** Allende was a democratically elected leader.

9. President Reagan's administration illegally circumvented Congress's Boland Amendment in order to
   (A) secretly fund Nicaragua's Contras
   (B) increase the U.S. nuclear stockpile
   (C) undermine Mikhail Gorbachev's reformist government
   (D) purchase arms for the Chinese Nationalists
   (E) invade Panama

ANSWER: **A.** Reagan claimed he was not aware of the actions of his subordinates whose support for the Contras was designed to topple Nicaragua's Sandinista government, despite the Boland Amendment's prohibition of such activities (*The American Pageant,* 12th ed., pp. 985-986/11th ed., pp. 1001-1002).

10. In order to prevent communist forces from toppling the
    governments of Greece and Turkey, the United States
    (A) sent combat troops to both nations at the end of World War II
    (B) initiated the Truman Doctrine
    (C) imposed a trade embargo on both nations
    (D) initiated the Marshall Plan
    (E) established NATO

ANSWER: **B.** The Truman administration sent millions in economic and
military aid to Greece and Turkey to assist them in their fight against
communist rebels (*The American Pageant,* 12th ed., p. 874/11th ed., p.
895).

Free-Response Questions

1. Compare and contrast the success of the containment policy
   during the Cold War. Select TWO of the following case studies:
   a. containment in Europe
   b. containment in Asia
   c. containment in South America

RESPONSE When asked to *compare,* you should identify commonalities;
when asked to *contrast,* identify differences. In discussing containment
in Europe, you may wish to first describe the containment policy and
then incorporate economic and military programs such as the Truman
Doctrine, the Marshall Plan, and the creation of NATO that sought to
achieve this objective. In discussing containment in Asia, you should
address the three major case studies of U.S. containment on that
continent: Chinese Civil War, Korean War, and the Vietnam War. For
South America discuss U.S. interventions, the reasons for these
interventions, and their outcomes. Three case studies should suffice.

2. Support or refute this statement:
   It is reasonable to assume that the actions, behavior, and
   policies of the Soviet Union following World War II caused and
   prolonged the Cold War.

RESPONSE In your essay, you can identify major actions taken by the
Soviets in the Cold War and evaluate whether they were reasonable
reactions on their part. For example, the development by the Soviets
of nuclear weapons, the creation of the Warsaw Pact, the decision to
place nuclear missiles in Cuba, and Soviet interventions in Hungary
and Czechoslovakia are some of the events that can be used to support
or refute the statement, given your interpretation of the Cold War.
Keep in mind that there are three basic interpretations around which a
thesis can be constructed: the Soviets caused and prolonged the Cold
War, the United States caused and prolonged the Cold War, or both
are responsible.

Part III

Practice Tests

Practice Test 1

AP UNITED STATES HISTORY EXAMINATION
Section I: Multiple-Choice Questions
Time—55 minutes
Number of questions—80

Directions Each question or incomplete statement below has five possible answers. For each question, select the best response.

1. Mercantilism refers to an economic policy that emphasizes
   (A) greater import levels and reduced export levels by the mother country
   (B) the reluctance to establish colonies due to the high cost of maintaining them
   (C) the principle of free trade and competition
   (D) establishing colonies and a favorable balance of trade for the mother country
   (E) greater autonomy for colonies

2. The Navigation Laws of 1660 and 1663
   (A) affected only the shipping of raw material to Great Britain
   (B) were strongly supported by American merchants
   (C) demonstrated the intention of the British government to direct colonial trade for the benefit of the American colonies
   (D) were designed to enhance Britain's economic position at the expense of the American colonies
   (E) were vetoed by King George because it was detrimental to the economic growth of the colonies

3. All of the following contributed to the expansion of U.S. industrialism in the late nineteenth century EXCEPT
   (A) the demise of the capitalist class as a political force
   (B) the existence of loose immigration laws
   (C) new inventions and technological advancements
   (D) the role played by government in this period in relation to big business
   (E) the presence of a large industrial workforce

4. In the Supreme Court case *United States v. E. C. Knight* (1895), the court ruled that
   (A) the actions of the E. C. Knight Company were unconstitutional given the wording of the Sherman Anti-Trust Act
   (B) neither the E. C. Knight Company nor the American Sugar Refining Company could be considered a monopoly
   (C) the Sherman Anti-Trust Act was unconstitutional
   (D) the E. C. Knight Company was engaged in commerce, not manufacturing, and therefore could not be regulated by Congress
   (E) child labor was unconstitutional in businesses that engaged in interstate commerce

5. A major reason why Al Smith lost the presidential election in 1928 was
   (A) his allegiance to Hoover's economic programs
   (B) his adherence to maintaining a balanced budget in the midst of a depression
   (C) his opposition to the Nineteenth Amendment
   (D) Franklin Roosevelt's lack of support for Smith's candidacy
   (E) Smith's Catholicism, which cost him Protestant votes

GO ON TO NEXT PAGE

6. Frances Perkins
   (A) was a major Republican opponent of the New Deal
   (B) was the Republican candidate for president in 1932
   (C) represented a radical challenge to FDR's New Deal
   (D) was FDR's vice president during his first term in office
   (E) was the first female cabinet member in U.S. history

7. Which of the following was NOT an objective of the Populists?
   (A) abolishing the graduated income tax
   (B) preventing the government from owning and operating the railroad
   (C) placing term limits on the president and vice president
   (D) placing limits on the mining and coining of silver
   (E) an eight-hour workday for industrial workers

8. Which of the following acts established the Civil Service Commission?
   (A) Interstate Commerce Act
   (B) Dawes Act
   (C) Pendleton Act
   (D) Bland-Allison Act
   (E) Sherman Anti-Trust Act

9. Which one of the following was a member of the Central Powers during World War I?
   (A) France
   (B) Britain
   (C) United States
   (D) Germany
   (E) Russia

10. Which of the following was passed while Wilson was president?
    (A) Mann-Elkins Act
    (B) Pure Food and Drug Act
    (C) Federal Reserve Act
    (D) Meat Inspection Act
    (E) Alien and Sedition Acts

11. Margaret Sanger was an important reformer who
    (A) campaigned to end child labor
    (B) sought to end racial segregation
    (C) attacked the abuses of trusts and monopolies
    (D) advocated for women's right to vote
    (E) advocated in favor of women's reproductive rights

12. "There is a common, widespread, and persistent stereotyped idea regarding the Negro and it is that he is here only to receive; to be shaped into something new and unquestionably better....Through his artistic efforts the Negro is smashing this immemorial stereotype faster than he has ever done through any other method he has been able to use...." This quote represents
    (A) the primary reason the KKK had so many members in the 1920s
    (B) the challenges made to prejudicial views by the Harlem Renaissance
    (C) the divisions that existed in the 1920s between urban and rural black Americans
    (D) FDR's crusade to improve the socioeconomic status of black Americans
    (E) a major reason why some criticized the New Deal for not doing enough to better the lives of lack Americans

13. The military turning point in the American Revolution occurred as a result of which of the following battles?
    (A) the Battle of Gettysburg
    (B) the Battle of Saratoga
    (C) Spain's decision to enter the war on the side of the British
    (D) the Battle of New Orleans
    (E) the Mexican attack on the Alamo

14. The Brain Trust was the name given to
    (A) President Franklin D. Roosevelt's political advisers
    (B) The nation's first Supreme Court justices
    (C) President Lyndon Johnson's advisers during the Vietnam War
    (D) A nineteenth-century monopoly broken up by the government
    (E) President Harding's political associates and advisers who were involved in the Teapot Dome scandal

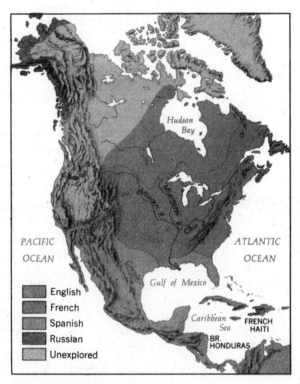

North America Before 1754

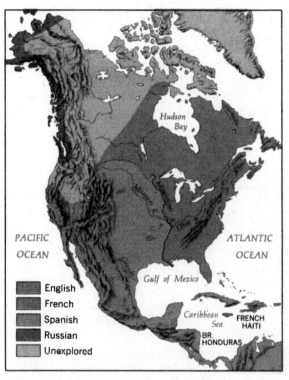

North America After 1763 (after French losses)

15. Which of the following was a factor in the U.S. decision to enter World War I?
(A) Japan's attack on Pearl Harbor
(B) Germany's invasion of Poland
(C) the Zimmerman note
(D) the *Panay* incident
(E) the DeLôme letter

16. Democratic party congressmen who opposed Lincoln's goal of forcefully restoring the Confederate States to the Union were called
(A) the Sons of Liberty
(B) the Axis Powers
(C) Copperheads
(D) Minutemen
(E) the American Expeditionary Force

17. The maps above indicate that
(A) before 1754 the Spanish controlled most of the northeastern part of North America
(B) before 1754 the English controlled all of the territory that borders the Atlantic Ocean

(C) the French gained the most territory by 1763
(D) France had lost most of it territorial possessions in North American by 1763
(E) Russia had tripled its land holdings in North America by 1763

18. After the Civil War the North was characterized by all of the following EXCEPT
(A) a growing industrial economy
(B) a steady flow of immigrants that greatly increased the North's labor pool
(C) a high protective tariff
(D) social turmoil as millions of northerners were displaced by the war
(E) a politically powerful industrial capitalist class

GO ON TO NEXT PAGE

19. All of the following are associated with economic and political corruption in the post-Civil War era EXCEPT
    (A) Crédit Mobilier
    (B) Teapot Dome
    (C) the attempt to corner the gold market by financiers Fisk and Gould
    (D) Boss Tweed and Tammany Hall
    (E) the Whiskey Ring

20. The precedent for using federal troops to break up a major strike was set by
    (A) Abraham Lincoln in 1862
    (B) Rutherford Hayes in 1877
    (C) Grover Cleveland in 1894
    (D) Theodore Roosevelt in 1901
    (E) Franklin D. Roosevelt in 1945

21. Thomas Paine's pamphlet *Common Sense*
    (A) supported the idea that the colonies would benefit by remaining in the British Empire
    (B) argued for reconciliation between Britain and the American colonies
    (C) repudiated the goal of achieving independence from Britain
    (D) emphasized the virtues and advantages of a constitutional monarchy
    (E) provided intellectual justification for American independence

22. In the Rush-Bagot Treaty of 1817
    (A) the Great Lakes region was demilitarized
    (B) France agreed to settle boundary disputes with the United States over control of the Mississippi River
    (C) Britain refused to treat the United States as a political and military equal
    (D) all of the issues that led to the War of 1812 were resolved
    (E) the United States and France agreed to a military alliance

23. Which of the following would NOT have been supported by a southern expansionist in the antebellum period?
    (A) the Walker expedition
    (B) the Ostend manifesto
    (C) the attempt to acquire Cuba
    (D) the Wilmot proviso
    (E) the Adams-Onis Treaty

24. Which of the following is associated with a Border State during the Civil War?
    (A) Tennessee was a Border State
    (B) a state that did not have slavery but still joined the Confederacy
    (C) Western states that were untouched by the war
    (D) those states that refused to stay in the Union or join the Confederacy
    (E) states that had slavery but did not secede

25. Which New Deal agency gave legal protection to labor unions, set up the National Labor Relations Board, and gave workers the right to bargain collectively?
    (A) FERA
    (B) CCC
    (C) Section 7A of the NRA
    (D) CWA
    (E) REA

26. Britain's Proclamation of 1763
    (A) prevented the American colonies from trading with France
    (B) prevented the American colonists from moving west of the Appalachian Mountains
    (C) required the colonists to purchase tea from only the British East India Company
    (D) subordinated American economic interests to those of British capitalists
    (E) ended all hostilities between Britain and France

27. Huey Long
    (A) was the leader of the Sons of Liberty before the American Revolution
    (B) helped found the American Federation of Labor and was responsible for unifying it with the CIO in 1935
    (C) ran unsuccessfully for president three times in the late nineteenth century
    (D) was commander of Union forces in the American Civil War
    (E) was a Louisiana senator who posed a political challenge to FDR's reelection until he was assassinated in 1935

28. The Bonus Army
    (A) demanded that the federal government pay their World War I bonuses immediately rather than wait until 1945
    (B) was sent by President Wilson to France in 1917 to help the Allied Powers defeat the Central Powers
    (C) was the name given to those workers who were rewarded by business owners for refusing to join a union
    (D) was composed of those Americans who had fought in both world wars
    (E) was organized in 1861 to suppress the rebellion of the Southern states that had seceded from the Union

29. Those Northerners who traveled to the South following the Civil War, some for personal gain and some to help reform the South, were derisively referred to as
    (A) scalawags
    (B) Coxey's Army
    (C) the Army of the Potomac
    (D) carpetbaggers
    (E) progressives

30. The "Revolution of 1800" refers to
    (A) the industrialization of the United States
    (B) the victory of the Americans over the British
    (C) the election of Thomas Jefferson
    (D) the abolition of the slave trade in the United States
    (E) the election of Andrew Jackson

31. War hawks were
    (A) Americans who demanded that the United States invade China in the Korean War
    (B) those congressmen who supported the war against Britain in 1812
    (C) loyalists during the American Revolution who took up arms in support of the king
    (D) a Native American tribe that attempted to stop the westward expansion of the Americans in the early nineteenth century
    (E) British politicians who favored supporting the Confederacy in the Civil War

32. Which of the following was an abolitionist who believed in using violence to destroy the institution of slavery?
    (A) Harriet Tubman
    (B) Marcus Garvey
    (C) Frederick Douglass
    (D) John Brown
    (E) Elijah Lovejoy

33. The Know-Nothings were
    (A) Confederate spies during the Civil War
    (B) a nativist movement in the mid-nineteenth century
    (C) Americans who organized boycotts of British goods before the Revolution
    (D) anarchists who were arrested by the government during the First Red Scare
    (E) those who refused to testify when called to do so by the House Un-American Activities Committee

34. The president of the Confederate States of America was
    (A) Frederick Douglass
    (B) Robert E. Lee
    (C) Jefferson Davis
    (D) John Brown
    (E) John Wilkes Booth

35. The Hartford Convention was convened
    (A) by New Englanders who opposed the War of 1812
    (B) in order to prevent the South from seceding
    (C) by women's rights advocates in the mid-nineteenth century
    (D) in order to organize a colonial response to the Coercive Acts
    (E) by labor leaders in order to advocate for the eight-hour workday

36. Which of the following is NOT associated with the American System?
    (A) It was developed by Henry Clay.
    (B) It was strongly supported by Southern political leaders.
    (C) It promoted funding for the Second Bank of the United States.
    (D) It would allow for protective tariffs.
    (E) The federal government would fund canal and road construction.

GO ON TO NEXT PAGE

37. The Fifteenth Amendment to the U.S. Constitution
    (A) gave eighteen-year-old citizens the right to vote
    (B) gave women the right to vote
    (C) made the sale, distribution, and consumption of liquor a federal offense
    (D) abolished slavery
    (E) guaranteed the right to vote for any American citizen regardless of race or color

38. The first motion picture to use sound was
    (A) *The Great Train Robbery*
    (B) *The Jazz Singer*
    (C) *Nanook of the North*
    (D) *The Sheik*
    (E) *Birth of a Nation*

39. Jackie Robinson
    (A) broke the color barrier in major league baseball
    (B) helped to organize a boycott of the 1980 Olympics
    (C) was a famous jazz musician in the 1920s
    (D) was a literary figure associated with the Harlem Renaissance
    (E) was an important political leader in the Populist movement

40. Which one of the following ideas would the Puritans have rejected?
    (A) Education is unimportant.
    (B) Material success is a sign of moral superiority.
    (C) Everyone is encouraged to interpret the Bible.
    (D) The Puritans are the chosen people.
    (E) Evil must be wiped out through harsh punishments.

41. The Puritans
    (A) were satisfied by all of the changes made by the Church of England
    (B) wished to separate from the Church of England
    (C) believed in predetermination
    (D) sought to proselytize among the Native American tribes for the Church of England to build an empire
    (E) were eventually forced to leave the American colonies due to religious persecution

42. Which one of the following is NOT a reason for U.S. participation in the Spanish- American War?
    (A) Spanish dictator Franco's friendship with Nazi Germany
    (B) the explosion of the USS *Maine* in Havana Harbor
    (C) yellow journalism
    (D) humanitarian support for the Cuban people who were victimized by Spanish General Weyler
    (E) an effort by the U.S. government to stabilize conditions in Cuba in order to benefit American industries

43. Which of the following actions hurt President Wilson's efforts to win Senate approval for the League of Nations?
    (A) his failure to take a Republican party leader on the treaty mission to France
    (B) his refusal to meet with members of his own party who opposed ratification of the treaty
    (C) his inability to travel to Europe to meet with the other Allied leaders
    (D) his insistence that Germany and Austria not be admitted into the League
    (E) his inability to convince the other world leaders to make New York City the headquarters of the League

44. Which one of the following would best describe an *immediate* cause of World War I?
    - (A) the naval arms race between Britain and Germany
    - (B) colonial disputes
    - (C) Germany's invasion of Poland
    - (D) the assassination of Archduke Francis Ferdinand
    - (E) Germany's violation of Belgium's neutrality

45. The Anaconda Plan
    - (A) was the Democratic party's response to the Whig party's support for the American Plan
    - (B) was the Union's military strategy for defeating the Confederacy
    - (C) was designed during the Eisenhower administration to increase funding for atomic weapons research
    - (D) was designed by the federal government in the 1950s to integrate public schools
    - (E) was President Roosevelt's design for attacking the problems that caused the Great Depression

46. If one were to argue that the United States pursued a policy of neutrality from 1919 to 1933, which of the following would support that view?
    - (A) signing of the Kellogg-Briand Pact
    - (B) the Open Door Policy
    - (C) the Dawes Plan
    - (D) failure to join the League of Nations
    - (E) the Washington Naval Conference

47. The major goal of the Neutrality Acts of 1935, 1936, and 1937 was to
    - (A) prevent the United States from becoming involved in another global conflict
    - (B) address the economic effects of the Great Depression
    - (C) assist the Fascist nations by not helping Britain
    - (D) keep European nations from interfering in the China

    - (E) make certain Japan did not embark on a policy of territorial expansion

48. Which one of the following was an effect of the Revolutionary War?
    - (A) the establishment of a constitutional monarchy
    - (B) the confiscation of Loyalists' property
    - (C) the acquisition of Canada by the United States
    - (D) the recognition of the Second Continental Congress as the legitimate government of the United States
    - (E) the demand by all Americans for a strong central government

49. A weakness of the Articles of Confederation was that
    - (A) it had no legislative branch
    - (B) some states were not permitted to join as long as they maintained slavery
    - (C) it decided to form a military alliance with Great Britain
    - (D) too many amendments were ratified, diluting the power of the government
    - (E) nine of thirteen states were needed to pass legislation

50. All of the following are accurate statements about the Bill of Rights EXCEPT
    - (A) the Bill of Rights was not part of the original Constitution
    - (B) the antifederalists opposed adding a bill of rights to the Constitution
    - (C) the Bill of Rights placed limits on the power and authority of the federal government
    - (D) the Bill of Rights reflected a fear of a strong central government
    - (E) the Bill of Rights was added to the Constitution as a compromise measure

GO ON TO NEXT PAGE

ROTHCO
FOR AMES NEWS PRESS

51. The political cartoon above dealing with the Reagan administration expresses the view that
   (A) Reagan resented how large the defense budget had grown
   (B) Reagan expanded federal aid to cities but not for the environment or Social Security
   (C) under Reagan federal funding for social programs was significantly cut
   (D) Reagan believed in balancing the federal budget so that it addressed social needs and the needs of the military
   (E) Reagan increased defense funding against his better judgment

52. The North Atlantic Treaty Organization and North American Free Trade Alliance are modern-day examples of the United States practicing
   (A) isolationism
   (B) neutrality
   (C) formal empire
   (D) internationalism
   (E) imperialism

53. "Bleeding Kansas"
   (A) refers to the attempt by the British to subjugate Americans who settled west of the Mississippi River
   (B) involved a pre-Civil War conflict between proslavery and antislavery forces to determine that state's status
   (C) describes the massacre of Native Americans by U.S. troops in the late nineteenth century
   (D) describes the effects of the Mexican-American War on residents of that state
   (E) was the name given to that state by Native Americans who were forced onto reservations in the early twentieth century

54. The event that sparked the outbreak of the American Civil War was
    (A) the Confederate invasion of Pennsylvania in 1863
    (B) Lincoln's assassination by a pro-Confederate sympathizer
    (C) South Carolina's attack on Fort Sumter
    (D) the military skirmishes at Lexington and Concord
    (E) Lincoln's issuing of the Emancipation Proclamation

55. Which one of the following can be considered a radical trade union?
    (A) Industrial Workers of the World
    (B) American Federation of Labor
    (C) International Ladies' Garment Workers Union
    (D) Congress of Industrial Organizations
    (E) United Mine Workers Union

56. Which of the following dates best corresponds to the Gilded Age?
    (A) 1776-1800
    (B) 1861-1865
    (C) 1870-1900
    (D) 1917-1929
    (E) 1945-1970

57. Which of the following occurred during the presidential administration of George Washington?
    (A) the nullification crisis
    (B) the War of 1812
    (C) the Whiskey Rebellion
    (D) the Louisiana Purchase
    (E) the XYZ Affair

58. Which one of the following was NOT one of Secretary of the Treasury Alexander Hamilton's economic programs?
    (A) Report on Public Credit
    (B) Report on Manufactures
    (C) chartering a national bank
    (D) protective tariff
    (E) tax on exports

59. Jefferson's purchase of the Louisiana territory from France was unexpected in that
    (A) he was a strict constructionist
    (B) the United States had recently broken off diplomatic relations with France
    (C) he agreed to pay an outlandish sum for the territory
    (D) most Americans opposed the purchase
    (E) he was opposed to territorial expansion

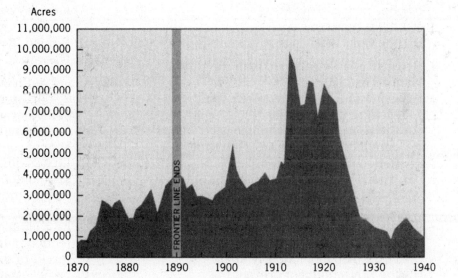

60. The chart above indicates that the most significant transfer of public lands to private ownership occurred in which of the following periods?
    (A) 1870-1880
    (B) 1880-1895
    (C) 1890-1905
    (D) 1905-1910
    (E) 1910-1925

GO ON TO NEXT PAGE

61. The *Dred Scott* decision
    (A) was a major factor in the U.S. government's decision to go to war against Mexico in 1846
    (B) weakened the fugitive slave laws
    (C) reconfirmed that African-Americans were not citizens
    (D) freed all the slaves in the border states
    (E) forbade the United States from trading with any nation that was at war

62. The radical Republicans are associated with which period in U.S. history?
    (A) the American Revolution
    (B) the Civil War
    (C) Reconstruction
    (D) the progressive era
    (E) the Cold War

63. Because of a Soviet boycott of the United Nations in 1950
    (A) Communist China was refused membership in the U.N.
    (B) the United States was able to convince the U.N. to establish the nation of Israel
    (C) troops were sent to assist South Korea after it had been invaded by communist North Korea
    (D) the United States and other Western nations refused to send their athletes to participate in the Olympics
    (E) the U.N. could not prevent the outbreak of hostilities that led to the Chinese Civil War

64. The first state to secede from the Union in 1860 was
    (A) Georgia
    (B) Florida
    (C) South Carolina
    (D) Louisiana
    (E) Texas

65. The rags-to-riches stories of the Gilded Age were written by
    (A) Upton Sinclair
    (B) Mark Twain
    (C) Horatio Alger
    (D) Harriet Tubman
    (E) F. Scott Fitzgerald

66. Ronald Reagan's military objectives included
    (A) the construction of an extensive antimissile satellite system
    (B) returning the Panama Canal to Panama
    (C) allowing the Soviet Union to join NATO
    (D) economic and military assistance to communist nations that ended their membership in the Warsaw Pact
    (E) military assistance to the Sandinista government in Nicaragua

67. The Camp David Agreement is associated with the presidency of
    (A) Richard Nixon
    (B) Gerald Ford
    (C) Jimmy Carter
    (D) Ronald Reagan
    (E) George H. W. Bush

68. Adam Smith condemned government regulation and intervention in the economy because:
    (A) he believed that the lower classes should control the economy
    (B) he was an anarchist
    (C) he maintained that government intervention usually favored the laboring class
    (D) he maintained that government tended to disrupt the competitive forces of the free market
    (E) he believed that government always sided with the capitalist class

69. The United States entered World War II
    (A) after the sinking of the *Lusitania*
    (B) after Japan's attack on Pearl Harbor, in Hawaii
    (C) after British Prime Minister Churchill told President Roosevelt that his nation would be conquered by Germany without U.S. help
    (D) after Japan invaded China
    (E) after Germany invaded Poland

70. In the Supreme Court case *Gibbons v. Ogden,* the Court ruled that
    (A) segregation was constitutional as long as facilities for the different races were equal
    (B) the closed shop was unconstitutional
    (C) state governments could not deny a citizen the right to vote in federal elections
    (D) Congress has the power to regulate interstate commerce
    (E) trusts and monopolies were in restraint of trade

71. The power and strength of industrial unions in achieving their objectives in a dispute with management can be clearly seen in which of the following strikes?
    (A) Lawrence Textile Workers strike
    (B) Homestead strike
    (C) Ludlow massacre
    (D) Haymarket riot
    (E) railroad strike of 1877

72. Which of the following Supreme Court cases was heard by the Marshall Court?
    (A) *McCulloch v. Maryland*
    (B) *Brown v. Board of Education of Topeka, Kansas*
    (C) *Plessy v. Ferguson*
    (D) *Dred Scott v. Sandford*
    (E) *United States v. Butler*

73. Other than President Clinton, who was the only other president to be impeached by the House of Representatives?
    (A) Richard Nixon
    (B) Jimmy Carter
    (C) Ronald Reagan
    (D) Andrew Johnson
    (E) Warren Harding

74. The Tet offensive is considered one of the turning points of
    (A) World War II
    (B) World War I
    (C) the Korean War
    (D) the Spanish-American War
    (E) the Vietnam War

75. The Norris-LaGuardia Act of 1932
    (A) placed strict limitations on immigration from Eastern and Southern Europe
    (B) made it a federal offense to strike during wartime
    (C) outlawed yellow-dog contracts
    (D) provided billions of dollars for the construction of an interstate highway system
    (E) established the eight-hour workday

76. All of the following groups characterize the New Immigration, or the second wave of immigration, from 1890 to1930 EXCEPT
    (A) Italians
    (B) Chinese
    (C) Russian Jews
    (D) Poles
    (E) Greeks

77. The Dawes-Severalty Act of 1887 was passed in order to
    (A) break up Native American tribes by offering them lands out west
    (B) limit Chinese immigration
    (C) outlaw labor strikes
    (D) prevent the government from engaging in deficit spending
    (E) maintain U.S. neutrality in the event of a European war

78. The only Democrat elected president between 1861 and 1912 was
    (A) Lyndon Johnson
    (B) James Garfield
    (C) Grover Cleveland
    (D) William McKinley
    (E) Chester Arthur

79. Which president initiated Operation Desert Storm?
    (A) George H. W. Bush
    (B) Ronald Reagan
    (C) Jimmy Carter
    (D) Bill Clinton
    (E) Gerald Ford

GO ON TO NEXT PAGE

80. The Saturday Night Massacre
    (A) was a turning point in the Vietnam War
    (B) was an event related to the Watergate scandal
    (C) led to the impeachment of President Clinton
    (D) convinced the United States to send troops to Panama to overthrow Manuel Noriega
    (E) was a riot outside the 1968 Democratic party convention in Chicago

STOP
END OF SECTION I

IF YOU FINISH BEFORE TIME IS CALLED, YOU MAY CHECK YOUR WORK ON THIS SECTION. DO NOT GO ON TO SECTION II UNTIL YOU ARE TOLD TO DO SO.

SECTION II: FREE-RESPONSE ESSAYS

Section II of the examination has two kinds of questions. Part A is the Document-Based Question, which you must answer. Part B and Part C each have two general free-response essay questions. You are to answer one essay question from Part B and one essay question from Part C. You will have a total of 130 minutes to complete the document-based essay and two free-response essays.

Part A: Document-Based Question (DBQ)
Mandatory reading time—15 minutes
Writing time—45 minutes

Directions The question below asks you to develop a coherent, well-structured essay that integrates information from nine documents with your own knowledge of the topic. You are not required to use information from all of the documents.

1. How do the attitudes and impressions expressed in the documents indicate that racism was still prevalent in the United States from World War I to the 1960s?

Document A: Black Migrants' Reasons for Relocation (1917)

Sir: I am writing you to let you know that there is 15 or 20 familys wants to come up there at once but cant come on account of money to come with and we cant phone you here we will be killed they dont want us to leave here & say if we dont go to war and fight for our country they are going to kill us and wants to get away If we can if you send 20 passes there is no doubt that every one of us will com at once. we are not doing any thing here we cant get a living out of what we do now some of these people are farmers and som are cooks barbers and black smiths but the greater part are farmers & good worker & honest people & up to date the trash pile dont want to go no where These are nice people and respectable find a place like that & send passes & we all will come at once we all wants to leave here out of this hard luck place if you cant use us find some place that does need this kind of people we are called Negroes here. I am a reader of the Defender and am delighted to know how times are there & was to glad to, know if we could get some one to pass us away from here to a better land. We work but cant get scarcely any thing for it & they dont want us to go away & there is not much of anything here to do & nothing for it Please find some one that need this kind of a people & send at once for us. We dont want anything but our wareing and bed clothes & have not got no money to get away from here with & beging to get away before we are killed and hope to here from you at once. We cant talk to you over the phone here we are afraid to they dont want to hear one say that he or she wants to leave here if we do we are apt to be killed. They say if we dont go to war they are not going to let us stay here with their folks and it is not any thing that we have done to them.

Source: Letter Daphne, Alabama, 4120/17, Emmet Scott, ed., "Letters of Negro Migrants of 1916–1918," Journal of Negro History, 4 (July 1, 1919), pp. 290–340.

GO ON TO NEXT PAGE

Document B: Percentage of Black Voting-Age Population Registered

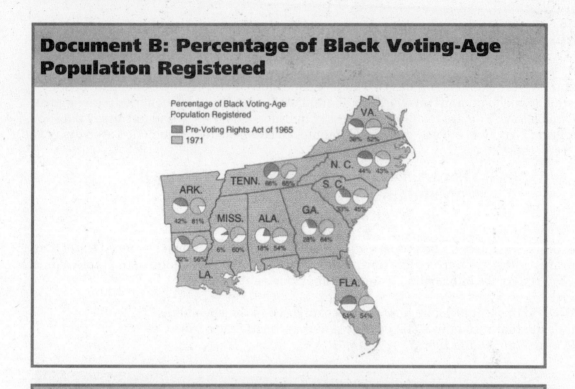

Document C: Congress on Racial Equality (CORE) Demonstration (mid-1950s to early 1960s)

Document D: Chicago Race Riot (1919)

The refusal of Policeman Daniel Callahan (white) . . . to arrest George Stuber (white) . . . last Sunday afternoon after the latter had knocked Eugene Williams, age 13 . . . from a raft as he was floating down Lake Michigan at Twenty-ninth street, fanned into action one of the worst race riots in the history of Illinois. Officer Callahan, it is charged, not only refused to make an arrest, but kept expert swimmers from reaching Williams. The news of Callahan's negligence reached the bathers at the Twenty-sixth street beach and a mob of fifty men marched to Twenty-ninth street to avenge the death of the boy. The patrolman's action so enraged the bathers that they pounced upon Callahan and commenced to pommel him. Callahan was chased to a drug store, where he summoned help. . . .

Source: Chicago Defender, *August 2, 1919, front page.*

Document E: French Directive: "Concerning Black American Troops" (1918)

1. We must prevent the rise of any pronounced degree of intimacy between French officers and black officers. We may be courteous and amiable with these last, but we cannot deal with them on the same plane as with the white American officers without deeply wounding the latter. We must not eat with them, must not shake hands or seek to talk or meet with them outside of the requirements of military service.

2. We must not commend too highly the black American troops, particularly in the presence of [white] Americans. It is all right to recognize their good qualities and their services, but only in moderate terms, strictly in keeping with the truth.

3. Make a point of keeping the native cantonment population from "spoiling" the Negroes. [White] Americans become greatly incensed at any public expression of intimacy between white women with black men. They have recently uttered violent protests against a picture in the "Vie Parisienne" entitled "The Child of the Desert" which shows a [white] woman in a "cabinet particulier" with a Negro. Familiarity on the part of white women with black men is furthermore a source of profound regret to our experienced colonials who see in it an over-weening menace to the prestige of the white race.

Source: W.E.B. Dubois, ed. "Documents of the War," The Crisis 28 (May 1919) Vol. 18: 1, pp. 16–18.

GO ON TO NEXT PAGE

Document F: Greensboro Sit-In (1960)

Document G: Mississippi School Classroom (1964)

Document H: Onlookers with the Burned Body of Jesse Washington, Waco, Texas (1916)

Document I: School Segregation

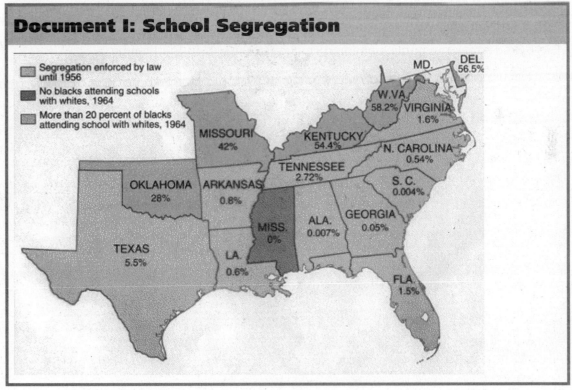

End of documents for Question 1.
Go on to the next page.

Part B and Part C: Free-Response Essay Questions
Writing time—70 minutes

Directions Answer TWO of the following questions, one question from Part B and one from Part C. It is recommended that you spend 5 minutes planning each essay and 30 minutes for writing. Write a well-structured, clearly written essay that provides sufficient evidence to support your thesis. Make certain to identify in the test booklet which essay questions you have selected.

Part B Select ONE question from Part B.

2. Analyze the relationship between Great Britain and its American colonies prior to 1763.

3. The ability and the willingness the Framers had for compromise was reflected in the creation of a constitution that successfully addressed the needs of the young republic. Explain how TWO of the following reflect the validity of this statement.
   a. representation
   b. slavery
   c. democratic rights

Part C Select ONE question from Part C.

4. Analyze the various groups, individuals, and movements that either challenged or presented an alternative program to President Franklin D. Roosevelt's New Deal.

5. Why did American public opinion turn against the war in Vietnam by the late 1960s?

END OF EXAMINATION

ANSWERS FOR SECTION I

ANSWER KEY FOR MULTIPLE-CHOICE QUESTIONS

1. D	17. D	33. B	49. E	65. C
2. D	18. D	34. C	50. B	66. A
3. A	19. B	35. A	51. C	67. C
4. D	20. B	36. B	52. D	68. D
5. E	21. E	37. E	53. B	69. B
6. E	22. A	38. B	54. C	70. D
7. B	23. D	39. A	55. A	71. A
8. C	24. A	40. A	56. C	72. A
9. D	25. C	41. B	57. C	73. D
10. C	26. B	42. A	58. E	74. E
11. E	27. E	43. A	59. A	75. C
12. B	28. A	44. D	60. E	76. B
13. B	29. D	45. B	61. C	77. A
14. A	30. C	46. D	62. C	78. C
15. C	31. B	47. A	63. C	79. A
16. C	32. D	48. B	64. C	80. B

Scoring The multiple-choice section counts for 50 percent of your examination grade.

EXPLANATIONS FOR THE MULTIPLE-CHOICE ANSWERS

1. ANSWER: **D**. Britain established colonies to promote its own economic self-interest (*The American Pageant,* 12th ed., p. 123/11th ed., p. 122).

2. ANSWER: **D**. The Navigation Laws were developed to increase the colonies' economic dependence on the mother country (*The American Pageant,* 12th ed., pp. 123-125/11th ed., pp. 122-123).

3. ANSWER: **A**. The capitalist class possessed considerable political power in the late nineteenth century (*The American Pageant,* 12th ed., pp. 542-543/11th ed., p. 549).

4. ANSWER: **D**. The case was seen as a victory for those who favored a laissez-faire policy by the government (*The American Pageant,* 12th ed., p. 543/11th ed., p. 550).

5. ANSWER: **E**. There was distrust on the part of some Protestants that Smith might be influenced by the Papacy in Rome (*The American Pageant,* 12th ed., pp. 764-765/11th ed., p. 783).

6. ANSWER: **E**. Perkins was appointed secretary of labor by FDR (*The American Pageant,* 12th ed., p. 787/11th ed., p. 805).

7. ANSWER: **B**. The Populists were in favor of government ownership of railroads, grain elevators, and storage facilities (*The American Pageant,* 12th ed., p. 613/11th ed., p. 619).

8. ANSWER: **C**. The Pendleton Act was passed in 1883 (*The American Pageant,* 12th ed., p. 515/11th ed., p. 528).

9. ANSWER: **D**. The other nations were members of the Allied Powers (*The American Pageant,* 12th ed., p. 697/11th ed., p. 714).

10. ANSWER: **C**. The act, passed in 1913, established the Federal Reserve System (*The American Pageant,* 12th ed., p. 692/11th ed., p. 708).

11. ANSWER: **E**. Sanger advocated for the distribution of contraceptives to prevent unplanned pregnancies (*The American Pageant,* 12th ed., p. 745/11th ed., p. 763).

12. ANSWER: **B**. The quote points out the important cultural contribution made by black artists, authors, and musicians associated with the Harlem Renaissance (*The American Pageant,* 12th ed., p. 748/11th ed., p. 764).

13. ANSWER: **B**. After the American victory France agreed to enter the war against Britain (*The American Pageant,* 12th and 11th eds., p. 171).

14. ANSWER: **A**. The Brain Trust was composed mostly of university professors such as Columbia University's Rexford Tugwell (*The American Pageant,* 12th ed., p. 779/11th ed., p. 797).

15. ANSWER: **C**. The German ambassador to Mexico promised that Germany would return land lost by Mexico in the Mexican-American War if that nation joined the Central Powers (*The American Pageant,* 12th ed., p. 706/11th ed., p. 723).

16. ANSWER: **C**. The leader of the Copperheads was Ohio congressman Clement Vallandigham (*The American Pageant,* 12th ed., pp. 468-469/11th ed., pp. 477-478).

17. ANSWER: **D**. As a result of its defeat in the French and Indian War, France lost all of its territory in North America except for French Haiti (*The American Pageant,* 12th ed., p. 116/11th ed., p. 114).

18. ANSWER: **D**. With the exception of the Battle of Gettysburg, the North was generally undamaged by the war (*The American Pageant,* 12th ed., pp. 500-501/11th ed., pp. 510-511).

19. ANSWER: **B**. The Teapot Dome scandal occurred under President Harding in the early 1920s (*The American Pageant,* 12th ed., p. 759/11th ed., pp. 776-777).

20. ANSWER: **B**. The use of federal troops helped put down the railroad strike of 1877 (*The American Pageant,* 12th ed., p. 511/11th ed., p. 522).

21. ANSWER: **E**. Among other issues, Paine repudiated monarchy and urged the American colonies to declare their independence from Britain (*The American Pageant,* 12th ed., p. 145/11th ed., p. 146).

22. ANSWER: **A**. Britain and the United States agreed to disarmament in the Great Lakes (*The American Pageant,* 12th ed., p. 240/11th ed., p. 239).

23. ANSWER: **D**. The Wilmot proviso would have outlawed slavery in new territories (*The American Pageant,* 12th ed., p. 388/11th ed., p. 398).

24. ANSWER: **A**. Tennessee joined the Confederacy (*The American Pageant,* 12th ed., p. 436/11th ed., p. 446).

25. ANSWER: **C**. This provision increased union membership (*The American Pageant,* 12th ed., p. 795/11th ed., p. 812).

26. ANSWER: **B**. The colonists deeply resented the act as many wanted to engage in fur trapping and land speculation west of the Appalachian Mountains (*The American Pageant,* 12th ed., p. 121/11th ed., p. 119).

27. ANSWER: **E**. Long's Share-Our-Wealth program threatened to siphon votes from Roosevelt (*The American Pageant,* 12th ed., pp. 785-786/11th ed., pp. 803-804).

28. ANSWER: **A**. President Hoover called out the U.S. Army to drive the marchers away (*The American Pageant,* 12th ed., p. 774/11th ed., pp. 790-791).

29. ANSWER: **D**. Although some were corrupt, carpetbaggers played an important role in helping emancipated slaves (*The American Pageant,* 12th ed., p. 492/11th ed., pp. 501-502).

30. ANSWER: **C**. After twelve years of federalist rule, the election of Jefferson (a Democratic-Republican) represented a fundamental shift in political party power (*Thc Amcrican Pagcant,* 12th cd., p. 215/11th ed., p. 212).

31. ANSWER: **B**. The war hawks were led by Henry Clay of Kentucky (*The American Pageant,* 12th ed., p. 229/11th ed., p. 227).

32. ANSWER: **D**: Brown and his followers captured the federal arsenal at Harpers Ferry, Virginia, hoping to start a slave insurrection (*The American Pageant,* 12th ed., pp. 422-424/11th ed., pp. 432-433).

33. ANSWER: **B**. The Know-Nothings believed that immigrants, especially Catholics, were undermining American democracy and driving down wages (*The American Pageant,* 12th ed., pp. 296, 415-416/11th ed., p. 425-426).

34. ANSWER: **C**. Davis's vice president was Alexander Stephens of Georgia (*The American Pageant,* 12th ed., p. 428/11th ed., p. 438).

35. ANSWER: **A**. The delegates threatened to secede from the United States because of their opposition to the war; however, the conflict ended before this could happen (*The American Pageant,* 12th ed., pp. 238-239/11th ed., p. 238).

36. ANSWER: **B**. Southerners generally opposed federal funding for internal developments (*The American Pageant,* 12th ed., pp. 240-242/11th ed., p. 238).

37. ANSWER: **E**. The Fifteenth Amendment was intended to permanently guarantee voting rights, especially for blacks in the South (*The American Pageant,* 12th ed., p. 491/11th ed., p. 500).

38. ANSWER: **B**. The movie was an instant hit and revolutionized the motion-picture industry (*The American Pageant,* 12th ed., p. 745/11th ed., p. 762).

39. ANSWER: **A**. Robinson broke into major league baseball with the Brooklyn Dodgers in 1947 and had a Hall of Fame career (*The American Pageant,* 12th ed., p. 891/11th ed., p. 912).

40. ANSWER: **A**. The Puritans placed a premium on education (*The American Pageant,* 12th ed., p. 79/11th ed., p. 76).

41. ANSWER: **B**. In the seventeenth century, after failing to convince the Church of England to reform itself, many Puritans chose to separate from that church (*The American Pageant,* 12th ed., p. 46/11th ed., p. 45).

42. ANSWER: **A**. Franco became dictator of Spain in the 1930s (*The American Pageant,* 12th ed., p. 811/11th ed., p. 830).

43. ANSWER: **A**. Republicans felt slighted when Wilson took only Democrats with him to France (*The American Pageant,* 12th ed., p. 719/11th ed., p. 736).

44. ANSWER: **D**. The assassination of the heir to the Austro-Hungarian Empire was the spark that ignited the war (*The American Pageant,* 12th ed., p. 696/11th ed., p. 713).

45. ANSWER: **B**. By using a naval blockade and dividing the Confederacy in half, the Union hoped to strangle the South into submission (*The American Pageant,* 12th ed., p. 456/11th ed., p. 466).

46. ANSWER: **D**. By not joining the League, the United States hoped to remain neutral in European affairs (*The American Pageant,* 12th ed., p. 723/11th ed., p. 741).

47. ANSWER: **A**. The Neutrality Acts were intended to prevent the United States from becoming embroiled in another European conflict such as World War I (*The American Pageant,* 12th ed., p. 811/11th ed., p. 830).

48. ANSWER: **B**. Loyalists, or Tories, had their property confiscated, though the Treaty of Paris required that they be compensated by the U.S. government (*The American Pageant,* 12th ed., p. 162/11th ed., p. 161).

49. ANSWER: **E**. It was very difficult to get nine states to agree on any piece of legislation (*The American Pageant,* 12th ed., p. 173/11th ed., p. 172).

50. ANSWER: **B**. The antifederalists demanded that a bill of rights be added to the Constitution (*The American Pageant,* 12th ed., p. 192/11th ed., p. 191).

51. ANSWER: **C**. Whereas Reagan significantly cut social programs, he substantially increased the defense budget (*The American Pageant,* 12th ed., pp. 980-981/11th ed., pp. 996-997).

52. ANSWER: **D**. The political objective of internationalism is to increase political and economic cooperation between nations (*The American Pageant,* 12th ed., pp. 877-878/11th ed., pp. 897-898).

53. ANSWER: **B**. "Bleeding Kansas" was a prelude to the Civil War as free-state and slave-state advocates attempted to determine the status of Kansas in regards to slavery (*The American Pageant,* 12th ed., pp. 412-414/11th ed., pp. 422-424).

54. ANSWER: **C**. Fort Sumter was the last major Union fort in the seceded states. The attack compelled Lincoln to call up troops to put down the

rebellion (*The American Pageant,* 12th ed., pp. 435-436/11th ed., pp. 445-446).

55. ANSWER: **A.** The IWW (or Wobblies) wanted to dismantle capitalism; other unions sought higher wages and a shorter workday (*The American Pageant,* 12th ed., p. 710/11th ed., p. 727).

56. ANSWER: **C.** Mark Twain gave the name to the period in 1873 (*The American Pageant,* 12th ed., p. 507/11th ed., p. 517).

57. ANSWER: **C.** The Whiskey Rebellion (1794) provided the executive branch the opportunity to use its power to put down domestic uprisings. Western Pennsylvania farmers refused to pay an excise tax on whiskey and proceeded to attack revenue collectors. President Washington nationalized the Pennsylvania militia, an act that so intimidated the rebel farmers that the uprising was quickly suppressed without bloodshed (*The American Pageant,* 12th ed., p. 196/11th ed., p. 195).

58. ANSWER: **E.** The Constitution forbids a tax on exports (*The American Pageant,* 12th ed., p. A38/11th ed., p. A8).

59. ANSWER: **A.** Jefferson applied the elastic clause (necessary and proper) to justify his purchase of the Louisiana territory despite his strict interpretive view of the Constitution (*The American Pageant,* 12th ed., p. 222/11th ed., p. 220).

60. ANSWER: **E.** By 1910 the U.S. government had significantly expanded the transfer of public lands to private ownership, reaching a peak by 1913 of approximately 10 million acres. The decline did not occur until 1925 (*The American Pageant,* 12th ed., p. 607/11th ed., p. 613).

61. ANSWER: **C.** The Supreme Court ruled that since Scott, a slave, was property, he could not sue for his freedom (*The American Pageant,* 12th ed., p. 417/11th ed., p. 427).

62. ANSWER: **C.** The Radical Republicans challenged President Johnson's Reconstruction plan (*The American Pageant,* 12th ed., p. 483/11th ed., p. 493).

63. ANSWER: **C.** The Soviets were boycotting the U.N. to protest the U.S. veto of Communist China's admittance into the organization. The United States took this opportunity to ask for a Security Council vote to assist South Korea (*The American Pageant,* 12th ed., pp. 883-884/11th ed., pp. 903-904).

64. ANSWER: **C.** South Carolina had been a hotbed of secession since the Nullification Crisis in 1832 (*The American Pageant,* 12th ed., p. 427/11th ed., p. 437).

65. ANSWER: **C.** Alger's stories espoused the view that through hard work and self-sacrifice anyone could be successful in the United States (*The American Pageant,* 12th ed., pp. 556, 578/11th ed., p. 563).

66. ANSWER: **A.** Known as Strategic Defense Initiative (SDI), or "Star Wars" to its critics, the program was an important military objective of the Reagan administration (*The American Pageant,* 12th ed., p. 982/11th ed., p. 998).

67. **ANSWER: C:** The Camp David Agreement ended the state of war that had existed between Egypt and Israel (*The American Pageant,* 12th ed., pp. 970-971/11th ed., pp. 981-984).

68. **ANSWER: D.** Smith maintained that if left alone the (capitalist) marketplace would regulate itself in terms of supply and demand, and prices and wages (*The American Pageant,* 12th ed., p. 123/11th ed., p. 122).

69. **ANSWER: B.** The Japanese launched a surprise attack on the U.S. Seventh Fleet stationed at Pearl Harbor on December 7, 1941. The next day Congress declared war on Japan (*The American Pageant,* 12th ed., p. 824/11th ed., p. 843).

70. **ANSWER: D.** Chief Justice John Marshall reaffirmed and broadened the government's power to regulate commerce (*The American Pageant,* 12th ed., p. 247/11th ed., pp. 248-249).

71. **ANSWER: A.** The textile workers received increases in wages, overtime pay, and other concessions from management.

72. **ANSWER: A.** The case was heard in 1819 (*The American Pageant,* 12th ed., p. 247/11th ed., p. 248).

73. **ANSWER: D.** Johnson ran afoul of the radical Republicans, who used his violation of the Tenure of Office Act as grounds for impeachment (*The American Pageant,* 12th ed., pp. 494-495/11th ed., p. 504).

74. **ANSWER: E.** Although a military victory for the United States and South Vietnam, the massive Tet offensive demonstrated that the end of the war was not in sight, as claimed by the government (*The American Pageant,* 12th ed., p. 937/11th ed., p. 937).

75. **ANSWER: C.** Labor had long wanted to abolish yellow-dog contracts, which compelled workers to sign an agreement that they would not join a union (*The American Pageant,* 12th ed., p. 772/11th ed., p. 790).

76. **ANSWER: B.** The Chinese Exclusion Act kept that ethnic group from immigrating to the United States in this period (*The American Pageant,* 12th ed., p. 513/11th ed., p. 525).

77. **ANSWER: A.** The plan was intended to make Native Americans individual property owners and thus break up tribal communal property (*The American Pageant,* 12th ed., p. 597/11th ed., p. 604).

78. **ANSWER: C.** Cleveland is also the only president to have been elected to two nonconsecutive terms (*The American Pageant,* 12th ed., p. 518/11th ed., p 531).

79. **ANSWER: A.** Under President George H. W. Bush, the United States and U.N. allies drove the Iraqi army from Kuwait (*The American Pageant,* 12th ed., pp. 995-996/11th ed., 1010-1011).

80. **ANSWER: B.** On October 20, 1973, President Nixon ordered that the special prosecutor in charge of the Watergate investigation be fired. When the attorney general and the deputy attorney general refused to carry out his orders, they were forced to resign. The event further tarnished Nixon's reputation (*The American Pageant,* 12th ed., p. 957/11th ed., p 975).

Answers for Section II, Part A: Document-Based Question (DBQ)

Below are short analyses of the documents. The italicized words suggest what your margin notes might include.

Document A In this letter to a northerner, *a desperate black Alabaman* pleads to be given the means to come to the North *to escape the discrimination, intimidation, and threats of violence* that defined the lives of black Americans in the South *around the time the United States entered World War I,* a conflict in which black soldiers fought nobly.

Document B This map and pie chart show that the *Voting Rights Act of 1965 enfranchised considerably more black southerners* than before the legislation was passed. Take note of *Mississippi as a stunning example of this change.*

Document C This photograph of *CORE* (Congress of Racial Equality) *members and supporters—blacks and whites--mobilizing* to promote equal rights. While the photo does not have a date, take note of the evidence that may provide you with a time frame. For example, one demonstrator is carrying a sign with the words *"We Shall Overcome,"* which was an *unofficial motto of the civil rights movement* in the 1950s and 1960s. Another demonstrator is carrying a sign that *demands equal education,* which may place this demonstration around the time the Supreme Court handed down its decision in *Brown v. Board of Education of Topeka, Kansas case.*

Document D This document discusses the *reaction of black Chicagoans* to the *murder of a young black swimmer* who had inadvertently drifted into a *segregated white bathing area* on Lake Michigan. The event *touched off one of the worst race riots in the nation's history.* The time and place of the riot indicate that even as late as the *post-World War I period northern blacks faced discrimination and segregation* like that found in the South, and they were *angered by their treatment* to the point where they *struck back at their oppressors.* In other words, *migration north was not synonymous with equality.*

Document E In this document the *French military* provides its troops with *advice regarding the complexities and nuances of American racism* so that they *would not antagonize or alienate the white American troops fighting in France.* Take note of the comment regarding *black officers, who were also relegated to a second-class status.*

Document F This photograph shows what happened to *black and white civil rights protestors* when they *attempted to integrate a segregated lunch counter* in Greensboro, North Carolina, in the early 1960s. *Humiliation is the tactic used by those who refuse to accept federal law and Supreme Court decisions outlawing segregation.* Using *peaceful, nonviolent resistance* as espoused by *Dr. Martin Luther King, Jr.,* the protestors in fact *compel the racist mob to act in a humiliating manner* by resorting to this type of reprehensible behavior.

DOCUMENT G This photograph shows a *volunteer white teacher* educating blacks in *1964* as part of *Freedom Summer.*

DOCUMENT H Taken in the early 1900s, this *photograph of the lynching and burning of a black man* has taken on an *atmosphere of amusement* judging from the facial expressions of the onlookers. You are left to draw your own conclusion about the *extent of "justice" meted out to black Americans* during this period in U.S. history.

DOCUMENT I While this *map shows some improvement in integrating public schools,* with the exception of Missouri, Oklahoma, Kentucky, and West Virginia, the *extent of improvement is negligible in the South. Contrast this map with Document B* (Black Registration in the South, 1964). *While Mississippi has registered a considerable number of black voters by 1965, schools in the state were still not integrated.*

One way to designate each document is by its basis—political, social, or economic. Keep in mind that some have more than one designation. This form of categorization can be seen below:

Political	Social	Economic
A	A	A
B		
C	C	C
	D	
	E	
F	F	F
		G
H		H
	I	

In developing your essay, you should incorporate the following historical information:

- The legitimization of racial segregation was articulated in the *Plessy v. Ferguson* decision in 1896, in which the Supreme Court ruled that as long as facilities were equal for the races, segregation was constitutional.
- A number of significant groups formed early in the twentieth century, among them the Niagara Movement in 1905, the NAACP in 1908, the National Urban League in 1911, and the United Negro Improvement Association in 1916.
- The rise in popularity of the KKK in the 1920s was profound.
- The Committee on Civil Rights was formed in 1946.
- The federal government and the military were desegregated in 1948.
- The Supreme Court decision in *Brown v. Board of Education of Topeka, Kansas* in 1954 was a watershed.
- Demographics changed as more and more blacks migrated north.
- Important black political leaders such as Dr. Martin Luther King, Jr., and Malcolm X emerged. In addition, after World War II more civil

rights organizations such as the Southern Christian Leadership Conference (SCLC), the Black Muslim movement, and, in the 1960s, the Student Non-Violent Coordinating Committee (SNCC) formed.

- The Montgomery bus boycott focused national attention on the plight of blacks.
- Nonviolent protests were aimed at segregated lunch counters, bus terminals, hotels, and other public facilities.
- Freedom Summer (1964) was an effort to register southern blacks to vote and provide educational support for the underfunded black communities in the South.
- Congress passed important legislation such as the Civil Rights Act of 1964 and the Voting Rights Act of 1965.

A Sample Essay

If you take the view that racism was prevalent from World War I to the 1960s, your essay might look something like this:

While some substantial gains were made in combating racism in the period from World War I to the 1960s, a legacy of racism and discrimination lingered in the United States in the 1960s. Despite the fact that President Wilson had claimed that the United States was fighting in World War I to "make the world safe for democracy," this obviously did not include black Americans, quite a few of whom actually were doing the fighting in Europe. In 1916, the year before the United States entered World War I, President Wilson won passage of the Jones Act, which gave Filipinos basic democratic rights, including universal male suffrage. The same cannot be said of Wilson's attitudes towards black Americans. As a Virginian he was steeped in the racial ideology of the South. To avoid offending those Americans, in both the North and the South, who opposed racial equality, the French military advised its troops not to treat black Americans soldiers as equal to white American soldiers. "We cannot deal with them [black officers] on the same plane as with white American officers without deeply wounding the latter" (Document E).

So poor were conditions for black southerners that they were relegated to living out their lives in quiet desperation as sharecroppers and tenant farmers. The material demands of the war provided some opportunities for blacks to migrate north if they could, as expressed in Document A, in which a desperate black migrant appeals for assistance to move his family to the North in order to escape the persecution, intimidation, and violence associated with the South in this period. For those blacks who challenged the status quo or who broke the law, a different kind of "justice" was meted out, as shown in Document H, a photograph of a black man who has been lynched and his body burned as a warning to other blacks. In fact, so frequent were cases of lynching during the World War I era that the NAACP would hang a banner outside one of its northern offices that read: "Today a black man was lynched in the South." Not surprisingly, the Ku Klux Klan experienced a massive rebirth during the postwar years. Yet this period witnessed the emergence of important black civil rights organizations such as the Niagara Movement, led by W. E. B. Du Bois.

Unfortunately, by World War II attitudes had not dramatically changed in the United States in regards to its black citizens. The nation, including the military, continued to be segregated (a condition legitimized by the *Plessy v. Ferguson* Supreme Court decision in 1896). It was not until after the war that the military and the federal government were desegregated. In 1954 the Supreme Court overturned *Plessy* in its landmark decision in *Brown v. Board of Education of Topeka, Kansas.* Yet, in 1964, Mississippi schools were still not integrated (Document I). Although it was now unconstitutional to segregate the races, racist attitudes take a longer time to die.

To be sure, there were successes along the way, such as the Montgomery bus boycott, led by Dr. Martin Luther King, Jr. Also various southern universities such as the University of Alabama were integrated. Added to this was the passage of the Civil Rights Act in 1964 and the Voting Rights Act the following year, which went a long way in integrating public schools in the South. As more and more blacks and whites began to protest against racial injustice, discrimination, and segregation, many in the South responded shamefully and at times violently, as expressed in the southern response to Freedom Summer (1964), which sought to register blacks to vote and provide educational assistance (Document G). We see this clearly in Document F, showing white segregationists attempting to humiliate those nonviolent protestors at a lunch counter in the South. Thus by the middle of the 1960s the government and civil rights activists had taken significant steps to address racial discrimination, but the attitudes of the World War I era continued unabated well into the 1960s.

COMMENT This essay effectively synthesized document information—six of the nine documents—with appropriate comments and analysis of important outside information relating to the topic. The view that racial attitudes were maintained throughout the period from World War I to the 1960s despite some important civil rights gains is sustained throughout the essay.

SCORING The DBQ essay counts for 45 percent of the total free-response grade, or 22.5 percent of the total examination grade.

ANSWERS FOR SECTION II, PART B AND PART C

QUESTION 2 Some would argue that the relationship between Great Britain and the American colonies prior to 1763 was based on salutary neglect. That is, Britain at this point had not placed restrictions on the colonists that were either exploitative or hard to avoid. Prior to 1763 the British had not yet imposed revenue-raising taxes on the colonies. In the French and Indian War the colonists aided the British in defeating France and its colonists, eventually helping the mother country expand its North American territory.

Others might argue that the relationship between Britain and the American colonies was far from neglectful or salutary. In fact the British sought to control and subordinate American trade and the American economy to its own needs. The Navigation Laws were a series of British laws that attempted to expand Britain's economy, often at the expense of the American colonies. Further, the British government imposed regulations on American industry that had the desired effect—from the British perspective—of stifling the growth of American capitalism.

In order to develop a strong thesis that indicates the relationship as one based on salutary neglect, you should build on the view that Britain had no strong desire to subordinate the American economy, nor did it yet have a need to compel the colonists to pay for the costs of empire. Although the French and Indian War did strain the relationship, the colonists and the mother country had similar objectives. To this end a discussion of the Albany Congress would be beneficial. Also, as for trade restrictions, a very good essay would point out that the British did not enforce the Navigation Laws and that Americans often violated the laws by smuggling commodities. To develop the perspective that the relationship between the colonists and Britain was strained prior to 1763, an effective essay would discuss the British policy of subordinating American capitalism to British capitalism. To support this view a discussion of specific British policies such as the Navigation Laws, Hat Act, Iron Act, and Wool Act is necessary. These acts were designed by Britain to prevent competition from its own colonies.

QUESTION 3 To many historians the brilliance of the Framers of the U.S. Constitution is that they were able to compromise on a variety of issues and concerns in the midst of class, sectional, and philosophical suspicions and tension. For example, since the states were not equal in size and population, the Framers had to determine a structure that would prevent a "tyranny of the majority" and a "tyranny of the minority." The Articles of Confederation had a unicameral legislature in which each state was granted one vote regardless of its population. Representation based on population would benefit states with large populations, like Virginia or Pennsylvania, while diminishing the influence of states with smaller populations, like Delaware and Rhode Island. Thus a two-house legislature was agreed to, one based on population, the other providing equal representation regardless of population.

The Framers also found a way to compromise over slavery, at least in a limited way. A slave was to be counted as three-fifths of a person for purposes of representation and taxation. After 1808 slaves could no longer be imported, thus ending the slave trade—but not slavery. That would be an issue for a later generation to resolve.

One of the more controversial aspects of the new government was the question of individual rights under the Constitution, which provided for a considerably stronger central government and executive branch than did the AOC. Having recently won its independence from a monarchical system, many Americans were concerned that the new government would abuse its powers and deny Americans the rights they assumed they had won in the Revolutionary War. These individuals insisted that basic rights be identified in the Constitution in the form of a bill of rights. Opponents claimed that because the people would elect their representatives, these elected officials would preserve their rights. What is more, opponents of a bill of rights claimed there was an assumption that all rights were protected under the Constitution and that the identification of certain rights would in fact limit citizen rights to a specific list. In the end the Bill of Rights was added in order to convince wary states to ratify the Constitution. Thus the Framers were able to compromise on a number of serious issues and establish a Constitution that has stood the rest of time.

An easy way to organize this discussion is to make references to the supporters of the ratification of the Constitution, the Federalists, and the opponents of ratification, the antifederalists. While there continues to be controversy over the various compromises made at the Constitutional Convention, in this essay you need to identify those compromises that shaped the Constitutional Convention. For example, you should discuss the Great Compromise, which provided for a two-house legislature: the House of Representatives (representation based on population) and a Senate (equal state representation). A brief discussion of federalism is also important to the quality of this essay, and though the options do not include states' rights, the political system created by the Framers reserved powers to the states, thus neutralizing some of the accusation that the Constitution would establish a tyrannical central government. To this end the term of the president was limited to four years; furthermore, the other two branches of government could check the power and authority of the chief executive.

As for slavery, the Constitution did not abolish the institution because the South would never have gone along with such an idea, especially because some of the southern delegates were themselves slaveowners. At the very least the slave trade was allowed to continue only until 1808. The southern delegates also maintained that they would be underrepresented in the new government. You should thus discuss the three-fifths compromise, which allowed for the South to count a slave as three-fifths of a person for purposes of representation *and* taxation.

In discussing the degree to which democratic rights would be preserved by the Constitution, you should point out that some Revolutionary War leaders such as Patrick Henry refused to attend the Constitutional Convention because they were suspicious of an attempt to establish a tyrannical government. For this reason a brief discussion of the controversy surrounding the addition of a bill of rights is necessary. Point out that the Bill of Rights was added after the Constitution was ratified, as promised by the supporters of ratification. If time permits, provide a brief discussion of several of these first ten amendments as a means of identifying specifically what rights needed to be protected.

QUESTION 4 Despite being elected to four terms, more than any other president in U.S. history, FDR was certainly not without his critics. Attacks came from both ends of the political spectrum—from those who were anxious about the expansion of government authority and spending during the 1930s, and those who maintained that the New Deal was undermining American capitalism or was not going far enough in addressing the maladies that plagued the nation. Some claimed that Roosevelt wielded unprecedented and dangerous powers that would upset the constitutional balances that prevailed between the branches of government. To be sure, FDR did not diminish these concerns when he introduced his Court-packing scheme in 1937.

Well before this ill-advised maneuver, however, Senator Huey Long, the powerful demagogue from Louisiana, had posed a significant challenge to FDR's reelection bid, in 1932. Long's Share-Our-Wealth plan was poised to steal some of the president's thunder by introducing a program that seemed to the millions suffering from the effects of the Great Depression an even more promising and far-reaching solution to their condition than that offered by the president. Others challenged Roosevelt as well, such as the "radio priest" Father Charles Coughlin and Dr. Francis E Townsend, both of whom offered economic plans that appealed to the suffering masses of Americans hurt by the collapse of the economy.

Liberals, socialists, and conservatives attacked the New Deal as well. On the one hand, those on the left of the political spectrum maintained that the New Deal was addressing almost exclusively the concerns and interests of white Americans, whereas conservatives contended that the New Deal was undermining the American free- enterprise system. Thus Roosevelt's New Deal philosophy and programs were contested by critics who offered what they considered to be a better, more comprehensive solution to the economic problems facing the nation and by critics who believed that FDR's solution to the Great Depression was worse than the problem itself.

In constructing your essay you should indicate that FDR and the New Deal at no time had universal support. In fact, from the time he took office and began his first Hundred Days Roosevelt was under attack from disparate forces. Coughlin, a onetime supporter of the New Deal, turned on Roosevelt, claiming the president was a tool of the moneyed elites, such as bankers and financial leaders, whom he claimed were responsible for the collapse of the economy. Townsend's plan was to establish a program to help the elderly and stimulate the economy by creating a program funded by a sales or transaction tax in which those over age sixty would receive $200 monthly on the condition they spend the stipend, thus stimulating demand and therefore increasing employment. As for Long, you should indicate that the Louisiana senator posed a significant challenge to Roosevelt's 1932 reelection bid by offering a program that guaranteed an annual income of $5,000 to every family, which would be funded by a tax on the wealthy.

It is important that you emphasize that attacks on the New Deal came from both ends of the political spectrum. Liberals and socialists, for example, attacked the New Deal for being probusiness and for neglecting the needs of those most hurt by the depression: the unemployed, minorities, and women. The right attacked the New Deal as a program that was systematically undermining American capitalism. To these critics the New Deal solutions to the economic maladies confronting the nation would be, in the long term, more dangerous than the Great Depression itself. The conservatives argued that the New Deal was dangerously expanding the power of the government to regulate business, that it was pro-labor and, what is more, was dabbling in what conservatives contended was a ruinous financial solution to the depression, deficit spending.

QUESTION 5 In the early 1960s the U.S. government had been attempting to bolster the government of South Vietnam economically and militarily. By 1964 U.S. involvement increased profoundly. That year President Johnson reported that U.S. warships had been attacked by North Vietnam in the Gulf of Tonkin. In the Tonkin Gulf Resolution Congress gave Johnson the funds necessary to repel future attacks, extending to the president what amounted to a blank check to wage war in Vietnam.

Over the next few years U.S. military intervention increased significantly. By 1968 the United States had over half a million troops in Vietnam. Between 1965 and 1968 the American public had begun to raise questions about the success of military operations in Vietnam. Protests began to break out as Americans increasingly sought a resolution to the war. The Tet offensive, launched by the North Vietnamese and Vietcong on January 30, 1968, was the final straw for many Americans. Despite claims by the administration that the end of the war was in sight, the Tet offensive indicated that this was not the case. By March 1968 the war had so divided the nation that Johnson chose not to run for reelection.

The new president, Richard Nixon, sought to reduce U.S. involvement while avoiding the impression that the United States was accepting defeat in Vietnam. His policy of Vietnamization was an attempt to pull the United States out of the war gradually. For many Americans this process was too slow; they favored an immediate withdrawal. Almost nightly television reports indicated the futility of sustaining operations in Indochina. As U.S. and Vietnamese casualties mounted and with no end to the war in sight, Americans began protesting in increasing numbers, fueled by the shocking report that U.S. troops had massacred South Vietnamese women and children in the village of My Lai. When Nixon expanded the war into Cambodia, antiwar protests intensified. Added to this was the publication of the Pentagon Papers by the *New York Times* and the *Washington Post,* which revealed how the government had misled the American people and provided false reports on events in Vietnam. By this point more Americans than not opposed continued U.S. intervention in Vietnam. Over time, American public opinion had shifted away from supporting to opposing the war, which in turn had influenced the U.S. government to end American involvement in the war.

In constructing this essay you should indicate the transformation that occurred within a relatively short period of time. That is, Americans had generally and initially supported U.S. military intervention in Southeast Asia as a necessary measure to contain the spread of communism. Television, however, played a major role in depicting the war in a way that became increasingly troubling for many Americans. Search-and-destroy missions, massive bombing raids on Hanoi, North Vietnam, the use of defoliants and napalm, and the destruction of South Vietnamese villages only added to the public's growing anxiety. Your essay should also point out the government's misleading claim that the end of the war was in sight. The Tet offensive in 1968 proved otherwise: the North Vietnamese and Vietcong had the ability to launch a massive attack on South Vietnamese cities and military bases. At home antiwar demonstrations were turning deadly. Students were killed by police and National Guard units on two such occasions: at Jackson State University in Mississippi and Kent State University in Ohio. Now Americans were dying *in* the United States over the war in Southeast Asia. The publication of the Pentagon Papers only intensified antiwar sentiment that, in turn, played a primary role in ending U.S. military involvement in Vietnam by 1973.

SCORING Together the two free-response essays from Part B and Part C count for 55 percent of the free-response essay grade, or 27.5 percent of your total examination grade.

Grade your essays on a score of 0–9.

8-9: EXCELLENT The essay has a clear thesis, is well written and organized, covers all aspects of the essay in depth, analyzes the question effectively, and supports the thesis with sufficient and relevant historical information. It may contain minor errors.

5-7: GOOD The essay has a clear thesis, though it is not as well developed as in an 8-9 essay. It has clear though not excellent organization. The essay covers only one aspect of the question in depth and does not fully indicate an understanding of the complexity of the question or topic. The analysis is not as well developed as in an 8-9 essay and makes limited use of relevant historical information. The essay may contain errors that do not affect the overall quality of the essay.

2-4: FAIR The essay either lacks a clear thesis or the thesis is confused or even missing. It is not well organized and exhibits weak writing. It does not indicate an understanding of the complexity of the question or topic, and it fails to support a thesis with sufficient historical information and/or analysis. It may contain significant errors.

0-1: POOR The essay has no thesis, poor structure and organization, is poorly written, lacks historical information and analysis, and tends to offer rhetorical comments. It contains both major and minor errors.

It is important that you be as objective as possible when evaluating your essays. You might ask a teacher, parent, fellow student, or friend to evaluate your essays for you.

CALCULATING YOUR SCORE

SCORING THE MULTIPLE-CHOICE SECTION

Use the following formula to calculate your raw score on the multiple-choice section of the exam:

$$\underline{\hspace{2cm}} - (\underline{\hspace{2cm}} \times 1/4) = \underline{\hspace{2cm}} \text{ (round to nearest whole number)}$$

    number   number   raw
    correct   incorrect   score

SCORING THE FREE-RESPONSE SECTION

Use the formula below to calculate your raw score on the free-response section of the exam:

$$(\underline{\hspace{1cm}} \times 4) + (\underline{\hspace{1cm}} \times 2.44) + (\underline{\hspace{1cm}} \times 2.44) = \underline{\hspace{1cm}} \text{ (round to nearest whole number)}$$

  DBQ   essay   essay   raw
           # 1   # 2   score

YOUR COMPOSITE SCORE

$$1.13 \times \underline{\hspace{2cm}} = \underline{\hspace{2cm}} \text{ (weighted multiple-choice score: NOT rounded)}$$

       multiple-   raw
       choice   score

$$2.73 \times \underset{\substack{\text{free-}\\\text{response}}}{\underline{\hspace{2cm}}} = \underset{\substack{\text{raw}\\\text{score}}}{\underline{\hspace{2cm}}} \text{ (weighted free-response score: NOT rounded)}$$

Once you have completed your calculations, add the two weighted sections (and round to the nearest whole number). You now have your composite score. Now see where your score falls in the Composite Score Range below. Remember that this score is an estimate of your performance on the College Board exam.

AP GRADES BY SCORE RANGE

AP Grade	Composite Score Range
5	114–180
4	91–113
3	74–90
2	49–73
1	0–48

Practice Test 2

AP UNITED STATES HISTORY EXAMINATION

Section I: Multiple-Choice Questions
Time—55 minutes
Number of questions—80

Directions Each question or incomplete statement below has five possible answers. For each question, select the best response.

1. The roots of intolerance that influenced the 1920s can best be seen in all of the following EXCEPT
   - (A) the conviction and execution of Ethel and Julius Rosenberg for passing on atomic secrets to the Soviets
   - (B) the imprisonment of Eugene Debs for violating the Espionage Act
   - (C) the Sedition Act of 1917
   - (D) the East St. Louis race riot
   - (E) the trial of IWW members

2. In the 1920s the reborn Ku Klux Klan
   - (A) focused its enmity entirely on black Americans
   - (B) identified with the qualities of urban and cosmopolitan values
   - (C) strongly endorsed women's rights, including the right to vote
   - (D) turned its wrath on Catholics, Jews, immigrants, and blacks
   - (E) became the voice of moderate social reform in the South and the Midwest

3. Keynesian economics
   - (A) was adopted by the Reagan administration in order to stimulate consumer demand
   - (B) is most associated with the policies of Herbert Hoover in the first two years of the Great Depression
   - (C) is synonymous with the Roosevelt administration's deficit spending to stimulate the economy
   - (D) was the justification for Hamilton's support for the Bank of the United States
   - (E) was blamed for causing the Great Depression

4. Which of the following was NOT part of the coalition that comprised the Populists in the late nineteenth century?
   - (A) free-silver advocates
   - (B) socialists
   - (C) anarchists
   - (D) Farmers' Alliance
   - (E) grain-elevator operators

5. Which of the following was NOT a problem that faced the United States *immediately* after the end of World War II?
   - (A) reconversion from wartime to consumer-based economy
   - (B) housing shortage
   - (C) inflation
   - (D) rebuilding sections of the nation that had been destroyed by the war
   - (E) unemployment

6. Richard Nixon's vice president, Spiro Agnew, was forced to resign his office because
   - (A) it was revealed that he had provided the Soviets with nuclear secrets
   - (B) the press reported that he had been a member of the Ku Klux Klan earlier in his political career
   - (C) he had helped to plan the Watergate break-in

(D) as governor of Maryland he had received payoffs from businessmen, which he did not report to the IRS

(E) Agnew had publicly opposed and criticized Nixon for visiting communist China

7. In the mid-nineteenth century, strong opposition arose in the United States to immigrants who came from
(A) Eastern Europe
(B) Russia
(C) the Mediterranean countries
(D) South America
(E) Ireland and Germany

8. Which of the following is consistent with President Lincoln's attitudes about slavery?
(A) He sought to contain the spread of slavery, not abolish it.
(B) He fought long and hard against the activities of the American Colonization Society.
(C) He encouraged Congress to ratify the Thirteenth Amendment, which drove Southern states out of the Union.
(D) He firmly believed that black Americans were equal to white Americans in every way.
(E) His opposition to slavery was moral, not political.

9. The Emancipation Proclamation
(A) ended slavery in the entire United States
(B) ended slavery only in the Border States
(C) was rejected by Southern congressmen who prevented Lincoln from issuing it
(D) abolished slavery in those states that were in open rebellion against the U.S. government
(E) was a major factor in the Southern states' decision to secede from the United States and form their own government

Evolution of Major Parties*

Year	Hamiltonians		Jeffersonians
c. 1792	Federalists		Democratic-Republicans
c. 1816	Death of Federalists		
c. 1820		Republicans One party: Era of Good Feelings	
c. 1825	National Republicans		Democratic-Republicans (Jacksonian Democrats)
1834	Whigs		Democrats
1854	Republicans		
	To Present		To Present

10. Which of the following statements about the flow chart above, which shows the evolution of the major parties, is INCORRECT?
(A) The Democrats evolved from the Whigs.
(B) The demise of the Federalist party occurred in 1816.
(C) The Jacksonian Democrats evolved from the Democratic Republicans.
(D) The Hamiltonians and the Jeffersonians evolved into the Federalists and the Democratic-Republicans.
(E) During the Era of Good Feelings there existed only one major political party.

11. General Douglas MacArthur was dismissed as commander of U.N. forces fighting in the Korean War because
(A) he claimed that the war could not be won
(B) he publicly criticized President Truman's handling of the war
(C) Republican conservatives in Congress believed he was too "soft" on communism
(D) he opposed the containment policy, preferring instead to co-exist with communist nations
(E) he launched an unauthorized attack on Communist China

12. The Taft-Hartley Act
(A) was warmly embraced by labor unions as legislation that favored

the rights of the nation's working class

(B) was passed by a Republican Congress over President Truman's veto

(C) limited immigration from South America and Asia

(D) made it a federal offense to advocate the overthrow of the U.S. government

(E) was a key feature of the progressives' goal of assimilating new immigrants into American culture

13. Which of the following is NOT associated with radical Republican Reconstruction?
(A) Jim Crow laws
(B) the Wade-Davis Bill
(C) the Fourteenth Amendment
(D) the Fifteenth Amendment
(E) the Tenure of Office Act

14. Which of the following initially supported the New Deal but later became a harsh critic of Roosevelt and the New Deal?
(A) the Ku Klux Klan
(B) Father Charles Coughlin
(C) Upton Sinclair
(D) the American Communist Party
(E) Senator Huey Long

15. This labor union was formed right after the end of the Civil War and was the first major union to organize workers regardless of their race, gender, or skill level.
(A) Knights of Labor
(B) American Federation of Labor
(C) Congress of Industrial Organizations
(D) National Labor Union
(E) Industrial Workers of the World

16. All of the following acts were passed in order to promote Britain's mercantilist policy EXCEPT
(A) the Virginia resolutions
(B) the Navigation Laws
(C) the Iron Act
(D) the Wool Act
(E) the Sugar Act

17. The Treaty of Tordesillas
(A) ended the French and Indian War
(B) gave to Spain control of the Mississippi River
(C) was the papacy's plan to prevent conflict between Portugal and Spain as a result of their competition to acquire colonies.
(D) allowed French Canadians to continue to practice Catholicism after the French and Indian War
(E) ended the Mexican-American War

18. The Populist party platform included all of the following EXCEPT
(A) land grants given to railroad companies not used by the railroads should be returned to the government
(B) a graduated income tax
(C) a gold- and silver-based currency
(D) the referendum
(E) government ownership of the railroads

19. Which of the following is associated with the post-World War II civil rights movement?
(A) *Plessy v. Ferguson*
(B) Black Codes
(C) Jim Crow laws
(D) *Brown v. Board of Education of Topeka, Kansas*
(E) *Williams v. Mississippi*

20. Which of the following is associated with the transcendentalist movement of the early nineteenth century?
(A) F. Scott Fitzgerald
(B) Henry David Thoreau
(C) Ernest Hemingway
(D) Mark Twain
(E) John Steinbeck

21. Which of the following did NOT occur during the Cold War?
(A) the U-2 incident
(B) the Palmer raids
(C) the Marshall Plan
(D) the Truman Doctrine
(E) the formation of NATO

22. This Supreme Court case upheld a state law limiting maximum working hours for women:
    (A) *Muller v. Oregon*
    (B) *McCulloch v. Maryland*
    (C) *William v. Mississippi*
    (D) *Munn v. Illinois*
    (E) *Texas v. White*

23. The impressments of American sailors was an important cause of
    (A) the American Revolution
    (B) the War of 1812
    (C) the Mexican-American War
    (D) the Spanish-American War
    (E) World War I

24. All of the following are groups of contemporaries EXCEPT
    (A) Abraham Lincoln, Charles Sumner, Jefferson Davis
    (B) Martin Luther King, Jr., John F. Kennedy, Malcolm X
    (C) Thomas Jefferson, Henry Clay, William McKinley
    (D) Theodore Roosevelt, William Howard Taft, Woodrow Wilson
    (E) Elizabeth Cady Stanton, Horace Mann, Lucretia Mott

25. The Gag Resolution was adopted by the U.S. Senate in order to
    (A) provide a greater opportunity for junior senators to speak
    (B) prevent senators from disparaging U.S. foreign policy
    (C) prevent political differences from turning violent
    (D) prevent a senator from engaging in a filibuster
    (E) prevent senators from discussing abolitionist proposals

26. The first Southern state to be readmitted into the Union during Reconstruction was
    (A) Virginia
    (B) South Carolina
    (C) Tennessee
    (D) Texas
    (E) North Carolina

27. As a result of the Spanish-American War, which of the following was ceded to the United States?
    (A) Haiti
    (B) Jamaica
    (C) Indonesia
    (D) the Philippines
    (E) New Guinea

28. Which of the following is NOT associated with the presidency of Jimmy Carter?
    (A) Limited Test Ban Treaty
    (B) inflation
    (C) the Iran hostage crisis
    (D) establishing the cabinet-level Department of Energy
    (E) the return of the Panama Canal to the Panamanians

29. Booker T. Washington
    (A) found an ally in the black civil rights movement in W. E. B. Du Bois
    (B) believed that blacks should forgo political equality until they achieved economic success
    (C) demanded that blacks receive full political, economic, and social equality without hesitation
    (D) was the first black American to be appointed to the U.S. Supreme Court
    (E) assisted Martin Luther King, Jr., in organizing the Southern Christian Leadership Conference

30. The Federal Reserve Act
    (A) removed all decisions regarding the economy from state control
    (B) established a large surplus of gold and silver specie to be used in times of national crisis
    (C) was the first major reform of the nation's banking system since the Civil War
    (D) was ruled unconstitutional by the Supreme Court
    (E) was established during the Nixon administration

31. Geraldine Ferraro
    (A) was the first female Speaker of the House
    (B) was the nation's first female cabinet member
    (C) helped organize the International Ladies' Garment Workers Union
    (D) was arrested in the 1950s for selling nuclear secrets to the Soviets
    (E) was the first woman to run for vice president

32. Which of the following statements best articulates President Andrew Jackson's policy towards Native Americans?
    (A) Jackson believed that Native Americans should be relocated outside the United States.
    (B) Jackson firmly supported the decisions handed down by the Marshall Court regarding Native Americans.
    (C) Jackson was arguably the best friend Native Americans had in the White House up to that point.
    (D) Jackson favored a policy whereby Native Americans would be forced to migrate west.
    (E) Jackson believed that the U.S. government had no authority to remove Native Americans from their land.

33. Which of the following best articulates the meaning of the Monroe Doctrine?
    (A) It reaffirmed the concept of self-determination for all nations.
    (B) It was used to justify U.S. intervention in World War I.
    (C) It warned the European powers not to attempt recolonization in the Western Hemisphere.
    (D) It became the basis for American isolationism in the early nineteenth century.
    (E) It established the principle that the United States was justified in attempting to create a global empire.

34. Marcus Garvey's Universal Negro Improvement Association
    (A) found considerable support among blacks in northern urban areas
    (B) was affiliated with the Freedmen's Bureau during Reconstruction
    (C) separated from Martin Luther King, Jr.'s Southern Christian Leadership Conference because King's organization was too moderate
    (D) attempted to organize a labor union that would include black and white workers
    (E) was successful only in rural southern communities

35. In order to ensure that his reform programs would not be ruled unconstitutional by the conservative majority on the Supreme Court, this president attempted to increase the number of Supreme Court justices from nine to fifteen.
    (A) Abraham Lincoln
    (B) Woodrow Wilson
    (C) Franklin D. Roosevelt
    (D) Richard Nixon
    (E) Ronald Reagan

36. In the nineteenth century the federal government helped to settle the Great Plains with the passage of this act:
    (A) the Newlands Reclamation Act
    (B) the Morrill Land Grant Act
    (C) the Forest Reserve Act
    (D) the Northwest Ordinance
    (E) the Homestead Act

37. In 1911 a horrific fire that killed over 140 workers, many young women, and led to reforms that addressed lax building codes occurred at the factory of which company?
    (A) McCormick Reaper Company
    (B) Rockefeller Oil Company
    (C) U.S Steel Company
    (D) Triangle Shirtwaist Company
    (E) Union Iron Mills

38. Which of the following statements best describes the U.S. government's policy in the Spanish Civil War?
    (A) The United States maintained a policy of neutrality.
    (B) The United States asked the League of Nations not to intervene.
    (C) The United States secretly provided Franco's forces with military supplies and economic aid.
    (D) The United States sent thousands of troops to act as a peacekeeping force.
    (E) The United States provided the Loyalists with weapons and supplies.

39. This president sent a naval force to fight against the Barbary pirates.
    (A) George Washington
    (B) John Adams
    (C) Thomas Jefferson
    (D) William McKinley
    (E) Theodore Roosevelt

40. "Article III: The Government of Cuba consents that the United States may exercise the right to intervene for the preservation of Cuban independence..." This is an excerpt from
    (A) the Zimmerman note
    (B) the Webster-Ashburton Treaty
    (C) the Treaty of Guadalupe Hidalgo
    (D) the Platt Amendment
    (E) the Teller Amendment

41. Which one of the following did President Andrew Jackson veto because he maintained it was unconstitutional?
    (A) the Agricultural Adjustment Act
    (B) the Tennessee Valley Authority
    (C) the Maysville Road Bill
    (D) the Wade-Davis Bill
    (E) the Taft-Hartley Act

42. Which of the following is NOT associated with the war in Vietnam?
    (A) General Douglas MacArthur
    (B) The Pentagon Papers
    (C) The Tet offensive
    (D) The Gulf of Tonkin incident
    (E) Ho Chi Minh

43. The Albany Congress of 1754 was an assembly of seven colonies that sought to improve relations with which Native American tribe?
    (A) Seminole
    (B) Iroquois
    (C) Sioux
    (D) Cheyenne
    (E) Apache

44. "Dixiecrats"
    (A) was the name given to pro-secession politicians on the eve of the Civil War
    (B) were Southerners who opposed the Reconstruction governments imposed on them by Congress
    (C) were Southern Democrats who voted for the Republican presidential candidate Ulysses S. Grant in 1868
    (D) were members of a Southern faction of the Democratic party who opposed their party's 1948 platform on civil rights
    (E) were Northern politicians who were opposed to abolition

45. Which of the following best characterizes the South in the antebellum period?
    (A) The majority of the white population was engaged in sharecropping.
    (B) It had a substantial middle class.
    (C) Vital to the South's economy was manufacturing.
    (D) Most of the South's population lived in urban areas.
    (E) The South was opposed to a high protective tariff.

46. Put the following in the correct order:
    I. Mexican Cession
    II. Louisiana Purchase
    III. Adams-Onis Treaty
    IV. Gadsden Purchase
    (A) II, III, IV, I
    (B) I, II, III, IV
    (C) I, IV, III, II
    (D) II, III, I, IV
    (E) IV, I, III, II

47. The Elkins Act of 1903
    (A) established federal shipping rates for railroad companies
    (B) was the nation's first minimum-wage law
    (C) placed millions of acres of forests under federal protection
    (D) established the nation's first federal income tax
    (E) strengthened the Interstate Commerce Act of 1887

50. The Essex decision, the *Leopard-Chesapeake* incident, and the Berlin Decree are all associated with events that led to
    (A) the War of 1812
    (B) the Mexican War
    (C) the Aroostook War
    (D) the Spanish-American War
    (E) World War I

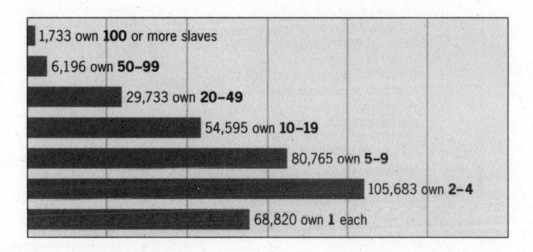

48. Critics referred to this as Seward's Folly:
    (A) an attempt by unscrupulous speculators to corner the gold market after the Civil War
    (B) the purchase of Alaska from the Russians in 1867
    (C) the establishment of an interracial commune in the 1830s
    (D) an attempt by a royal governor to enforce the tea tax following the Boston Tea Party
    (E) a leading abolitionist's effort to convince slave owners to sell their slaves to the federal government

49. In which of the following nations did the United States NOT intervene in the early twentieth century?
    (A) Nicaragua
    (B) Haiti
    (C) Mexico
    (D) Argentina
    (E) Cuba

51. Which of the following statements about the table above is INCORRECT?
    (A) The vast majority of slaveowners owned fewer than one hundred slaves.
    (B) Slightly less than 70,000 slaveowning families owned one slave.
    (C) The largest number of slaveowners owned between five and nine slaves.
    (D) Over 100,000 slaveowning families owned between two and four slaves.
    (E) Only a small percentage of slaveowning families owned one hundred or more slaves.

52. In the election of 1884 the Republican party was divided into conservative and reform-minded factions known as
    (A) Mugwumps and Half-Breeds
    (B) Jayhawkers and Border Ruffians
    (C) Dixiecrats and Progressives
    (D) Wobblies and Molly Maguires
    (E) Hawks and Doves

53. "Muckrakers" was a derisive term used by Theodore Roosevelt to describe
    (A) conservatives in his own party
    (B) his Democratic president and vice presidential opponents in the 1912 election
    (C) rebels in Cuba who were fighting against U.S. occupation
    (D) the Spanish military, which was accused of brutalizing the Cuban people
    (E) journalists whom he claimed were sensationalizing their stories of corrupt business practices

54. In his Farewell Address Washington recommended that
    (A) Native Americans should be moved to reservations out west where their safety would be ensured
    (B) the institution of slavery should be abolished
    (C) states' rights should be paramount to the laws of the federal government
    (D) the United States should maintain a policy of neutrality with other nations
    (E) the U.S. government should adopt policies to promote manufacturing and industry

55. Which of the following played a major role in the First Great Awakening?
    (A) Benjamin Franklin
    (B) George Whitefield
    (C) Elijah P. Lovejoy
    (D) Horace Mann
    (E) Thomas Jefferson

56. This event took place in 1794 when Pennsylvania farmers refused to pay an excise tax.
    (A) Bacon's rebellion
    (B) the actions of the Paxton Boys
    (C) the actions of the Regulators
    (D) the Battle of Wounded Knee
    (E) the Whiskey Rebellion

57. The first United States secretary of war (now defense) was
    (A) Thomas Jefferson
    (B) Ulysses S. Grant
    (C) Andrew Jackson
    (D) Henry Knox
    (E) Jefferson Davis

58. Which of the following would an advocate of states' rights NOT use to support his view?
    (A) the Kentucky and Virginia Resolutions
    (B) nullification
    (C) the Compact Theory of government
    (D) South Carolina Exposition and Protest
    (E) the decisions of the Marshall Court

59. One of the most famous perspectives in the study of U.S. history is Frederick Jackson Turner's frontier thesis, in which he claims that
    (A) the western frontier stimulated the growth of democracy
    (B) most Native Americans were willing to assimilate into American civilization
    (C) had slavery been prohibited in the West, the Civil War would not have occurred
    (D) the West developed manufacturing and industry at a greater rate than the Northeast
    (E) racial and religious disputes prevented the West from fully integrating with the rest of the nation until the twentieth century

Occupational Distribution of Workingwomen, 1900–1998*

	1900	1920	1940	1960	1980	1998
Total white-collar workers†	17.8%	38.8%	44.9%	52.5%	65.6%	73.8%
Clerical workers	4.0	18.7	21.5	28.7	30.5	38.9
Manual workers	27.8	23.8	21.6	18.0	14.8	9.7
Farm workers	18.9	13.5	4.0	1.8	1.0	1.0
Service workers‡	35.5	23.9	29.4	21.9	18.1	15.4

*Major categories; percentage of all women workers, age fourteen and older, in each category.
†Includes clerical, sales, professional, and technical workers, managers and officials.
‡Includes domestic servants.
(Sources: *Historical Statistics of the United States* and *Statistical Abstract of the United States*, relevant years.)

60. Which of the following was NOT a border state in the antebellum period and the Civil War era?
    (A) Kentucky
    (B) Ohio
    (C) Missouri
    (D) Delaware
    (E) Maryland

61. "From Stettin in the Baltic to Trieste in the Adriatic an iron curtain has descended across the continent." What did British Prime Minister Winston Churchill mean when he uttered these words in a speech in 1946?
    (A) The noncommunist nations should roll back communism wherever it exists.
    (B) There should be a thawing of relations between the Soviet Union and the Western allies.
    (C) Europe was divided between two hostile camps, the communist and non-communist nations.
    (D) The United States and Britain should restore international trade.
    (E) Through espionage, the Soviet Union was conspiring to acquire nuclear secrets from the West.

62. Which statement *accurately reflects* the information regarding the occupational distribution of workingwomen from 1900 to 1998 in the table above?
    (A) The percentage of service workers increased between 1900 and 1920, but then declined.
    (B) The percentage of manual workers has steadily increased from 1900 to 1998.
    (C) By 1998 clerical workers comprised the largest percentage of workingwomen.
    (D) The percentage of farm workers has steadily declined from 1900 to 1989.
    (E) The percentage of clerical workers was equal to the percentage of service workers until 1940.

63. This early-twentieth-century leader for educational reform espoused a "learn by doing" approach to education. He was also greatly influenced by a theory of educational knowledge known as pragmatism.
    (A) John Dewey
    (B) Horace Mann
    (C) Henry James
    (D) William Spencer
    (E) Walt Whitman

64. Upton Sinclair's *The Jungle* convinced Congress to
    (A) pass legislation barring slavery from any new territories west of the Mississippi River
    (B) pass the Pure Food and Drug Act
    (C) create the Agricultural Adjustment Administration
    (D) establish a cabinet position for a secretary of the interior
    (E) cut funding for the war in Vietnam

65. A major riot occurred in New York City in July 1863. One of the causes of the riot was
    (A) the terrible treatment of freed blacks by the citizens of the city
    (B) factory owners cut the wages of immigrant workers while leaving the wages of others intact
    (C) strong opposition to the military draft
    (D) the attempt by city officials to integrate the city's public schools
    (E) that banks closed their doors to prevent depositors from withdrawing their money after the stock market collapsed

66. An example of government corruption in the post-Reconstruction era is
    (A) the Watergate scandal
    (B) the Pentagon Papers
    (C) the Teapot Dome scandal
    (D) the Crédit Mobilier scandal
    (E) the Ludlow massacre

67. The Constitutional Convention's Great Compromise of 1787 addressed
    (A) the abolition of slavery
    (B) whether to grant women the right to vote
    (C) the need for a strong executive branch of government
    (D) whether to provide the federal government the power to tax imports
    (E) how states would be represented in Congress

68. The Republican party in the antebellum period comprised all of the following EXCEPT
    (A) Southern planter-slaveholders
    (B) Free-Soilers
    (C) Northern Democrats who felt betrayed by their party's support for the Kansas-Nebraska Act
    (D) members of the Whig party who favored containing slavery
    (E) various labor groups in the North

69. Charles Frémont
    (A) was placed in command of Union forces at the First Battle of Bull Run
    (B) was sent by President Buchanan to open Japan to U.S. trade
    (C) was the Republican party's first presidential candidate
    (D) was governor of South Carolina when it seceded from the Union
    (E) attempted to start a slave insurrection in the South in the eighteenth century

70. Which of the following is the name for President Harry Truman's reform program?
    (A) Square Deal
    (B) New Deal
    (C) the Great Society
    (D) the New Frontier
    (E) the Fair Deal

71. Which of the following actions did President Eisenhower take during his two terms as president?
    (A) He met with Churchill and Stalin at the Yalta Conference in 1945 to discuss post-World War II policies.
    (B) He sent troops to help South Korea after North Korea attacked it in 1950.
    (C) He became the first president to visit the Soviet Union in 1972.
    (D) He sent troops to integrate Little Rock, Arkansas' Central High School in 1957.
    (E) He placed a naval blockade around Cuba to prevent the Soviets from delivering nuclear missiles.

72. Which of the following made a significant contribution to assembly-line mass production?
    (A) Andrew Carnegie
    (B) Eli Whitney
    (C) J. P. Morgan
    (D) Henry Ford
    (E) Cornelius Vanderbilt

73. The Keating-Owen Act of 1916
    (A) legalized the use of rebates in the railroad industry
    (B) established the nation's first minimum-wage law
    (C) outlawed the closed shop
    (D) took the United States off the gold standard
    (E) barred from interstate commerce products made by child labor under the age of fourteen

74. At the end of the American Revolution (1783) the U.S. border extended to
    (A) the Mississippi River
    (B) the Appalachian Mountains
    (C) the Rocky Mountains
    (D) the Pacific Ocean
    (E) the Oregon Territory

75. Native Americans received their citizenship rights as a result of
    (A) the Dawes Act of 1887
    (B) the efforts of the American Indian Movement in the 1970s
    (C) the Fourteenth Amendment (1868)
    (D) the Civil Rights Act of 1964
    (E) an act of Congress in 1924

76. Which of the following improved U.S. relations with the Philippines?
    (A) the Platt Amendment
    (B) the Foraker Act
    (C) the Tydings-McDuffie Act
    (D) the Teller Amendment
    (E) the Jones Act

77. Which of the following groups of political leaders was opposed to U.S. entry into World War I?
    (A) Woodrow Wilson, William Jennings Bryan, Theodore Roosevelt
    (B) William Howard Taft, Francis Perkins, Henry Cabot Lodge
    (C) Wendell Wilkie, Franklin D. Roosevelt, Thomas E. Dewey
    (D) Jeanette Rankin, Robert La Follette, George Norris
    (E) Upton Sinclair, Huey P. Long, Harry S Truman

78. In 1947 President Truman responded to the request from two nations for military assistance to fight communist groups attempting to overthrow
    (A) France and Germany
    (B) Greece and Turkey
    (C) Spain and Portugal
    (D) Italy and Austria
    (E) Japan and Korea

79. Which of the following is NOT associated with a slave rebellion?
    (A) Ludlow massacre
    (B) Stono Rebellion
    (C) Nat Turner
    (D) Gabriel's Plot
    (E) John Brown

80. W. E. B. Du Bois was instrumental in helping to establish the
    (A) Congress of Racial Equality
    (B) United Way
    (C) Southern Christian Leadership Conference
    (D) National Association for the Advancement of Colored People
    (E) Black Panthers

STOP
END OF SECTION I

IF YOU FINISH BEFORE TIME IS CALLED, YOU MAY CHECK YOUR WORK ON THIS SECTION. DO NOT GO ON TO SECTION II UNTIL YOU ARE TOLD TO DO SO.

SECTION II: FREE-RESPONSE ESSAYS

Section II of the examination has two kinds of questions. Part A is the Document-Based Question, which you must answer. Part B and Part C each have two general free-response essay questions. You are to answer one essay question from Part B and one essay question from Part C. You will have a total of 130 minutes to complete the document-based essay and two free-response essays.

Part A: Document-Based Question (DBQ)
Mandatory reading time—15 minutes
Writing time—45 minutes

Directions The question below asks you to develop a coherent, well-structured essay that integrates information from nine documents with your own knowledge of the topic. You are not required to use information from all of the documents.

1. To what extent did American society's views of women change from the World War I era to the mid-1970s?

Document A: Barbie Doll Fashions (1960)

BUSY GAL
(without doll) #981
Two-piece red linen suit with striped jacket lining. Red and white striped cotton sun-back blouse. Open-crown hat, to match blue belt and shoes. Glasses. Two fashion drawings inside artist's portfolio. The set, $2.50

#981

COTTON CASUAL
(without doll) #912
Sparkling navy and white stripe cotton play-dress. Contrasting ribbons accent the Empire line. White summer shoes. $ 1.00.

#912

Document B: Birth Control Review

Document C: TV Show "Father Knows Best" (1953–1963)

GO ON TO NEXT PAGE

Document D: Betty Friedan, The Feminine Mystique (1963)

The suburban housewife--she was the dream image of the young American woman and the envy, it was said, of women all over the world. The American housewife--freed by science and labor-saving appliances from the drudgery, the dangers of childbirth and the illnesses of her grandmother. She was healthy, beautiful, educated, concerned only about her husband, her children, her home. She had found true feminine fulfillment. As a housewife and mother, she was respected as a full and equal partner to man in his world. She was free to choose automobiles, clothes, appliances, supermarkets; she had everything that women ever dreamed of.

In the fifteen years after World War II, this mystique of feminine fulfillment became the cherished and self-perpetuating one of contemporary American culture. Millions of women lived their lives in the image of those pretty pictures of the American suburban housewife, kissing their husbands goodbye in front of the picture window, depositing their stationwagonsful of children at school, and smiling as they ran the new electric waxer over the spotless kitchen floor. They baked their own bread, sewed their own and their children's clothes, kept their new washing machines and dryers running all day. They changed the sheets on the beds twice a week instead of once, took the rug-hooking class in adult education, and pitied their poor frustrated mothers who had dreamed of having a career. Their only dream was to be perfect wives and mothers; their highest ambition to have five children and a beautiful house, their only fight to get and keep their husbands. They had no thought for the unfeminine problems of the world outside the home; they wanted the men to make the major decisions. They gloried in their role as women, and wrote proudly on the census blank "Occupation: housewife." . . .

Document E: Suffrage Poster, Pre-1919

Document F: National Organization for Women Statement of Purpose (1966)

The purpose of NOW is to take action to bring women into full participation in the mainstream of American society now, exercising all the privileges and responsibilities thereof in truly equal partnership with men.

NOW is dedicated to the proposition that women, first and foremost, are human beings, who like all other people in our society, must have the chance to develop their fullest human potential. We believe that women can achieve such equality only by accepting to the full the challenges and responsibilities they share with all other people in our society, as part of the decision-making mainstream of American political, economic and social life.

We organize to initiate or support action, nationally, or in any part of this nation, by individuals or organizations, to break through the silken curtain of prejudice and discrimination against women in government, industry, and professions, the churches, the political parties, the judiciary, the labor unions, in education, science, medicine, law, religion and every other field of importance in American society. Enormous changes taking place in our society make it both possible and urgently necessary to advance the unfinished revolution of women toward true equality now. With a life span lengthened to nearly 75 years it is no longer either necessary or possible for women to devote the greatest part of their lives to child-rearing, yet childbearing and rearing--which continues to be a most important part of most women's lives--still is used to justify barring women from equal professional and economic participation and advance.

GO ON TO NEXT PAGE

Document G: Women Depicted in Various Occupations (1915)

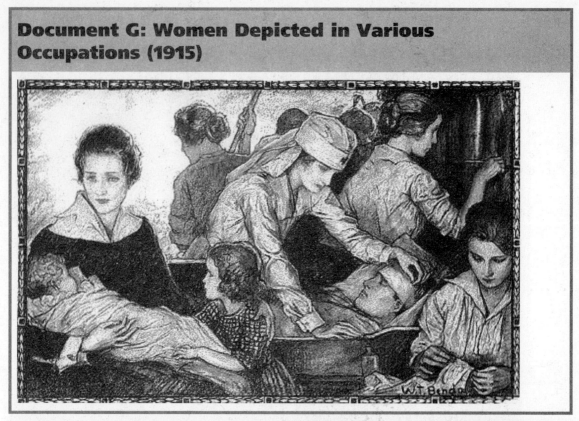

Document H: Women in the Work Force, 1950–1992

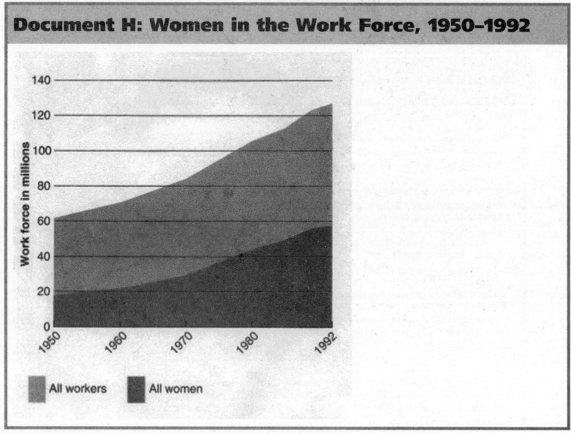

Document I: Women's Liberation March, 1976

End of documents for Question 1.

Part B and Part C: Free-Response Essay Questions
Writing time—70 minutes

Directions Answer TWO of the following questions, one question from Part B and one from Part C. It is recommended that you spend 5 minutes planning each essay and 30 minutes for writing. Write a well-structured, clearly written essay that provides sufficient evidence to support your thesis. Make certain to identify in the test booklet which essay questions you have selected.

Part B Select ONE question from Part B.

2. To what extent was the period following the War of 1812 an "Era of Good Feelings"?

3. Analyze the role social reformers played in addressing the social, economic, and political maladies that faced the nation in the antebellum period.

Part C Select ONE question from Part C.

4. To what extent did the coalition that comprised the Populists achieve its goals?

5. Despite the mixed records of Presidents John Kennedy, Lyndon Johnson, and Richard Nixon and the divisions within the civil rights movement, the 1960s is a notable decade in U.S. history for the profound successes of the black civil rights movement. Assess the validity of this statement.

END OF EXAMINATION

GO ON TO NEXT PAGE

ANSWERS FOR SECTION I

MULTIPLE-CHOICE ANSWER KEY

1. A	17. C	33. C	49. D	65. C
2. D	18. C	34. A	50. A	66. D
3. C	19. D	35. C	51. D	67. E
4. E	20. B	36. E	52. A	68. A
5. D	21. B	37. D	53. E	69. C
6. D	22. A	38. A	54. D	70. E
7. E	23. B	39. C	55. B	71. D
8. A	24. C	40. D	56. E	72. D
9. D	25. E	41. C	57. D	73. E
10. A	26. C	42. A	58. E	74. A
11. B	27. D	43. B	59. A	75. E
12. B	28. A	44. D	60. B	76. C
13. A	29. B	45. E	61. C	77. D
14. B	30. C	46. D	62. D	78. B
15. D	31. E	47. E	63. A	79. A
16. A	32. D	48. B	64. B	80. D

Scoring The multiple-choice section counts for 50 percent of your examination grade.

EXPLANATIONS FOR THE MULTIPLE-CHOICE ANSWERS

1. ANSWER: **A.** The Rosenberg trial took place in the 1950s during the Cold War (*The American Pageant,* 12th ed., p. 880/11th ed., p. 901).

2. ANSWER: **D.** While maintaining its animosity towards blacks, the KKK was strongly opposed to the immigration of large numbers of Jews and Catholics who came to the United States in the early twentieth century (*The American Pageant,* 12th ed., p. 730/11th ed., p. 749).

3. ANSWER: **C.** British economist John Maynard Keynes argued that government must become a purchaser of goods and services, which would involve the government initially spending more money than it took in (*The American Pageant,* 12th ed., pp. 800-801/11th ed., pp. 818-819).

4. ANSWER: **E.** Populists generally favored government ownership of grain-elevator and storage facilities, which the owners of these facilities opposed (*The American Pageant,* 12th ed., p. 613/11th ed., pp. 619-620).

5. ANSWER: **D.** The United States was physically untouched by the war (*The American Pageant,* 12th ed., p. 853/11th ed., p. 874).

6. **ANSWER: D.** Agnew had been accused of corruption and failing to report income to the IRS when he was governor of Maryland (*The American Pageant,* 12th ed., p. 956/11th ed., p. 975).

7. **ANSWER: E.** The antebellum nativist movement organized as a reaction to German and Irish (Catholic) immigrants, whom nativists accused of undermining American culture (*The American Pageant,* 12th ed., p. 415/11th ed., p. 425).

8. **ANSWER: A.** Lincoln stated that while opposed to the institution of slavery, he would not risk the break up of the Union to end it. He was, however, opposed to its expansion (*The American Pageant,* 12th ed., p. 430/11th ed., pp. 439-440).

9. **ANSWER: D.** The Emancipation Proclamation did not apply to the Border States for fear of driving them out of the Union (*The American Pageant,* 12th ed., p. 458/11th ed., p. 468).

10. **ANSWER: A.** The Democrats were the political opponents of the Whigs between the 1830s and the 1850s; they did not evolve from the Whigs (*The American Pageant,* 12th ed., p. 197/11th ed., p. 196).

11. **ANSWER: B.** Truman fired MacArthur because, unlike Truman, the general wanted to attack China and then criticized the president's handling of the war (*The American Pageant,* 12th ed., p. 885/11th ed., p. 905).

12. **ANSWER: B.** The act profoundly limited labor's collective bargaining powers. Truman vetoed it, but it was passed over his veto by the Republican majority in Congress (*The American Pageant,* 12th ed., p. 859/11th ed., p. 881).

13. **ANSWER: A.** Jim Crow laws segregated blacks and whites. The radical Republicans sought to correct such abuses (*The American Pageant,* 12th ed., pp. 510-511/11th ed., p. 522).

14. **ANSWER: B.** Coughlin, who helped form the Union party which was opposed to FDR and the New Deal, initially used his popular radio show to advocate for the New Deal (*The American Pageant,* 12th ed., p. 785/11th ed., p. 803).

15. **ANSWER: D.** The NLU was open to workers in the industrial and agricultural sectors as well (*The American Pageant,* 12th ed., p. 550/11th ed., p. 557).

16. **ANSWER: A.** The Virginia resolutions criticized British policies in the colonies (*The American Pageant,* 12th ed., pp. 207, 264/11th ed., pp. 205, 263).

17. **ANSWER: C.** The papacy was concerned that the two Catholic nations would war against each other in their attempt to colonize the New World (*The American Pageant,* 12th ed., p.16/11th ed., p. 15).

18. **ANSWER: C.** Populists did not want U.S. currency to be backed by deflationary gold specie. Instead they favored a more inflationary silver currency (*The American Pageant,* 12th ed., p. 617/11th ed., pp. 633-636).

19. **ANSWER: D.** The *Brown* decision (1954) overturned the *Plessy* decision, making segregation unconstitutional (*The American Pageant,* 12th ed., p. 895/11th ed., p. 914).

20. **ANSWER: B.** Thoreau was a close friend of Ralph Waldo Emerson, the best known of the transcendentalists (*The American Pageant,* 12th ed., p. 341/11th ed., pp. 349-350).

21. **ANSWER: B.** The Palmer raids occurred in the First Red Scare following World War I (*The American Pageant,* 12th ed., p. 729/11th ed., p. 747).

22. **ANSWER: A.** *Muller* is considered a landmark decision (*The American Pageant,* 12th ed., p. 670/11th ed., p. 688).

23. **ANSWER: B.** British warships stopped American ships and took off sailors they claimed were British citizens (*The American Pageant,* 12th ed., p. 226/11th ed., p. 224).

24. **ANSWER: C.** McKinley was president long after the other two had died (*The American Pageant,* 12th ed., p. 620/11th ed., p. 638).

25. **ANSWER: E.** The Gag Resolution was adopted in 1836 in order to prevent debates regarding the abolition of slavery (*The American Pageant,* 12th ed., p. 367/11th ed., p. 375).

26. **ANSWER: C.** Tennessee was readmitted to the Union in 1866 (*The American Pageant,* 12th ed., p. 490/11th ed., p. 499).

27. **ANSWER: D.** The Philippines proved the most contentious of the issues to be settled in the peace negotiations (*The American Pageant,* 12th ed., p. 636-637/11th ed., pp. 654-655).

28. **ANSWER: A.** The Limited Test Ban Treaty was signed in 1963 (*The American Pageant,* 12th ed., p. 923/11th ed., p. 942).

29. **ANSWER: B.** Referred to by critics as the "Great Accommodator," Washington emphasized vocational training as a means to make blacks economically independent and therefore more easily accepted by white America (*The American Pageant,* 12th ed., pp. 573-575/11th ed., pp. 580-581).

30. **ANSWER: C.** The Federal Reserve Act of 1913 was also known as the Owen-Glass Act (*The American Pageant,* 12th ed., p. 692/11th ed., p. 708).

31. **ANSWER: E.** The Mondale-Ferraro ticket was defeated by the Republican ticket of Reagan-Bush in 1984 (*The American Pageant,* 12th ed., p. 984/11th ed., p. 1000).

32. **ANSWER: D.** Jackson despised Native Americans and sought to relocate them, by force if necessary, in the West (*The American Pageant,* 12th ed., pp. 266-267/11th ed., pp. 224-225).

33. **ANSWER: C.** The Monroe Doctrine warned European nations that attempts to colonize in the Western Hemisphere would be viewed as a threat to U.S. national security (*The American Pageant,* 12th ed., p. 253/11th ed., p. 252).

34. ANSWER: **A**. Garveyism was associated with Black Nationalism. Garvey established UNIA to encourage black pride (*The American Pageant,* 12th ed., p. 748/11th ed., pp. 764-765).

35. ANSWER: **C**. Distressed that the Supreme Court overturned two of his most important reform programs, the AAA and the NIRA, Roosevelt devised a plan to add justices to the Court. The scheme drew harsh criticism and it was withdrawn (*The American Pageant,* 12th ed., pp. 798-799/11th ed., p. 816).

36. ANSWER: **E**. The Homestead Act of 1862 provided for the sale of 160 acres of land in the West for a modest price if the settlers stayed on the land for five years (*The American Pageant,* 12th ed., p. 603/11th ed., pp. 610-611).

37. ANSWER: **D**. One hundred forty-six workers trapped on an upper floor of the Triangle Shirtwaist Company in New York City died when the building caught fire. Negligent safety standards and inadequate safety inspections made it impossible for them to escape (*The American Pageant,* 12th ed., p. 672/11th ed., p. 688).

38. ANSWER: **A**. Although President Roosevelt sympathized with the Loyalist side, his hands were tied by the 1930s Neutrality Acts (*The American Pageant,* 12th ed., pp. 811-812/11th ed., pp. 829-830).

39. ANSWER: **C**. American ships and crew were being captured by the Barbary pirates (from Northern Africa) and held for ransom. Jefferson sent ships to protect American shipping (*The American Pageant,* 12th ed., pp. 219-220/11th ed., pp. 217-218).

40. ANSWER: **D**. The controversial Platt Amendment in effect made Cuba a U.S. protectorate (*The American Pageant,* 12th ed., p. 639/11th ed., p. 657).

41. ANSWER: **C**. Jackson claimed the bill was unconstitutional because it would require federal funding for an intrastate road.

42. ANSWER: **A**. MacArthur is associated with World War II and the Korean War (*The American Pageant,* 12th ed., pp. 840 and 884/11th ed., pp. 860-862, 904-905).

43. ANSWER: **B**. The colonies also hoped to organize with the Iroquois a defense of the British colonies against the French and their Native American allies (*The American Pageant,* 12th ed., pp. 113-114/11th ed., p. 112).

44. ANSWER: **D**. The Dixiecrats walked out of the Democratic party convention and ran their own candidate (*The American Pageant,* 12th ed., p. 881/11th ed., pp. 901-902).

45. ANSWER: **E**. Because the South had little manufacturing, it did not require a protective tariff. Furthermore the planter class purchased foreign-made goods, which would increase in price as a result of a tariff (*The American Pageant,* 12th ed., p. 263/11th ed., pp. 262-263).

46. ANSWER: **D**. (*The American Pageant,* 12th ed., pp. 220-222, 394, and 404-405/11th ed., pp. 218-22, 401-405, 414-415).

47. **ANSWER: E.** The act required railroads to charge only the published rate and made secret rebates illegal (*The American Pageant,* 12th ed., p. 673/11th ed., p. 690).

48. **ANSWER: B.** Secretary of State Seward purchased Alaska for two cents an acre ($7.2 million), for which he endured harsh criticism (*The American Pageant,* 12th ed., pp. 496-497/11th ed., pp. 505-506).

49. **ANSWER: D.** Disorder and revolution in Nicaragua, Haiti, and Cuba precipitated American intervention (*The American Pageant,* 12th ed., p. 684/11th ed., p. 698).

50. **ANSWER: A.** The three events played a role in increasing hostilities between the United States and Britain that ultimately led to the War of 1812 (*The American Pageant,* 12th ed., p. 226/11th ed., pp. 224-225).

51. **ANSWER: D.** The largest percentage of slaveowners in 1850 owned between two and four slaves (*The American Pageant,* 12th ed., p. 353/11th ed., p. 364).

52. **ANSWER: A.** Blaine led the Half-Breeds. Mugwumps were Republicans who bolted (*The American Pageant,* 12th ed., pp. 507-508/11th ed., pp. 517-518).

53. **ANSWER: E.** Roosevelt had borrowed the term from John Bunyan's *Pilgrim's Progress* to describe the journalistic exposés of Lincoln Steffens, Ida Tarbell, and others (*The American Pageant,* 12th ed., pp. 666-667/11th ed., pp. 684-685).

54. **ANSWER: D.** Washington advised that the United States establish economic and not political ties with other nations (*The American Pageant,* 12th ed., p. 201/11th ed., pp. 199-200).

55. **ANSWER: B.** Whitefield was a Calvinist minister who was instrumental in the First Great Awakening in the late eighteenth century (*The American Pageant,* 12th ed., p. 97/11th ed., p. 94).

56. **ANSWER: E.** Pennsylvania farmers refused to pay an excise tax on whiskey imposed by Secretary of the Treasury Alexander Hamilton (*The American Pageant,* 12th ed., p. 196/11th ed., p. 195).

57. **ANSWER: D.** Knox was Washington's secretary of war (*The American Pageant,* 12th ed., p. 192/11th ed., p. 191).

58. **ANSWER: E.** The Marshall Court strengthened the powers of the federal government, often at the expense of the states (*The American Pageant,* 12th ed., pp. 218-219/11th ed., p. 216).

59. **ANSWER: A.** Turner's *The Frontier in American History* espoused the view that the West promoted individualism and democracy (*The American Pageant,* 12th ed., pp. 606-607, 622/11th ed., pp. 614, 621).

60. **ANSWER: B.** Border States were slave states that did not secede from the Union (*The American Pageant,* 12th ed., pp. 436-437/11th ed., pp. 446-447).

61. **ANSWER: C.** Churchill's speech, given in Fulton, Missouri, warned the West that the Soviets and their allies were adversaries of the

United States, Britain, and their allies; Europe was now divided between two antagonistic camps (*The American Pageant*, 12th ed., p. 873/11th ed., p. 893).

62. **ANSWER: D**. Although a substantial percentage of workingwomen in 1900 worked on farms (18.9 percent), by 1998 the percentage of women who worked on farms had declined to only 1 percent (*The American Pageant*, 12th ed., p. 909/11th ed., p. 928).

63. **ANSWER: A**. Dewey articulated the principles of progressive education (*The American Pageant*, 12th ed., p. 737/11th ed., p. 755).

64. **ANSWER: B**. Sinclair's novel about the horrid and unsanitary conditions in Chicago's meatpacking industry angered the American public and Congress. The Pure Food and Drug Act (1906) was passed in order to address these problems (*The American Pageant*, 12th ed., p. 675/11th ed., p. 691).

65. **ANSWER: C**. The rioters were mostly Irish-Americans who took out their anger on the city's black population (*The American Pageant*, 12th ed., p. 446/11th ed., p. 456).

66. **ANSWER: D**. The Crédit Mobilier scandal involved fraud on the part of U.S. congressmen (*The American Pageant*, 12th ed., p. 504/11th ed., p. 514).

67. **ANSWER: E**. The Great Compromise provided for a bicameral legislature, the Senate and House of Representatives (*The American Pageant*, 12th ed., p. 180/11th ed., pp. 178-180).

68. **ANSWER: A**. The planter-slaveholding class sought to expand the institution of slavery. Their policies were inconsistent with the Republicans (*The American Pageant*, 12th ed., pp. 413-417/11th ed., pp. 423-427).

69. **ANSWER: C**. Frémont lost to Democrat James Buchanan (*The American Pageant*, 12th ed., p. 417/11th ed., p. 427).

70. **ANSWER: E**. Truman outlined the Fair Deal in 1949 (*The American Pageant*, 12th ed., p. 883/11th ed., p. 903).

71. **ANSWER: D**. Eisenhower was enforcing the Supreme Court's decision in *Brown v. Board of Education of Topeka, Kansas* (*The American Pageant*, 12th ed., pp. 895-896/11th ed., p. 914).

72. **ANSWER: D**. The Ford Motor Company used the assembly line to mass-produce automobiles such as the Model T (*The American Pageant*, 12th ed., pp. 739-740/11th ed., pp. 757-758).

73. **ANSWER: E**. Two years later, in *Hammer v. Dagenhart*, the Supreme Court ruled the Keating-Owen Act unconstitutional.

74. **ANSWER: A**. As a result of the Treaty of Paris, U.S. territory ended at the Mississippi River (*The American Pageant*, 12th and 11th eds., pp. 161-162).

75. **ANSWER: E**. Congress acted to grant Native Americans their citizenship rights after the Dawes Act of 1887 failed (*The American Pageant*, 12th ed., p. 597/11th ed., p. 605).

76. **ANSWER: C.** The act (1934) provided for the eventual independence of the Philippines, which finally occurred in 1946 (*The American Pageant,* 12th ed., p. 807/11th ed., p. 826).

77. **ANSWER: D.** The three political leaders opposed U.S. entry for a variety of reasons—a large German-American constituency, a belief that the United States had been manipulated into the war by financial interests, and the view that there was no reason to go to war against Germany (*The American Pageant,* 12th ed., pp. 706-707/11th ed., p. 724).

78. **ANSWER: B.** The Truman Doctrine was a key feature of the containment policy in the years immediately following World War II. It provided assistance to nations, such as Greece and Turkey, that were fighting against "armed minorities"—meaning communist rebels (*The American Pageant,* 12th ed., p. 874/11th ed., pp. 894-895).

79. **ANSWER: A.** The Ludlow massacre was a violent attack on striking mine workers by mine company security guards and Colorado militiamen in 1914.

80. **ANSWER: D.** The NAACP was formed in 1910 (*The American Pageant,* 12th ed., pp. 574-575/11th ed., pp. 581-582).

ANSWERS FOR SECTION II, PART A: DOCUMENT-BASED QUESTION (DBQ)

Below are short analyses of the documents. The italicized words suggest what your margin notes might include.

DOCUMENT A The *Barbie Doll* has been a phenomenon in the toy industry since its *introduction in the late 1950s,* and since then millions of young girls have owned one. While the original designer of the doll intended it to go beyond the limitations of earlier dolls, critics contend that it *represents a modern-day version of the eighteenth-century concept of the Cult of Domesticity.* They contend that Barbie is depicted first and foremost for her *physical attributes* (for example, her model's shape). It should be noted that the "Busy Gal" doll portrayed in the document may in fact be employed or is seeking employment as an artist or designer.

DOCUMENT B This powerful magazine cover for *Birth Control Review,* edited by the most famous advocate for birth control, Margaret Sanger, depicts the *plight of women* who have *no access to birth control, a life of despair* weighted down by *"unwanted babies."*

DOCUMENT C This still photo from one of the most popular *family television shows* of the 1950s and 1960s illustrates the *quintessential post-World War II white middle-class family.* The photo (like the show itself) obviously *does not suggest significant discord;* everyone knew his or her place within the nuclear family, and they are *untouched by the realities of the era:* the Cold War, the nuclear arms race, the civil rights movement, and U.S. foreign policy. In short it is the way white middle-class America wanted to see itself.

DOCUMENT D In her book, *The Feminine Mystique,* Betty Friedan *attacks the view of the American woman as equal to men based solely on the material quality of her life.* She *caustically presents the view that women had no concerns outside those that affected the material happiness of their own families.*

DOCUMENT E The designer of this *poster* (possibly created before the ratification of the Nineteenth Amendment) felt compelled to *use babies to appeal to men to support women's suffrage.* The message is this: Not only do *women want and need to have the right to vote,* but the *future generations will depend on it as well.*

DOCUMENT F The National Organization for Women (*NOW*) has been one of the primary national organizations for women's rights since it was founded in 1966. Over the years it has *attacked stereotypes, attitudes, and discrimination that have negatively shaped women's lives.* In the document the NOW *statement of purpose indirectly attacks earlier perspectives such as the Cult of Domesticity, Republican Motherhood, and possibly even the Barbie Doll itself.* The political sentiment being expressed is *a demand for equality in politics and government nearly fifty years after the ratification of the Nineteenth Amendment.* Laws change, but attitudes take longer to change. NOW was obviously tired of waiting.

DOCUMENT G This *idealistic drawing portrays the varied roles women played in early-twentieth-century* America. *From our perspective it reveals the narrow range of women's work* in this time period. Central to the drawing is the *woman as mother and as caregiver to the helpless and injured.* However there is some recognition of the *manual labor associated with women's work* in the early part of the twentieth century. Perhaps *the little girl* watching her mother caring for the baby *may be seeing how her own life will someday unfold.*

DOCUMENT H This chart shows that the number of women in the workforce grew at a rate higher than the rate for general employment. *All workers doubled in number, whereas women in the workforce tripled.* Of course the chart *does not tell* us what *type of labor* women were doing.

DOCUMENT I This photograph is quite revealing in that the year is *1976 and women are still demanding "equality" and complaining that they are "second-class citizen(s),"* over half a century after the Nineteenth Amendment. Given the date, it is possible they are advocating in favor of the *Equal Rights Amendment.*

One way to categorize your documents so that they reflect the nature of the question being asked is to group as negative those documents that reflect, say, the way society's attitudes regarding women did not change and group as positive those that reflect change. Some documents reflect both a negative view and a positive view. Also a document may not be identified with one perspective or another, but that does not mean that it cannot be used in defending your thesis.

Remember that you provide meaning and perspective to the documents based on your own attitudes and understanding of U.S. history. Below is a categorization of the documents based on changes in attitude:

Negative Documents (Attitudes did not change)	Positive Documents (Attitudes did change)	Neutral Documents
A	A	
B		
C		C
	D	
E		
	F	
G		
	H	
I	I	

In developing your essay, you should incorporate the following historical information:

- Attitudes regarding the role of women in American society such as the Cult of Domesticity and Republican Motherhood were common.
- There were antecedents to the twentieth-century women's movement—for example, the Seneca Falls Conference.
- Women's rights, such as the right to vote and the legalization of birth control methods and devices, were national issues in the early twentieth century.
- The Nineteenth Amendment, which gave women the right to vote, was ratified in 1920.
- After World War II, stereotypes of women's place in the family and society were widely expressed in popular culture and consumerism.
- In the 1960s women's rights activists such as Betty Friedan, author of *The Feminine Mystique,* facilitated the challenge to attitudes that left women subordinated despite the educational and professional advances they had made over the years.
- The Equal Rights Amendment was not ratified, and the Supreme Court's ruling in *Roe v. Wade* continues to be questioned.

A Sample Essay

If your view is that society's views of women changed in the twentieth century, your essay might look something like this:

Over the course of much of the twentieth century, various reform movements, including the women's rights movement, sought to address the inequalities of American life. Key to gaining political, social, and economic rights was the transformation in attitudes that shaped the American public's views of women. To be sure, women throughout the nation's history have sought to challenge stereotypes, attitudes, and conditions that have shaped their lives. For example, women who organized the Seneca Falls Conference (such as Elizabeth Cady Stanton and Lucretia Mott) sought to challenge attitudes that limited the role of women—for example, the eighteenth-century Cult of Domesticity and in the nineteenth-century Republican Motherhood. In the case of the former, women were expected to develop and adhere to the following characteristics: piety, purity, submissiveness, and domesticity. A small step in the right direction came with the advent of the notion of Republican Motherhood in which women, though disenfranchised, were given a political role: to raise the next generation of politically minded males who fully understood the importance of and responsibility to God, family, and country. Yet, as Document G reveals, the responsibilities of women had not changed that much by the early twentieth century. Women's work was still limited mainly to that of caregiver to the helpless and injured.

By the twentieth century, many women were discontent with the slow pace of change. True, the Nineteenth Amendment enfranchised women, but given their primary task of bearing and rearing children, most women were unable to improve their lives as a result of traditional stereotypes and unwanted pregnancies. One reformer, Margaret Sanger, took the bold step of publicly advocating for access to birth control methods, (Documents B and E), a highly controversial crusade in the first decades of the twentieth century. Later this crusade would expand to the right to have an abortion to end an unwanted pregnancy, which the Supreme Court ruled constitutional in the *Roe v. Wade* case of 1973. Access to contraceptives for married couples in all fifty states had been legalized only eight years earlier.

Following ratification of the Nineteenth Amendment in 1920, many women believed that the goal of the women's rights movement had been met; they did not seek to radically challenge the social and ideological attitudes that were so deeply ingrained in American life. Others, such as Elizabeth Paul, took the next step, advocating for an Equal Rights Amendment to the Constitution, an objective that would challenge attitudes in a political battle in the 1970s. Following World War II America seemed to settle back into a sense of conformity in which everyone knew his or her role in the nuclear family, as evidenced by the television show aptly titled to suggest this era's attitudes: "Father Knows Best" (Document C). Another modern-day version of the "ideal woman" can be seen in the emergence of the Barbie Doll (who admittedly seemed to transform her persona over the years as attitudes about "women's work" changed).

In the early 1960s, society's perceptions and attitudes about women's roles was challenged by Betty Friedan, whose landmark book, *The Feminine Mystique*, exposed how societal forces such as intellectual and professional oppression left many middle-class women angry and frustrated. Attitudes, however, were indeed changing. The following year the 1964 Civil Rights Act was passed; this prohibited discrimination on the basis of, among other factors, gender. In 1966 the National Organization of Women was founded in part to "advance the unfinished revolution of women toward true equality now" (Document F). But as more women played an active role in social programs and movements, they found that even within these reform-minded organizations perceptions of women's work reflected a pre-World War II attitude. Consequently it was deemed necessary to resuscitate the crusade for an Equal Rights Amendment (Document I). Unfortunately for advocates of the ERA, attitudes had not changed dramatically enough. Anti-ERA forces led by, among others, Phyllis Schlafly, a conservative Republican, contended that the amendment would break down all differences between the genders.

Undoubtedly attitudes regarding women had changed profoundly in the first five or six decades of the twentieth century. But as is the case with all reform movements, attitudes must change enough so that more democratic legislation can follow. So it is for the women's right movement.

COMMENT This essay effectively synthesizes outside information—the writer's knowledge of the nineteenth-century women's rights movement, the ideological influences on women in the eighteenth and nineteenth centuries, as well as twentieth-century movements such as the legalization of birth control and the growing activism of women in the formation of NOW. The document information is also used effectively to depict post-World War II popular and consumer attitudes towards women.

SCORING The DBQ essay counts for 45 percent of the total free-response grade, or 22.5 percent of the total examination grade.

ANSWERS FOR SECTION II, PART B AND PART C

QUESTION 2 Many historians see the years following the War of 1812 as a time when nationalism flourished because Americans unified behind common economic and political objectives. As the nation expanded industrially and as the sections were integrated (especially the North and West) because of the development of national roads and canals, a sense of greater self-sufficiency prevailed. To a certain degree these sentiments and developments generally defined the years immediately after the war. But if there was an Era of Good Feelings, it was very short lived. The elimination of the Federalist party did much to give Americans the impression that they were unified.

Following the War of 1812 the Federalist party began to disappear as a viable political alternative to the Democratic-Republicans. The Federalists had only themselves to blame. Well before the war they had passed the undemocratic Alien and Sedition Acts. These pieces of legislation sought to deny Americans their First Amendment right to criticize the government and, by extending the time period before one could become a citizen, neutralized the political power of many new immigrants, who would probably have voted for the Democratic-Republicans. The Federalists further alienated many Americans because of their activities during the War of 1812, which they fervently opposed. In fact some New England Federalists actually sold supplies to the British during the war. Equally controversial was the calling of the Hartford Convention in 1814, at which the delegates discussed the possibility of amending the Constitution to require a two-thirds vote by Congress for a declaration of war. A number of the delegates even discussed secession. With the end of the war many Americans chastised the Federalists for their actions. Soon, at least on the national level, the Federalists imploded, leaving only the Democratic-Republicans. In fact the Democratic-Republican president, James Monroe, was reelected in 1820, having won all but one electoral vote.

Yet, though there was only one major national political party, Americans were still divided as economic and political tensions prevailed, thus limiting the longevity of the assumption that Americans were unified. The issues that had divided the nation before the war continued to shape the political debate after it: the tariff controversy, the establishment of a national bank, tax-supported infrastructural development, the availability of land, and, of course, slavery. The tariff of 1816 (the first in the nation's history) serves as a good example. New England, which had not yet developed a substantial industrial sector, opposed the tariff, whereas the South and West favored it as an expression of national unity and the means for expansion of the nation's economy. (Southern political and economic leaders, however, would condemn subsequent protective tariffs as detrimental to their sectional interests.) The rechartering of the Bank of the United States, a part of Clay's American System, would soon divide the nation as well—the South came to strongly oppose it.

When in 1820 Missouri was prepared to enter the Union as a slave state and thus affect the political balance that prevailed in the Senate, a further sectional division reemerged. The year before this crisis the nation had been devastated by a financial panic, and the focus of the blame was on the Democratic-Republicans, who controlled government. Soon, from the ashes of the old Federalist party a new political party, the National Republicans, emerged to challenge the power of the Democratic-Republicans. By 1824, although all four candidates for the presidency were Democratic-Republicans, divisions within the party and the nation had emerged. Probably by this point the Era of Good Feelings had run its course.

This approach lays out a clear thesis supported by sufficient background information on the reasons why the Federalist party collapsed after the War of 1812. It is important to point out that the period was referred to as the Era of Good Feelings because there was only one major national party, the Democratic-Republicans. It is also important to point out that the period was short-lived because of ongoing controversies—the tariff, the Bank of the United States, and the expansion of slavery—and that the tariff and slavery soon replaced a sense of national unity with sectional concerns.

QUESTION 3 In the antebellum period, the decades prior to the Civil War, a vast array of social, economic, and political problems affected the level of democracy in the nation. There are two sources of reform: the federal, state, and local governments can enact legislation that addresses these maladies; and grassroots movements can mobilize citizens, often at the local level, to bring about particular reforms. From the 1820s to the 1850s, reform-minded groups organized, many of which involved middle-class women, to combat the various problems, among them gender inequality, as women had been relegated to a second-class status; slavery; inhumane prison conditions; the inhumane treatment of the mentally ill; the absence of an educational system for all but the nation's wealthier citizens; and the problems associated with the expansion of urban America.

Reformers held certain assumptions about how to address these problems, but ultimately they were distilled into one broad objective: expanding democratic rights. In order to address the inequality that women experienced, advocates such Elizabeth Cady Stanton and Lucretia Mott organized a meeting of like-minded reformers. Meeting in Seneca Falls, New York, in 1848, they drew up a "Declaration of Sentiments," which had as its cornerstone the demand for the vote. It was hoped that other positive developments such as property rights for women would come about as a result of achieving this goal. Women also were involved in the abolition movement, led by William Lloyd Garrison, Harriet Tubman, and Frederick Douglass. Unfortunately, reform—especially the abolition of slavery—never took root in the stagnant socioeconomic and political structure of the South. Although the Civil War achieved what the abolitionists were unable to accomplish in the antebellum era, they nevertheless kept the nation's attention on the "peculiar institution" through, for example, Garrison's newspaper, *The Liberator*. Other reformers such as Dorothea Dix were appalled at the treatment of the nation's mentally ill, many of whom were brutally treated or abandoned to live out their existence in degradation and despair; they were successful in bringing about some reforms by eliciting funding for better facilities. Prisoners as well were brutalized, which compelled some reformers to seek out more humane treatments and to establish institutions that would make a prisoner a more productive member of society by instilling a sense of morality and discipline. Other reformers sought to improve the working and living conditions of the growing urban working class. The development of trade unions would face considerable obstacles. Nevertheless the Massachusetts supreme court did rule in favor of the right to organize in *Commonwealth v. Hunt*. Another major goal, one that would certainly have an impact on the future evolution of American democracy, was the work of Horace Mann and other educational reformers, who helped to bring about the Massachusetts model of tax-supported public schools.

The impact of the reformers who organized grassroots movements to address those features of the nation that needed to be democratized was mixed. Yet the antebellum reformers raised the consciousness and pricked the conscience of many Americans regarding these problems, and they took active steps to remedy them.

The nature of reform and the undemocratic conditions that existed in the antebellum period are a good place to start your essay. In discussing the reform movements and major reformers, it is important to point out that the Age of Reform was a mostly Northern phenomenon. Equally significant is the connection between attempts to remedy these problems and the ultimate objective of further democratizing the nation. Further, it is important to point out that while some reforms were not achieved, the antebellum reformers did lay the foundation for future reforms by raising the political, social, and economic conscience of their fellow citizens.

QUESTION 4 The Populists were indeed a coalition—that is, separate groups that came together in order to advance their collective political interests. The movement and party comprised a wide range of organizations and movements such as the Grangers, Farmers' Alliance, Greenback party, Knights of Labor, Free Silver party, Socialists, prohibitionists, women's rights groups, and even anarchists.

Because there were so many factions, establishing a platform for the Populist party was not easily accomplished. Yet most favored a loose or soft money policy, in which currency would be inflated in order to drive up farm prices, allowing farmers to pay off loans. The Populists also sought greater government intervention on behalf of farmers. To this end they supported local, state, and federal legislation that would place regulations on railway shipping rates and grain-elevator and storage facilities. For laborers the party supported the passage of laws that would reduce the twelve-hour workday, which was common in many sectors of private enterprise. In short, to develop the perspective that the coalition was effective, you should point out the successes of the movement—for example, inflating currency, achieving some forms of federal and state regulations, as well as immigration restrictions to reduce the labor pool and, it was hoped, inflate wages. You should also point out that the coalition had drawbacks in that its strength lay with the agrarian component of the movement, thus marginalizing the less potent forces in the coalition.

An effective essay is one that presents the Populists as an organization and as a political party that organized in response to industrialism and to the cooperation between big business and government that prevailed in the late nineteenth century. In articulating the view that despite its diversity the coalition was able to achieve some of its goals, you should discuss the passage of Granger Laws in a number of states and the passage of the Interstate Commerce Act and the Bland-Allison Act. To address the failures of the Populists, include a discussion of key events such as the Resumption Act of 1875, the Supreme Court's ruling in *Wabash v. Illinois,* and Granger Laws.

QUESTION 5 The 1960s witnessed significant successes in the civil rights movement. Various accomplishments came about as a result of government actions and laws; others were the result of grassroots activities by black leaders such as Dr. Martin Luther King, Jr. President Kennedy, for example, sought to address the conditions under which many urban blacks lived by calling on Congress to provide funding for urban renewal, but Congress did not act on these concerns. Kennedy's narrow victory in the 1960 presidential election made him cautious about pursuing a civil rights agenda that might alienate the southern members of his own party. Yet Kennedy did use the power of the federal government in helping to integrate the University of Mississippi in 1962 and the University of Alabama in 1963, despite strong segregationist opposition in those states.

Considerable achievements occurred under Kennedy's successor, President Lyndon Johnson. For example, despite strong southern opposition, Congress passed the Civil Rights Acts of 1964 and 1965. The acts addressed segregation and the use of Reconstruction-era tactics to prevent blacks from voting—namely, the poll tax. Also in 1965 the Voting Rights Act was passed, which further dismantled state obstacles to participating in the electoral process.

President Nixon, on the other hand, had been elected in large part by Americans disenchanted by the turmoil of the 1960s and opposed to such programs as school busing to achieve racial integration. He therefore sought to roll back some of the gains made in the civil rights movement.

Conversely a major impetus for the civil rights movement came from black Americans and their leaders. Dr. Martin Luther King, Jr., believed that the best way to achieve equal rights for black Americans was by peaceful nonviolent resistance. Utilizing the boycott, for example, King and the black residents of Montgomery, Alabama, achieved success in integrating that city's public transportation system. He and other leaders also organized major peaceful demonstrations and marches to generate universal awareness of the plight of the nation's black citizens. Other black leaders took a more confrontational approach. Some, such as Malcolm X and Elijah Muhammad, opposed integration and tapped into black nationalism; they tended to criticize Dr. King as being too moderate and a lackey to whites. Like Malcolm X, Stokely Carmichael and the Black Panthers and the Student Non-Violent Coordinating Committee (SNCC) sought more radical objectives. Thus the black civil rights movement was divided over objectives and methods that would improve the lives of black Americans.

While black Americans continue to struggle for racial, political, and social equality, the movement can look back to the successes of the 1960s, when the government passed important legislation, when some blacks organized to bring about a change in government policies, and when other blacks stimulated a sense of black pride that is necessary for this segment of our society to reach what Dr King referred to as "the promised land."

If you support the statement on which the question is based, make certain to discuss Kennedy's support for urban renewal and increased funding for civil rights programs and enforcement, but which was generally unsuccessful because of a reluctant Congress. The first few years of Johnson's presidency were marked by the passage of key civil rights legislation, which you should point out was an essential part of his Great Society reform program. It is important to point out key legislation such as the Civil Rights Act of 1964 and the Voting Rights Act of 1965; the first act prohibited segregation in all public facilities and established the Equal Opportunity Commission to combat employment discrimination. That same year the Twenty-fourth Amendment was ratified, which finally abolished the poll tax. The following year Congress abolished the literacy test with the passage of the Voting Rights Act of 1965, which was the result, in part, of mass demonstrations organized by King and other civil rights activists. Finally, discuss the reaction to the civil rights gains in the mid-1960s as seen by the election of Richard Nixon, whose rhetoric and actions appealed to southerners opposed to federally imposed integration. The divisions within the black civil rights movement require attention to show that blacks themselves had different definitions of what the movement represented.

SCORING Together the two free-response essays from Part B and Part C count for 55 percent of the free-response essay grade, or 27.5 percent of your total examination grade.

Grade your essays on a score of 0-9.

8-9: EXCELLENT The essay has a clear thesis, is well written and organized, covers all aspects of the essay in depth, analyzes the question effectively, and supports the thesis with sufficient and relevant historical information. It may contain minor errors.

5-7: GOOD The essay has a clear thesis, though it is not as well developed as in an 8-9 essay. It has clear though not excellent organization. The essay covers only one aspect of the question in depth and does not fully indicate an understanding of the complexity of the question or topic. The analysis is not as well developed as in an 8-9 essay and makes limited use of relevant historical information. The essay may contain errors that do not affect the overall quality of the essay.

2-4: FAIR The essay either lacks a clear thesis or the thesis is confused or even missing. It is not well organized and exhibits weak writing. It does not indicate an understanding of the complexity of the question or topic, and it fails to support a thesis with sufficient historical information and/or analysis. It may contain significant errors.

0-1. POOR The essay has no thesis, poor structure and organization, is poorly written, lacks historical information and analysis, and tends to offer rhetorical comments. It contains both major and minor errors.

It is important that you be as objective as possible when evaluating your essays. You might ask a teacher, parent, fellow student, or friend to evaluate your essays for you.

CALCULATING YOUR SCORE ON THE PRACTICE TEST

SCORING THE MULTIPLE-CHOICE SECTION

_____ − (_____ × 1/4) = _____ (round to nearest whole number)

number correct — number incorrect — raw score

SCORING THE FREE-RESPONSE SECTION

Use the formula below to calculate your raw score on the free-response section of the exam:

(____ × 4) + (____ × 2.44) + (____ × 2.44) = ____ (round to nearest whole number)

DBQ — essay #1 — essay #2 — raw score

YOUR COMPOSITE SCORE

1.13 x _____ = _____ (weighted multiple-choice score: NOT rounded)

         multiple-   raw

         choice   score

2.73 x _____ = _____ (weighted free-response score: NOT rounded)

        free-   raw

        response   score

Once you have completed your calculations, add the two weighted sections (and round to the nearest whole number). You now have your composite score. Now see where your score falls in the Composite Score Range below. Remember that this score is an estimate of your performance on the College Board examination.

AP GRADES BY SCORE RANGE

AP Grade	Composite Score Range
5	114–180
4	91–113
3	74–90
2	49–73
1	0–48